LEAPFROGGING
DEVELOPMENT?

SUNY series in Global Politics
James N. Rosenau, editor

LEAPFROGGING DEVELOPMENT?

The Political Economy of Telecommunications Restructuring

J. P. SINGH

State University
of New York
Press

Published by
State University of New York Press, Albany

© 1999 State University of New York

Production by Susan Geraghty
Marketing by Nancy Farrell

Printed in the United States of America

For information, address State University of New York
Press, State University Plaza, Albany, N.Y., 12246

Library of Congress Cataloging-in-Publication Data

Singh, J. P., 1961–
    Leapfrogging development? : the political economy of
telecommunications restructuring / by J. P. Singh.
        p.   cm. — (SUNY series in global politics)
    Includes bibliographical references and index.
    ISBN 0-7914-4293-4 (alk. paper)
    ISBN 0-7914-4294-2 (pb : alk. paper)
    1. Telecommunication policy—Case studies. I. Title. II. Series.
    HE7645.S56 1999
    384—dc21   98-43558
                                                                CIP

10 9 8 7 6 5 4 3 2 1

"... And the souls in Plato riding up to heaven in a two-horse chariot would go in a Ford car now," she said.

"Or a Rolls Royce: Plato was an aristocrat!"

"Quite! No more black horse to thrash and maltreat. Plato never thought we'd go one better than his black steed and his white steed, and have no steeds at all, only an engine!"

"Only an engine and gas!" said Clifford.

—D. H. Lawrence, *Lady Chatterly's Lover*

*To my mother
and the memory
of my father*

CONTENTS

List of Tables, Figures, Map, and Boxes   *xiii*

Important Terms   *xv*

Abbreviations   *xvii*

Preface   *xxi*

PART I   The Political Economy of Restructuring

Chapter 1   Introduction   3

    The Questions   3
    The Leapfrogging Thesis   4
    The Argument In Brief   8
    The Plan   14
    The Importance   15

Chapter 2   The Argument Explained   19

    The Context for Telecommunications Restructuring   19
    The Political Economy of Telecommunications   33
    Conclusion   45

PART II   Telecommunications Restructuring in Seven Countries

Chapter 3   Telecommunications Restructuring in Catalytic
and Near-Catalytic States   49

    Catalytic States: Singapore, South Korea   51
    Near-Catalytic States: Mexico, Malaysia   71
    Conclusion   86

Chapter 4   Telecommunications Restructuring in
Dysfunctional and Predatory States   89

    Dysfunctional States: China, Brazil   89
    Predatory States: Myanmar   106
    Conclusion   108

PART III   Telecommunications Provision and Restructuring
in India: 1851–1998

Chapter 5   Indian Telecommunications: Shadow
of the Empire, 1851–1984   115

    Colonial Communications   116
    The State of the State (1947–1984)   122
    Slow Growth and Entrenched Interests in
        Telecommunications: 1950–85   127
    Demand for Telecommunications Services Since
        the Mid-1970s   133
    Conclusion   137

Chapter 6   Indian Telecommunications: Service
Enhancement, 1984–91   139

    The Indian State (1984–91)   139
    Major Policy Changes and Challenges   141
    Service Enhancement   152
    Liberalization of Manufacturing   158
    Conclusion   162

Chapter 7   Indian Telecommunications: Privatization and
Liberalization, 1991–98   165

    The Indian State (1991–98)   166
    Growing Demands for Services and Restructuring   170
    Major Policy Changes   174
    Services Privatization and Provision   183
    Conclusion   194

PART IV   Conclusion

Chapter 8   The Myth and the Reality of Leapfrogging   201

    The Myths of Leapfrogging   203
    The "Reality" of Political-Economic Context   214

Notes   231

References   263

Index   283

LIST OF
TABLES, FIGURES,
MAP, AND BOXES

TABLES

1.1 Selected Studies Linking Telecommunications to
    Development By Level of Analysis   7

1.2 Studies Showing Benefits of Telecommunications According
    to User Groups   9

2.1 The Arguments   20

2.2 State Decision-Making Processes   43

3.1 Types of States, Pressures, and Outcomes in
    Telecommunications Restructurings   52

3.2 National Telecommunication Infrastructures   57

3.3 National Telecommunication Infrastructures:
    Specialized Services   59

3.4 Asian Specialized Services: Current Rates and Projections
    (Media Reports)   60

5.1 Telephone Subscribers in India (1882–1951)   120

5.2 Telephones per 100 Population (January 1951)   121

5.3 Population and Telephones in Major World Cities
    (January 1951)   121

5.4 Total Central Plan Investment Outlays for
    Telecommunications   128

5.5 Telecommunication Infrastructure in India (1951–1985)   133

5.6 Growth of International Telecommunications Traffic
    in India (1980–1997)   134

5.7 Demand for Telephones in India (1978–1996)   136

6.1   Distribution of Population and DELs   155

8.1   Growth and Efficiency Indicators for Telecommunications   206

8.2   Theories of Communications and Information:
Representative Works   208

8.3   Provision of Telecommunication Services According
to User Group Demands and State Supply   225

FIGURES

1.1   Flow Chart of Factors Determining Telecommunications
Restructuring   13

2.1   Provision and Membership Conditions for Club Goods   36

6.1   Policy, Regulatory, Operations Chart
(Telecommunications Sector in India, 1986)   145

6.2   Policy, Regulatory, Operations Chart
(Telecommunications Sector in India, 1989)   146

8.1   State Determination of Provision and Membership
in Clubs   217

MAP

5.1   Telegraph Map of British India (1855)   116

BOXES

3.1   Telecommunication Restructuring in Singapore   54

3.2   Telecommunication Restructuring in South Korea   63

3.3   Telecommunication Restructuring in Mexico   72

3.4   Telecommunication Restructuring in Malaysia   80

4.1   Telecommunication Restructuring in China   91

4.2   Telecommunication Restructuring in Brazil   98

IMPORTANT TERMS

Basic services: Telecommunications services (such as telephone service) where the content of the message is not altered during transmission

Value-added services: Telecommunications services (such as data switching) where the message is altered during or for transmission

Specialized services: (As used in this book) services other than telephone provided over terrestrial and nonterrestrial networks (therefore, cellular is specialized)

DELs/Mainlines: Direct Exchange Lines or Mainlines refer literally to the last wire (for example, copper) from the telephone pole bringing service to customer premises. May provide more than one telephone connection

ABBREVIATIONS

Assocham	Associated Chambers of Commerce and Industry (India)
BJP	Bharatiya Janata Party (India)
CII	Confederation of Indian Industry
CCITT	Comité Consultaf International Telgraphique et Telephonique (International Telegraph and Telephone Consultative Committee—permanent body in ITU)
C-DoT	Centre for the Development of Telematics (India)
CCP	Chinese Communist Party
CPE	Customer Premises Equipment
CUGs	Closed User Groups (India): term used to define shared use and resale of leased circuits in India
DACOM	Data Communications Corporation (South Korea)
DELs	Direct Exchange Lines (excludes PBXs)
DoE	Department of Electronics (India)
DoT	Department of Telecommunications (India)
EAPBX	Electronic Automatic Private Branch Exchange (also known as PABX)
EISPAI	E-mail and Internet Service Operators Association of India
EPB	Economic Planning Board (South Korea)
FCC	Federal Communications Commission (United States)
FDI	Foreign Direct Investment
FICCI	Federation of Indian Chambers of Commerce and Industry
GATS	General Agreement on Trade in Services
GATT	General Agreement on Tariffs and Trade
GDP	Gross Domestic Product
GNP	Gross National Product
GPSS	Gateway Packet Switching System (connects Indian users with international telecommunications networks)

HCL	Hindustan Cables Limited (India)
IAS	Indian Administrative Service
IBRD	International Bank for Reconstruction and Development (The World Bank)
IBS	International Business Service (satellite links provided by Intelsat connecting users to global satellites)
ICS	Indian Civil Service
IIFT	Indian Institute of Foreign Trade
HVIF	International Monetary Fund
INC	Indian National Congress
Inmarsat	International Maritime Satellite Organization
IPSA	Indian Paging Service Association
Intelsat	International Satellite Communications organization
ISD	International Subscriber Dialing (international direct dialing)
ISDN	Integrated Services Digital Network
ISI	Import Suliititution Industrialization
ITI	Indian Telephone Industries
LDCs	Less Developed Countries
ITU	International Telecommunications Union
JTM	Jabatan Telekorn Malaysia
KTA	Korea Telecom Authority
MAFF	Market Opening Fact Finding Talks (U.S.–South Korea)
MNCs	Multinational Corporations
MoF	Ministry of Finance (India)
MPT	Ministry of Posts and Telecommunications (China)
MTNL	Mahanagar Telephone Nigarn Limited (public sector telecommunications monopoly for Bombay [Mumbai] & Delhi)
NASSCOM	National Association for Software and Service Companies (India)
NCB	National Computers Board (Singapore)
NIC	National Informatics Centre (India)
NICs	Newly Industrializing Countries
NII	National Information Infrastructure
NITB	National Information Technology Plan (Singapore)

NTP	National Telecommunications Policy (India)
NRIs	Non-Resident Indians (Indian nationals living outside India)
NWICO	New World Information and Communication Order
PABX	Private Automatic Branch Exchange
PAN	Partido Acción Nacional (Mexico)
PAP	People's Action Party (Singapore)
PCOs	Public Call Offices (India)
PILs	Public Interest Litigations (India)
PRI	Partido Revolucionaro Institucional
PSDN	Packet Switched Data communication Network
PSTN	Public Switched Telephone Network
PTT	Post, Telegraph, and Telephone (historical acronym for government monopolies in this area)
RABMN	Remote Area Business Message Network (a PSDN in India)
RBOCs	Regional Bell Operating Companies (United States)
Rs.	Rupees
SCT	Secretaría de Communicaciones y Tranportes (Mexico)
STD	Subscriber Trunk Dialing or Direct Distance Dialing (DDD)
STM	Syarikat Telekorn Malaysia
SWIFT	Society for Worldwide Interbank Financial Transactions
TEMA	Telecommunications Equipment Manufacturers Association (India)
TCIL	Telecommunications Consultants of India, Limited
TRAI	Telecommunication Regulatory Authority of India
TNEs	Transnational Enterprises
UMNO	United Malays National Organization
USTR	United States Trade Representative
VANs	Value-added Networks
VIKRAM	A proposed PSDN in India
VSAT	Very Small Aperture Terminal (satellite based)
VSNL	Videsh Sanchar Nigam Limited (India's public sector international carrier)

WANs	Wide Area Networks
WTO	World Trade Organization
X.25/X.75	Protocols used by ITU to permit communication between different users

PREFACE

The talk of national and global information infrastructures now fills the halls of development policy-making. Once considered luxuries for the developing world, telecommunications are now touted as strategic priorities by scholars as well as policymakers. As telephones, satellite terminals, fax machines reach consumers from remote areas to high-tech export enclaves in the developing world, this prioritization can hardly be seen as benefiting only elites. However, as this book shows, the causal links between telecommunications and development remain unclear unless we examine how telecommunications services are demanded and how they are supplied.

Most of telecommunications and development literature suffers from examining the supply side of service provision while paying lip service to the demand side. Typical studies note how X amount of telecommunications services lead to Y amount of development benefits without examining how X comes about and who demands or does not demand X in the first place. At times, infrastructural growth itself is taken as a proxy for development. This book departs from such texts on technology and development by emphasizing both demand and supply.

It is argued here that a telecommunications infrastructure leads to development in a few cases only where the state as a supplier is a successful catalyst (a rare condition) among various user groups who either accede to the state line or pressure it to meet their demands for services for specific purposes. The state's function must always be analyzed in terms of its links with user groups which demand telecommunication services. In short, this book contextualizes the possibilities of development with telecommunications in the political economy of user group service provision.

As this book goes into press, the World Bank has just released its much delayed *World Development Report 1998/99: Knowledge for Development*. While acknowledging that communication technologies have proliferated the world over, it argues, among other things, that one of the keys to understanding their role is to examine how knowledge (as systematized information) is disseminated and how groups acquire and utilize this knowledge. The delay in the report's release was significant because it reflected the contention within the World Bank about the appropriate role of the information infrastructures and the meaning of 'knowledge' (often distributed over these infrastructures).

Just as the World Bank has now come to emphasize how knowledge is acquired and distributed by societal groups, this book also underscores the importance of demand as well as supply of telecommunication service provision. The book ends with how telecommunication services are being provided and their possible implications for development. While it shows how information infrastructures are coming about, it does not provide a rigorous treatment of how exactly they lead to particular types of development. Instead it concentrates on the likely losers and beneficiaries from telecommunications restructurings Thus, the contribution of the book lies in outlining an oft-missed first step in our calculations, and not in repeating the steps that have already been taken.

I have incurred several debts in writing this book. The University of Southern California's interdisciplinary program in Political Economy and Public Policy allowed me to study international development issues rigorously without confining myself to the narrow bounds of any one academic discipline. The enthusiasm for interdisciplinarity promoted by this program is, hopefully, reflected positively in the pages that follow. The guidance given by my mentor, Jonathan D. Aronson, stands out. He motivated me to study telecommunications and also to find a balanced mix between theory and policy so that my contribution would be relevant for the myriad of difficult choices facing decision-makers in the developing world. Jeffrey Nugent pushed me toward developing a conceptual framework with insights from institutional economics and public choice literatures. Sandra Ball-Rokeach introduced me to important insights from communication and sociological traditions. I also thank John Odell whose passion for international political economy and whose methodological sensitivities I have tried to emulate.

I have gained from two particular institutional affiliations while writing this book. My work as a Research Associate at the Center for Telecommunications Management at USC's School of Business Administration exposed me at close quarters to the world of telecommunications. My academic position at the University of Mississippi, funded by the BellSouth Foundation until 1998, also allowed me to keep in touch with the dynamic world of telecommunications policy that intersects academia, business, and policy-making bodies. I thank the BellSouth Foundation for the research funds made available to me.

This book would not have covered the shoving and jostling of politics and economics were it not for the forthright and long interviews telecommunications officials gave to me in several countries. In particular, I would like to thank officials of Asia-Pacific Telecommunity (Bangkok) and telecom officials in Singapore, Malaysia, and India. Officials at MTNL, VSNL, NIC, and DoT in India made reams of data and information available to me. I am especially grateful to Sam Pitroda who encouraged me with this project even though he must have realized in interviews that I did not quite agree with him on everything. Bjorn Wellenius and Peter Stem helped in giving me useful contacts in the developing world. Ranjit Singh of *Telematics India* provided several research resources and tips. I am indebted to Ashok Advani for making the archives of his trade journal *Business India* available to me during several research trips to India. I have also benefitted from participants' discussions on the India-gii listserv maintained by "cyberactivist" Arun Mehta.

Many colleagues have read parts of previous drafts. Two in particular, Jana Harrison and Alice H. Cooper, told me things about the draft that, at times, I did not want to hear but nonetheless helped to improve its quality. I would wish such meticulous colleagues upon myself and others any day for the sake of good scholarship. Others who gave me feedback include Thomas Biersteker, Sandra Braman, Katrina Burgess, Donald Crone, John Elliott, Robert Friedheim, Richard French, Jeffrey Hart, Christine Kearney, Alan Melchior, Mary Beth Melchior, Bella Mody, Eli Noam, Jim Rosenau, Jagdish Sheth, Bill Shughart, Tim Shaw, Ronald Steel, and Dianna Tussie. Jill Keesbury and Monique Moléon provided valuable research assistance. Neetha Rao helped with proofreading. I have presented papers drawn from this project at the International Studies Association, the Telecommunications Policy Research Conference, the American Political Science Association, the Congress of Political Economists, the Claremont Colleges political economy group, and the Columbia Institute for Tele-Information, and gained immensely from the discussions at these fora. Finally, the enthusiastic staff of SUNY Press (especially Zina Lawrence, Susan Geraghty, and Nancy Farrell) paid meticulous attention to the book's production and encouraged me to improve the book's quality.

On a personal note, I thank my parents for instilling the love of education in me. I dedicate this book to my mother and the memory of my father. My sister and her family always encourage me with loving words. Uncle Meji remains an inspiration. I must also thank M. J. Parel, my political science and economics teacher at my high school, The Lawrence School, Sanawar, in helping me dedicate myself to development questions at an early age with his poetic intensity. Most of all, not a day passes now without deep gratitude on my part for having a caring, giving, and intellectual partner in Chuck Johnson. Chuck is my muse.

I would have repaid my debt to the people mentioned above and others if my efforts help in any way to make even a small dent in the quest for answers to the problem of development. It is a pitiful paradox that just as we talk of the splendors of "the Information Revolution," a majority of the world's population must live below standards befitting human dignity.

PART I

The Political Economy of Restructuring

CHAPTER 1

Introduction

The *dernier cri* of the developing world's strategic options is now considered telecommunications. Beginning with the early 1980s, many developing countries made telecommunications a development priority and launched ambitious restructuring initiatives ranging from enhanced telecommunications service provision to introduction of varying degrees of market competition in the telecommunication sector.[1] Telecommunications infrastructures are now seen as imperative for the future prosperity of developing countries. The International Telecommunications Union noted more than a decade ago that "telecommunications may be viewed not simply as one technology among others, but as the neural system of a society."[2] Distribution of information, the key function performed by telecommunications, is important for market efficiency. Telecommunications restructurings are thus seen as important barometers in the shift among developing countries toward market-based economies and are often posited as technologies that can help developing countries "leapfrog" or accelerate their pace of development and "connect" with the world economy while also facilitating economic and other transactions in the domestic sphere.

THE QUESTIONS

Restructuring initiatives such as accelerated service enhancement, liberalization, and privatization, challenging the historical state-run monopolies in telecommunications in developing countries, are now widespread but many important questions regarding these changes remain partially or wholly unanswered. How can we understand the links among subsectoral, sectoral, and economy-wide restructuring efforts? How can we account for the differences in the pace (fast/slow), scope (comprehensive/piecemeal), and the sequence of delivery of restructuring initiatives? Which societal groups will benefit the most from these restructuring efforts? There is considerable scholarship on comparative macroeconomic efforts but we still need theoretical studies of sectoral restructurings (especially those examining their links with subsectoral and macroeconomic restructurings and explaining the variations specified in the second question). It is only after providing answers to the first two questions that we can understand the links to development implied by the last question.

This book shows that most LDC states are unable to resolve the myriads of pressures they face for telecommunication restructurings to effect accelerated or "leapfrogging" development. The scope, pace, and sequencing of restructuring varies according to whether the state responds to subsectoral (hereafter micro) level pressures from heterogeneous groups or to macro-level cohesive or plural pressures from coalitions of groups. Micro-heterogeneous and macro-plural pressures usually result in piecemeal, slow, and capricious restructuring because most states are unable to react fast or comprehensively in the face of myriad demands. On the other hand, cohesive pressures on a few states that act as "catalysts" among groups, can result in fast, comprehensive, and demand driven change.[3] Micro and macro pressures are not exclusive and the state might, for example, respond to micro rural pressures while addressing cohesive macro pressures from businesses and other groups in urban areas.

Catalytic states are hard to come by in LDCs. Therefore, telecommunications restructuring initiatives in most developing countries remain slow, piecemeal, and capricious. The political economy of restructuring restricts the provision of telecommunications to a few societal groups. After more than a decade of restructurings, it is not clear that telecommunications are quite the leapfrogging technologies they were made out to be. Considerable scholarship on comparative telecommunications restructurings now indicates that the links between telecommunications and development are not straightforward. This book shows that development depends on who demands telecommunications services, who supplies them, and how they are supplied. The links between telecommunications and development will remain unclear unless we are able to provide reasonable answers to important questions that link telecommunication restructurings with micro- and macroeconomic efforts and also account for the differences in restructurings among the developing countries. While there is plenty of scholarship on telecommunications restructuring and on telecommunications and development, this may be one of the first book-length treatments explicitly linking development with the types of restructurings taking place.

THE LEAPFROGGING THESIS

The phrase "leapfrogging development" reflects the belief, especially in the 1980s, among policymakers and theoreticians that information technologies, especially telecommunications, can help developing countries accelerate their pace of development or telescope the stages of growth.[4] This results from the modernization and expansion of telecommunications infrastructures in developing countries. The infrastructure, in turn, feeds into demand for telecommunications services by other sectors of the economy.

The telecommunications literature uses the word "leapfrogging" in three ways. First, it is meant to imply that telecommunications can help developing countries skip over the stages of development and become members of a postindustrial society. Second, leapfrogging is used in "an engine of growth" sense to mean that telecommunications can help developing countries accelerate their pace of development.[5] Finally, leapfrogging is used in a technical sense to signify skipping over the technological frontier or product cycle.[6] Often the word "leapfrogging" is used interchangeably in both technological and economic ways.[7]

At a theoretical level, an increasing demand for telecommunication services due to changes in global and domestic economic structures is well documented.[8] Among other things, the strategic role information plays in better decision making, creation of markets, reduction of transaction costs, decentralization of organizational hierarchies, and controlling the patterns of distribution, consumption, and production is noted by these works.[9] These factors account for the growing demand for telecommunication services.

Empirically, the linkages between telecommunications and economic development are explored in a range of quantitative and qualitative studies. Empirical studies range from crude economic models correlating indices of development with indices of telecommunications infrastructure and services[10] to detailed qualitative case studies outlining the role of telecommunications in providing a diversity of social and economic services, especially to remote and rural areas.[11] At a more sophisticated quantitative level, studies show the backward and forward linkages of telecommunications in an economy using input-output tables or the telecommunications multiplier.[12] The precise causal mechanism between telecommunications and development, however, is something that is assumed or asserted rather than explored by these studies.

In order to better specify the links between telecommunications and development, a case can be made for measuring economy-wide benefits from telecommunications based on which user groups are the beneficiaries from telecommunications restructuring. Demand for telecommunications services is usually disaggregated by governments and telecommunications in terms of user groups, but the literature on telecommunications and development does not comprehensively posit economy-wide benefits by tallying benefits obtained by these groups. As calculations about user groups are an intrinsic part of studying demand and supply of telecommunications services, it makes sense then to posit benefits in a similar manner. It also helps to show if the benefits from telecommunications are correlated to the sources of demand. Telecommunications policy-making models are usually supply driven, not surprising given the strength and the key role played by governments and telecommunications monopolies in developing countries. A focus on user groups returns us to the sources of demand that, if taken into account, might produce more benefits than a pure supply-driven model.

How Telecommunications Benefits

It needs to be remembered that tallying user-group benefits is but one of the ways of calculating benefits from telecommunications. Overall, table 1.1 presents selected studies at the three levels of analysis usually employed to test the role of telecommunications in development. In general, the studies definitely posit a strong link between telecommunications and development. This link is brought out by these studies in two major ways:

First, at the level of the user group, the benefits from telecommunications are measured for a specific user group in an economy according to the various uses of telecommunications for the agents involved, be they individual business firms or an entire sector. In many ways, techniques measuring consumer surplus at the individual level are but an extension of this analysis, in that the value that consumers place on telephone service, for example, is strongly dependent upon the various uses of the telephone to these consumers.

Second, the causal link is explored at the economy-wide level. Single equation models note the positive correlation between indices of telecommunications service provision (e.g., telephones per 100 population) and those of economic development (e.g., GNP). Structural models identify the linkages of telecommunications to the rest of the economy. The latter technique is especially useful for three reasons: (1) it shows that telecommunications serves as an input to just about every sector in the economy; (2) the benefits from telecommunications to development are independent of the level of development of the various countries studied (because the relative weight of telecommunications use among various sectors varies little among these countries); (3) the studies help to identify sectors such as retail, transport, hotels, tourism, and banking that consume telecommunications services more than others.

The usefulness of economy-wide studies can be increased by incorporating analysis from user-group level. In order to identify how an economy is affected by telecommunications, we need to know who is

TABLE 1.1

Selected Studies Linking Telecommunications to Development by Level of Analysis

	Individual/ Microeconomic	Sectoral/ User Group	Economy-wide: Correlational	Economy-wide: Structural anal.
Representative Work	Chs. 8 & 9 Saunders 1983	Hudson 1981 Tyler 1981 Parker 1980	Hardy & Hudson 1980 Stone 1991	Ch. 5: Saunders DRI/McGraw Hill 1991
Type of Analysis	Quantitative/Descriptive: involving estimates of consumer surplus	Quantitative/Descriptive: indicators of telecom density compared with indicators of dev.	Correlations between indicators of telecom. and development	Input-output analysis showing backward & forward linkages
Major Finding	• Telecom. benefits best assessed by those demanding access to telecom.	• important for social Delivery • lack of telecom: cost on industry • savings in transportation costs	• telecom: greater dev. benefit in LDCs than DCs • telecom increases GDP more in areas with low telecom density	• telecom is an input in every industry • identifies sectors with high telecom intensity
Weaknesses	• Snapshot view of development: no indication of dynamic processes underlying demand & supply	• Partial analyses difficult to generalize • Dynamic processes missing	• Implies rather than explores causality	• Causality exogenously assumed

affected the most by the telecommunications supply and who demands it the most. Telecommunications development analysis at the level of the user group is helpful here because it identifies the various uses of telecommunications by individual groups and thus delves deeper into the causal links between telecommunications and development.

Table 1.2 summarizes some of the findings vis-à-vis these user groups. These groups are not mutually exclusive and are presented here only for analytical clarity. Thus, an exporter may also be a small-sized firm and a large user could be one of the government administration services. Furthermore, we only have a scattered and, at times, group-specific idea of benefits of telecommunications. There is no single study that incorporates the links of telecommunications with development for the whole economy from the point of view of user groups. Therefore, the table draws upon several different studies to examine the uses of telecommunications to the various groups.

Designing telecommunications policies to benefit specific user groups brings in politics. The studies that have identified benefits of (mostly) telephone service to various groups of users have done so in a kind of sociopolitical vacuum. They have been concerned with the uses of telephones once provided or the potential uses of telephones if provided (in the future). None of them (at least in those works that analyze development questions) investigate the dynamic processes of demand and supply underlying telecommunication (telephone) service provision.[13] It may even be argued that these works assume Pareto optimality in telephone service provision whereas the state-run telecommunications sectors in developing countries are full of market distortions. Thus, these analyses are only partially able to answer the three questions posed at the beginning of this chapter that are of paramount importance if we are to fully examine the role of telecommunications in development.

THE ARGUMENT IN BRIEF

Different user groups demand different telecommunication services and benefit from their provision in different ways. The scope, pace, and sequencing of restructuring initiatives varies according to whether the state responds to subsectoral (micro) level pressures from heterogeneous groups or to macro-level cohesive/plural pressures from coalitions of groups. At a micro level, telecommunications services (entailing user-group benefits) can be conceptualized as club goods, whose supply, in most LDCs, is determined by the state. (Reasons for this institutional intervention are explained in the next chapter.) A club good is one where members sharing certain common characteristics come together

TABLE 1.2.
Studies Showing Benefits of Telecommunications According to User Groups

User Group	Representative Work	Benefits of Telecom.
1. Urban Residential	Chs. 10–11: Saunders 1983	Demand for telecom highest among highly educated and high-income people
2. Rural Users	Parker et al. 1989	Helps diversify economic base of rural America, much of it through externalities
3. Small or Medium-Sized Businesses	Tyler 1981	Business costs incurred in Kenya due to lack of telecom (e.g., supply cost, managerial costs): sales loss for industry & services
4. Large Users	NTIA 1992	Several examples of large users (e.g., banks, retailers) reaching markets and linking business units
5. Government Administrations	Kochen 1982 Ch. 7: Saunders 1983	• Computer conferencing for central planning • Substitution of telecom for travel • Administrative efficiency
6. Public/Private Social Delivery Systems	NTIA 1992 Saunders 1983 ITU 1983	Telecom helps deliver health services, education, emergency services, etc.
7. Exporters	IIFT 1988	Telephone/telex traffic and international trade: parallel growth rates, former growing faster than latter

voluntarily to provide themselves with a good (e.g., a country club). Clubs can be identified on the basis of type of service consumed (voice, data, etc.) or on the basis of user-group attributes (the classification used in this book). The terms *clubs* and *user groups* are used interchangeably in this book. The important user groups/clubs (as shown in table 1.2 above) are: large and small business users, exporters, urban and rural residential users, government administrations, and social delivery systems (education, healthcare, emergency services). Unless clubs can form a cohesive coalition, heterogeneous clubs' demands remain weak and pull the state in several directions in meeting their special interests, usually resulting in piecemeal and slow restructurings.

At sectoral and macroeconomic (hereafter both referred to as macro) levels, clubs might come together to form single cohesive or plural coalitions including other interest groups in telecommunications (sometimes in conjunction with other sectors of the economy) that try to wrest telecommunications service provision away from the state. User clubs, for example, might solicit the help of manufacturers, actual or potential service providers, transnational businesses, international organizations, and foreign governments in making their case. These interest groups (including telecommunication clubs) face many collective action problems in petitioning for their demands at the macro level because of group heterogeneity and intangibility of future benefits. On the other hand, telecommunications restructurings in the form of liberalization and privatization are demanded by these groups precisely because, in most cases, state-run telecommunication monopolies are deemed to be inefficient (or resource constrained) in their supply of telecommunication services. A few of these groups also seek to gain from the opening of business opportunities for them from restructuring the sector. Thus, a cohesive coalition, if it comes about, can in specific circumstances lead to comprehensive, fast, and demand-led restructuring.

Telecommunications restructuring entails how states traditionally supplied services through their post, telegraph, and telephone monopolies (commonly known as PTTs) and how states are responding to the pressures for change. States are influenced by political objectives in the supply of telecommunications services. The influence of state decision-making processes means that the workings of supply and demand of telecommunications services may not follow the economic criteria of Pareto efficiency (or optimality) where someone can be made better off without making anyone worse off. Neoclassical economists, such as Sandler and Tschirhart, acknowledge that state/institutional supply of club goods is nonoptimal, but they do not present a model of institutional decision-making.[14] States vary in the degree of efficiency their policy produces. However, a few states (termed catalytic in this book) will

supply services with obvious links to demand and to areas of high productivity and, therefore, approach conditions of efficiency even if they
remain suboptimal. Catalytic states are not beholden to any group and
possess enough resources to effect development agendas. But most states
in LDCs are not catalytic and can be classified as near-catalytic, dysfunctional, or predatory. Dysfunctional states, which are almost always
special-interest dominated, are the most commonly found LDC states,
and are thus examined at length in this book.

The conceptual connections made above between micro- and
macro-restructuring processes are effected in large part by building on
analysis developed by Olson[15] that helps to synthesize two important
theoretical traditions in political economy. Rational choice institutionalism explains political-economic change by focusing on individual preferences. Historical institutionalism shows how existing institutions constrain or even shape individual and societal preferences.[16] Olson's
analysis of special interest organizations, encompassing interest organizations and state responses, helps us synthesize the two facets of new
institutionalism.[17] The distinction between micro- and macro-level activity in this book is analogous to Olson's between "special" and "encompassing" interest groups. Olson writes that while the former focus on
getting benefits only for themselves, the latter encompass substantial
portions of societies leading to widespread benefits.[18]

This book builds on Olson's analysis in three ways. First, club-
goods analysis is employed conceptually to bring rigor to what Olson
calls special interest groups. Sandler in fact notes that Olson's special
interest–group analysis contains "the rudiments of club theory."[19] Second, while examining LDCs we cannot assume that special interest
groups necessarily demand market-displacing favors or favors that do
not reward society as a whole. As most markets in LDCs are heavily regulated or nonexistent, a few special interest groups (or clubs) may in fact
focus on removal of regulations.[20] This is important for analyzing mar-
ket-creation at the micro level. Third, the book makes explicit connections between micro- and macro-level activities while these connections
are more or less peripheral to Olson's work.[21] However, this book
focuses more heavily on the macro contexts of sectoral and subsectoral
restructurings than vice versa.

A caveat about placing the institutional determinants of change mentioned above in three long-run influences is necessary. These are
ideational, technological, and economic changes that impact the preferences of interest groups and states. These determinants are not ignored in
this book, but as shown later, they are incorporated as incentives in the
preference formation of institutional actors.[22] Ideational influences in
LDCs include the weakened hold of existing ideas (such as inward-ori-

ented development strategies and Keynesianism[23]) or the diffusion of neo-classical ideas among the decision-making elite. The role played by the Bretton Woods institutions (IMF and IBRD) and American universities in training neoclassical economists is important in this context.[24] As for technology, in the context of telecommunications, the old argument was that high fixed costs of telecommunication infrastructure only allowed for the operation of a monopoly (the "natural monopoly" argument). Changes in technology that lowered the costs of providing telecommunications services (for example, microwave links) allowed for new firms to contest markets or parts of markets controlled by monopolies.[25]

In addition, economic conditions, termed "objective factors" by Belassa, are important for pushing developing countries toward economic restructuring.[26] Political scientists, particularly, take economic crises as their point of entry in examining the shift among LDCs toward neoliberal economic strategies.[27] Waterbury shows how deep economic crises allow a state to bring in a "change team" that is comprised of "technocrats with few or no links to the political arena," allowing the state to usher in rapid economic restructurings.[28] The impetus given to telecommunications (in trying to "connect" with world markets) in the 1980s may be understood in this regard. To be sure, demand for telecommunication services in LDCs did increase due to attempts to join international markets or to reform their domestic ones. Developing countries spent about 0.6 percent of their GDPs (about $12 billion) on telecommunications by the end of the 1980s, a 100 percent increase from the 0.3 percent they were spending at the beginning of the decade.[29]

Ideas, technology, and economic conditions define the environment in which the politics of clubs, collective action, and state decision-making are played out.[30] These conditions by themselves then only provide the context for the political economy of restructuring and not its resolution.[31] Ultimately macroeconomic or telecommunications restructuring in developing countries is a problem of demand and supply resolved thorough the means of state authority, which remains the dominant supplier or the prime architect of such efforts. The analysis that follows explains how the scope, pace, and sequencing of restructuring initiatives in telecommunications are shaped by: (1) the access of clubs to the state, which often leads only to slow, piecemeal, and capricious restructuring; (2) collective action by telecommunications clubs and other sectors at a macro level, which only in a few cases can lead to fast, comprehensive, and demand-led change; and (3) differences in restructuring initiatives depending on whether the state is catalytic, dysfunctional, or predatory. Figure 1.1 summarizes the argument. The analysis is consistent with current studies [32] that, instead of prescribing minimal roles for the state in an economy (as in neoclassical economics), focus on the particular con-

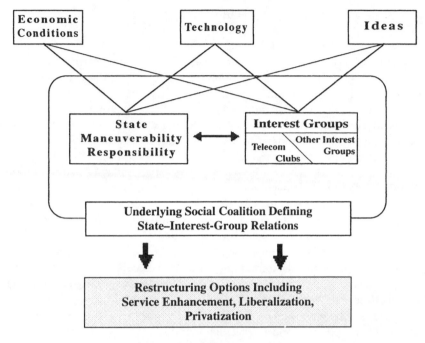

FIGURE 1.1
Flow Chart of Factors Determining Telecommunications Restructuring

texts under which state intervention leads to predatory behavior or prosperity and on how the state might prepare itself for giving up its role as a supplier of goods and services.

Finally, piecemeal change cannot be understood with piecemeal analysis. Subsectoral, sectoral, and macroeconomic restructurings are not discrete entities. State monopoly in telecommunications was itself part of a macro strategy of inward-oriented development in which the state role was dominant. Moves away from this strategy are, likewise, part of emerging social coalitions or party systems in LDCs that include private domestic and international business, the services sector, parts of middle income urban groups, and a variety of international pressures. It is for this reason that figure 1.1 places the political economy of telecommunication restructuring (ideational, technological, economic, and political factors) within the wider backdrop of economy-wide coalitions in LDCs. Whether or not emergent policies benefit the new social coalitions or interest groupings will depend less on the efficacy of an ideal economic strategy and more on the institutional context of its implementation and consolidation.

THE PLAN

A two-tiered approach is followed for the research design. The first step explains variation across cases and the second step explains variation within a case by the use of the same explanatory variables. Developing countries are making disparate choices for restructuring their telecommunication sectors. Part II of the book, the first step, examines the political economy of these choices in seven developing countries in several broad issue-areas in telecommunications. The method of structured focused comparison is used, by picking cases according to the variation in explanatory variables: the countries are selected on the basis of state types (catalytic/near-catalytic/dysfunctional/predatory) and the types of pressures on these states (heterogeneous at micro level and cohesive/plural at macro level). The chapters bring out the commonalities and differences among them for the purposes of generalizability. The validity of this method lies in finding evidence for propositions through their confirmation in a large number of cases while also remaining sensitive to the differences among the cases to ascertain the causes for variation.[33] In Alexander George's words, this method can "increase the likelihood of discovering causal patterns between various outcomes of the dependent variable and various configurations of independent and intervening variables."[34]

The propositions in this book would be valid if they explained not just the variation across cases but also within cases over time as well. Why, for example, are countries able to liberalize one subsector (say, cellular) before others (basic telephone service)? What explains the particular timing of restructuring in a given time period versus another when it may have been tried but abandoned? The cases discussed in part II of the book provide partial answers to these questions. Ideally, in order to get complete answers, all seven cases discussed in part II would have to be explained in terms of variations through time of many types of telecommunications restructurings carried out by these countries. Given the time and resources needed to do such a study, Eckstein suggests a simpler method when "there is unfortunately no close relationship between the simplicity of propositions and the ease or economy of testing them."[35] Thus, a plausibility study of multiple observations within a single "most likely" case is carried out.[36] The single case chosen is that belonging to the class of pluralistically pressured-dysfunctional states. Part II of the book in particular, and common sense in general, dictates that the transition from centrally planned/state-directed economies to market liberalization usually involves dysfunctional states trying to arbitrate plural pressures.[37] Chapter 4 concludes that the case of a dysfunctional state (Brazil in this chapter) with heterogeneous pressures at the micro level and a plurality of pressures at the macro level, may be the most representative for developing countries. In fact, the other cases observed in part II of the book seem to be converging toward such a class of cases in the 1990s. Testing for variation within dysfunctional-pluralistic pressured cases is then of particular 'real world' relevance. Eckstein notes for such most-likely cases "that the theory could hardly be expected to hold widely if it did not fit closely there."[38] Part III of the book treats India as a crucial generalizable case for the purposes of such validation in three successive chapters: one on Indian telecommunications from colonial days to early 1984, another on slow restructuring from 1984–91, and a third on crisis-driven restructuring from 1991 onwards.

Why India? The country is widely regarded as the classic and oldest case of an import-substitution industrialization strategy now trying to liberalize and enter world markets. It offers the case (even more than Brazil) of a typical inward-oriented country undergoing economic transition with multiple pressures on a state that lacks maneuverability and responsibility. In fact, it could even be conceived as a near-catalytic state until the late 1960s when it became dysfunctional (such a transition now holds for many of the cases examined in chapter 3 of this book). India made telecommunications a development priority in 1984 and now accounts for the highest investment expenditure on telecommunications among the developing countries.[39] As one of the first low-income countries to make telecommunications a development priority along with measures toward liberalization and privatization, the country's experiment with telecommunications (among other sectors) is also being watched closely.

The research design used in this book is a variation on the mix of quantitative-qualitative research design (a large-n, small-n combination) that is often advocated for getting robust results. King, Keohane, and Verba advocate combinations of both strategies.[40] This book takes their advice, albeit within a qualitative research design context. In fact, there is no a priori case for believing that large-n, small-n combinations are only useful in quantitative-qualitative research design contexts (even though one can agree on validating small-n results through large-n studies or expanding on large-n results through details on small-n). Thus, part III of the book, with its multiple case studies, serves as the first test of causal inferences across seven cases but part IV tests these for variations within a single case. However, let me once again emphasize that the ultimate validity for the propositions advanced in this book will lie in testing them in detail across a large number of cases in the future.

THE IMPORTANCE

New hopes for development are being placed on strategies of liberalization and privatization in developing countries. Much has also been made specifically of telecommunications as a "leapfrogging technology" that would help developing countries accelerate their pace of development and become part of global markets. These scenarios need to account for the role politics plays in these efforts. Kindleberger calls these "the relationships between economic interest and political power."[41] Specifically, we need an appreciation of the political mechanisms of states to understand how societal preferences are articulated and arbitrated. In the words of another theorist: "Creating markets is politically dangerous."[42]

As scholars, we care about inconsistencies and contradictions in economic restructuring efforts but we are less successful in explaining them. These explanations are also important to policymakers, businesses, and societal groups.[43] The framework proposed in this book qualifies pressures for change by showing how these pressures are seldom rationalized and how in many circumstances they remain weak, resulting in piecemeal, slow, and inconsistent changes. The elite driven nature of most restructuring coalitions also explains why benefits are slow to trickle down to the masses unless their support is important for state legitimacy.

Theoretically, the book synthesizes club goods, collective action, and historical institutionalist political economy literatures to explain telecommunication restructuring. This is necessary to examine not only how group preferences impact the state, but how the state responds to and shapes these preferences in turn. Historical institutionalist analysis contextualizes the findings of rational choice analysis that posits outcomes approaching optimality given group preferences. Clubs and coalitions dealing with institutionalized authorities like the state can seldom expect political markets to work as effectively as economic markets. Catalytic states are able to play a dirigiste role here, but dysfunctional special-interest–driven states are like biased referees, while predatory states seldom care about external preferences.

At a policy level, the book contextualizes the findings of many studies that posit the benefits from increased investments in telecommunications. As developing countries restructure their telecommunications sectors, this study provides a useful framework for examining the relative influences of various economic, ideational, technological, and political factors. By themselves, each of these influences provides a partial explanation. This book combines them in a theoretically driven demand and supply framework to provide a better explanation. The book then places the current thinking on the "information revolution" in developing countries in a political-economic context. It provides a framework for judging the optimistic as well as pessimistic claims being made about the effects of the information revolution in developing countries. Much of the literature on telecommunications comes with a supply push technology bias. This book looks at how the supply of these services benefits the various groups who are demanding them and at how these demands are being met at all. The documentation of micro- and macro-level user-group pressures in this book tries to correct the relative empirical neglect of these issues in the telecommunications literature.[44] "Leapfrogging" implies that telecommunications will help developing countries accelerate their pace of development or skip the stages of development. Which user groups get these services first and how do they do so will be important for determining whether or not these countries "leapfrog."

CHAPTER 2

The Argument Explained

This chapter first explores the influence of economic conditions, ideas, and technology on telecommunication restructurings in general. The three variables were considered briefly in the last chapter. They provide the context for restructuring telecommunications and explain the origins of preferences for interest groups and the state. In brief, changes in the underlying national and international economic structure, and the available pool of ideas and technology provide incentives and disincentives for demands by user groups (and other interest groups) and supply by the state. The chapter then turns to the central theme of this book, namely micro- and macro-level pressures upon different types of states for restructuring. This political economy is provided to show how certain types of pressures and states are better suited for fast, comprehensive, and demand-led restructuring than others. But in most cases, states (termed dysfunctional in this book) are unable to effectively resolve the intensity and the variety of demand pressures. The access of politically powerful user clubs and other interest groups to the state and the state's concerns with maintaining its legitimacy are paramount conditions influencing restructuring efforts. Table 2.1 lists the main arguments explained in this chapter.

THE CONTEXT FOR
TELECOMMUNICATIONS RESTRUCTURING

The motivations for telecommunications restructuring are explained by economic conditions, and changes in ideas and technology. Economic conditions are further subdivided into the domestic production structure and globalization for analytical purposes (though both reveal domestic and international influences). The three factors examined here specify the overall direction of change by constraining the set of options that developing countries have available.[1]

Economic Conditions: Domestic Production Structure

The high priority given to telecommunications by policymakers in developing countries now is in stark contrast to the near neglect this sector

TABLE 2.1
The Arguments

Telecommunication restructuring applies to service enhancement, liberalization, and privatization and the accompanying organizational, regulatory, and policy changes.

Context for Restructuring Affecting Demand and Supply

Severe domestic economic crises (entailing international help or bailouts, and selling of lucrative state-run enterprises) or increasing globalization will push the state toward restructuring according to the priorities dictated by international actors or rules framed at the global level (and weaken the constituencies favoring state-run/inward-oriented development strategies).

The ascendance of liberal ideas and the rate of technological innovation strengthen the case for telecommunication restructuring while weakening the arguments favoring PTTs.

Demand for Restructuring

Micro Level: Because individual (user group) clubs are voluntary, remain dispersed, and may have few incentives to petition the state collectively, pressures at this level are often too weak to move the state resulting in marginal restructurings.

Macro Level: Coalition/s of interest groups (including those part of economy-wide coalition/s) can effectively petition the state collectively though the pace, scope, and demand-led nature of restructuring is contingent on the coalition/s' degree of access to the state's decision-making processes.

Supply of Restructuring

One of the following three will apply:

1. A *catalytic state* (with high degrees of maneuverability and responsibility) will not only meet user demands but also play a dirigiste role in shaping future preferences including those of powerful special interests (which, while present in catalytic states, are seldom able to dominate state agendas) resulting in fast, comprehensive, and demand-led restructuring.

2. A *dysfunctional state* (with low degree of maneuverability and varying degrees of responsibility) meets the demands of a few or many user groups who dominate the state although provision is neither efficient nor optimal (and contingent on the state effectively arbitrating coalitional pressures where they are plural).

2a. Subsidiary argument: A dysfunctional special-interest–driven state with myriad pressures (at club and coalitional levels) is most prevalent in the developing world. This accounts for the slow, piecemeal, elite or supply-driven nature of telecommunication restructurings in developing countries.

(continued on next page)

TABLE 2.1 *(continued)*

3. A *predatory state* (with a high degree of maneuverability and absence of responsibility) seldom meets user demands or takes any developmental initiatives.

Constraint Affecting Demand and Supply

Choices states make are sometimes as dependent on the micro and macro levels of interaction with specific interest groups as they are on the degree of state concern with construction of its legitimacy or consolidation of power.

---

suffered in the development strategies until the late 1970s in almost all LDCs. An inward-oriented development strategy (also known as import-substitution industrialization or ISI) was the dominant strategy adopted by developing countries until the late 1970s and early 1980s.[2] However, long before the ISI strategies were dismantled in the developing world, a number of international organizations and other advocates had been pressuring developing countries to make telecommunications a priority, and many were beginning to do so. Brazil and Singapore made telecommunications a development priority in the 1970s and South Korea and India did so in the early 1980s. It would then be incorrect to assume, as is often done now when telecommunications are thought of as "technologies of globalization," that telecommunications had to wait for worldwide liberalizations to be considered important for development. The brief history provided below serves to provide an appropriate context.

Telecommunications and ISI   Among the big economic development debates of the immediate postcolonial era, telecommunications was seldom mentioned among the key sectors slated for a thrust in development strategies or in central plans.[3] Telecommunications investments in LDCs, at least until the mid-1970s, were usually around 0.3 percent of the GDP (which doubled to 0.6 percent by the end of 1980s).[4] Five reasons (not mutually exclusive) might be mentioned to explain the lack of importance given to telecommunications. First, the policy emphasis on satisfying "basic needs" made the supply of food, drinking water, and electricity more pressing than the need for telephones. Second, the economic development discourse was set up in terms of primary and secondary sectors and other sectors such as the services or the tertiary ones (which would include telecommunications) received marginal importance. Third, it was not until the early 1970s that studies (see tables 1.1 and 1.2) began to examine the positive impact of telecommunications on development. Fourth, telecommunications occupied a low place of importance even among many developed countries, as could be seen from the low density of telephones in many European countries. There were few international pressures to improve telecommunications. Finally, the telecommunications bureaucracies set up during the colonial days catered to elite interests. With their jobs secure in postcolonial administrations, they had no incentive to supply telecommunication services to the masses or to try to change policy thinking on these issues.

The emerging importance of telecommunications within ISI might be traced to two factors: recognition of the importance of communications in general (including radio, TV, media) to the development process (of which the studies mentioned in tables 1.1 and 1.2 were a part), and secondly, the explicit importance given to development of telecommunications in the call for correcting the communication/information imbalances between the North and the South. Wilbur Schramm's *Mass Media and National Development* (1964) was seminal in its attempt to link development with the spread of information, hence literacy and education, through mass-communication instruments.[5] While Schramm's ideas might have been limited to mass communication initially, they did highlight the importance of information to development. This led directly to examining the information imbalances within and beyond LDCs, especially between industrialized and developing countries. This later came to be known as the "communication gap."[6] These events also coincided with and provided impetus internationally to the demand for a New World Information and Communication Order (NWICO) to accompany the New International Economic Order.[7]

The idea of a NWICO was launched formally after the 1976 Colombo meeting of the Non-Aligned countries and the 1976 Nairobi 19th General Conference of UNESCO. Initially, the NWICO laid importance on correcting the one-way flow of negative news and information from LDCs to DCs. But by the time of the MacBride Commission Report, the influential work *Many Voices, One World* (1980), developing self-reliant communication infrastructures within LDCs became important. The MacBride Commission wrote that

> communication be no longer regarded merely as an incidental service and its development left to chance. Recognition of its potential warrants the formulation by all nations, and particularly developing countries, of comprehensive communication policies linked to overall social, cultural, economic and political goals. Such policies should be based upon inter-ministerial and inter-disciplinary consultations with broad public participation. The object must be to utilize the unique capacities of each form of communication, from interpersonal and traditional to the most modern, to make men and societies aware of their

rights, harmonize unity and diversity, and foster the growth of individuals and communities within the wider frame of national development in an interdependent world.[8]

In as much as international market imbalances are linked to imbalances in information, the emphasis upon telecommunications was apparent in international trade and services issues where access to and control over information became primary concerns.[9] The need for a viable telecommunications infrastructure with the growing importance of international trade became increasingly recognized.[10] What emerged from NWICO were ideas emphasizing self-reliance in individual LDCs and collective reliance across them. Many authors and organizations during the 1970s, while not expressly endorsing NWICO, recognized the importance of self-reliance in telecommunications and also emphasized making transfers of technology from developed countries more suitable to LDCs.[11] Before NWICO, Mowlana notes that the "[R]esearch emphasis on developing nations usually stressed how to communicate Western ideas and models *to* these countries, not how to communicate *with* them."[12]

To sum up, the NWICO-ISI line of thinking shows that telecommunications was becoming increasingly recognized as a priority even before LDCs began moving away from an ISI strategy in the 1980s. Thus, it could be argued counterfactually that, LDCs would have continued to make telecommunications a priority even without abandoning ISI.[13] For example, IBRD reports recognize that changes in telecommunications thinking began to emerge around the mid-'70s before ideas of privatization and deregulation had become popular among LDCs.[14] The studies commissioned by the International Telecommunication Organization to examine the links between telecommunications and development led the organization to declare 1984 as the International Communication Year. ITU's Maitland Commission Report urged developing countries to put a telephone within a short distance of every member of their population.[15] One could add, however, that this thinking did not come into being fully until the ISI strategy was considerably more in disrepute by the 1980s and developing countries (along with the Soviet Union and Eastern Europe) abandoned it.

Moving Beyond ISI   The slow economic gains effected through ISI called the efficacy of the entire strategy into question. The low level of investment in telecommunications in developing countries did not meet the high demand for even basic telecommunications services and continued to be low despite high rates of return in telecommunications.[16] Moreover, the number of telecommunications services demanded by domestic and international users multiplied manifold. In the meantime, technological change and globalization of markets (discussed later) broke down the traditional "natural monopoly" argument that called for high levels of investment usually taken up by LDC states. It was becoming apparent to policymakers (and many academics) that not only was telecommunications of utmost importance to development, but that the traditional ISI model that rested on the state-run monopolies or PTTs was inappropriate to meet the growing demand for telecommunications services.

The basic gist of the thinking critiquing ISI, as articulated in several reports, was threefold. First, they attempted to show that no matter how elaborate the central plans, capital resources remained scarce for sectors included in the plans while others have had to be excluded due to lack of resources. The Consultative Committee on Telephones and Telegraph (CCITT), an important advisory body within the ITU, noted that in spite of the importance of telecommunications to building the national economic infrastructure, it was consistently plagued with underinvestment: "a permanent shortage of investment funds . . . leads to capital rationing which can be quite arbitrary in effect. This often results in the treasury of the country allocating a given sum to telecommunications, even though a much larger amount would be warranted."[17] Not limiting himself to any particular sector, Vernon notes that while in theory state enterprises might have promoted growth and development, in practice most of the resources were diverted toward rescuing financially troubled enterprises.[18]

Second, drawing upon the studies linking telecommunications to development, national planning agencies (while making telecommunications a priority) realized the inability of their resource constrained state-run telecommunications sectors to provide enhanced investments or better services.[19] At a general level, public enterprises in LDCs during the 1970s recorded heavy deficits, coupled with huge borrowings in the capital markets.[20] Studies show the relative inefficiency of the public sector vis-a-vis private enterprises with the latter accounting for high rates of return, higher labor productivity and profits, and lower production costs. Belassa notes that "the absence of clear-cut objectives for managers and state intervention in firm decision-making" were the two basic conditions for examining the relative efficiency of the state-run sector.[21]

Third, telecommunications became important as the services or tertiary sector began to receive importance. It was noted earlier that development strategies of LDCs were once preoccupied with primary and secondary sectors. However, in spite of the low importance given to services, their dynamism and productivity lies in the fact that the biggest growth rates in LDCs (as well as developed countries) in the postwar era were recorded in the services sectors. These sectors constitute areas such as banking, finance, travel, tourism, distribution networks, telecommunications, and media. Services are now estimated to account for 66 percent of the GDP in high-income countries, 35 percent in low-income economies, 52 percent in middle-income economies, and 63 percent in the world as a whole.[22] Furthermore, the growth rates of the services sectors have been far higher than that of agriculture and industry, for both developed and developing countries. These growth rates in fact increased in the 1980s as more and more countries moved toward an export-oriented strategy. Rapid flows of information are important for making the services sectors efficient and competitive. "Telecommunication services are at the heart of any modern service economy. Indeed the merging of computers, communications, and product technologies is creating a world information economy."[23]

By the late 1970s, given the need to make telecommunications a development priority and the resource constraints states faced, *we would expect that the economic crises generated by the ISI would allow many states to usher in new economic strategies (including those in telecommunications) by, for example, weakening the hand of ISI constituencies and strengthening the outward-oriented ones.*

The 1980s became a decade when not only did telecommunications become a development priority but moves toward involving the private sector in telecommunications service provision and equipment manufacturing began to be considered. It was becoming clear that government-run telecommunication monopolies were too inefficient or resource-constrained to provide enhanced telecommunication services (in spite of their high rates of return) and a move toward the market (through liberalization and privatization measures) was deemed necessary. It would be a win-win situation. States could raise revenues by selling off these monopolies while private businesses would be afforded additional opportunities. The market orientation being given to these sectors in developing countries in the context of globalization attracted international attention. A focus on the latter helps to understand how the emerging global economy influences telecommunications restructurings.

Economic Conditions: Globalization

It is now readily acknowledged that telecommunications is a way for developing countries to "connect" with the world markets and adjust to the emerging global rules governing these markets. The term "globalization" captures this dynamic. At a broad level, globalization, which picked up pace in the late 1970s, signifies the emergence of international markets, the associated beneficiaries, patterns of interdependence or dependence, and the sociopolitical processes sustaining these markets. In the context of this book, globalization refers mostly to the influence upon telecommunications restructurings of the actors and rules sustaining world markets. Globalization implies that given the rapid changes taking place in production, LDCs must improve their telecommunications sectors if they are to play any role in world markets. Globalization is also directly connected with interdependence defined as "situations characterized by reciprocal effects among countries or among actors in different countries."[24] Thus, in a world of emerging or existing tightly knit markets, telecommunications are a key to smooth information flows that are crucial for the markets to work efficiently.[25]

The globalization perspective is presented somewhat prescriptively by neoclassical economists who argue that an export-oriented or outward-focused strategy is better suited for development (and becoming part of the global economy) than an ISI or an inward-oriented strategy.[26] The economists' argument implies that LDCs have a choice and they can opt to stay out of the world system if they so wish.[27] Scholars in international relations are divided on the question of whether the pressures of globalization would automatically make developing countries take certain actions including those leading to telecommunication restructuring. For now these perspectives are combined here to present four major globalization aspects (again, not mutually exclusive) that in turn necessitate the improvement of telecommunications sectors in LDCs.[28]

1. The coordination of the current complexity of the international division of labor, sometimes termed post-Fordism, depends on rapid flows of information that make telecommunications a necessity.[29] The current international division of labor is such that the traditional notion of comparative advantage and product cycle with nation-states specializing in the production of commodities must now be transformed to account for two profound changes. First, the final product might reflect the specialization or value added by several nations rather than one. Technological innovation is making it "increasingly advantageous for multinational corporations to spread production around the globe."[30] Second, the introduction of new technologies, especially microelectronics, is making uncompetitive industries in a few countries competitive again. This is happening in "downstream industries" in the product cycle where LDCs traditionally claimed comparative advantage. Thus "producers with access to newest technologies in industries as diverse as automobiles, textiles, and machine tools are defining new production frontiers that give them an absolute cost advantage over competitors relying on older technologies."[31] In as much as LDCs are becoming part of the global economy (or are already a part of it) they must invest in these technologies, too, to remain competitive.

2. Global economy at present is characterized by intense competition not just in the number of firms operating in any industry but also in the way that the firms create their market shares through product differentiation and flexibility of production.[32] Thus firms may create a competitive advantage over others by their use of information technologies. These technologies can help to reduce costs, improve quality, and provide value added and competitive intelligence. These intrafirm tasks, most of which require tremendous coordination, are dependent on information networks.

3. Telecommunications are important for the producing firms not just to keep in touch with fluctuations in world demand (or elasticities) but also to keep the distribution channels efficient. Sometimes it is even pointed out that trade is moving the capitalist world toward homogenized consumption patterns, where market shares would depend upon the ability of the firm to deliver the same product with slight differences in different countries at the same time.[33] Gereffi notes that the rise of global commodity chains "are rooted in transnational production systems, which link the economic activities of firms to technological, organizational, and institutional networks that are utilized to develop, manufacture, and market specific commodities."[34] The importance of information technologies for sustaining these networks is self-evident. An estimated one third of world trade is now in fact intrafirm trade.[35]

4. Developing countries are also responding to the emerging norms and rules governing telecommunications in a globalized world economy in restructuring their telecommunications sectors. The WTO accord signed by 69 countries in February 1997, agreeing to time schedules for liberalizing and privatizing their telecommunication sectors, is an important illustration of this phenomena. The global norm here is clearly free trade that the WTO was able to translate into rules governing telecommunications.

Returning now to the degree of autonomy states possess vis-à-vis global influences, the question is whether developing countries are socialized in to the global liberal economy or they are doing so of their volition.[36] Many neo-Marxists, social constructivists, and power-theory scholars argue the former whereas liberal internationalists argue the latter position.[37] In the former perspective (of which there are many variants), the powerful set up the rules of the game and the weak suffer what they must even though occasionally they might protest. Krasner writes that international telecommunication norms and rules reflect the underlying distribution of power in the world.[38] Rules emerge in areas where nation-states either agree or can co-opt others into agreeing with them.

Liberal internationalists argue that norms and rules, even when they might reveal the influence of powerful actors, may neither mean that the weak are suffering nor that only the strong states are calling all the shots. In fact, Keohane and Nye examine issue-structures rather than global power structures to examine how particular norms and rules emerge in particular issue areas.[39] Cowhey writes that the international telecommunications rules were epitomized in the past by the series of multilateral negotiations that led to the formation of the International Telecommunications Union (ITU) and the International Telecommunications Satellite Organization (Intelsat). This regime gave pride of place to government-run PTTs and also "fostered an epistemic community devoted to the idea of a 'natural monopoly' for telephone services."[40] According to Cowhey, two specific changes globally have caused this regime to move toward more market and trade–oriented ideas for the future. These are: technological changes that have eroded the natural monopoly argument, and demands by large users, computer and electronic firms, and service companies to open up the telecommunications service and equipment manufacturing market to competition.[41] To this we may add that, in the context of developing countries at least, the economic crises induced by their erstwhile ISI strategies made it possible for them to now accept (or accede to) the outward orientation at the heart of globalization.[42]

The proof of the pudding is in the eating. The evidence presented in the four empirical chapters will show the respective roles played by the strong (in forcing or not forcing) and the weak (in acquiescing or adjusting) to global pressures. The focus of this book is clearly on comparative telecommunications restructurings. In as much as different developing countries reveal differences in the pace, scope, and sequencing of restructuring initiatives, one may at least conjecture for now that developing countries have not given into any totalizing logic of globalization.[43] Nonetheless, the context of globalization is important for understanding the preferences of domestic and international actors in telecommunication restructurings. International actors such as ITU, IBRD (significant in the LDC context), transnational enterprises and other international and large users are thus modeled as interest groups (or user groups as the case may be) that impact upon domestic political processes.[44]

Finally, given the combination of domestic production structure and globalization influences, we can expect that developing countries will not only make telecommunications a priority but also move away from an ISI strategy while doing so. *Where economic crises are severe (entailing international bailouts or help) or globalization influences strong, we*

*can expect that countries will restructure according to the prerogatives
of international actors or rules framed at the global level (and weaken
the hand of actors favoring inward-oriented development strategies).*

Ideas and Technology

Economic restructuring in general, and telecommunications in particular, is seldom mentioned without citing the influence of ideational or technological factors that helped to weaken the entrenched constituencies of erstwhile economic groupings. Casualties include the failure of the inward-oriented development strategies in developing countries and the weakened hold of Keynesian state intervention ideas in general.[45] Zacher and Sutton acknowledge these influences in their work, calling recent ideational influences "the *zeitgeist* of neoclassical economics and deregulation."[46] Similarly, technology-based explanations are at the heart of older arguments about "natural monopoly," and their breakdown in the current context is located in technological factors.

Ideas   There are two levels at which ideas may influence telecommunications restructuring in developing countries. At the sectoral level, there may be policy emulation, catching-up, or ideational competition ("who will liberalize first" type) that leads to adoption of particular ideas. At a broader level, ideas guiding policymakers for the economy in general may trickle down to the telecommunications sector.

1. Sectoral Level Ideas   Ideational emulation and trickle down have always informed the choices countries make for their telecommunication sectors. The influence of ideas in making telecommunications a development priority and rationalizing the operations of telecommunication monopolies was noted earlier (tables 1.1 and 1.2) as in ITU making 1984 the International Communications Year or the World Bank releasing a major report on telecommunications in 1983.[47] It is no coincidence or surprise that as developing countries began in the 1980s to restructure their telecommunications sectors, they looked toward other countries' experience for guidance. Initiatives such as introducing competition or privatization in the telecommunications sector were not a big part of telecommunication policy in the world until the mid-1980s. It was only after such restructuring took place in developed countries in the early 1980s (breakup of AT&T, privatization of British Telecom and Japan's NTT) that it became a standard fare of options to be advocated for developing countries. Starting with the Mexican PTT Telmex's privatization in December 1990, advocacy of liberal sectoral policies became de rigueur for interested parties: multilateral institutions, developed country governments, transnational enterprises, and a few technocrats and businesses in developing countries. A World Bank strategy paper released in 1992 outlines three areas of major thrust for Bank support in telecommunications: developing competition, increasing private sector participation, and developing regulations that enhance the other two objectives.[48] Beginning with the late 1980s, developing-country policymakers studied and were advised about other countries' experiences on these matters. Those countries with well-framed telecommunications policies, high telecommunications densities, and ambitious restructuring programs received a lot of attention.[49]

That there was considerable dissemination of ideas and information about telecommunication restructuring in the 1990s is not in dispute. The degree to which it actually influenced policy is hard to measure. On the other hand, the extent to which we can trace explicit policy statements made by user groups and states with implicit or explicit references to these ideas will help to show that ideational influences matter.

2. *Neoclassical Ideas*   The move toward a more market-oriented industry structure in telecommunications is also explained by the diffusion of neoclassical ideas supporting market systems in general among the decision-making elite and (to a lesser extent) the societal groups in developing countries. Two quotations serve to illuminate this phenomena:

> The internationalization of economic training, through the Bretton Woods institutions and the graduate departments of American and European universities, has clearly increased the viability of orthodoxy by creating a cadre of economists in many developing economies who can understand its outlines and are attracted (in part) to its coherence.[50]

> Ideas may have an independent explanatory role by way of a number of different transmission mechanisms. First, there may be general contagion effects and policy emulation. . . . Second, there may be a "trickle-up" process where ideas gain initial acceptance among academic economists, who subsequently press their policy advice on the political leadership.[51]

The position taken by the World Bank and the International Telecommunications Union vis-à-vis the move toward market-oriented mechanisms in the provision of telecommunications services and equipment seems to be consistent with the quotations above. It is also now noted that the new coalition of large users, microelectronics firms and computer manufactures that challenged the PTT-dominated model in telecommunications "turned to the organizing principle of free trade as a guide for reform."[52] The spread of neoclassical ideas would also seem to be consistent with the diffusion of technology and innovations literature in as much as ideas may be regarded as innovations (or technologies in a broad sense of the word). By definition, diffusion is deemed to be a "process by which (1) an innovation (2) is communicated through certain channels (3) over time (4) among the members of a social system."[53]

In spite of the seeming consistency of the last paragraphs with the two quotations that preceded it, two caveats are necessary. First, it is hard to assign an exogenous role to ideas without contextualizing them in economic conditions. Biersteker, too, acknowledges that while neoclassical ideas had been around for a long time, they "took a particular systemwide shock [mostly economic] to prompt a major reversal in thought."[54] The World Bank studies, for example, specifically note the failure of public enterprises to provide telecommunications services. The market-oriented coalition described by Cowhey finds its rationale not just in market-oriented ideas but in an industry structure that worked against their favor. Even diffusions literature that may be taken to lay emphasis on supply of innovations as opposed to the demand for them acknowledges that, "[I]t is unthinkable to study diffusion without some knowledge of the social structures in which potential adopters are located as it is to study blood circulation without adequate knowledge of the structure of veins and arteries."[55] Second, studies that assign an exogenous role to ideas alone (as in Keynes' famous dictum about the academic scribblers influencing even the madmen in authority) are taking a particularly long-term view of phenomena that would need to be broken up into the short run of political-economic conditions to make sense. Thus, Altschuler, who attributes liberalization of telecommunications to the ascendance of ideas about deregulation in general, fails to specify the role of the human agencies that led to this ascendance.[56]

The point is simple; economic ideas cannot be disengaged from the underlying social and economic structure that makes for their adoption or rejection. The fact is that neoclassical ideas have been around for a long time and while their adoption now may certainly be due to the effects on the decision-making elite and academicians in developing countries, it is no coincidence that this should happen after the failure of the ISI strategy than before it.[57] Social coalitions may also block the adoption of specific ideas or innovations.[58]

Technology   Technological innovations have challenged the traditional notion of a natural monopoly in telecommunications revered by PTTs worldwide including the developing countries. This natural monopoly argument rested on the fact that telecommunications infrastructures required large investment for economies of scale and scope, thus imposing high costs of entry. But changes in technology that lowered the costs of providing telecommunications services (for example, microwave links) allowed for new firms to enter markets or parts of markets controlled by monopolies. Aronson and Cowhey note that "there has been so much investment in fiber optic, microwave, and private satellite systems that future contestability seems assured. If nothing else, once a fiber optic cable is laid, someone can buy it if the original builder goes bankrupt. The 'fire sale' lowers entry costs for the next generation."[59] The fact that the first few service markets to be challenged in developing countries were specialized and value-added services can be attributed to technology that provided an opportunity for potential service providers to enter the telecommunications market while letting the government-run telecommunication entities retain their monopoly in basic telephone services.

Equipment manufacturers also challenged the practices of PTTs to either manufacture equipment on their own or order it through their historic networks of preferred suppliers, an arrangement termed "political telematique" by Noam.[60] In fact in many developing countries (and in many developed countries), the liberalization of the equipment-manufacturing market preceded that of the services market. In the United States, the Hush-A-Phone decision in 1956 that allowed for a muting device to be attached to the mouthpiece, and the Carterphone decision allowing for non-AT&T telephones to be attached to AT&T networks in 1967, are taken as seminal cases opening the AT&T-dominated equipment-manufacturing market for competition. Similarly, FCC granted MCI the right to provide private-line connections between St. Louis and Chicago in 1969 based on the potential of a new technology, namely microwave instead of land-based lines. In many LDCs, potential or existing manufacturers applied pressures on the government to liberalize equipment manufacturing soon after telecommunications was made a priority. Given the strength of international equipment firms, the latter also lobbied LDC governments directly or through their home governments for equipment market liberalization. The role played by the United States Trade Representative (USTR) in officially opening the South Korean equipment market following the Market Opening Fact Finding (MAFF) talks in 1987 is an important example.

More recently, as data communications spread in the developing world, the blurring of lines between telecommunications and computers (dubbed "telematique" by Nora and Minc[61]) also pose a challenge for telecommunications monopolies because computer and microelectronic industries have always been more competitive, the software market being close to perfect competition in some cases.

Technological change explains how it created a constituency for potential providers for provision of telecommunications services and equipment. It is a good point to start when looking for the sources of change in industry structures. However, technological change has been taking place in telecommunications for a long time. The point is explicitly stated by Cowhey when he notes that technological change invalidated the natural monopoly claim as "a self-evident truth after the early years for many parts of telecommunications. . . . [O]ne of the turning points in the regulation of communications came when economists began to grow suspicious of many of the cost claims of engineers."[62] As with economic and ideational factors, we have to trace out the influence of technological change upon user groups and other interest groups to examine the precise timing, scope, and direction of technological influences in each country examined. The case is succinctly stated by Landes: "Invention may follow genius, but production follows demand."[63]

In short, *the ascendance of liberal ideas and the rate of technological innovation strengthen the case for telecommunication restructuring while weakening the arguments in favoring PTTs.* But we need to chart the influence of ideas and technology upon human agencies to understand the path of these influences specifically.

THE POLITICAL ECONOMY OF TELECOMMUNICATIONS

The discussion so far gives a clue to "why" telecommunications restructuring is taking place but is missing the "how" and "by whom." The latter requires us to trace the influence of economic factors, ideas, and technology through political-economic institutions and processes. This section explains how micro user-group (club) level and macro coalitional (plural or cohesive) level pressures impact the state and how the latter responds to these pressures even while shaping them in turn.

Clubs and States

Before explaining how club-level heterogeneous pressures are resolved by states, it would behoove us to understand the importance and nature of telecommunications as a club good.[64] Apart from the obvious fact that club goods are merely a formal way of focusing on user groups, a focus on them is useful for three other reasons. First, club-goods analysis helps us understand the logic behind how influential minorities might appropriate most of the benefits of particular restructuring initiatives. Buchanan's seminal paper on club-goods also noted that club-goods theory is relevant wherever there is a membership limit to any economic activity.[65] Second, as rationales for state intervention are usually based on public-goods characteristics, and rationales for market authority are based on private-good characteristics, a club-goods scenario might help contextualize public policy appropriately. For example, if a particular telecommunications service (say a data network) benefits only business users then obviously it is incorrect to characterize telecommunications exclusively as a private or a public good. Telecommunication lies on the spectrum between a private good that is individually supplied and consumed, and a public good from whose consumption no one can be excluded and that suffers from no congestion or crowding with additional consumers. Third, club-goods analysis is particularly useful for analyzing important restructuring processes underway in LDCs as it can be applied to most infrastructural facilities and utilities and attendant political coalitions. A telecommunication infrastructure is a club good that can be jointly supplied by its members who can share the cost of provision of the good (for example, through installation costs) and exclude nonmembers. In reality, clubs organize as firms who attract members by listing their prices (entry and usage fees).[66]

Although it is a club-good, many analysts tend to portray telecommunications infrastructure as a public good, focusing on positive externalities that result in enhanced societal benefits beyond those of members from the telecommunications network.[67] But this analysis can be used as a rationale for any number of goods to be called public goods. This was precisely the case with the growth of public-sector enterprises in developing countries.[68] Moreover, the elite-driven nature of telecommunication restructuring in most LDCs means that externalities are not quite as far-reaching as sometimes posited.[69] Public goods analyses also ignore the crowding effects from telecommunications that make telecommunications a nonpublic good. Crowding or congestion effects, arising from the poor quality of the network or long waiting lists for connections, are of particular importance in noting the club-goods character of telecommunications in developing countries, in as much as they exclude potential or existing members from consuming services.

Telecommunications is not a private good either. Those classifying telecommunications as a private good examine congestion effects.[70] A good is perfectly congested when its consumption precludes the consumption of it by another. But telecommunications is not perfectly congestible (or it is only 'partially rival' to use another economics term). One person's use of the network does not necessarily preclude its use by another either at that time or in the future.

Telecommunications is an interesting example of a club-good because its provision has always necessitated institutional intervention. The reasons for institutional intervention in the supply of a club-good are well documented though seldom studied thoroughly. (This book's contribution lies not just in detailing the institutional intervention mechanisms for telecommunications but using them to generalize for other kinds of club goods in the conclusion.) Historically, such intervention in telecommunications came in the form of the state because it could marshal the capital needed for the high level of fixed costs and because telecommunications was seen as prestigious enough for direct state intervention.[71] The continued state interest in preserving its role was also motivated by the high rates of return the telecommunication monopolies generate, allowing state treasuries to use telecommunications as "cash cows."[72] Beyond historical factors, a centralized authority like the state can also resolve several other dilemmas in situations such as telecommunications, where the clubs' populations are made of heterogeneous members (user groups), the good in question is a multiproduct one (existence of several types of telecommunications services), where increasing returns to scale exist, and where a good is not perfectly divisible.[73] Heterogeneous populations have difficulty with setting goals and reaching decisions and multiproduct clubs necessitate the supply of several goods (services in this case) that may not be demanded by all clubs' members.[74] In both cases, the central authority can help to regulate levels of membership and provision in clubs. Where increasing returns are present, marginal cost pricing will not help to recover costs because average costs are higher than marginal costs.[75] A central authority can help to recover costs by instituting a flat rate membership fee apart from the regular utilization charge. Indivisible goods must be shared by consumers and jointly produced by them allowing for either club-goods provision or institutional intervention.

Standard club-goods analysis (without accounting for institutional provision) shows how the size of the club (formally known as membership condition) and quantity of the goods supplied (provision condition) are determined simultaneously to yield a Pareto optimal solution. It is possible to progressively increase the total members in a club as long as the benefits of a marginal increase in membership are equal to or greater than the marginal costs. Conversely, it is possible to go on increasing services as long as they are supported by increased memberships. Each condition is derived independently relative to costs and benefits (of provision and membership as the case may be) to get what economists term partial equilibrium. Taken together, they provide us with general equilibrium (see fig. 2.1). In situations where optimal provision is less than optimal membership, it may be possible to increase provision by increasing membership. In situations where optimal provision is greater than optimal membership, the provision may need to be reduced so that the costs to membership are not greater than the benefits.

The institutional politics of club-goods seldom follow the criteria of efficiency and instead allow for influential groups to benefit. The political influence of clubs in telecommunications is concentrated predominantly among business users and government administrations. Residential users, while in dire need of services especially in urban areas, often

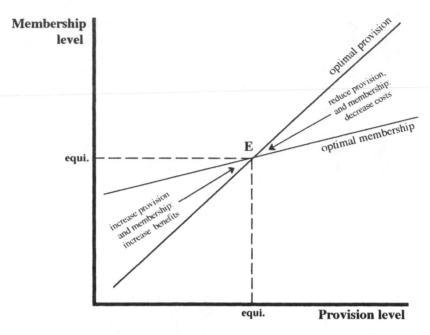

FIGURE 2.1
Provision and Membership Conditions for Club Goods

have less influence than business users. This is explained by the particular nature of the telecommunications sector as well as the nature of club activity. An issue like telecommunications tends to find interested constituency among specialized clubs rather than the general populace.[76] Thus, historically, national telecommunications monopolies found it easy to favor these specialized groups "because state enterprises are ultimately controlled by politicians and government can more easily compensate public enterprises for the costs of accommodating these powerful interest groups."[77] This seldom resulted in optimal provision because political calculations seldom approximate equilibrium costs and benefits. Membership and provision levels are thus different from ones that would be dictated by economic markets. To assume that the state will supply the club-good under optimal circumstances implies that the state has no other agenda apart from selflessly supplying the good in question. State decision-making processes, as we will see later, are important here.

Because individual clubs are voluntary, remain dispersed, and may have few incentives to petition the state collectively, telecommunications service enhancement, liberalization, and privatization in many LDCs is piecemeal, slow, and capricious. As noted earlier, clubs in telecommunications can be differentiated along user group and type of service characteristics, all of which lead to several clubs and heterogeneous outcomes. Thus, it may be easier for an individual club such as business users to petition for their demands to the state through their trade organizations than it is for them to come together with other user clubs. Clubs will then try to obtain individualized privileges at a subsectoral level rather than collectively try to transform the supply structure altogether because of collective action problems. While club demands may be buffered by prevailing economic, technological, and ideational conditions, clubs can be easily ignored by the states unless they are politically powerful. In formal political economy terms, efforts to transform the supply structure at club-level are weak. First, such efforts at the individual club-level may be insufficient to alter existing rules. Second, incentives for clubs to be part of a larger coalition within the telecommunications sector or other sectors may be lacking. Even with collective action forthcoming many clubs might still not be members of coalitions. In the latter case, micro-heterogeneous club pressures must be analyzed simultaneously with macro pressures, as is usually the case with residential user clubs in urban and rural areas existing alongside other coalitions in LDCs.

Third, club-level changes tend to be narrow in scope even if momentarily they fit the needs of the club involved. Usually they result in incremental enhancement of service provision to individual users groups or they are stopgap measures meeting particular demands in the short run. This would account for the availability of specialized services to elite users in a number of developing countries. For example, Motorola provided cellular service in Kinshasa. Data Communications Corporation (DACOM) was originally licensed in Korea in April 1982 to provide data services to a particular set of users. But such measures are seldom rationalized in terms of their relation to macroeconomic policies though they might later lead to formulation of general policies. They may even be contradictory in principle or practice. Thus, whereas the state might be professing a spartan use of scarce resources, private line dedicated networks operated by influential and large corporate and government users might proliferate. Such short-run measures also usually remain woefully inadequate to meet the prevalent or pent-up sources of demand beyond those of a few users. When provision and membership is determined by power, it is seldom consistent or comprehensive.

Collective Action and States

In this section we examine if telecommunications user-clubs are able to come together to form a cohesive coalition demanding change or remain dispersed (in many groups or plural coalitions). The extent of cohesion influences the degree of pace, scope, and sequencing of restructuring. A cohesive coalition may encompass sectors other than just telecommunications inasmuch as a new set of property rights (a collective good) must emerge. In the form of liberalization and privatization, these property rights are now being demanded by various interest groups including those in telecommunications. In telecommunications, this means multiproduct clubs coming together perhaps with other sectors to press for changes ("alliance valence" in Gourevitch's terminology[78]). But heterogeneous groups have a hard time coming together and demanding a collective good. An individual club's incentive to join an alliance is diminished by the fact that benefits from joining a coalition may be incalculable or low. The incentive to free ride becomes high.

A few incentives for collective action at the sectoral or macroeconomic levels do exist especially as a result of economic, technological, and ideational influences mentioned earlier. First, economic crises in many LDCs, largely a result of former state-led development policies during the 1980s, made collective action imperative. The severity of the debt-induced economic crisis in Mexico after 1982 made it easier for the Mexican state to give in to the demands for liberalization measures and eventually telecommunications privatization in 1989. In India, the failure of the state to provide much needed telecommunications services led slowly to the formulation of coalitions of users, potential service providers, and equipment manufacturers to demand liberalization of service provision in the 1980s. Liberalization picked up speed after a severe balance of payments crisis in 1991 weakened the influence of groups supporting the status quo. Second, the effect of changes in ideas and technology might prompt collective action too. In many developing countries, changes in technology empowered groups to demand liberalization of equipment manufacturing and specialized services, and to question national monopolies. It resulted in the breakdown of the closely knit relationship between government run telecommunications monopolies and their equipment suppliers. States respond to ideational change themselves in emulating policies followed in other countries. The third incentive for collective action may come from a failure of activities at the micro level, which prompts user-clubs to become part of macro-level coalitions. Although cohesive user group coalitions (at least in the formal institutional sense) do remain rare in the developing world, it is not rare to find particular clubs' demands supported by potential providers, equipment manufacturers, and international organizations.

Macro telecommunications restructuring (including economy-wide restructuring of which telecommunications may be a part) results from

*the degree of access of the coalition/s of interest-groups to the decision-
making processes of the state.* While this may sound similar to the activity of clubs, the difference is in the scope of change required and the
problems of collective action faced by these groups. For example, while
at the club-level large business users may demand the provision of dedicated data networks from the state, at a sectoral (or at a macroeconomic level) they may also be part of an industry-wide coalition
demanding the privatization of these and other services.

Distinguishing the results of club-level activity from that of collective-action coalitions may now be stated concretely. The answer comes
from a detailed look at the decision-making processes of the state. It is
here that we can discover the ultimate intent of restructuring and the
groups that this restructuring is meant to appease in the state's construction of its legitimacy. Furthermore, clubs usually concentrate on
getting their demands met from the existing institutions. Where they join
forces with other clubs to transform this structure, the problem becomes
one of collective action. Three possible results are often found in developing countries:

1. Club demands are granted by the state in those areas where they
   face little opposition from the state's own bureaucracies. Thus, privatization of cellular services in response to business demands might
   be easy because the service has never been bureaucratic turf and the
   state lacks vested interest in supplying cellular services itself.

2. Privatization of basic telephone or equipment markets where the
   bureaucracy is heavily involved, on the other hand, may need pressures beyond those of an individual club and thus collective-action
   problems arise. However, like in Rousseau's stag hunt (where individual hunters go off hunting for rabbits rather than sticking
   together to find a stag), it may still remain beneficial for clubs to
   seek their share of the pie though the existing state-run structure
   than it is for them to come together in the hope of a bigger pie to
   come in the future through a transformation of that structure.

3. In a few cases the state provides telecommunications services in
   accordance with its own priorities regardless of external demands
   (explained in the next section). Residential user-clubs, while usually
   not part of any coalition, tend to benefit from states' legitimacy prerogatives.

An example regarding export interests and their influences is illustrative. Less developed countries usually have better international services than they have domestic ones. This is mainly due to the access of

exporters, transnational enterprises, and multilateral institutions to the decision-making processes of developing country states. Exporters generally do better than corporate or government large users (although a few large users are also exporters), because they tend to be well organized as interest groups historically. They may have a history of state lobbying for export related favors and they are most likely to employ ideational arguments (a pro-liberalization argument, for example) to hold their numbers together and also to lobby the state. With the globalization of world markets and the attendant competition and division of labor, an inefficient telecommunications infrastructure imposes high costs on the coordination of their productive activities. Being the highest foreign exchange earners, they occupy a privileged position with state decision-makers. State decision-makers, in turn, also may be courting transnational enterprises that place high priority on telecommunications.[79] States may also be under pressures from multilateral institutions to improve their international telecommunications services, pressures that may come appended with loans and grants from these institutions.

The predominance of export interests over those of any other economic interests explains the availability of sophisticated telecommunications services along China's coast, particularly Guangdong and Fujian, which are tied up economically with Hong Kong and Taiwan. It also explains Singapore's international telecommunication ties. It explains the relative efficiency of international services compared to domestic services in Brazil, Indonesia, and India, all of whom have separate providers for international services, partly due to their colonial and semicolonial (in Brazil's case) legacies and partly due to the importance of export and import interests.

The attention paid to both clubs and coalitions in this book is consistent with efforts to integrate societal level variables in political economy analyses in general and telecommunications in particular. Telecommunications literature frequently refers to user demands but more or less limits itself to either anecdotal evidence or needs of large users alone. For political economy as a whole, a recent study notes how institutionalist analyses often overemphasize the state to the relative neglect of how states are able or unable to accommodate multiple and overlapping societal forces.[80] In order to bring in societal actors, this book follows the stringent criterion suggested by Haggard for doing so. "One strategy is to begin deductively, identifying the groups likely to be favored by a particular strategy. . . . A much more stringent criterion for demonstrating societal influence involves showing how groups overcome dilemmas of collective action, gain access to centers of decision-making, and exercise influence."[81]

State Decision-Making Processes

How are micro- and macro-level pressures, especially where they are multiple or conflicting, resolved through the state? States are revenue and power maximizers. Provision of telecommunications services is a subpart (often a minuscule part) of this agenda. It would then be unrealistic to expect that the state's motives for supplying telecommunications services will coincide with those of the demandeurs or result in efficient outcomes. North sums up the issue well in a larger context: "[I]t is exceptional to find economic markets that approximate the conditions necessary for efficiency. It is impossible to find political markets that do."[82]

Attempts to explain the politics of restructuring by focusing on formal political institutions like those existing in developed countries is not possible, as the existence of permanent or highly developed institutions is an untenable assumption to make in many developing countries. Because of the uniqueness of formal institutions in each country, comparative analyses also become difficult.[83] Similarly attempts to explain outcomes by focusing on regime type (pluralist, statist, corporatist, etc.) are fraught with difficulties.[84] Economy-wide studies show that it is incorrect to assume that a particular regime would necessarily adopt a particular development strategy.[85]

The historical institutionalist tradition pinpoints three relevant aspects of state decision-making processes that are relevant for us to analyze the inner workings of the state in LDCs and also to provide cross-national comparisons.[86] (The three aspects can also be seen as constraints upon societal choices.) The first aspect concerns state autonomy or the degree to which the state is independent from (or not captured by) interest groups or the population at large in carrying out its actions. The second characteristic, known as state capacity, concerns the degree to which the state is actually effective in its actions, which in turn depends on its cadre of officials and other resources (financial, institutional, historical circumstances). Finally, the degree to which state actions are development oriented is dependent on the history of state interest and involvement in development issues. The first two aspects relate to institutional aspects of development. The third aspect is specified historically and comes close to being a "behavioral" factor, but in as much as the degree of state involvement in development issues becomes permanent, it can be taken to inform our understanding of institutional characteristics.[87] Either way, the historical institutionalist tradition clearly points toward analyzing institutions in their environmental and historical context, and thus the development orientation of a state would hardly be inconsistent with it.[88]

This book builds upon the preceding concepts to speak of state "maneuverability" and "responsibility" to highlight how state autonomy and development agendas are impacted by varying degrees of state capacity and legitimacy of state institutions.[89] State responsibility is almost always a historical outcome and must be viewed in the context of state legitimacy.[90] Placing state responsibility in the context of construction of legitimacy and state capacity distinguishes it from what has been called a "developmentalist state."[91] The constraint of legitimacy also means that state plans in telecommunications are often at the mercy of the overall political-economic climate. Unless sectoral or economy-wide pressures are intense, states may move very slowly toward addressing the problems of telecommunications. "Maneuverability" takes into account state resources and capacity, and the embeddedness of the state in societal relations while leaving it room to impose its agenda and shape societal choices.[92] First, without capacity, state autonomy means nothing and thus both dimensions are necessary in positing maneuverability. Second, maneuverability can only be analyzed with reference to societal actors as autonomy and divisiveness in state decision-making are often reflective of the state's bases of support.[93] Third, state maneuverability can often be reduced by divisions within the state ranks or by strong bureaucracies who may not tow the line of political power holders. In telecommunications, state enters the picture in three ways: as a policymaker, as a service provider, and as a user. As the three tasks are performed by different agencies with varying degrees of clout within the state, harmony of interests cannot be expected, often resulting in lack of maneuverability for elite decision-makers. All in all, the varying combinations of maneuverability and responsibility in the developing world posit three state types:

1.   A catalytic state can both maneuver and be responsible. It shapes an active developmentalist agenda with respect to vital societal interests. *A catalytic state will not only meet user demands but also play a dirigiste role in shaping future preferences including those of powerful special interest, (which, while present in catalytic states, are seldom able to dominate state agendas).*

2.   A dysfunctional situation follows if the state has either limited maneuverability or varying levels of responsibility. A lack of maneuverability (with or without a lack of responsibility) will produce a state that is either dominated by special interests or is unstable or both, though it can (under special circumstances) act responsibly in carrying out development initiatives. In reality, most states in developing countries have some degree of maneuverability as the most powerful actors in their polities; otherwise they

could not survive. Therefore, *special-interest domination is applied here in the strict sense of a few interest-group preferences being dominant on the state agenda or reflected in state resources diverted toward these preferences. A few or many (depending on the context) user demands are met in this scenario although provision may be neither efficient nor optimal.* The state may also supply these services to other groups because it helps the state increase its legitimacy.

2A. A subsidiary argument made in this book (especially in the empirical chapters) is that *a dysfunctional state with myriad micro- and macro-level pressures is the most representative of the LDCs. This accounts for their slow, piecemeal, elite- and supply-driven nature of telecommunication restructurings.*

3. *An absence of responsibility with a high degree of maneuverability produces a predatory state that seldom meets user demands or takes any developmental initiatives.*[94] Table 2.2 summarizes these results.

Two important contextualizations, one concerning state maneuverability and the other concerning state legitimacy, are necessary to further

TABLE 2.2
State Decision-Making Processes

	Maneuverability	*Responsibility*	*Examples*
Catalytic State	High	High	Singapore S. Korea
			Near-Catalytic: Mexico Malaysia
Dysfunctional State	Low	Variable	Brazil China India (1967–95)
Predatory State	High	None	Myanmar (Burma) Congo (Zaire)

Key:
Maneuverability: The state's ability to impose its own agenda and shape societal choices.
Responsibility: Commitment to development while helping the state increase its legitimacy.

Both maneuverability and responsibility need to be situated historically.

highlight the propositions made above. First, the maneuverability of states, especially those of dysfunctional ones, may be boosted at times due to a number of factors. (*a*) States might be afforded "windows of opportunity" to shape policy agendas, independent of special interests, because of situations such as serious macroeconomic crises and changes in leadership. These windows, in turn, allow leaders to bring in change teams of technocrats to build and implement new agendas.[95] But windows close fast and, therefore, such change is often short lived. (*b*) Even dysfunctional states, as mentioned earlier, do possess limited degrees of maneuverability. They can command vast bureaucratic machineries and were active historically in shaping the development politics of their countries. Ironically, pockets of maneuverability for dysfunctional states come not from exercising state capacities responsibly toward developmental goals, but through the legacy of prior periods of state intervention that have left the politicians in charge of dismantling the behemoth structure of rules and regulations to institute restructuring, a power often misused by them for personal gain.[96]

Second, crises of legitimacy, entailing nonacceptance of state institutions and officeholders, in the developing world now extend to catalytic, dysfunctional, and predatory states, further complicating analyses of institutional decision-making processes. States that had been able to marginalize social groups now find themselves in an increasingly untenable situation vis-à-vis their legitimacy. Thus, the South Korean state classified as catalytic in this book, has experienced everything from student riots to trade union strikes and middle-class dissatisfaction and is finding itself increasingly resource constrained in terms of effecting outcomes. No longer able to marginalize these groups, the state has tried to appease these groups through various mechanisms. Provision of telecommunication services may be understood in this regard. The South Korean waiting list for telecommunication services, which exceeded half a million in 1980, was brought close to zero by the end of the decade. This is also the case in providing services to rural ethnic Malays in Malaysia, a near-catalytic state. In India, a dysfunctional special-interest driven state, a pro-rural strategy (essential for any party to come to power) guided Rajiv Gandhi administration's (1984–91) and subsequent administrations' commitment of resources to rural telecommunications projects after it was made a development priority. In India, the state also uses a pro-rural rhetoric to deflect the demands of urban groups.

It should be now clear that telecommunication restructurings at the state level are linked with state struggles for power and legitimacy. Ultimately the particular combinations of state-type and types of pressures on the state mean that demands or pressures from interest groups alone will not automatically create their supply in state hands. State actions are always reflective of the larger sociopolitical backdrop. *Choices states make are sometimes as dependent on the micro and macro levels of interaction with specific interest groups as they are on the degree of state concern with construction of its legitimacy or consolidation of power.* But legitimacy may not be accorded just because the proposed restructuring takes place.[97] States in many developing countries, as well as in Eastern Europe and the former Soviet Union, continue to face crises of legitimacy even after restructuring efforts. Restructuring may also not actually take place in spite of state rhetoric that is designed to buy legitimacy. States in developing countries are often caught in a desperate struggle to survive and state legitimacy is a slow exercise in rhetorical politics, implementation failures, and mixed successes.

The next two chapters explain the arguments made in this chapter with reference to seven case studies (which include all cases mentioned in table 2.2 except for India and Congo). These seven cases were picked according to state types (two for each state-type explained except for predatory states) and according to the types of pressures (macro plural or cohesive). Each state-type is therefore further distinguished by the type of pressures on the state. Micro heterogeneous pressures are explained for each country.

The types of state and variety of macro pressures present us with different sets of outcomes that are consistent across similar cases. There is no great plurality of pressures in telecommunications upon Singapore, Mexico, China, and Myanmar in terms of the basis of their support or legitimacy.[98] Restructuring initiatives (if any) in these states are more streamlined and trouble free than for the other three cases. South Korea, Malaysia, and Brazil represent plural pressures. Restructuring initiatives here often run into a number of problems, especially for dysfunctional states such as Brazil. Catalytic and near-catalytic states, though, are able to play a decisive role in shaping the overall policies governing telecommunication restructuring. Even with plural and heterogeneous pressures, catalytic states like Korea or near-catalytic ones like Malaysia, at least in the short-run, are able to play a dirigiste role in shaping societal preferences toward streamlined outcomes.

CONCLUSION

Economic, technological, and ideational factors influence the preferences of societal groups and states and provide incentives or disincentives for particular strategies. In the empirical chapters that follow, the influence of these factors is not analyzed separately for each country but, where appropriate, they are mentioned to explain group preferences. However, these factors are important starting points for analyses. As Haggard and Kaufman note: "Failure to take initial conditions and constraints into account can lead to irrelevant comparisons and misleading prescriptions."[99]

Theoretically, this chapter shows that we cannot expect that a centralized authority such as the state will supply telecommunication services efficiently, but its actions in concert with external pressures (in as much as it meets their demand) may help it approach efficiency rather than deviating from it. This explains the apparent paradox that even states that are special-interest dominated will undertake telecommunication restructuring initiatives that result in provision of services to groups beyond the ones who have direct access to the state. Furthermore, the state might have to provide these services to maintain its power.[100] At the micro level, in formal club terms, the state can not only restrict or enhance membership and provision (to suit its prerogatives) but it can cross-subsidize various groups in society that might further interfere with optimal provision. Furthermore, states will respond more effectively to macro cohesive coalitions but the latter come about only in special circumstances. Where it is difficult to marginalize workers, rural areas, and other interest groups in politics (as in South Korea, Malaysia, Brazil), plural coalitions arise making it difficult for states (even catalytic ones) to respond effectively. The following chapters will show how the task of development is getting increasingly complicated in developing countries due to the hold of special interests upon states and the rising tide of pluralistic coalitions (even those states that lacked it earlier). Thus, many states are now becoming dysfunctional states facing pluralistic pressures.

PART II

Telecommunications Restructuring in Seven Countries

CHAPTER 3

Telecommunications Restructuring in Catalytic and Near-Catalytic States

Part II of this book examines telecommunications restructuring in seven countries categorized according to the different types of pressures and states. Pressures at the macro level can be cohesive or plural while states examined are catalytic, near-catalytic, dysfunctional, or predatory. Seven countries are examined: Singapore (cohesive pressures/catalytic state), South Korea (plural pressures/catalytic state), Mexico (cohesive pressures/near-catalytic state), Malaysia (plural pressures/near-catalytic state), China (cohesive pressures/dysfunctional state), Brazil (plural pressures/dysfunctional state) and Myanmar (pressures invalid/predatory state). Heterogeneous pressures at the micro level are examined for all states.

While the countries examined in this chapter may now be called newly industrializing countries (NICs), in as much as they were all considered "developing" countries when their telecommunication restructuring began, their experience is relevant for this book. Furthermore, as noted in chapter 2, many developing countries continue to look at the experience of the present-day NICs to model their own economic strategies including those dealing with information technologies. This chapter thus examines the case of two cases each of catalytic and near-catalytic states.

Each country in this chapter and next is described with reference to the arguments developed in the first two chapters. The context for restructuring is traced to economic conditions and, where applicable and readily apparent, the influence of ideas and technology. Economic conditions, in particular, enter the picture in two different ways. First, many of the demands for restructuring are located in the economic profile for countries. Most noticeably, demand for telecommunications services grows in countries as business activity picks up and middle income groups grow. Second, economic conditions also influence supply conditions. Resource-strapped states often sell off lucrative telecommunications enterprises in order to ease their fiscal difficulties. Economic crises fueled by external debt in countries like Brazil and Mexico in the 1980s left them with no choice but to move toward their telecommunication monopolies' privatization. Many developing countries now also rely on auctioning licenses for other sections of the telecommunications market (like cellular, paging, data services) in order to raise revenues for the government. Economic conditions also influence supply of restructuring in as much as the state believes that an injection of market discipline is necessary to make telecommunications monopolies perform effectively in domestic or international markets.

While referring to these economic, technological, and ideational influences alone, chapters 3 and 4 emphasize the political economy behind the demand and supply of telecommunication restructuring. These politics explain the timing, scope, and pace of restructuring efforts. Each country section below first describes the macropolitical economy of the country before turning to the phases of restructuring with reference to this political economy. In most countries, during the first phase of restructuring, service-enhancement initiatives come about in response to powerful user-clubs. During phase two, as demand pressures continue to build up, coalitions arise (and, in some cases, economic conditions become worse), and other initiatives like liberalization and privatization come about (usually because of the limited success of government monopolies with service enhancement).

A word of caution is needed here about user-group demand estimates as presented in this and successive chapters. In spite of all the claims made about demand-driven changes in telecommunications in several studies and by policymakers, most often these claims about demand are asserted rather than shown. Historically, national telecommunications carriers did not keep demand estimates (beyond simple crude estimates of waiting lists and a few other indicators) and if they did (or do), they are extremely reluctant to part with these estimates (perhaps for political reasons). Thus, there is very little in terms of systematic cross-national or time-series data available internationally that can help us compare demands from various user groups across countries. Therefore, demand is gauged in this book in several ways. The two most often used indicators of demand in this book are (1) waiting lists for different types for services if they can be found, and (2) accounts of direct lobbying by different user groups. Other indicators of demand used here include number of subscribers for various services, special studies (of demand) carried out by national or international organizations, accounts (sometimes complaints) in the media, and data gathered doing field interviews. Trade media are usually quite alert to demands by business users and, where available, such studies are cited. All in all, this book, by relying on such scattered and sparse sources of demand estimates, still gives only a rough sketch of these demands. On the other hand, it is hoped that even such estimates are better than merely asserting them. Table 3.1 summarizes the arguments made in part II of the book for all seven states and the pressures that they face.

CATALYTIC STATES

Catalytic states possess vast amount of resources and enough autonomy from domestic and international actors providing them enough maneuverability to effect their "responsible" development agenda. Historically, the responsibility in catalytic states comes from building their legitimacy through delivering on economic growth. Catalytic states facing cohesive pressures have an easier time effecting this agenda than those with plural pressures. Either way, catalytic states are able to shape the agenda of domestic political forces.

Singapore

Singapore's telecommunication restructuring is streamlined and shaped by the powerful Singaporean state, which plays a key role in shaping societal preferences and intervenes directly in the economy. The role played by the state is so central to Singapore's economy that it is possible to discount the demands that the state faces. The role of the state, however, provides the macro backdrop against which the preference given to MNCs and the current international strategy of Singapore Telecom need to be traced. Nonetheless, the state makes sure that all of its population receives telecommunication services, in turn ensuring the legitimacy of the state.

The origins of the catalytic Singaporean state can be traced to colonial rule under the British and the consolidation of the state after its independence under its dominant single party, the People's Action Party (PAP). Singapore was founded (in 1819) as a trading hub for East Asia and lacking any domestic capital, the city was dominated by foreign capital.[1] The city was part of Malaysia from 1963–65 but achieved independence, mostly because its trading interests would have suffered under the Malay federation (and partly because its affluent Chinese majority posed a threat to the emerging power base of ethnic Malays in the federation). Since 1965, Singapore's politics, within the historically defined trajectory of trade and export-led development, reveal the influence of PAP and its leader Lee Kwan Yew.

Lee Kwan Yew, who served as prime minster until 1990 and continues to hold a cabinet portfolio, epitomizes Singapore state's ability to guide the workings of its economy with a view toward exploiting its particular advantage in being a hub-city for commerce. Lee consolidated his

TABLE 3.1

Types of States, Pressures, and Outcomes in Telecommunications Restructurings

Type of State	Variety of Pressures*	Country	Restructuring Outcomes** (presented roughly in the order they begin)
1A. Catalytic	*Macro cohesive*: international business. *Micro het.*: latent societal pressures.	Singapore	• Impressive infrastructural provision • Comprehensive policies • Singapore Telecom privatization smooth
	Macro (somewhat) plural: domestic & int. business pressures. Trade unions. *Micro het.* : urban users, latent rural pressures	South Korea	• Impressive infrastructural provision • Comprehensive policies (underlying process difficult) • Nepotism in liberalization, Worker strikes
1B. Near-catalytic	*Macro cohesive*: economic crisis pressures contained through PRI, pro-liberalization coalition strong *Micro het.*: urban/rural residential	Mexico	• Somewhat impressive growth in services (1990s) • TELMEX privatization smooth • Regulatory policies emerging (but with difficulty) • Future liberalization might be rough
	Macro plural: powerful ethnic Malay and Chinese (business) coalitions. *Micro het.*: Federal provinces, rural/urban residential	Malaysia	• Impressive growth in services (after corporatization) • Earlier liberalization/privatization smooth • Comprehensive and regulatory policies emerging • Now "privatization run amok"

(continued on next page)

TABLE 3.1 (continued)

Type of State	Variety of Pressures*	Country	Restructuring Outcomes** (presented roughly in the order they begin)
2 Dysfunctional: (special interest domination)	*Macro cohesive:* coalition of government ministries, foreign manufacturers *Micro het.:* rural/urban residential (often suppressed or marginalized), provinces	China	• Very low teledensity • No comprehensive policies/but telecom prioritized • Ambitious service enhancement program • Emerging powerful service providers: smooth transition
	Macro plural: disparately powerful business groups, export interests *Micro het.:* urban users, latent rural pressures, provinces	Brazil	• Low teledensity (compared to others in Lat. Am.) • No comprehensive policies/but telecom prioritized • Ambitious service enhancement program (esp. urban) • Messy, special-interest driven, complex liberalization
3. Predatory	*None:* state lacks legitimacy	Myanmar	• Extremely low teledensity • Services concentrated in Yangon & among select few

* Macro (sectoral) demands are either cohesive or plural; Micro level are always heterogeneous (referred to as "micro het." above).

** Comprehensive policies among outcomes refer to consistency of telecommunication restructuring with overall development initiatives and also to formulation of policies and regulations governing the restructured telecommunications sectors.

BOX 3.1

Telecommunication Restructuring in Singapore

Phase/Date	Restructuring Initiative	Explanation
First Phase/1970s	Service enhancement	State reduces waiting lists in turn increasing legitimacy
Second Phase/1980s	Provision of sophisticated services	State responding mainly to pressures from MNCs and its bureaucracy in making Singapore competitive internationally.
Third Phase/ Late 1980s	• International service provision • Partial privatization • Liberalization of cellular/terrestrial telephony	Pressures from international markets and international organizations (e.g., WTO). Initiative seen necessary to give Singapore Telecom a global orientation and become a stronger regional player.

power through his dominance of the PAP and via governmental agencies that he founded for the purpose of economic development. PAP, founded in 1954, initially followed a moderate course in politics and was supported by the country's middle class, private business, and parts of labor. By the time Singapore gained independence in 1965, PAP had practically silenced the left-wing labor movements in the country and gained authority in appointing and running the affairs of the labor union that was sympathetic to it. As Singapore's private business was weak, the state could then effectively direct the workings of the main social cleavages in the country. "A politically and economically weak entrepreneurial class meant that the state and foreign firms would have to play a central role in Singapore's industrialization."[2] The state built its administrative capacity since the early 1960s by recruiting civil service employees from the best students graduating from the National University of Singapore.[3] The agency founded with the aim of directing economic development was the Economic Development Board (founded in 1961), preeminent in the arena of industrial policy and later helping plan Singapore's telecommunication strategy. Singapore in the three decades following independence then reveals "a relatively autonomous state, a highly centralized and interventionist economic policy-making apparatus, a weakened left, and a tamed labor."[4]

Given that its domestic capital was weak, foreign capital featured prominently but did not dictate Singapore's economic strategy in this regard. Lee clearly favored foreign capital in economic plans but the latter was not politically powerful enough to dominate the state. Singapore's infrastructure and its elite bureaucracy responded foremost to the interests of foreign capital. These infrastructural facilities include the city's port (the second busiest after Hong Kong), the highly modern Changi airport, and sophisticated telecommunications.

Singapore's telecommunications has gone through three restructuring phases.[5] In the first phase lasting until the late 1970s, telecommunications responded to business and societal needs via an expansion of the infrastructure.[6] During the second phase, during the 1980s, telecommunications became part of the state's pro-active strategy to carve out a competitive advantage for the city-state. The last phase began in the late 1980s and is characterized by Singapore's attempts to play a prominent international role in telecommunications, and by a partial liberalization of the telecommunications sector.

First Phase of Restructuring   This phase was characterized by service enhancement and reduction of waiting lists for telephone connections. State legitimacy in Singapore rests ultimately on its ability to deliver a high standard of living to its citizens. The two groups at the micro level that matter to the state in terms of telecommunications include the Singapore society and international business groups. The latter are often the only actors emphasized in examination of Singapore's telecommunications but it is important to remember that Singapore's two-year waiting period for telephones in 1972 (which included society at large) was brought down to less than two weeks in 1979.[7] By 1980, Singapore had the highest teledensity in the developing world (see table 3.2) (while now its penetration rates are comparable to those of any in the developed world). Similarly, in the 1980s, the benefits of ISDN or broadband networks in Singapore, when provided were universal. This belies the frequently made assumption that the only groups that matter to the state in Singapore are MNCs. As we will see, they do matter but not exclusively so.

Second Phase of Restructuring   The first comprehensive plan drawn up by the state that affected telecommunications was the so-called Second Industrial Revolution launched in 1979. The strategy focused on deepening and extending Singapore's entrepôt advantages by utilizing and creating a competitive advantage in high technology. Services such as banking, financial services, and tourism were emphasized and a new drive was launched to attract MNCs. There are over 650 MNCs in Singapore, many of them with regional headquarters. These MNCs played a key role in shaping Singapore's international competitiveness. Telecommunications and information technologies would play a key role in this strategy. The National Computers Board (NCB) was established in 1980 to direct the country's information technology policies (interestingly enough as part of the ministry of finance that would help to synchronize the telecommunications policies with overall development ones). Singapore also pioneered the use of many technologies in the late 1970s and early 1980s including digital exchanges, fiber optics and ISDN trials (latter began in Singapore in 1976). Many value-added services were introduced and rates reduced for existing services as part of the Second Industrial Revolution.

The National Information Technology Plan (NITP) was started in 1986 with the aim of making Singapore an information society. The NCB (which included academics and planners in finance, computers, and economic development) began in 1983 to include members from Telecommunication Authority of Singapore (TAS).[8] By the time of NITP announcement in 1986, an "information communication infrastructure" was recognized as vital for Singapore's information society strategy. Earlier plans were given a renewed thrust and easily implemented given the coordination among ministries of finance (NCB), trade and industry, communications, and the EDB. By 1989, Singapore could

TABLE 3.2
National Telecommunication Infrastructures

Country	Main Lines (Per 100 Population)			Waiting List (000)			Largest City Main Lines (1995)				Waiting Time (yrs.)	Teleaccessibility (1995)		Projected Teledensity 2,000 (Per 100)
	1980	1990	1995	1980	1990	1995	Population (% of total)	Main lines (% of total)	Tele-density	Rest of country tele-density	1995	Resident main lines per 100 households	Pay phones per 1,000 inhabitants	
Singapore	25.98	38.96	48.18	4	0.7	0.2	100	100	47.85	47.85	0	>100	10.41	64.58
S. Korea	7.34	30.97	41.47	604	1.0	—	24.5	33.7	52.86	33.09	0	>100	6.85	55.44
Mexico	3.73	6.55	9.58	409	1,044	196	16.4	36.1	11.62	6.74	0.3	33.2	2.68	14.61
Malaysia	2.95	8.97	16.56	133	82	140	8.4	9.5	14.31	14.73	0.3	60.2	4.93	31.83
China	0.2	0.6	3.35	164	689	1,400	1.1	4.6	14.03	3.23	0.2	7.9	0.7	19.27
India	0.33	0.6	1.29	447	1,961	2,277	1.3	12.7	10.15	0.95	1.3	na	0.25	2.78
Brazil	3.93	6.5	8.51	3,250	428	n.a.	10.2	17.4	12.72	6.88	0.7	20.5	2.27	9.99
Myanmar	0.1	0.17	0.35				7.1	46.3	2.06	0.18	n.a.		0.02	0.59

Source:

International Telecommunication Union, *Yearbook of Telecommunication Statistics*, various years.
International Telecommunication Union, *World Telecommunications Indicators on Diskette.*

boast of 100 percent ISDN. Cellular service was introduced in 1982 and by 1991 the city had fifty thousand mobile telephones. Data network facilities were extended to Singapore's bureaucracy and commercial facilities. Private networks emerged for important services and industries.[9] But the biggest emphasis for NITP was international services and Singapore began to invest heavily in regional and international telecommunication links such as submarine networks. Instead of just being an entrepôt, Singapore now planned on playing a different type of international role, that of making its own firms (such as Singapore Telecom, Singapore Airlines) important in the world markets.

Third Phase of Restructuring   The third phase of Singapore's telecommunication strategy, starting in late 1980s, may be identified as a taking on of the international role identified above, and a partial liberalization of the state monopoly in telecommunications that was necessitated by this role. (By 1995, 47.5 percent of Singapore Telecom's revenues came from international services.)[10] Singapore's drive in telecommunications in the 1980s took place under governmental auspices but in order to play an international role, the firm needed to present itself as a corporate and commercial entity.[11] Singapore Telecom, unlike other revenue-strapped telecommunication carriers undergoing privatization, was not short on investment funds because of the carrier's big internal surpluses. Privatization was also not necessary to ease governmental deficits.

Only partial privatization was necessary to send the right signal to international markets. A carefully orchestrated privatization of around 11 percent of the stock (down from the initial announcement of 20–25 percent) took place in 1993. The trade media dubbed it as "the most prestigious international equity deal of the year."[12] Only about 2 percent of the stock was allowed to be held by foreigners and 89 percent of the firm continued to be government owned. Twenty-five percent of the stock will be sold by 2002 and the government announced in 1997 that local and international telephony will also have competition by the year 2000 with a foreign investment component of 49 percent in the new provider. Three consortia bid for the new license.

Singapore Telecom was granted a fifteen-year monopoly in basic services in 1992 (which will now end on April 1, 2000 instead) but other services such as cellular and paging were opened to competition on April 1, 1997. Local and international telephony will also have competition by the year 2000 with a foreign investment component of 49 percent. (The first licensed provider is a consortium including British Telecom and Japan's NTT.) The privatization and global orientation of Singapore Telecom, along with liberalization steps taken by the government,

TABLE 3.3
National Telecommunication Infrastructures: Specialized Services

| | Cellular Subscribers (Per 100 Population) | | Paging Subscribers (Per 100 Population) | | Information Technology | | | |
| | | | | | Internet Hosts | | | Personal Computers |
Country	1990	1995	1990	1995	1991	1995		1995
Singapore	1.91	10.25	12.3	32	484	22,769		430,000
S. Korea	0.19	3.66	1.0	21.5	1,506	29,306		4,857,000
Mexico	0.08	0.75	0.06	0.27	284	3,787		2,400,000
Malaysia	0.49	4.99	0.34	0.74	17 (1992)	4,194		750,000
China	—	0.30	0.04	1.4	569 (1994)	2,146		2,600,000
India	—	0.01	—	0.02	79 (1992)	788		1,100,000
Brazil	—	0.88	n.a.	n.a.	308	20,113		2,100,000
Myanmar	—	0.004	—	—	—	—		—

Source: International Telecommunication Union, *Yearbook of Statistics: Telecommunication Services, Chronological Series 1986–1995,* Geneva, 1997.

TABLE 3.4
Asian Specialized Services: Current Rates and Projections
(Media Reports)

	Cellular Penetration Rates* (per 100 population)		Info. Tech. Penetration Rates** (per 100 population/1997)	
	December 1997	December 2000	PCs	Internet Usage
Singapore	18.2	33.6	21.9	8.82
S. Korea	12.3	22.9	11.1	0.48
Malaysia	10.4	16.9	3.9	0.52
China	0.9	2.6	0.4	0.03
India	0.05[†]	0.26[‡]		

* *Far Eastern Economic Review*, June 4, 1998, p. 56.
** *The New York Times*, April 13, 1998, p. C1.
[†] Department of Telecommunications, India, data collected by author.
[‡] *Business India*, June 5–18, 1997.

are repeated almost as a mantra by Singapore Telecom's officials along with steps being taken internally to reorganize the firm as a customer and market-oriented corporation.[13] Singapore Telecom now competes (quite ferociously) with Mobile One (partly owned by Cable & Wireless and Hongkong Telecom) in cellular and slashed its rates by one third as Mobile One captured 10 percent of the market within two months of operation.[14] There were 230,000 subscribers in 1994 accounting for only 8 percent market penetration,[15] which increased to 10.25 percent by 1995 and 18.2 percent by December 1997.

Apart from the steps mentioned above, by the 1990s, Singapore Telecom began actively investing overseas and seeking global alliances. As telecommunications markets opened, it saw itself as a major regional player and as having a competitive advantage in providing services in developing and newly industrializing countries such as Tanzania, India, and China. By 1995, it had sixteen joint ventures in fifteen countries. It also sought to promote itself as a regional hub for broadcasting services (attracting HBO, Discovery, etc.) and for other satellite-based telecommunication services. But Singapore's global strategy was received with caution. Foreign investors remained skittish about the firm's overseas ventures. Its Philippines venture was losing money, it was pulling out of India, and its investments in China remained low. Its alliance with AT&T (called World Partners along with Japan's KDD and a few European partners) has fared badly globally. Nonetheless, Singapore played a key role in information technology measures announced by the WTO including hosting summits to this effect in Singapore in December 1995. It is a signatory to the WTO accord in telecommunication announced February 1997 and plans to open its market for foreign competition in the year 2000.

Singapore's comprehensive program in telecommunications has been shaped by a catalytic state that directly has to respond to only a few external pressures. While MNCs have direct access to the state and societal pressures are more indirect, the state does respond to both in providing basic services. In boasting of its present and future communication services, Singapore increasingly speaks of itself as "an intelligent island." A 100 percent fiber optic network is expected to be available by 2005. But as with large users elsewhere, 30 percent of the users account for nearly three fourths of all telecommunication traffic while only about 2 percent of the traffic comes from the bottom 30 percent users.[16] It is also undeniable that foreign firms operating in Singapore are slated to receive the best of telecommunications services with all other user groups coming second in terms of priority.

It may be added that even with a MNC-oriented coalition in Singapore, the state's working is made easy by the fact that it faces no opposing pressures. Furthermore, it has "contained" the micro heterogeneous pressures quite well as is evident from the greater than one hundred main lines available per 100 households (table 3.2). Political opposition itself remains quite weak and marginalized but may grow if its economy suffers a huge setback from the Asian financial crisis. In 1998, its economic growth rate was expected to be between 0.5 to 1.5 percent (down from the double-digit growth rates Singapore traditionally boasted). The state announced in mid-1998 that it would launch a huge pump-priming program with $1.2 billion slotted for infrastructural projects (including subsidizing telecommunication services).[17]

As Singapore moves toward providing the latest generation of interactive services, it also poses another problem for the state that has traditionally regulated information flows in the country. It now seems caught between wanting to provide services but also controlling information content. Singaporeans are, for example, not allowed to own satellite dishes and there are restrictions on speech and media in the country. On the other hand, the state has encouraged broadband proliferation and interactive services. Singapore One, a project jointly conceived by Singapore Telecom and Singapore Cable Vision, will thus provide a broadband network to all 800,000 Singapore households by the end of 1998.[18] Similarly, the number of people using the Internet in Singapore is also high by Asian standards (although this may also be due to the dominance of the English language on the World Wide Web) (table 3.4). One scholar notes the "irony" that "there is an inherent conflict between the democratization of information creation and access and the government's long-standing determination to control closely the information citizens receive."[19] The state's ability to implement its strategy is predicated on its strict control of the society and, in the context of telecommunications, information flows. *The Guardian* noted in 1994 that "one irony is that the information revolution that Singapore is pioneering may become the Trojan horse that upsets the political and cultural repression of the regime."[20]

South Korea

The dirigiste nature of the Korean state enabling it to shape and, in certain cases, marginalize societal preferences is reflected in the country's telecommunications sector. The state barely addressed urban and business pressures in telecommunications until the early 1980s when telecommunication restructuring began. By the 1990s, these pressures not only made the restructuring accelerate but the converse was also true in that the state was finding it increasingly difficult to shape the micro heterogeneous and macro plural pressures upon itself. The latter came from the domestic and international interest-group coalitions along with worker unrest, which made the democratizing South Korean state's task difficult.

The context for the Korean state involvement as well as the direction of economic change were dictated historically. The maneuverability and the responsibility of the Korean state can be traced back to the feudal bureaucratic tradition of the Yi dynasty (1392–1910) and the build-up of administrative capacity, which helped the Japanese dominate Korea (1905–1945).[21] The history shows the origins of state autonomy, capacity, and direct role in economic tasks that are now sometimes taken to be analogous to the Korean dirigiste state. While Japanese occupation did not benefit Korea, the buildup of state capacity and an economic infrastructure under colonial rule did later help Korea with industrialization. In fact, both telegraph (introduced 1885) and telephone (introduced 1898) helped the colonial administrators until 1945.

South Korea's postwar economic strategy was consolidated under Park Chung Hee's rule (1961–79). Given Korea's colonial past, while the external help provided by the United States enabled the Koreans to build and sustain the economy in the 1950s, Koreans remained suspicious of foreign influences. Park thus inherited a state apparatus that in the 1950s (under Synghman Rhee) was beginning to work closely with domestic industry while at the same time marginalizing rural elites and labor. Park deliberately moved South Korea toward economic independence by encouraging domestic industrialization and, after overcoming

BOX 3.2

Telecommunication Restructuring in S. Korea

Phase/Date	Restructuring Initiative	Explanation
First Phase/ 1980s	Service enhancement	Economic growth (1960s onwards) and subsequent socioeconomic crises (late '70s/early '80s) strengthen demands and state's concern with maintaining legitimacy.
First Phase/ 1980s	• KTA Corporatization in 1982 • Creation of DACOM for data services • Domestic technology development	Responding to *chaebol* (top domestic business) oriented coalition for provision of data and other sophisticated services. *Chaebol* profited from state's initiative in technology development.
Second Phase/ Late 1980s	Liberalization of specialized services market and provision of sophisticated services	Mostly in response to domestic business coalition but continued liberalization must account for the international liberalization coalition. Value-added service also liberalized in response to pressures from the United States.
Second Phase/ Late 1980s	Ongoing privatization of Korea Telecom	In response to demand pressures but resisted heavily by workers. Pressures for middle-income groups also continue to build up as they see themselves not benefiting much from restructuring initiatives.

an initial hesitance, favoring South Korea's family-owned businesses (*chaebol*).[22]

Park's strategy of import substitution industrialization with a view toward an export-push took off by the mid-1960s. From 1965 to 1980, industry grew at an average annual rate of 16.4 percent each year while merchandise exports grew at an average rate of 27.2 percent.[23] The strategy was sustained by the inherited administrative capacity and further centralization and consolidation under the president and his economic advisors (the Blue House). Park set in place the preeminence of the executive authority in the country. The most significant innovation was the formation of the Economic Planning Board (EPB) in June 1961, a key agency for designing and executing the Korean economic strategies to date. (EPB was merged with the ministry of finance in December 1994 and became the Board of Finance and Economy.) Moreover, Park further marginalized or eliminated groups that would challenge his authority. These included not just societal actors like workers and rural areas but also opposition political parties that were banned in 1972. A de facto military state existed in Korea during the 1972–79 period that ended with Park's assassination and widespread societal uprisings including students, workers, and middle-income groups. The infamous Spring 1980 Kwangju student uprising and its brutal repression epitomized the societal upheaval.

Telecommunications was not a development priority during Park's regime but many legacies of this period are important for understanding the impetus given to this sector during the 1980s. First, the overall technology policy was fast becoming a cornerstone of Korea's thinking about its future economic growth. Agencies like the Blue House and EPB played a direct role in designing these policies.[24] Other agencies important for technology policy included the ministry of commerce and industry (which later became ministry of trade, industry, and energy) and the ministry of science and technology (MOST). Important telecommunications-related research institutes established in the 1960s included Korean Institute of Science and Technology (KIST) and the Korean Electronics and Telecommunications Research Institute (KETRI). These agencies were well placed and prepared to guide the telecommunications sector in the 1980s. While the strategy model was top-down (beginning with the Blue House and EPB, telecommunications policy nonetheless resulted from consultations with other ministries, research institutes, and businesses, making it less monolithic at times than it seems. Secondly, ideationally the Korean society and state were committed to building self-reliance in technology and industry. Not only were Korean "infant industries" like Samsung and Goldstar protected to develop homegrown technologies, but technology policies were also put in place to develop a highly educated workforce, and supported through the foundation of state R&D institutions.[25] Thirdly, it was Korea's economic conditions that tipped the Korean state toward restructuring telecommunication. By the late 1970s, Korean industrialization had produced growing numbers of urban middle-income groups that were beginning to demand telecommunication services. Finally, the economic crisis of the late 1970s led directly to political and social unrest, the assassination of Park, and a shift in economic strategy of Korea in the 1980s toward satisfying the demands of middle-income groups. (The economic crisis included high inflation rates, a fall in real wages, a growing fiscal deficit, declining terms of trade, and a high external debt.[26]) In the words of one major analyst of Korean telecommunications: "The decade of the 1980s formed a virtual historical crucible in which the telecommunication revolution coincided with several political realities."[27]

First Phase of Restructuring   Korean telecommunications service enhancement and partial liberalization, which characterized its first period of restructuring, were in response to urban residential groups and its business conglomerates. The main micro heterogeneous demands for telecommunication services in the South Korean context came from urban residential users and domestic businesses whose demand for telecommunication services increased given economic growth.

The urban residential demands are easily documented. Nearly 80 percent of Korea's over 44 million people live in urban areas with Seoul accounting for a quarter of the country's population and another quarter of the population living in cities above 750,000 people.[28] The high per capita income made it possible for the population to demand basic goods and services. The waiting list for telephones exceeded five million lines in 1982, hardly a number that could be ignored.[29] Furthermore, large segments of the Korean population were politically mobilized during the ending years of the Park regime and political instability ensued after his death.

Meanwhile, Korean industry, which at this time became increasingly export oriented, demanded an increasingly sophisticated set of services. The role of large users in Korean economy is also especially significant. Fifteen percent of the GNP is produced by the biggest thirty *chaebol* and the top 108 corporations (less than 1 percent of the total exporters) are responsible for two thirds of the total exports.[30] The impetus given by the state to the telecommunications-intensive electronics industry alone in the 1970s accounted for a high demand for telecommunication services.[31] The electronics and software industries became major players in the 1980s. Larson notes that the information sector of the economy grew at 28.6 percent per annum during the 1980s (which was quite above the overall growth rate of the country), that electronics and telecommunications overtook textiles as the country's top exports by 1986 and that, by 1994, Samsung was the biggest exporter overall.[32]

Under President Chun Doo Hwan (1979–87), an aggressive restructuring program was launched in conformity with the technical, ideational, and economic trends noted above. There can be no denying that the policies pursued since 1980 to appease important user groups were embedded in societal preferences.[33] The widespread diffusion of telephones during the Chun administration was a direct result of the state's need to construct its legitimacy with the promise of a high economic standard of living. Thus, the waiting list for telephones was eliminated by 1987 in accordance with the country's "one telephone per household" policy. The year 1983 was singled out by the state as ushering in "the period of the development of the information industry."[34] There were 8.8 million main lines in 1986, triple those in 1980, and public phone booths increased from 58,000 in 1980 to 138,000 in 1986.[35] Table 3.2 gives other indicators of growth.

The telecommunications sector was also liberalized to provide enhanced telecommunication services and the government owned provider separated from the ministry of communications. Korea Telecom Authority (KTA) was corporatized (as a public sector corporation) in 1982. But restructuring was fraught with difficulty in a country "where being a governmental employee is a long-honored tradition, even though the separation raised the salaries of employees transferred to KTA and created job opportunities."[36] In response to business demands, a private entity, 33 percent owned by KTA, known as Data Communication Corporation (DACOM) was also launched in 1982 for the data communications and other value-added services.

Consistent with its overall economic strategy of responding to domestic business demands, Korea also sought to be self-reliant in telecommunications. Its research capabilities combined with the productive capacities of its *chaebols* played a big role in helping it achieve this goal in the early 1980s. KETRI was merged with another institute created in 1979 called KIET (Korea Institute of Electronics Technology) to create telecommunications' premier R&D department called Electronics and Telecommunications Research Institute, or ETRI. The most impressive Korean achievement in the technology arena was the development and commercialization (in 1985) of a sophisticated electronic switch called TDX resulting from a joint effort among ETRI, KTA, and four private corporations. (Another ETRI achievement was the development of the CDMA cellular technology since 1992, which boosted the efforts of businesses like Samsung, Hyundai, and LG to start exporting this technology by 1996.) The export efforts were further supported by the Ministry of Information and Communications in sponsoring export delegations to countries like Mexico, Argentina, and Brazil.[37]

Second Phase of Restructuring   A second phase of Korean restructuring can be identified during the late 1980s and was a little more chaotic than the first, given the variety of pressures and Korean political instability. Two telecommunication-oriented coalitions began to emerge in this period, putting considerable pressures on the state for service enhancement and sectoral liberalization. The first coalition included domestic large-business private users and equipment manufacturers, while the second one consisted of international pressures. External pressures came from foreign service providers and governments to liberalize the Korean market. In particular, the United States made telecommunications a key part of the bilateral Market Access Fact Finding (MAFF) talks launched with Korea in 1987. Opening the Korean equipment, value-added, and specialized services markets were of special importance to the United States (given the politicization of its deficit in equipment and fears that its liberalization before others would allow the U.S. market to be exploited).

The domestic coalition may now be further profiled. Apart from the importance attached by the top *chaebols* to telecommunication services in general, demand for leased lines and data-based services were particularly strong. A 1986 survey by the Korean Information Industry Association (KIIA) found that 53 percent of leased lines were finance related, nearly one third were general businesses, while governmental agencies accounted for the rest.[38] Eighty-five corporations that had formed the Computer and Communication Promotion Association (CCPA) asked the Ministry of Communications (MOC) in December 1987 to allow for shared use and resale of leased lines. Most significantly, by the late 1980s, both KTA and DACOM favored liberalization that would allow them to start providing and become competitive in value-added and data communication markets[39] (which, as noted earlier, were also the thrust of bilateral talks with the United States). The Korea Information Society Development Institute (KISDI), established in 1988 and affiliated to the MOC, after consultations with members of the government, industry, and academia, advised the MOC to open up the market for competition. KISDI spearheaded the Korean government's thinking and strategy about shaping the future of the "information society" in the country. However, MOC itself seems to have taken mostly industry groups into consideration in formulating its competition policies.[40]

The domestic and international pressures led to another reorganization of the Korean telecommunications market, again shaped decisively by the executive, especially the EPB. A number of legislative obstacles were overcome between 1989–91 but President Roh Tae Woo (1987–92) faced a number of political problems and therefore the main implementation of the restructuring programs came during President Kim Young Sam's tenure (1992–98).

The Korean state has walked a fine line in meeting the demands of the domestic and international coalitions without giving them too much power. Ideationally, Korea chose the Japanese model of strict regulation and limited competition in facilities-based providers and fewer restrictions in non-facilities-based, specialized, and value-added services providers. International access was allowed to the value-added market with foreign equity limited to less than 50 percent until January 1, 1994. However, the basic telecommunication market was reserved for the domestic coalition where the state, while giving valuable access to the *chaebol*, also sought to regulate the latter's market share. KTA, renamed Korea Telecom or KT, gave up its share of DACOM when privatized on January 1, 1991, allowing a duopoly market structure to emerge. KT competes with the privately held DACOM in international service and domestic long-distance service provision.

Furthermore, cellular, value-added, and specialized service markets were liberalized. The government-owned cellular operator Korea Mobile Telecom Corporation (KMTC) was privatized along with the introduction of another private cellular operator. Korea Mobile Telecom Service now competes with Shingsei Mobile Telecom (a subsidiary of a consortium led by the powerful Pohang Iron and Steel). In hindsight, the state did not do such a good job of keeping the *chaebol* at arms length. A notorious scandal erupted with charges of nepotism involving both Roh Tae Woo (1987–92) and Kim Young Sam (1992–98) in awarding cellular licenses in the early 1990s to the *chaebol* led by Sunkyong. (The latter was eventually placated with a lucrative share of Korea Telecom.) Nonetheless, as tables 3.3 and 3.4 show, cellular growth in South Korea has been rapid especially after 1995 (presumably after the corruption scandals were exposed). Similar results can be seen in the paging market, which seems to have exploded after liberalization.

Korea's approach toward KT privatization has been cautious, the state hedging not just between the two coalitions mentioned above but also between pressures from other *chaebol,* militant pressures from Korean workers, and others from urban groups. Korea Telecom was slated for privatization in 1990 but this did not take place until 1993 when the government decided to sell a 10 percent share each year. Plans to privatize the remaining 80 percent share in 1995 were met with strikes by the workers (KT has almost 60,000 workers). President Kim

Young Sam described it as equivalent to "an attempt to overthrow the state," itself indicative of how seriously the state views these pressures.[41] KT's privatization, which is now beginning to happen, was on the agenda for the last five years, and is still marred by worker resistance like the nationwide worker strikes in December 1996 – January 1997.

Apart from domestic and international business coalitions, the Korean state continues to respond to wider societal pressures. The worker resistance noted above was in fact part of the growing social and political instability in the country that continued to alienate certain social groups. In spite of the universal service enhancement measures undertaken under Chun's rule (during the first phase of restructuring) and continued thereafter, the state's main basis of support continued to be among the conservative business groups. But under President Roh, "business-government relations became decidedly more strained as government came under increased pressure to distance itself from the *chaebol*."[42] Noting a similar context for societal demands in telecommunications, one report underscored that while "the country has experienced remarkable economic growth during the past few decades, social unrest has never subsided, or more precisely speaking has been continually aggravated, mainly because of skewed income distribution."[43]

The influence of societal pressures can be traced in the number of planned steps announced by the state for introducing universal "information society" services that, according to one survey, are recognized by nearly 90 percent of the Korean population to be essential.[44] In terms of data services, the ministry of information and communications or MOIC (renamed by President Kim during his December 1994 ministerial reorganization) intends to introduce "one [data] terminal per household" by the year 2000 by which time 10 million intelligent terminals were slated for distribution. While providing a broad array of information services like e-mail, social delivery services like education (held in much importance by the Korean population) may play a big role, too. However, as table 3.4 shows, only 0.48 percent of the population used the Internet although 11.1 percent had PCs. On the other hand, in the 1980s, universal telephone service, which was initially introduced in urban areas, was quickly introduced in rural areas, too, effectively eliminating any disparities in the country for telephone provision. In the 1990s, MOIC introduced information services to rural administrations by distributing data terminals to agencies such as the post offices and in planning to create regional databases.[45] But, for value-added and specialized services, wide disparities remain between Seoul and other cities and also between urban and rural areas.[46]

In summary, the Korean state effectively managed the domestic pressures for telecommunications restructuring until the late 1980s for service enhancement and partial deregulation. It eliminated waiting lists and provided essential services to its businesses. But during the 1990s, it was showing strains in trying to reconcile the domestic business, international business, and wider societal pressures for sophisticated services and introduction of competition and privatization. Korean workers also resisted restructuring efforts. The state agencies continued to play a role in shaping telecommunications plans but with difficulty. The presence of myriad pressures and the severe economic crises of the early 1980s and since 1997 distinguish South Korea from Singapore in making the task of restructuring difficult. Charges of nepotism haunted the Roh and Kim administrations in awarding cellular licenses. KT privatization became increasingly difficult due to worker protests. Given that societal unrest continues to increase, it seems that the state has been far more successful in accommodating the domestic and international business demands than the societal ones. While societal demands become intense, the executive's capacity to effect economic change while keeping itself relatively insulated continues to decrease. In the meantime, international pressures on South Korea continue to rise. As a signatory to the WTO telecommunications accord signed on February 15, 1997, Korea has promised market access to foreign corporations in all areas by 1998. Thirty-three percent market access in facilities-based providers is promised until 2001 when 49 percent will be given. Twenty percent share of KT will be allowed until 2001 and increased to 33 percent thereafter.[47] South Korea, like Singapore, sees itself as playing a global and regional role in telecommunications and thus the WTO accord was seen as opening up equipment and services markets to Korean firms.[48]

Finally, the international bailout of South Korea by international agencies and foreign government amounting to nearly $60 billion, following its banking and currency crises since 1997, is itself predicated on Korea's opening its economy further. The new President Kim Dae Jung (1998–) after coming to power in February, while having close ties to labor, saw labor unrest as the biggest threat to Korean reform. By June 1998, Kim Dae Jung's window of opportunity seemed to be closing as the Korean Confederation of Trade Unions with 550,00 members became increasingly aggressive and threatened to strike. At the same time, the new presidency was also seen as "a chance to dismantle the cozy ties between government and business that both created Korea Inc. and set it up for a fall by protecting it from moderating market forces."[49] Shortly after coming to office, Kim did succeed in getting labor legislation passed and opened enquires into several *chaebol* while lifting restrictions on foreign investment. But the 1998 growth rate was expected to be a negative 4.7 percent and the state may find it increasingly hard to appease the labor, business, and other social groups.[50]

NEAR-CATALYTIC STATES

Near-catalytic states maintain institutions that can respond quite well to societal demands and even help to shape them, but are less successful than their catalytic counterparts in Singapore or (even) South Korea in framing comprehensive polices defining the role of information technologies in their societies. Near-catalytic states are also not always assured of support from their domestic constituents (or marginalizing them when the support is not forthcoming). Therefore, restructuring initiatives in these states often run into problems.

Mexico

The Mexican state reveals enormous institutional stability and ability to carry key political actors with it. In telecommunications, it has carried out an impressive restructuring program in the 1990s, which nonetheless remains less ambitious than those of catalytic states. Its policy and regulatory initiatives often trail its other initiatives like privatization, making it difficult to manage this change effectively from above. Whether or not this restructuring program will continue to work smoothly depends on the degree to which Mexican politics remain stable. The coalition of domestic business, urban, and rural interests that the Mexican state was able to hold together since the 1930s is now coming undone. Nonetheless, this coalition did define the agenda of Mexican politics, including telecommunication restructurings, in the past.

Mexico, like Singapore, was been dominated by one political party for the last seventy years, which accounts for the centralization and consolidation of Mexican politics.[51] The Partido Revolucionaro Institucional (PRI) founded in 1929 has been the de facto ruler at the federal level and, until recently, at most of the state levels, too. PRI's political strength has allowed it to run an otherwise federal structure of government in a unitary fashion and also eliminate the importance of the legislature that historically was controlled by PRI until July 1997. Thus, Mexican politics revolved around the figure of the president, the executive branch, and powerful technocrats appointed by the president.

PRI helped the executive maintain a tight grip on and contain major societal actors and launch economic efforts. As the party tracing its origins to the Mexican revolution, PRIs's early leaders such as Lazaro Cárdenas built party strength through the support of the peasantry and workers. A degree of state responsibility can be traced historically in Mexico. The party strategy was predicated on generating high rates of growth for maintaining legitimacy. In the postwar period, PRI helped the successive presidents launch a very successful drive for import-sub-

BOX 3.3

Telecommunication Restructuring in Mexico

Phase/Date	Restructuring Initiative	Explanation
First Phase/ Late 1980s	• TELMEX Privatization • Specialized service privatization	State responding to liberalization coalition (domestic and international businesses) while being able to contain/marginalize other pressures on left and right that remain latent.
Second Phase/ 1995–	• Liberalization of the entire telecommunication sector (especially long distance provision) • Further privatization of services (satellite, radio, etc.)	State responds to the "internationalist" coalition mentioned above but finds its work difficult due to pressures from right and left. State also has difficulty at times putting together regulatory polices to govern these restructurings.

stitution industrialization, which made the state close to the domestic industrial elite while at the same time counting on labor for support to launch its policies. The period between the mid-1950s and late 1960s is known as the period of "stabilizing development," which produced favorable macroeconomic indicators. The development strategy was tightly controlled by the "technicos" in the Ministry of Finance and Bank of Mexico (later Central Bank), which continue to occupy a pre-eminent position in the Mexican economy. A slow down of economic growth and distributive concerns led to protests in 1968. Under the *sexenios* of the two successive presidents, Luis Echeverría (1970–76) and Jose López Portillo (1976–82), the state's role in the economy increased as it stepped in as a direct producer and undertook investments funded by its oil exports as well as international loans.

After the severe debt and fiscal crises that started in 1982, the Mexican economy began to move away from an ISI strategy as the Mexican state consolidated its position. The economic crisis made it possible for PRI (without losing significant labor support initially) to appeal to the business groups, which, fearful of the radical elements in PRI, had started to support the right wing party Partido Acción Nacional (PAN). Overall, the Mexican state acted responsibly in reconstructing its legitimacy in the 1980s.[52] Under PAN and big business prodding, Mexico joined GATT under López Portillo. While liberalization polices continued under Miguel de la Madrid (1982–88), the most significant challenge to PRI's policies came in 1988 when Carlos Salinas de Gortari won by just 50.39 percent of the vote (compared to earlier PRI candidates such as Madrid's 74.4 percent in 1982 and López Portillo's 94.4 percent in 1976). Salinas, a former budget and planning minister, deepened Mexico's liberalization further by bringing in a "change team" of technocrats committed to a market-oriented philosophy.[53] (This included the appointment of a "deregulation czar" who reported directly to the president and the council of economic minsters and is credited with pushing together many of the deregulations between 1988–92.)[54] By the early 1990s, the Mexican economy was recovering and PRI had effectively countered the PAN challenge. But economic problems surfaced again under the Ernesto Zedillo administration (1994–), making PAN's position stronger on the right and PRD's on the left.

Mexican telecommunications parallels the phases of the Mexican political economy detailed above. Prior to Mexico's ISI phase, telecommunications was privately run except for a brief period after the revolution when the state took over one of the two dominant telephone providers.[55] Telephone service was introduced in 1878 and the origins of Telmex, the present dominant provider in Mexico, can be traced to 1903 when the Swedish firm Ericsson in cooperation with a Mexican capitalist founded Mexeric. In 1947, Mexeric became Teléfonos de Mexico, S.A. (Telmex) while bringing other investors on board. The period from 1947 until 1990 (when Telmex was privatized) represents the rise and decline of the ISI phase in telecommunications. The state played a strong role in ensuring infrastructural development especially since the 1960s and it took over majority control of telecommunications under Echeverria (it controlled 48 percent until 1972).

As in other countries, a mix of economic, ideational, and techno-logical factors prompted the Mexican state toward Telmex privatization and liberalization of specialized services. The severity of the economic crisis is especially significant in Mexico's case, as it allowed the state to reorient its strategy from ISI toward liberalization and outward orientation. The economic crisis weakened the dominant economic constituencies in Mexico and the state could move directly toward privatization of its telecommunication carrier. The privatization would raise high revenues for the government (burdened by external debt), while a market orientation for the state monopoly would make it more responsive to user demands. PRI's courting of business groups which translated into telecommunication initiatives is also important. Ideationally, under the Salinas and Zedillo administrations, the technocrats, many of whom were educated in U.S. universities and are neoclassically trained economists, helped to shape the liberalizing strategy. The newfound privilege of these technocrats further weakened the hold of the ISI constituency over decision-making while allowing for an internationalist strategy to take its place.[56] Finally, technologically Mexico was able to liberalize the market for specialized services without posing a threat to the dominant network under Telmex. Wireless, private network, and other specialized services were liberalized along with privatization in 1990.

First Phase of Restructuring   Until the 1980s, in spite of the state's direct role in telecommunication provision, most user-group demands were unmet in Mexico, even though Telmex was one of the most efficiently run public sector enterprises in the country, and was one of Mexico's biggest employers (second only to Brazil in terms of its size in the developing world's telcos).[57] As such, Telmex was a classic PTT, unresponsive to demand pressures and acting as a "cash cow" for the treasury. The state also was able to contain or marginalize dissenting pressures. Provision of services was concentrated in the politically powerful Mexico City, which still accounts for more than one third of the main lines (see table 3.2). Nationally, waiting lists were enormously high (close to one million by the time of privatization). Telephone service reached less than one fifth of the homes. The telecommunication rate of growth itself fell to 6 percent in the 1980s from 14 percent earlier.[58] The waiting list in 1990 was more than double that of 1980s (table 3.2). Mexico was preoccupied with its external debt problems through most of the 1980s and thus in spite of pressures from user groups, its telecommunication restructuring did not begin until the late 1980s.

Pressures from urban areas and business groups were important for Mexican restructuring but overall the pressures were not as heterogeneous as they might seem. The strength of the PRI helped it control workers while catering to business preferences. In fact, the only coalition that effectively got the state's ear in the late 1980s was the pro-liberalization domestic and international groups. Furthermore, the strength of the PRI increased with the "window of opportunity" provided by the economic crisis of the early 1980s that initially weakened the influence of groups opposed to liberalization. (Nonetheless, it must be remembered that historically telecommunication restructuring began in Mexico just as PRI's position began to weaken as was apparent during the Salinas and Zedillo elections.)

Catalytic states can be identified by the degree to which they can shape important comprehensive restructuring initiatives. By privatizing Telmex the state could earn revenues to help ease its fiscal situation (even though it meant losing a "cash cow") while also designing incentives to enhance service provision. In Mexico's case, the privatization program was preceded by an internal restructuring of Telmex, dealing with phasing out an inefficient tariff structure (replacing it with a form of price cap regulation) and bringing the management and labor in line with the government's steps toward privatization. The privatization took place in December 1990, turning over a majority 51 percent share to a consortium that included a domestic shareholder (as required by law) Grupo Carso along with Southwestern Bell (now SBC Communications) and France Telecom. The total revenue generated in 1990 was $1.78 billion followed by additional sales of $2.27 billion in 1991 and $1.35 billion in 1992, making Telmex one of the most hotly traded stocks on New York Stock Exchange.

Given the state's need to build its legitimacy among disparate groups by the end of the 1980s, it instituted regulations to ensure service provision nationwide. Main lines were to grow at 12 percent a year and growth rates for towns varying according to their sizes were laid down along with requirements for public telephones. The waiting period for telephones was to be brought down to six months by 1996 and to one month by the year 2000. Telmex would lose its monopoly over long-distance by the end of 1996 (actually lost it on January 1, 1997) and it had no obligation to interconnect for local calls until 2025 making it a monopoly in domestic provision until then. The local loop was actually opened to competition in June 1995 though problems remain with implementing this law.

In spite of the restructuring, Telmex retains a reputation as an overpriced and inefficient firm. Installation charges for residential telephones are alternatively reported from $150[59] to $240 and $415 for businesses,[60] all several times more expensive than Mexico's more affluent neighbor up north. Waiting lists that were over one million in 1990 have not been eliminated and at times customers must wait up to two years for a telephone (table 3.2). Only one third of Mexican households have a telephone.

Liberalization also took place for specialized services in 1990. The most comprehensive was cellular deregulation for which Mexico chose a duopoly model (analogous to the one in the United States) allowing one provider to compete with Telmex in each of the nine regions in the country except for Mexico City, which already had two providers. Apart from a number of Baby Bells from the United States, foreign providers included Motorola, Bell Canada, and, later, AT&T and MCI. Data communication services were also liberalized, the state permitting the proliferation of private networks. But as table 3.3 shows, cellular, paging, and Internet markets grew very slowly, mostly because of the licensing and regulatory hurdles (including opposition from Telmex) that the ministerial regulator/policymaker could not overcome, in turn delaying the operators. However, the Mexican cellular market was expected to expand from 690,000 customers in 1995 to over 1.6 million in the year 2000.[61]

Second Phase of Restructuring   The second phase of Mexican restructuring, following the initial privatization and liberalization, began in 1995 and reveals the difficulties facing the Mexican state in the 1990s. As with its erstwhile ISI strategy, the success and legitimacy of Mexico's neoliberal strategy was predicated on economic growth and PRI's ability to hold its constituents and pro-liberalization coalition together. The early 1990s were good for Mexico and came to be regarded as a liberalization "success story." But a drastic devaluation of the peso in December 1994 resulted in inflation, unemployment, high interest rates, and a $27 billion aid package from the United States and IMF. The economic crises cost PRI its internal solidarity, with the old guard questioning Mexican market opening. At the same time, PRI lost some ground to PAN, most significantly in the 1995 elections when it lost three of the four governorships.[62] The economy picked up in 1996 but only with a considerably weakened PRI that among other things was also rocked by corruption scandals involving the Salinas family. In the July 1997 elections, PRI lost it majority in the national parliament for the first time in history. PAN also began to control six governorships including states with industrial growth centers such as Monterrey and Guadalajara.

The increasing plurality of domestic and international players in the market coupled with PRI's weakened power base means that the cohesive pressures and near-catalytic nature of Mexican politics in telecommunications might be coming apart. The case for the "internationalist" coalition was buffered by the formation of NAFTA in 1993, which threw open the Mexican telecommunications market to the United States (much as the MAFF talks had done in South Korea). On the other hand, dissatisfied workers and rural areas were beginning to coalesce around the left of center PRD in Mexico. Mexico City began to be governed by Cuauhtemoc Cárdenas, the PRD leader, in 1997. Thus, now the Mexican regulators were faced not only with the new market applicants as a result of NAFTA, but were also trying to deal with other applications that were pending, and, finally pressures from powerful international and domestic businesses for long-distance telephony became intense.[63]

The 1997 liberalization of Mexico's $3.5 billion long-distance market is instructive here and presents a mixed picture.[64] On the positive side, the government policy and regulatory agency, the Secretaría (ministry) de Communicaciones y Transportes (SCT), in spite of its slow start as a reorganized regulator, did adequately work out most of the features of the 1997 liberalization (such as interconnection and tariffs), well in advance. An interconnection ruling was passed in June 1994 and a new regulatory law was enacted in June 1995 to make way for the 1997 liberalization. The 1995 law actually allowed competition in the entire sector including local, long-distance, cellular, satellite, and cable. (The total telecommunications market in Mexico was valued at $11.3 billion.[65])

But the Mexican state was also trying to build its legitimacy among domestic and international businesses, which no longer lent it automatic support. Significantly, private operators were first started in the commercial capital Monterrey in January 1997 (perhaps for courting PAN bases of support) followed by Mexico city in April.[66] More than 60 cities would get competition in 1997. Telmex was asked to separate the local and long-distance accounts for customers. The field was crowded by luminaries like AT&T and Bell Atlantic, indicative of the strength and potential of the Mexican economy. On the other hand, SCT also seemed to be overwhelmed with this market opening which was not the case in 1990. For example, it had decided not to intervene in interconnection negotiations between Telmex and other firms, instead relying on draft regulations, but by March 1996, it had to settle the increasingly contentious issue between Telmex and the seven newly licensed providers.

This time SCT was dealing with a plurality of actors whose preferences diverged. Players like AT&T and MCI could not be tamed like Telmex could be in the past and the market tactics used by both to bring down access charges or capture customers raised significant fears among government officials and competitors.[67] In the meantime, Telmex got increasingly aggressive in defending its turf because by July 1998 it had lost 28 percent of Mexico's long-distance market to competitors. There were seven major domestic-international business alliances (featuring all the major U.S. long-distance providers) pitted against Telmex. These included: Avantel (Banamex & MCI), Alestra (Alfa Telecom and AT&T), Unicom (Bancomer, Telefonica, and GTE), Iusatel (Bell Atlantic and Iusacell).[68]

By 1998, the interconnection issue between Telmex and, by then, the two dominant challengers in the Mexican market (Avantel and Alestra represented by their U.S. agents MCI and AT&T) threatened to derail the liberalization process. It also reveals the influence of plural actors in Mexican politics.[69] Both MCI and AT&T complained of the high interconnection tariffs being charged by Telmex (including a 58 percent fee for expanding networks in the socially disadvantaged regions). Both firms stepped up their pressures by complaining to the U.S. Trade Representative (USTR) and FCC. The former was asked to put pressures on account of NAFTA and WTO accords and the latter was asked to withhold a license to Telmex and its partner Sprint for an international long distance service.[70] (AT&T and MCI were unable to get the Telmex-Sprint license withheld.) MCI threatened to withhold its $700 million investment plans in Mexico, a country then in the process of making many overtures toward attracting MNCs. At one point, Telmex physically pulled out sixty-nine circuits belonging to MCI on its premises.

Many of the regulatory problems could not be resolved because of the absence of an independent regulator competent enough to arbitrate these issues. The 1995 law stipulated that many of the SCT powers would be turned over to a new regulatory commission. This commission was created in August 1997 as Comisión Federal de Telecomunicaciónes (COFTEL) and became functional in April 1998. Under Javier Lozano, the new chairman, the Commission moved swiftly to resolve the interconnection tariffs issue. It replaced the 58 percent surcharge with a fixed fee of $422 million for infrastructure expansion and also reduced the other interconnection charges.[71]

In conclusion, the Mexican state in the past, mainly through its capacity vis-à-vis PRI's strength, was able to institute policies well. Telmex privatization is a case in point of the state responding to internationalist pressures. But this position is now changed. Given the reduced ability of the Mexican state to play a near-catalytic role in the Mexican economy and the fears about future economic growth, it is not clear whether the markets will evolve as smoothly as they did in the past. SCT and now COFTEL have had problems in instituting liberalization policies and many operators have been delayed in their operations as a result. This is most visible in table 3.3, which shows the slow diffusion of cellular and paging in Mexico between 1990 and 1995.

The current market opening is also devoid of an overall national debate or planning on the shape of information society in Mexico in the future, unlike Singapore or South Korea.[72] While the state seeks to respond to the internationalist coalition, its capacity is weakened by PRI's eroding power base and challenged by interest groups on the right and left of PRI (although PRI did make a few electoral gains in the July-August 1998 elections). On the other hand, its economy remains strong with GDP growth expected to be 6.5 percent for 1997 and above 5 percent for 1998.[73] Nonetheless, pluralist politics (dubbed "wide open and confused" by *The Wall Street Journal*)[74] are here to stay in Mexico.

Malaysia

Malaysia represents the case of a near-catalytic state more or less pushing through its telecommunication restructurings with its administrative clout but nonetheless having to satisfy disparate constituencies in doing so. Demand pressures on the Malaysian state come from its socioeconomic cleavages, which include Malaysia's multi-ethnic society, rural-urban divisions, and, to some extent, federalism or regional breakdowns. Malaysian pluralism often makes telecommunication restructurings difficult, and at times, biased in favor of politically powerful groups.

Malaysian socioeconomic pluralism needs to be evaluated against the context of a historically maneuverable state that developed both in capacity and autonomy before and during the colonial period. Well-developed empires followed by successive periods of European colonial rule (which began in 1511) were responsible for a centralized state and also a tradition of independence in the provinces that could not have been integrated into the state without a modicum of autonomy. In particular, British rule, which began through Penang in 1786 and Singapore in 1819, resulted in a strong civil service and a railways and telegraph infrastructure that would help the British control the provinces and exploit Malaysia's economic potential in extractive industries. (Telegraph was introduced in 1876 and Kuala Lumpur had its first telephone exchange in 1891.)[75]

After independence from the British in 1957, Malaysia not only had a strong civil service but a tradition of centralized control from Kuala

BOX 3.4

Telecommunication Restructuring in Malaysia

Phase/Date	Restructuring Initiative	Explanation
First Phase/ Mid-1980s	Service enhancement	Pressures from business concerns and also from the waiting lists of rural and urban users
First Phase/ Mid-1980s	Corporatization of dominant carrier and awarding of equipment and infrastructural contracts	Apart from demand pressures (businesses, rural/urban), the state was responding to its need to build its legitimacy among ethnic Malays. State effectively managed to contain worker dissent.
Second Phase/ 1990s	Privatization of dominant carrier and liberalization of specialized services	Restructuring efforts often run into trouble (nepotism/too many licenses awarded) because of the access of ethnic Malay coalition to state. Also pressures from international interests, ethnic Chinese business coalition, as well as rural and urban residential areas continue.

Lumpur, which was continued by the Malaysian elite after wresting control from the British.[76] In the postindependence period, power coalesced around the multiparty coalition known as the National Front (or Barisan Nacional) which is dominated by the United Malays National Organization (UMNO). So far UMNO has dealt quite effectively with internal and external challenges to its dominance in national politics. Ethnic riots in 1969 were followed by the announcement of the New Economic Policy which sought to correct the economic imbalance between the ethnic Malays (known as *bumiputeras*) and the economically dominant Chinese.[77] This ensured UMNO longevity through support by the largest constituency in the country. However, this also ensured effective economic discrimination against the Chinese.

UMNO's internal problems came to a head in the 1986 elections when most of the Chinese voted for the Chinese-based Democratic Action Party (DAP), which, in combination with other parties, could have led to a two-party system in Malaysia. This possibility resulted in leadership challenges to Mahathir Mohamad, who was both the prime minister and leader of UMNO. Mahathir strengthened his control over UMNO through a variety of measures leading to a situation that has been characterized as "creeping authoritarianism."[78] The latter is also underscored by the fact that "the arsenal that the government possesses to entrench itself in power is far greater than would be considered proper in normal circumstances in a fully democratic country."[79]

The legitimacy of the Malaysian state, has eventually rested on the strong economic growth in the county, which, except for a hiatus in the early 1980s, has been rapid since the 1970s. In spite of the problems with pluralism mentioned above, Malaysia now counts among the high end of the middle-income countries. The state's ability to direct this growth is unquestionable but historically it is also rooted in the commercial and trading activities associated with Malaysia before and during the colonial rule. If anything, state control over the economy has allowed it to redirect the surpluses and opportunities for participation preponderantly toward *bumiputeras* while the high growth rates themselves have helped non-Malays gain, too.[80] The slowdown of economic growth in the early 1980s, when the state sought to redirect economic growth by investing in heavy industry, was also taken as a lesson by the government to trust private investment instead of its own initiatives. But disagreements between the state and businesses are seldom severe enough for the latter to denounce the political regime.[81]

First Phase of Restructuring   The pressures building up for telecommunications since the 1970s are consistent with the overall socioeconomic profile of the country. In Malaysia's case, user-group pressures of political importance include those from businesses, government administrations, and urban/rural residential areas (each of which can be further subdivided along ethnic and provincial lines). Malaysian industry's strong economic profile accounts for the state-of-the-art telecommunication facilities available in its centers of growth, including the growth corridors that allow Malaysia to transact business or coproduce with its neighbors. These include the 1965 international cable venture known as SEACOM that allowed the country to interconnect directly with Hong Kong, Japan, and Guam initially.[82] More recently, Malaysia has collaborated on two regional industrial growth hubs with sophisticated telecommunication services. One encompasses Johor (Malaysia), Riau (Indonesia), and Singapore and the other includes Penang and the northwestern peninsular Malaysia, along with northern Sumatra (Indonesia) and Southern Thailand.[83]

Rural users are important for the Malaysian state, as the rural population accounts for 46 percent of the total in contrast to an average of 27 percent for upper-middle-income countries (Mexico is 75 percent urban).[84] Also, Malaysia's ethnic Malay population is concentrated in rural areas. Thus, Malaysia's official policy in its rhetoric at least displays a rural bias even though it is not always borne out by numbers. For example, rural teledensity was 3.8 in 1994 against a national total of 14.9.[85] On the other hand, with Kuala Lumpur accounting for less than one sixth of the total main lines in the country, it attests to the diffusion of telephones in the country as a whole (see table 3.2 for comparison with other countries). Most significantly, table 3.2 shows that over 60 percent of households in Malaysia have access to a main line. Even if exaggerated (ITU reports figures provided by governments), this number shows the importance to the Malaysian state of building its legitimacy widely.

The government-run department of telecommunications (known as Jabatan Telekom Malaysia or JTM) provided telecommunication service in Malaysia for thirty years after 1957 when the department was corporatized in 1986 with the eventual goal of privatization that began in 1990. The pre-corporatization period was marked by a variety of pressures and economic difficulties experienced by JTM. The waiting list for telephones, which stood at 176,000 in 1970, crossed the one million mark in 1986 in spite of the rapid increase in main lines, prompting consumer pressures for service enhancement including letters to the media.[86] In addition, efforts to decentralize the department to meet regional priorities or to outsource infrastructural projects to private concerns were only partially successful. Equipment and personnel shortages along with long waiting lists continued.

The most important case of subcontracting in the pre-corporatization period was the awarding of four licenses worth more than $1 billion for laying of 1.76 million main lines between 1983 and 1988 to *bumiputera* contractors. The project remained controversial from the start. Apart from the clear ethnic favoritism, the contractors were unable to meet their obligations and only one sixth of the main-line targets had been fulfilled by 1991, three years after the initial closing date for the projects.

During the mid-1980s, the government of Mahathir Mohamad, which by now was clearly committed to an export-oriented strategy fueled by private investment, decided to emulate the privatization trend in countries like the United Kingdom and Japan in response to pressures for service enhancement.[87] The Telecommunications Act of 1950 was amended in 1985 to prepare for corporatization, the latter effected on January 1, 1987. A new entity called Syarikat Telekom Malaysia (STM) came in to being (which began to be called Telekom Malaysia after privatization in 1990). The efficiency with which laws were passed and workers accepted privatization is often noted by officials.[88] Officials summarize the contribution of Mahathir Mohamad in terms of his strong personality and institutional factors: "The prime minister does not want warlords."[89] Another notes the influence of a good and efficient civil service to implement policy "rationally and beautifully."[90] These claims notwithstanding, there is now ample evidence that corporatization succeeded because of the hold of UMNO over the Parliament rather than because of an overwhelming political consensus. Workers' representatives were not consulted and initially their chief organization, the National Union of Telecom employees (NUTE) with twenty-two thousand members striked and picketed. Eventually the workers were offered lucrative terms of stay with STM or retirement. JTM, the original provider, was restructured as a regulatory body. Critical officials also note that due to the vested interest of the Ministry of Energy, Telecommunications and Posts, plans to vest JTM with autonomy (by, for example, placing it under purview of another ministry such as industry) could not be realized.[91]

Second Phase of Restructuring   The post-corporatization period is marked not only by the partial privatization of STM but also the liberalization of the Malaysian telecommunication market as a whole. Twenty-five percent of Telekom Malaysia's stock was privatized and while the corporation still has problems meeting waiting list demands, it had become a profitable entity by 1993. Most of the opposition to restructuring the dominant provider had diminished by the time of privatization and most of the energies of user and other interest groups in the 1990s were focused on the liberalizing market structure.[92]

The market liberalization exercise was marked both by trying to satisfy the potential providers of telecommunications (and favoring *bumiputeras*) while also trying to appease the various user groups. The biggest challenge was meeting the service demands of rural users for whom provision costs are high while marginal revenues are low. Overall, in spite of service enhancement, Malaysia's waiting list for telephones, which decreased in the 1980s, increased again in the 1990s, from 82,000 in 1990 to 140,000 in 1995 (table 3.2). Finally, Telekom Malaysia, as could be expected from a dominant incumbent provider, indulged in a number of practices that made matters difficult for new entrants. Interconnection with Telekom's network and high charges were a major problem.

The liberalization of the cellular industry, in particular, illustrates the themes underlined in the last paragraph. The government sought to leapfrog the technological frontier and assured rural areas that cost-effective cellular service would soon be available to them. The next step was to license cellular service providers that would then compete with Telekom's own cellular service provider ATUR (introduced in 1985). The first provider to be commissioned was Celcom (a *bumiputera* concern) in 1989, which by 1995 controlled 75 percent of the cellular market. But by 1995, seven licenses had been issued for mobile telephony alone, leading many observers to term it a case of "privatization run amok."[93] The case extended beyond cellular. TRI (the holding company for Celcom) geared itself for providing international service (a Telekom Malaysia monopoly) to its customers. Binariang, another cellular provider (with a 20 percent share by US West) was to provide domestic and international services, too. In addition, Time Communications was licensed to lay out a 1,000 kilometer fiber optic network for local service and hoped to provide international services. All in all there were eight providers for cellular, fixed line, and satellite-based services. The government had also licensed thirty-two paging providers. "The stampede for licenses seems to have overwhelmed the government. Having dispensed permits freely, in some cases to political favorites, ministers appear to have realized belatedly how big a problem they had created for themselves."[94] Another former official admitted: "Licensing appears to be a political process to please all masters."[95]

By mid-1995, Mahathir Mohamad personally intervened in the overcrowded telecommunications market declaring that the government would like to see mergers or consortia develop. Along these lines the first move Telekom Malaysia made was in June 1996 when it bought out a 70 percent share in one of the cellular providers (Malaysian Resources Corporation or MRCB). The fact that the market got so out of control is explained by the pluralistic nature of Malaysian politics, but the fact that the state can step in to try to streamline this market is explained by the state's near-catalytic nature. Thus, unlike Mexico in this regard, the messy market politics are not reflected in the expansion of the cellular phone services although paging growth has been slow (tables 3.3 and 3.4).

Another example of the near-catalytic nature of Malaysian state is the framing of Vision 2020, whether or not entirely reasonable, by the Mahathir government which foresees placing Malaysia with the other highly industrialized countries by the year 2020. In telecommunications, densities upwards of forty main lines per 100 people (like in the industrialized countries) are envisioned. Malaysia has also started moving toward leapfrogging the technological frontier with state support to try to fulfill this vision. Of particular importance here is a project nick-named "Multimedia Super Corridor" costing $8 to $15 billion that would comprise a ten to thirty square mile city south of Kuala Lumpur full of state-of-the-art multimedia technologies putting Malaysia on the map with places like Silicon Valley.[96] But the supply push nature of this experiment is suspect in a pluralistic society. Furthermore, economically Malaysia suffered a severe blow to its currency and financial crisis in mid-1997, calling into question large state expenditures on projects like these.

Malaysia is also positioning itself to become an international provider beyond its borders. Collaborative projects along its borders were mentioned earlier. Telekom Malaysia has now also invested in telecommunications operations in countries like Malawi, India, Bangladesh, and China. It sees its experience in enhancing infrastructures in developing countries as giving it a lead in competing against providers from developed countries.[97] Malaysians are also always cognizant of their neighbor Singapore, which has started playing a similar role in international telecommunications.[98] Malaysia, which stands to benefit from the WTO accord in telecommunications, will be one of the first newly industrializing countries to put the accord to effect. Market access and foreign investment (which will be limited to 30 percent) are to be provided to foreign providers by 1998. In turn, Malaysia hopes to gain from international opportunities for its own providers.

The Malaysian state continues to play a strong and effective role in its society. But the pluralistic pressures it has always faced and the difficulty with arbitrating those pressures distinguish the Malaysian state from its near-catalytic counterpart in Mexico, which has begun to deal with pluralistic pressures only recently.[99] The one-party-dominated catalytic system in Mexico was coming undone in 1997 with opposition parties gaining control of the legislature. The Malaysian state has always walked a fine line among its various ethnic groups and federal provinces.

Beginning in July 1997, the Malaysian state's legitimacy (built on an economic foundation since the 1969 riots and subsequent policies) faced a strong challenge from the currency devaluation and financial crisis. While the growth rate was 7.8 percent in 1997, it was only expected to be around 2 percent in 1998.[100] Fissures were beginning to develop in the ruling coalition by mid-1998 over the course of future economic policies including one between Mahathir Mohamad and his powerful deputy premier Anwar Ibrahim. Nonetheless, the maneuverability of the Malaysian state in the past allowed it to cater to both its *bumiputeras* and Chinese coalitions while giving preferential treatment to the former.[101] It also responded to direct pressures from urban areas and indirect pressures from rural areas. Finally, unlike the weakened Mexican state in the 1990s, the powerful Malaysian state (at least until the banking and financial crisis of 1997 hit) was moving toward the framing of comprehensive "information society" type policies.

CONCLUSION

The four cases in this chapter offer several similarities and contrasts. Catalytic and near-catalytic states on the whole are quite successful with their service enhancement initiatives and launching of liberalization and privatization ones. However, here the catalytic states with their enormous maneuverability and responsibility are more successful than their near-catalytic counterparts. Malaysia continues to feature long waiting lists and a messy liberalization process while Mexico's second wave of restructuring is messier than its first. States like Singapore and Mexico featuring cohesive pressures also have an easier time pushing through restructuring initiatives than ones with myriad pressures like South Korea and Malaysia.

Similarities and contrasts are available for catalytic states depending on the pressures they face. Both states responded quite well to the coalitions that they favored, the internationalist coalition in Singapore's case and the *chaebol*-oriented domestic coalition in South Korea's case. Both of them framed comprehensive "information society" type policies and carried out initiatives to streamline their regulatory structure. But South Korean restructuring was made difficult by its pluralistic pressures. First, its restructuring proceeded more slowly as the state sought to redress many wants that built up in the 1990s, especially as its democratization began to proceed. Second, by mid-1990s, the South Korean state was beginning to show increasing stress as its privatization of Korea Telecom was stalled and political crises surrounding earlier telecommunication restructuring became public news.

Near-catalytic states offer interesting comparisons, too. Both Mexico and Malaysia lagged in service provision and framing of regulatory and comprehensive policies (the latter especially during the second phase of restructuring). But the initially cohesive pressures on Mexico made its privatization exercises smoother in the first phase though this may not be the case in the second phase. The smoothness of corporatization in Malaysia was not so much due to its pressures (which were plural) but because in many ways the Malaysian state reveals more capacity and autonomy than the Mexican state. Thus, whereas since the late 1980s, PRI faced an attrition of its power base, Malaysia's Mahathir Mohamad has consolidated state power through authoritarian policies and appeasing to its traditional constituencies including the *bumputera* groups. This accounts for the apparent paradox of the simultaneous presence of the dirigiste role of the Malaysian state in shaping telecommunications policies while at the same time presenting a much more nepotistic restructuring process, both in contrast to Mexico's.

However, all the states examined above showed enough tensions in the 1990s in terms of being unable to contain, respond to, or marginalize pressures (as the case may be) to indicate that these states may no longer be able to play catalytic or near-catalytic roles in their economies. Here the South Korean and Mexican states were closer to moving away from their catalytic and near-catalytic roles respectively than the Singapore and Malaysian states. In the latter states, authoritarian policies continued to marginalize many pressures but it was not clear for how long these polices could continue. The Malaysian state in particular faced significant challenges to its legitimacy with the economic crisis that started mid-1997 and that the state sought to assuage through a combination of populist and authoritarian policies reminiscent in some ways of Brazil's (which will be examined in the next chapter).[102]

CHAPTER 4

Telecommunications Restructuring in Dysfunctional and Predatory States

This chapter first explains the cases of two dysfunctional states, one facing macro cohesive pressures and the other plural ones. It then describes a predatory state for which pressures do not matter. (Table 3.1 summarizes these cases.) Unlike their catalytic and near-catalytic counterparts, dysfunctional states have a hard time effecting restructurings, while predatory states do not even undertake them.

Theoretically, this chapter concludes that the case of a dysfunctional special-interest–driven state with a plurality of pressures (Brazil in this chapter) is the most generalizable (or most representative) for developing countries at present. The chapter proposes the examination of a pluralistic pressured dysfunctional state in detail. At the demand level, this chapter (like the last one) also shows how powerful clubs (large business users, government administrations, exporters) are able to get services before other user clubs (residential users) who lack access to the state. The same holds true for coalitions that arise out of these powerful clubs.

DYSFUNCTIONAL STATES

Dysfunctional states lack maneuverability and are, therefore, usually special-interest driven. The last part needs clarification. Historically, many developing countries inherited vast bureaucratic machineries and other resources. Thus, state capacity is quite high but state autonomy may be lacking. Furthermore, these states might actually play a large role in their society based on their commitment to development. Not lacking state capacities, many of the development programs actually may be easy to implement even if these programs ultimately benefit a few user groups or special interests that dominate the state.[1] But unlike catalytic or near-catalytic states, dysfunctional states seldom succeed in providing services to the society at large.

China

China may at first seem like an odd choice for a special-interest–dominated state for telecommunications because the state seems so insular. Its highly authoritarian and centralized decision-making procedures, however, reveal the influence of powerful groups (most of them located within the government itself) that accounts for everything from awarding of lucrative economic contracts (including those in telecommunications) to widespread corruption within the government. No clear vision in terms of integrating the telecommunication sector with the overall development strategy or trajectory has emerged, although state estimates for future service enhancement and telecommunication investment are high.

A highly bureaucratized and centralized state is as much a product of centuries of Chinese imperial history as it is of the 1949 communist revolution. Chinese bureaucrats or mandarins had existed for hundreds of years aiding the state with its agenda.[2] Communist China was able to build on this tradition by recruiting officials to its cadres. The nearly 50 million strong Chinese Communist Party (CCP) thus represents both legacy and departure. The reach of the Party is pervasive enough to weaken any opposition to state legitimacy. But the centralized bureaucratic tradition in China, while formal in its hierarchies, also reveals informal elements. Of particular importance are political "connections" (*guanxi* in Chinese) that allow many officials and their relatives and friends to profit from this system.

The centralized nature of the Chinese state and its instruments of domination like the CCP, however, do exhibit both tension and evolution.[3] Struggles within the Chinese state are visible even during the highly centralized Mao period (1949–76). Mao himself responded to pressures for reform in implementing programs like the "Great Leap Forward" (1958–60). The latter, however, degenerated into brutal Stalinist type repression of Chinese people and a famine that took 20 to 30 million lives. A second program, the "Cultural Revolution," began in the late 1960s and sought to purge society of reformist elements. However, reformers like Deng Xiaoping were, after Mao's death, able to introduce elements of capitalism and international market opportunities into China (especially after 1978). The reformist movement in China, along with the efforts to open China, may itself be seen as leading to the protests and repression following political demonstrations and killings in Tiannenman in 1989. It is this coalition of interests (within and outside the Chinese state) favoring China's connections with the world economy that has not allowed the state to respond effectively to other interests in society.

The post-Deng China after 1996 continues to deal with the tensions of a highly centralized system that must also respond to market-opening measures, the latter being a feature of Chinese political economy for over two decades now. The 1997 CCP plenary further underscored

BOX 4.1
Telecommunication Restructuring in China

Phase/Date	Restructuring Initiative	Explanation
First Phase/ Mid-1980s	Service enhancement and growth of rival providers to MPT	Demand for services grows as business activity picks up in the 1980s especially along China's eastern coast. "Reformist" coalition consists of these domestic and international businesses supported by powerful state officials.
Second Phase/ Mid-1990s	Autonomy to regional providers	Need to contain regions through devolution of autonomy and also because MPT continued to weaken in the decade before.
Second Phase/ Mid-1990s	Privatization/partial liberalization of specialized services (cellular, paging, Internet)	Pressures from the "reformist" coalition mentioned above.

China's market experiment in outlining China's privatization plans, which would lead to all but 1,000 of China's 370,000 enterprises being privatized.[4] "The irony of politics in China in the post-Tiananmen period is that although the CCP still rules, communism seems dead."[5]

Apart from the obvious tension and evolution of the Chinese state vis-à-vis its reform processes at the central level, China also must deal with centrifugal tendencies from its twenty-two provinces, five autonomous regions, and three federally governed territories. Imperial China often devolved power to the provinces to maintain legitimacy. Postcommunist China dealt with the provincial question by strengthening the reach of the Party in the provinces and at the county level through recruitment as well as administration.[6] CCP's "accumulated political capacities" have allowed it to maintain provincial control while participating in national development projects.[7] If these pressures could no longer be contained, they would pose a significant threat to the international-oriented "reformist" coalition.

Chinese telecommunications parallel the development of the state in China. Historically, an elaborate system of communication was necessary for maintaining imperial control, and postal and courier services can be found from the days of the Han dynasty (206 B.C. to A.D. 446).[8] Telegraph and telephone were introduced in the 1870s but China only had 193,000 urban lines (there were no rural phones) in 1949, though there was a 180,000 km long-distance network including one connecting Beijing with Shanghai.[9] Teledensity was 0.05 in 1949. Communist China ignored telecommunications until the 1980s, with only brief spurts of modernization mostly concentrated around cities like Beijing.

First Phase of Restructuring   Demands for telecommunication services grew severalfold with the market liberalization that began with Deng Xiaoping. These demands tended to be concentrated and articulated prominently by administrative and business (large) users. It is not that the rest of Chinese society does not demand telephones, but the Chinese state is able to marginalize these pressures easily. By one estimate, there were only one thousand "private phones" in China in 1980.[10] While this figure may sound exaggerated, ITU data shows that as late as 1990, only 28 percent of Chinese households had phones as opposed to 70 percent in 1995.[11] The picture becomes clear when it is realized that most of China's telephones are located in administrative offices, with teledensity in rural areas being 0.17.[12] (Table 3.2 documents the growth of Chinese waiting lists.) Thus, demand pressures in China are both cohesive and streamlined and both reflect, as well as shape, state priorities with efficacy. "The reform coalition consists of a powerful group which includes the major manufacturing and user ministries, large national users, local governments and interest groups, and international equipment suppliers and service operators."[13]

The insulated nature of Chinese politics accounts for the narrowness as well as the existence of a "reform coalition" among its privileged groups. (A small number of privileged groups would find it easy to form a coalition.) Foremost among the partners of this restructuring coalition are powerful ministries or government departments with access to the ultimate decision-making authority, the State Council or the cabinet. Thus, the first four ministries to be granted permission to build their own networks in 1976 were coal, petroleum, water, and railways (the latter and the People's Liberation Army had other networks in place already). Banks and airlines were the next to follow. In equipment manufacturing, the historic rivalry is between the Ministry of Posts and Telecommunications (MPT) and the politically favored Ministry for Machine Building and Electronic Industry (MMBEI). The latter has helped to coalesce the opposition to MPT into a single force that sees its interests aligned with the reform coalition.

The high economic growth rates in China and opening to the international market have also resulted in demand from the restructuring coalition for sophisticated and specialized telecommunication services. The demand by large users is especially significant because many of them sought to bypass the MPT network by hooking up with other carriers, such as the contract signed between AT&T and China's domestic airline (CAAC) for a VSAT based network.[14] The presence of high demands in economic hothouses along China's eastern coast (especially in provinces such as Fujian and Guangdong and in special economic zones for export) have resulted in provision of services like paging, dedicated business networks, and domestic VSAT services in these areas.[15] Places such as Beijing accounted for nearly 100,000 of the 850,000 on the waiting list for telephones in 1988.[16]

In the meantime, just as the state moves toward providing services to large users and high growth areas, rural and non-eastern areas continue to be neglected in telecommunications. While there are only a few studies showing the demand for telephones in rural areas, there is enough evidence to note the distribution of telephones among rural-urban areas and what one author calls the "core" (eastern and coastal) and "peripheral" areas.[17] Only 21 percent of China's telephones were in rural areas in 1988. The gap had worsened since 1965 when the rural-urban ratio was 1:1.6 (with a rural teledensity of 0.29) while it was 1:3.3 with a rural teledensity of 0.86 in 1988.[18] Furthermore, nearly half (46.2 percent in 1988) of the telephones were in the seven coastal provinces (Guangdong, Beijing, Jiangsu, Lianing, Shandong, Zhejing, and Shanghai) whereas remote and less developed areas like Xinjiang, Guizhou,

Qinghai, Ningxia, Hainan, and Tibet accounted for only 4.2 percent of the total.[19]

As for specialized services, cellular began proliferating in Eastern areas with a roaming service connecting Guangdong, Beijing, and Hong Kong.[20] There were 6.84 million cellular customers in China by 1997.[21] Of particular importance here is a government policy that marginalizes rural and peripheral areas from planning, a luxury that only a centralized state like China can enjoy. (Brazil and India, as shown later, are unable to avoid dealing with these pressures.) The official policy in China, on the other hand, did seem to encourage rural areas to invest in telephones with collective funds, hardly a possibility for economically disadvantaged regions. And a few provinces did take the lead in collaborating with foreign providers such as with Cable and Wireless in Shenzen starting in 1984.

Telecommunications was made a development priority in China following the opening of its economy under Deng Xiaoping. China's seventh five-year plan, starting in 1985, which formalized China's burgeoning international links, also made telecommunications a strategic priority. The availability of services in eastern and coastal provinces may be traced to this period although the spurt in the increase of teledensity did not come until the 1990s (table 3.2). In 1986, China specifically announced a program for pushing high-tech developments in seven issue areas including information technologies.[22]

MPT, established in 1949, was the monopoly domestic and international services provider in China, but, as mentioned earlier, it now works with several other large user providers, rival ministries, and provincial administrations for service provision. MPT controls thirty provincial posts and telecommunication administrations in its twenty-one provinces, five autonomous regions, and four municipalities. It also must coordinate the activities of over twenty-five hundred enterprises that make up the R&D and manufacturing wing of telecommunication service provision. MPT has seen its central position eroded because of the increasing autonomy of provinces in planning and operating their networks, leading observers to conclude that MPT leads "a confederation of thirty separate provincial and municipal bureaus."[23] In terms of equipment manufacturing, MPT was first challenged by MEI though the latter's position has now declined with the entry of international equipment manufacturers like Alcatel, AT&T, Northern Telecom, NEC, Nokia, Philips, Samsung, Mitsubishi, Seimen's, Hitachi, Fujitsu, and Motorola. By the end of 1997, there were sixteen joint ventures in telecommunication equipment manufacturing.

The politics of streamlined restructuring in China may be noticed in the outcomes resulting for the "reform coalition" in China. Instead of competing pressures and disparate networks, the ministerial providers have matched up with international providers, and two powerful service providers, Liantong and Jitong, have emerged as a result.[24] Liantong or the United Telecommunication Corporation, began in 1992 and included the MEI, and the ministries of railways and energy. By 1994, Liantong began offering mobile services in four cities even though MPT had successfully defeated their proposal for service provision earlier through the State Council in 1993. Liantong hopes to provide 10 percent of China's long-distance traffic and a third of its mobile traffic in the future. Jitong is controlled by twenty-six state institutions and will provide value-added services in the future. Both providers are matching up with foreign equipment manufacturers and service providers.

Beginnings of the Second Phase   The second phase of Chinese restructuring starting in the mid-1990s continues the devolution of power to provincial bodies and alternative providers. Privatization of a few services may also be allowed. Apart from the networks built by large users, provincial autonomy in building networks is important. It accounts for the accelerated deployment of services in eastern and coastal areas. In the mid-1990s, AT&T and Singapore Telecom planned on building business user and fixed-line networks in Shanghai. The ministry of radio, film, and television will also provide telephony in the future. The seemingly centrifugal nature of the network is in fact not quite so, given its hierarchical structure and the ultimate controls through Beijing's elite central decision-making bodies like the State Council. Thus, foreign providers have actually been kept quite disciplined by Beijing and even the steps announced by the September 1997 CCP plenary excluded most of terrestrial telecommunications from the list of sectors to be deregulated and privatized.

Given the September 1997 CCP announcement by President Jiang Zemin, a few notable telecommunication restructurings have come about in specialized services. The most important is the partial privatization of China Telecom, a cellular provider for the heavily industrialized Guangdong and Zhejiang provinces (although in February 1998 it also acquired the Jiangsu Mobile and was expected to announce another $33 billion in acquisitions by the year 2000).[25] The China Telecom sale was seen as the bellwether for the September 1997 CCP announcement and came about in October 1997. It was the largest stock offering in Asia outside of Japan (raising $4 billion) and created the fifth largest cellular firm in the world. Nevertheless, its politics reveal the difficulties the Chinese state might have in letting go of its control. MPT retains 77.61 percent interest in the firm (apart from other regulatory controls) and the sale raised far fewer dollars than expected (the Chinese state was also widely believed to have asked for too much, an all too common phenomena among many states selling lucrative enterprises). China Telecom will also compete in Guangdong and Zhejiang with two other state carriers: Unicom (a firm controlled by several state enterprises) and Great Wall (jointly owned by MPT and the People's Liberation Army).

The very strength and size of the China market is bound to bring many pressures to bear. China Telecom itself, which had only about 2.5 million customers in 1997, expected to increase to 10.7 million subscribers by the year 2000 for Guangdong and Zhejiang alone (accounting for over one quarter of the total cellular subscribers in the country) (see tables 3.3 and 3.4). The MPT also planned on providing a telephone in every village of the country by 2000 (itself a monumental task but reflected in the projected teledensity of 19.27 in table 3.2). Meanwhile, the telecommunication instrument of choice may be the low-cost paging instruments that are proliferating widely in China (see table 3.3). There were 17.4 million pagers in China by 1995. Paging codes are being used by consumers to send particular messages to each other and the public call offices are usually crowded with consumers trying to return phone calls.[26] There were over a hundred foreign manufacturers selling pagers in China in 1997. The Internet has been slow to diffuse in China. Apart from MPT and state controls (over content of messages), the English language dominance of the Internet remains another problem. Therefore, the largest subscription to Internet comes from foreign-owned businesses with government departments and academic institutions coming close behind. MPT provides services through ChinaNet (which started in April 1995). Other providers include GB Net owned by Jitong Corporation and networks put in place for academic purposes. The most watched-for entry here was that of the U.S. firm Netscape, which planned on starting business in China soon.

The tightly controlled telecommunication restructuring in China, however, may become difficult in the future as its political system adjusts to the post-Deng and post–Hong Kong eras along with successive international pressures (such as China's pending application for membership with the WTO) and those generated internally. China has by far the most ambitious service enhancement program in the world, with projected teledensity of 19.27 in the year 2000, a sixfold increase from 3.35 in 1995 (which was itself a nearly sixfold increase from the teledensity in 1990) (see table 3.2). Whether or not China can reach its targets in the year 2000 or beyond depends on how well it controls its political pressures. The neat ordering of its "reform coalition" can break down with China's inability to control its provincial or reformist pressures and as international manufacturers and providers get aggressive. Summing up China's development experience with special reference to telecommunication, Milton Mueller notes that China's "development is thus driven by a jarring dialectical tension between economic freedom and political authoritarianism, between decentralization and centralization, between capitalist practice and socialist ideology."[27]

Brazil

The similarity and contrast between Brazilian politics and those of China convey a sense of how two states with vast capacities and, at times, high degrees of responsibility nonetheless are ultimately dissimilar, given the plurality of pressures on the Brazilian state as opposed to the relatively cohesive pressures that China faces. This critical difference leaves us with a picture of a Brazilian state either courting and catering only to the elite interests that keep it in power, or gridlocked in trying to cater to all interests at once. In both cases, societal interests are seldom fully met leading to widespread dissatisfaction with state policies, including those in telecommunications. Coalitional pressures in Brazil's case come from its inward-oriented versus outward-oriented business groups (the latter more powerful), while micro heterogeneous pressure comes from federal provinces and urban and rural residential users. These pressures did move the state toward service enhancement during the first phase of restructuring, with slow moves toward liberalization and privatization in the second phase.

State power was consolidated and centralized in Brazil after the establishment of *Estado Novo* (New Republic) by Getúlio Vargas in 1930, who benefited from the divisions among the historically powerful governors to end Brazil's semicolonial state that had existed since 1808.[28] Provincial governors did not become powerful in Brazil until the 1980s but other special interests took their place during and after the Vargas regime. In particular, pressures from social and military elites continued to preoccupy the attention of successive regimes even as they tried populist measures to build a consensus for their policies in the society at large. Therefore, regime instability has been a regular feature of Brazilian politics, which have alternated between periods of populism and authoritarianism (or both simultaneously), the latter through either extreme centralization or military rule.

The special-interest–driven nature of Brazilian politics stands out in all political writings. The descriptions provided by successive dependency theorists beginning with Andre Gunder Frank in the late 1960s can in fact be conceived of as special-interest domination.[29] The early dependency writers emphasized the inequality of exchange relations between the (industrialized) core and the (underdeveloped) peripheral economies but more importantly they pointed toward dominant elites in

BOX 4.2

Telecommunication Restructuring in Brazil

Phase/Date	Restructuring Initiative	Explanation
First Phase/ Late 1970s	Service enhancement	State responding to long waiting lists from business and urban residential demands in turn arising out of the high economic growth rates of the 1970s. Service enhancement was slow given lack or resources and competing interests.
Second Phase/ Late 1980s	Liberalization and privatization of niche/specialized markets	Internationalist business coalition able to sway state, though often opposed by inward-oriented businesses and federal provinces wanting all the benefits to themselves. Regulatory authority lacking, legal disputes many.
Second Phase/ Late 1980s	Moves toward corporatization and privatization of Telebrás	Supported by internationalist coalition but opposed by workers and other political parties.

whose interest it was to keep these exchange relations in place. Sophisticated dependency writers, many of whom focused on Brazil, not only conceptualized these relations in class terms but also argued that the core includes the capitalist classes in the industrialized and the underdeveloped areas, thus deepening our understanding of the mechanism by which these exchange relations are sustained.[30] The state was posited as enforcing the interest of the dominant classes in the periphery. Evans' analysis of Brazilian development builds on the "pact of domination" thesis to examine the "conflict and cooperation among representatives of international capital owners, of local capital and top echelons of state apparatus" given in terms of what Evans called the "triple alliance."[31] While dependancy theory has been soundly critiqued for many reasons including difficulties with empirical verification and generalization,[32] its basic insight into the special-interest–driven nature of Brazilian politics is shared by other writers.

Evans notes that during the ISI period, which lasted until 1964, Brazil's dependence on imports was just changed by the need for foreign capital to produce these imports in Brazil instead, thus merely changing the particular form of special-interest domination. The role of foreign investment in Brazilian development has been dubbed by a few writers as the period of "import reproduction" instead of substitution. The import substitution policies that Brazil more or less followed had, by the early 1960s, resulted in a drop of industrial output, balance of payment difficulties, and domestic inflation.[33] The economic crisis of the early 1960s continued until the military government of Castello Branco took power in 1964. The economic crisis had provoked a social crisis and, in the words of Evans, "[A]s in the 1930s, the necessity of making the revolution from above before someone else succeeded in starting one from below was a compelling motivation."[34]

Military rule lasted over two decades until 1985 when elections took place. Branco and his successors ruled with an iron fist. In spite of the high economic growth rates during this period, wealth mainly accrued to the elite and by the early 1980s, Brazil was in the throes of another economic crisis.[35] Inflation was rampant, growth rates had declined, and foreign debt was above $80 billion. Meanwhile, the attempts at redemocratization (*abertura*) by Branco's successors fed into growing social unrest especially in Brazil's provinces. The 1982 gubernatorial elections brought the antimilitary PMBD to power in a number of southern provinces. In 1985, the PMBD candidate Tancredo Neves won the presidential elections but died before taking power. Instead, Jose Sarney, whose party (the PFL) supported PMBD after breaking off from the pro-military party (PDS), came to power. Nonetheless, Haggard and Kaufman note that the Neves election is consistent with the pluralistic political pressures in Brazil that cannot be contained. The consolidation that began with Vargas came undone with Neves as "grassroots opposition movements weakened the corporatist pillars of the old order."[36]

The decade following the Sarney presidency features first, the breakdown of the Brazilian system due to its factional politics and, second, the partially successful attempts, under the Cardoso presidency since 1994, at addressing Brazil's intractable political and economic problems.[37] By the time of Cardoso's election, both the politics (with corruption scandals and factional warfare) and economics (with slow growth and inflation) were coming undone. Neither the party system nor the governments could contain the resulting political-economic unrest. The Cardoso election was significant in that he was well respected and was able to pull together a coalition to effect important policies. Cardoso's first success was with a new monetary plan (called the "Real Plan" after the new currency that was introduced) that helped to bring down inflation.[38] While the coalition of parties pulled together by Cardoso gave the regime some institutional stability, its longevity was in question by 1997 as groups began to jockey for influence again and party discipline remained weak. Even as the long-delayed program of making Brazil's over five hundred state-owned enterprises efficient through privatization picked up under Cardoso, many investors remained wary of the Brazilian economic restructuring process.[39]

Resistance to restructuring also comes from opposition parties and trade unions, the latter long known to thwart such initiatives in Brazil. As a result, regulatory and legal institutions, necessary for ensuring smooth and impartial restructuring, remain weak.[40] Nonetheless, privatization of state enterprises had generated $15 billion by mid-1997 including $4.71 billion raised from cellular privatizations.[41] About $80 billion are expected by 1998, which includes $40 billion expected from the telecommunication monopoly privatization and liberalization.

Brazilian telecommunications history is reflective of the centrifugal Brazilian politics, the attempts at consolidation, and the vicissitudes of the economy. Until the mid-1960s, the power to grant licenses for telecommunications was divided between local and state (for regional operators) and the federal government (for long-distance and international).[42] Brazil's military rulers nationalized the over one thousand privately owned local telecommunication firms in 1966 and a period of consolidation began with the founding in 1972 of Telecommunicacoes Braselieras S.A. (or Telebrás as it is popularly known) providing domestic services and Embratel (another Telebrás subsidiary) providing international and interstate long-distance services. Telebrás began to supervise consolidated regional operating companies (ROCs), which soon numbered twenty-eight due to the desire of every region to have its own carrier and because of the granting of political privileges to various interests.[43]

First Phase of Restructuring   As the Brazilian economy grew under the military regime, the demand for telephones increased. In 1976, the government invested a sizable sum of $3.44 billion in telecommunications. This early spurt given to telecommunications meant that Brazil with its over 6 million lines would have the largest telecommunication system in the developing world by 1980 (China had about 3.5 million). Even in 1995, after slow growth during the 1980s, Brazil's over 12 million main lines (closely followed by the nearly twelve million lines in India) were second only to China's, which by then had nearly 41 million main lines.[44] However, given its population of over 159.2 million in 1995, the teledensity of 7.48 was much lower than other major Latin American countries such as Argentina (15.99), Mexico (9.58), or Uruguay (19.56).[45]

The enhanced investments in telecommunications barely met the demand for telecommunication services given the economic growth rates in Brazil during the 1970s. Thus investments carried out in the first wave of telecommunication service enhancement in Brazil were insufficient even though it must be credited with being one of the first developing countries to have realized the importance of telecommunications. An early study in Brazil showed that telecommunications density was strongly correlated to the product of the services sector in the economy suggesting that there were latent or explicit pressures from this sector on the telecommunication system.[46] By 1980, for the economy as a whole, there was a registered waiting list of three and a quarter million telephones (table 3.2), a situation that did not improve much during the 1980s when Brazilian telecommunication expenditures declined. Major economic centers like Sao Paulo and Rio de Janeiro suffered the worst with long waiting lists (Sao Paulo alone needed one million connections by 1990) and congestion on their inter- and intracity networks. The low quality of service and very high tariffs marred the national network as a whole. The "Own Your Telephone" scheme, which was to enable faster installation through consumers capitalizing and owning their main lines, was a failure with a backlog of four hundred thousand requests in 1990 out of the registered demand of above one million. Nonetheless, these schemes did allow the Brazilian telephone system to grow at rates of 20 percent or more a year for a little while.[47] But installation of these telephones could take as long as two years with premium prices ranging upwards of $3,000. As a result, a black market in telephones had started in major cities (a business telephone in Sao Paulo cost $10,000).[48]

With urban telephony and its elite interests posing such a problem, rural areas (with nearly one third of Brazil's population) hardly figured anywhere in the planning even though the government had announced a service enhancement program for rural areas in 1977, making it one of their top priorities. While the government calculated that at least a 150,000 lines were needed immediately for rural areas, only 20,000 had been installed by 1985.[49] Telephones were simply unavailable at any price in the rural areas even through the subscription schemes. Other initiatives taken by the government stayed at the level of rhetoric as far as rural areas were concerned. (Populist politics in Brazil have seldom really dealt with the underlying problems.)

Second Phase of Restructuring   Brazilian telecommunications remained stagnant or, by some measures, became worse during the 1980s due to Brazil's political and economic problems. The government continued to treat Telebras as a "cash cow" in the early 1980s, appropriating the surpluses to finance its debt and other areas.[50] But Brazilian inflation added to the economic woes as returns from services depreciated. The slow growth of Brazilian telecommunications during the late 1980s is well summarized by Wellenius as resulting from "government price controls that did not allow Telebras to fully recover costs and generate surpluses for reinvestment, an increasingly outdated policy of industrial autarky resulting in high cost of equipment and slow technological change in the network, and Telebras' organizational structure that gives the individual state enterprises insufficient managerial and financial autonomy to be run as modern businesses."[51]

Meanwhile, the demands from large users and other interest groups for service enhancement and other sectoral restructurings continued to grow up to the end of 1980s. For example, as the worldwide cellular industry took off by the late 1980s, business users began to demand this service as a substitute for the terrestrial networks. Demand for fax machines was so high that the U.S. embassy calculated that 10,000 contraband fax machines had been brought into the country.[52] Data services were available but at very high costs. Dedicated lines, for example, to the United States through AT&T and Embratel, cost anywhere between $9000 and $15,000 per month and still a waiting list of 11,000 customers existed.[53] Meanwhile, the regional Telebrás operators hardly ever provided efficient services. Rio de Janeiro's operator was termed a "national disgrace" by Brazil's telecommunications minister as late as 1998.[54]

A host of international service providers and equipment manufacturers were also applying pressures individually, collectively, and through their home governments for market opening. The Bush administration, for example, applied pressure on the Collor government (1989–93, which succeeded Sarney's) as it began to consider market opening steps. U.S. firms wanting market entry included AT&T, Motorola, GTE, Bell Atlantic, Ameritech, and BellSouth. Other foreign firms included Northern telecom, NEC, and Ericsson (equipment imports accounted for nearly a third of the Brazilian market).[55]

By the time of the Collor administration, restructuring was clearly on the agenda but its slow progress thereafter reveals the same plurilateral pressures that marred the political-economic scenario in Brazil as a whole. Furthermore, service enhancement was delayed given Brazil's political succession problems and economic crises. In particular, even as restructuring began, it first benefitted the privileged groups and specialized markets. The coalition with access to the Sarney, Collor, Franco (1993–94) and, to a great extent, the Cardoso administrations, was one made of large domestic and international large business users, and other interest groups such as equipment manufacturers, foreign governments, and international organizations such as the World Bank. Within Telebrás itself, workers who received lifelong employment resisted restructuring moves and their cause was taken up by nationwide trade unions and political parties.

Technological change, which would allow many of the demands of large users to be met through specialized markets such as data communications and cellular, was the initial alternative to comprehensive restructuring. One study assessing Brazilian telecommunications in the early 1990s noted: "Niches of investment opportunities for the private sector in Brazilian telecommunications will be confined to specialized applications of high technology, e.g., cellular telephony, high-speed data communications, and value-added networks (VANS), which as of 1991 are beyond the technical and financial capabilities of Brazilian companies."[56] The lack of resistance from Telebrás to the privatization of these services was another factor that enabled such initiatives to be launched.

In hindsight, Brazil has been only partially successful in streamlining telecommunications service enhancement and restructuring initiatives even in the "niche" markets. Collor's predecessor, Jose Sarney, had actually begun the process by partially deregulating data services in 1988. Embratel initially joined with Sprint and AT&T to provide these services. But up until 1997, prices for data services remained high and long waiting lists continued to exist. Brazil's 400,000 Internet users in 1997 as well as those calling internationally paid high prices, the latter running four to ten times the actual cost.[57]

Cellular privatization began in 1991 and paralleled that of data communications and other value-added services. (Earlier, a private operator had been allowed to provide cellular service in Sao Paulo in late

1990.) The 1991 privatization would allow networks to be installed in Rio de Janeiro and Brasilia and then be expanded to cover Sao Paulo, Curitiba, Porto Alegre, Belo Horizonte, and Salvador. In 1992, demand was estimated to be around half a million for these networks of which 60 percent was located in Sao Paulo, a city accounting for 70 percent of Brazil's data traffic and 60 percent of its telephone traffic.[58] In 1997, one half of Sao Paulo's businesses were without any kind of service and nationally the waiting list for cellular was upwards of 7 million (see table 3.3 for other data).[59] Meanwhile, while cellular privatization had raised $4.71 billion by 1997, investors were put off by the high prices for cellular licenses and problems with the formation of an independent regulatory authority. (The latter, however, was just about ready to start functioning in late 1997.) Other problems included legal and administrative disputes and the delayed granting of one of the two licenses in Sao Paulo (AirTouch Communications of the United States versus Telia of Sweden with the latter getting the license in March 1998). The legal battles caused yet another delay in license sales in August 1997 with the bidding not resuming until April 1998 (more than seven years after liberalization first began). In the meantime the second licensee in Sao Paulo, BCP Telecumincacoes (a BellSouth and Grupo Safra joint venture) began service in May 1998 (seven years after the licensing process began!).

Restructuring of Telebrás has been far more difficult than that of specialized markets even though the thinking for it began in the late 1980s. But over the last decade, in spite of overcoming many hurdles, opposition to Telebrás had continued to increase. The idea of privatizing Telebras and dividing it into seven regional holding companies was floated during Collor's regime and the National Communications Secretariat (SECOM) was created to facilitate this task.[60] However, trade union and bureaucratic pressures and Collor's own impeachment in October 1992 stalled privatization moves. Itamar Franco, with precarious political legitimacy, decided against privatization and the debate was not reopened until Cardoso came to power. One sure sign of Cardoso's seriousness of purpose was the appointment of the outspoken Sergio Motta, a close friend of Cardoso's, as communications minister.[61] Another major problem with the privatization of Telebrás was Article XXI of the constitution of 1988, which protected state-owned telecommunications. (Earlier loopholes, specifically exceptions for smaller investments, allowed specialized services to be provided without a constitutional amendment but Telebras posed special problems because of its trade unionism and bureaucratic constituencies.) The "General Telecom Law" was finally enacted in 1997 (after congressional approval in August 1995) giving the government a go-ahead with comprehensive liberalization.[62] The new regulatory agency, Brazilian Telecommunications Agency, was also given a charter in late 1997 to facilitate the transition. The growing sentiment for privatization in Brazil also came from the privatization of cellular and other services, which increased the constituency of these efforts in Brazil. In particular, Telebrás's cellular operations were seen to be increasingly inefficient (in an otherwise competitive segment of the market) without privatization. Finally, given the finances of the Brazilian government, the government needed the money from privatization.

The plan called for privatization within a year for the rest of the Telebrás' government-owned stock (nearly 20 percent of the firm, which gave the government a majority voting share) and the division of Telebrás (excluding Embratel, which will be sold separately) into three terrestrial telephony and nine cellular companies (nicknamed "baby brases"). The three terrestrial providers, the most important part of the privatization, would be for the south-central region (Telesul), the northern region (Telenorte), and Sao Paulo (Telesp), the last being the most wanted of them all. The privatization was expected to bring in $20 billion in 1998. Many political problems needed to be overcome for privatization but, after successive delays, July 29 was fixed as the date for the stock offering. Of paramount importance were the October 1998 elections, which made the government overly cautious in carrying out the privatization program. Although the Brazilian economy was on stable footing in 1998 (especially as compared to East Asia, its past history of hyperinflation, and its own averted Real crisis in October 1997), the growth rate was only expected to be 1.2 percent in 1998 (down from 3.2 percent) in 1998 and the unemployment rate in the industrial Sao Paulo stood at 16 percent.[63] Cardoso's rival Luiz Inacio Lula da Silva was already challenging the trade unions to picket state offices. It was due, first, to political pressures like these that the Cardoso administration asked for a high minimum asking price for Telebras stock.[64] Second, the many regulatory issues regarding longevity of licenses, interconnection, and tariffs, among other things, needed to be worked out. Brazil has chosen a duopoly model for competition. Not only would Telebrás be broken up, but another competitor allowed for services in the regions. This is as much in response to pressures from domestic and international business coalitions as from federal provinces. Third, Brazilian trade unions are known for launching legal challenges at the last minute and the sale could be delayed or complicated further.

The July 29, 1998 privatization brought in $18.85 billion for the Brazilian government, far exceeding the minimum asking price of $11.51, in turn increasing Cardoso's electoral chances in the scheduled October 1998 election.[65] The sale proceeded in spite of protests on the streets and threats by workers. It was the largest privatization in Latin America. *The Wall Street Journal,* while dubbing the sale to be of "Amazonian importance," noted that "nobody thought the government could stick to its July timetable for the sale with national elections looming in October."[66] The biggest international winner was Spain's Telefonica, which won the Telesp and two other cellular licenses. Others included Portugal Telecom, Telecom Italia, and MCI.

Brazil not only offers a contrast to China in terms of its slow pace of restructuring given its political pressures but, quite significantly, also to Mexico which also found itself in a severe debt crisis beginning August 1982. However, given the nature of its state and the cohesive pressures it faced, Mexico was able to introduce restructuring more easily. Given high rates of economic growth, Brazil's service enhancement program in the late 1970s (which also came during an authoritarian phase when many demands could be marginalized) was initially successful but soon trailed behind long waiting lists. Particularly bruising economically was the hyperinflation rate, which stood at 2,500 percent in 1993 (brought down to 5 percent by 1998). Cardoso is widely credited for bringing a measure of economic stability and launching restructurings in a country long accustomed to fractional politics and a chaotic economy. However, pluralistic pressures since the 1980s have still pulled the Brazilian state in many directions slowing down the liberalization and privatization initiatives.

PREDATORY STATES: MYANMAR

Predatory states seldom respond to any societal pressures, which usually take the form of opposition to the entrenched regime. Even when these states do respond, it is to appease or to court an extremely limited number of groups that help them stay in power. Cases of predatory states are hard to find for the reason that it is hard to maintain state legitimacy under such circumstances. But predatory states do exist. Mobutu Sese Seko's Zaire (now Republic of Congo) or the military-led Myanmar (formerly Burma) are such cases. Myanmar is examined in detail.

Myanmar has gone from being one of the richest states in Asia to being one of the poorest.[67] Burma with its vast natural resources was of strategic importance to the British. By 1855, Burma had a vast telegraphic network (see map 5.1) and Rangoon (along with Bombay, Calcutta, and Madras) was one of the first places on the subcontinent to receive telephone service in 1881. (There were seventeen subscribers in Rangoon in 1881 out of the subcontinental total of 244!)[68] A radio link was established between Rangoon and Madras in 1936 as security concerns in Burma grew with Japanese activity in China.

Burma achieved independence from the British in 1948 but has had authoritarian rule since 1962 when U Ne Win wrested power. The worst of the repression started in September 1988 when a military group, calling itself the State Law and Order Restoration Council (SLORC), seized power. While SLORC replaced the rhetoric of socialism with that of free enterprise, the regime remains as unresponsive to societal pressures as its predecessor. Elections in 1990 that would have brought Aung San Suu Kyi (Nobel Peace Prize winner in 1992) to power were ignored and the leader placed under house arrest.

There is opposition to the regime domestically and internationally but SLORC more or less represses or marginalizes these pressures, often through violent means. Aung San Suu Kyi symbolizes this opposition to the regime and remains under house arrest. There are a few international pressures from governments and international organizations but there are also those willing to overlook SLORC's record of human rights abuses and political repression. While countries like the United States continue to call for a boycott of Myanmar, others like the ASEAN (Association of South East Asian Nations) admitted Myanmar to its membership in July 1997. Furthermore, many firms continue to do business in resource-rich Myanmar (Unocal's $1 billion 416-mile-long natural gas pipeline is the most prominent). Competition among firms to do business in Myanmar made several Japanese firms appeal to their government to tone down its criticism of the SLORC regime.[69] But there are also a few firms that have either pulled out of Myanmar because of their political practices or refused to go there.[70]

Data and accounts of telecommunications in Myanmar are limited but all of them point toward the lack of services or clear bans on particular types of services. The country's teledensity of 0.35 per 100 population is one of the lowest in the world (along with 0.08 of Republic of Congo). With a population of 45 million, Myanmar has a total of 157,843 main lines of which more than 46 percent are located in the capital Yangon (formerly Rangoon). There are fewer than eighty thousand main lines for the rest of the country. Figures for the second biggest city, Mandalay, are unavailable but it probably accounts for a big percentage of the eighty thousand. In other words, telecommunications services for the more than 80 percent of the population that lives in rural areas are virtually nonexistent. While officials argue that geographical conditions entail special difficulties in laying down terrestrial links in Myanmar's rural terrain, this argument ignores the possibility of leapfrogging technologies like microwave communications.

Many studies point out the extent of unfulfilled demand in Myanmar. Early empirical studies quoted in an influential book by World

Bank cites several instances where transportation or human labor costs could have been avoided if a minimal level of telecommunications services were present.[71] This same study shows elsewhere that as early as 1977, the Burmese authorities were willing to crack down on people obtaining illegal connections (though letting them keep these connections after paying heavy fines). Some 520 such cases were found by the telecommunication authority in 1977 when the registered waiting list for potential subscribers extended to 15,545.[72] Current estimates of the waiting list are unavailable but given the lack of availability of services, one can safely conjecture that the waiting lists are longer than before.

There's also evidence of demand for specialized services. Beginning in December 1993, cellular service was first introduced in Yangon for up to two thousand users and later in Mandalay for up to one thousand.[73] There were a total of two thousand users in 1995. The low numbers indicate the elite audience to which this service caters. The ministry of communications regulates data communication strictly. SLORC's "The Computer Science Development Law" is relevant here. It makes the ownership or use of fax machines or modems without the ministry's permission a punishable crime with up to fifteen years in jail.[74] One of the first cases coming to international attention as a result of this law was that of Denmark's honorary consul, who died in prison after being sentenced to three years for unauthorized ownership of fax machines and main lines. There were only 1,339 fax machines in the country in 1995.[75]

So far, domestic and international telecommunications service enhancement has only impacted Yangon and Mandalay. The gainers have been prominent SLORC officials and a few businesses. But even the large business demand for telephones and connections especially with neighboring countries continues to be unmet (or ignored).[76] Thus, in spite of the increase in teledensity from 0.17 to 0.32 in the last five years, Myanmar cannot be considered a case of having made telecommunications a development priority or planned any restructurings. The World Bank notes: "Given the political situation in Myanmar, there is no reason to expect any substantial service market liberalization in either the near, medium, or long term."[77]

CONCLUSION

The political economy of telecommunication restructuring examined for the seven countries in the last two chapters reveals important similarities and differences. Even though the cases point out broad trends, they do provide the first bit of confirming evidence for the book's propositions.

Economic conditions explain the impetuses for demand and supply in all cases. They explain how the Mexican and Malaysian states were able to move toward a liberalization and privatization agenda after their respective economic crises. On the other hand, South Korea and Singapore moved toward privatization and liberalization, not so much because of economic crises but because of globalization influences, though the economic crisis in South Korea in the early 1980s did lead to service enhancement. Singapore Telecom moved toward privatization as it sought to play a globally active role. In South Korea's case the international coalition began to get its way in the 1990s. The 1997 economic crisis in South Korea is sure to further strengthen the position of this coalition as the state accedes to these pressures in order to obtain international loans. There was no economic crisis in China and globalization pressures did not become strong until the mid-1990s. Therefore, the country had barely moved in the direction of privatizing its telecommunications. In Brazil, given the economic crisis, we should have expected a result similar to Mexico's, but here the political differences in the two countries outweigh the economic factors. Brazil's pluralistic and somewhat gridlocked politics thwarted all attempts toward privatizing the monopoly. Interestingly enough, the picture presented also runs contrary to popular perceptions about privatization of lucrative enterprises being a way for developing countries to earn quick revenues. Only in Brazil and Mexico, both facing severe debt crises in the 1980s, were these strong considerations. And only Mexico was able to act on this opportunity. Brazil's privatization program continued to be derailed by its politics. Thus, even the lure of a "quick buck" needs to be evaluated against the slowness of politics in this country.

The absence of coalitional pressures explain the limited scope of restructuring efforts during the first phase of the process. In particular, they also explain the lack of priority given to residential users in countries such as Mexico, Brazil, and China. While it may seem that service enhancement is proceeding smoothly, this is not always the case, given long waiting lists at the end of this phase and the inability of the state to undertake any other comprehensive measures to meet demands. Thus, restructuring efforts during the first phase are mostly limited to either service enhancement or partial liberalization of specialized services. Dominant monopolies do not want to give up their privilege of supplying terrestrial services but are less resistant to giving up specialized services (which they may not be supplying in the first place) leading to partial liberalization of "niche markets." The latter factor needs to be located in technological influences, too. Technological innovation allows for new providers and equipment manufacturers to contest parts of markets earlier claimed by the dominant monopoly. Ideational factors, too, help interest groups as well as states strengthen their hand in carrying out certain initiatives. Sectoral level ideational emulation was clearly present in South Korea borrowing from the Japanese model, Malaysia from the Japanese and British models, and Mexico from that of the United States.

Telecommunications restructurings during the second phase are usually marked by coalitional pressures that are often strengthened by the failure of disparate groups to get their demands met at the user-group level. In fact, market-based alternatives in most developing countries are now perceived by demand groups and policymakers as helping to boost sectoral performance. Those countries with cohesive pressures here have an easier time delivering on the demand than those with plural pressures. This partly accounts for the smoothness and the fast pace of restructuring efforts in states like Singapore and China. States facing plural pressures such as South Korea, Malaysia, and Brazil often feature combinations of delays, limited scope, and high degrees of nepotism in their restructuring efforts. Mexico features both scenarios: the early restructuring featured cohesive pressures, while the second phase is somewhat marred with increasingly pluralistic pressures.

Finally, telecommunication restructuring needs to be located and understood from the point of view of the type of state carrying it out. Catalytic states or those facing cohesive pressures have an easier time than dysfunctional special-interest–dominated ones. Thus catalytic or near-catalytic states in general are able to carry out fast paced, comprehensive, and demand-led restructurings but even within this category, those facing cohesive pressures are able to do so more effectively. Dysfunctional states are able to cater mostly to those interest groups that dominate their agenda, but even here cohesively pressured China makes for smoother restructuring than pluralistic pressured Brazil.

All states in their supply of restructuring reveal the overall constraint of maintaining legitimacy. The supply of telecommunication services to residential users in many countries can be explained by this feature. Similarly, the slowness of restructuring in pluralistic pressured countries is to be partly understood in terms of the difficult time these states face in consolidating power among disparate groups.

While the cases studied above provide evidence for confirming the book's propositions across cases, there is still need to show how these propositions hold within a particular case. In order to explain the timing, pace, and sequence of delivery of restructuring initiatives in a particular country, much more detail than what has been supplied above is needed. But as chapter 1 noted, detailed studies of all seven cases are beyond the scope of this book. Therefore, the next three chapters document restructuring efforts in the most representative case found in the developing world today, that of a pluralistic-pressured dysfunctional state.

As one developing country after another undergoes the dual transition of political and economic liberalization, most of them are now approximating states faced with pluralistic pressures. Even catalytic or near-catalytic may find it difficult to play their respective roles in the future. Cohesive pressures, whether they were brought about by dominant single-party or authoritarian systems, are now becoming a luxury of the past. Furthermore, elite pressures are often dominant on their agenda, initially making the states special-interest driven. Second, catalytic states are themselves breaking down no longer able to play the kind of decisive role that they played in their economies in the past. Thus, this chapter concludes that the case of a special-interest–driven dysfunctional state is perhaps most representative of the developing world today and needs to be studied deeply.

The next three chapters take up the case of one currently special-interest–driven dysfunctional state, namely India, to study in depth how such a state would manage its restructuring processes internally. As noted above (and in chapter 1), such intimate acquaintance with one case is necessary to completely understand the restructuring dynamics. Brazil is not studied for three reasons, apart from the fact that it is already described here in this chapter: First, Brazil's economic conditions although fairly typical of the developing world in terms of economic crises are also different in terms of the severity of its debt crisis and its linkages with the world economy in the past. India offers the case of a typical inward-oriented country and one that faced economic pressures more representative of developing countries in that they were not as severe as those of Brazil. Second, Brazil for all its economic problems is a middle-income country and thus to remove any suspicions in terms of generalization (in terms of being the "most likely" case) for the developing world, India is studied. Lastly, India also offers us the chance to examine how a near-catalytic state became dysfunctional, which, as argued above, might be the case of other states today.

PART III

Telecommunications Provision and Restructuring in India: 1851–1998

CHAPTER 5

Indian Telecommunications: Shadow of the Empire, 1851–1984

The three chapters in part III evaluate the case of a dysfunctional state, namely India. This chapter shows how the monopolies in telegraphs and telephones fared during the British days and contributed to the centralized administrative traditions in India. While telegraphs received importance, the telephone network remained underdeveloped and continued to be so in the postcolonial period. Growing demands for telecommunication services since the 1970s finally resulted in marginal reorganizational changes and service enhancement in the latter part of the 1980s. However, most comprehensive restructurings followed the economic crisis of 1991 and as the pressures for these services strengthened. The presence of multiple coalitions and interest groups made the task of the Indian state particularly difficult.

The history of telecommunication monopolies worldwide (which came into being soon after the telephone was invented in 1876), and their protection from the state, are frequently cited to explain why restructuring was difficult in the 1980s. This chapter evaluates this claim for India. It steps back to the spread of telegraph in colonial India since 1851, which allowed the British to maintain control and deepened centralized governance in the country. The spread of telephone, on the other hand, was limited because of technological limitations and because the British could not control telephonic communications as they could telegraphic ones. During the immediate postcolonial Indian state, 1950–67 (termed Nehruvian state here),[1] telecommunications was classified as a luxury and received low priority. By the late 1960s, the consensus around an inward-oriented development strategy, which the Nehruvian state laid in place, was coming undone and the state found it increasingly hard to maintain legitimacy. After 1967, it did so with a combination of populism and appeasing special interests. Even slow economic growth rates in India by the 1970s had resulted in a sizable industrial sector and a middle class. These groups pressured the state for telecommunication service enhancement, which, among other things, accounts for telecommunications becoming a development priority in India in 1985.

COLONIAL COMMUNICATIONS

Colonial-era telegraph and telephone are reviewed here, which resulted in telecommunications becoming a low priority in postcolonial India administered by a monopolistic bureaucracy.[2]

The Development of the Telegraph in Colonial India

The Revolt of 1857 against the East India Company by sections of the North Indian society touched off a period of consolidation of British rule in India. The telegraph and railways aided this consolidation and increased British administrative control. The East India Company saw the advantages of the telegraph soon after its invention and it remained a vital infrastructure allowing for centralized control by the British.

MAP 5.1
Spread of Telegraph in the British Empire in India (1855)

Source: Adapted from Shridharni (1953)

The introduction of telegraphs began in 1851,[3] connecting the head-quarters of the East India Company in Calcutta with Diamond Harbor, a distance of 50 kilometers.[4] Map 5.1 shows that by 1855, telegraph routes traversed the major administrative centers of control. By 1857, there were sixty-eight hundred kilometers of telegraph lines connected to forty-six receiving offices.[5] Telegraphs thus preceded the railways in India, though both grew rapidly thereafter.[6]

The Revolt of 1857 was led by Mughal princes and feudal aristoc-racy hurt by economic and political policies of the East India Company. The troops of the East India Company quelled the revolt; the telegraph played an important role, summoning troops from far-flung provinces. The revolting soldiers destroyed 1479 kilometers of telegraph lines. Dal-housie, the Company's Viceroy in India, noting the importance of tele-graph during the revolt termed it "such an engine of power."[7] "Electric Telegraph saved India," he declared.[8]

The Revolt of 1857 ended East India Company's direct political control over India.[9] Following Queen Victoria's Proclamation of 1858, India was brought under direct British rule in 1861. As part of "Pax Brittanica," India's political and economic interests were tied to those of Britain.[10] A source of administrative support came from the increasing numbers of Indians educated in the western tradition.[11] This education produced an army of English-speaking clerks and lawyers well versed in British legal practices, who later became loyal members of the Indian Civil Service [ICS]. Education also produced the nationalist movement's political leadership, initially a "timid annual gathering of the English-speaking intelligentsia."[12] Indians employed in the British bureaucracy, especially the Indian Civil Service, offered no threat to the Raj. Their numbers were small. They were pro-British and removed from Indian social life. Later they were criticized by the nationalist movement for betraying fellow Indians.[13]

The telegraph continued to be the mainstay of imperial communi-cations until 1947. It was made a government monopoly by the Electric Telegraph Act of 1854 to consolidate British administrative control. For strategic reasons, few Indians were allowed into the telegraph service during the nineteenth century.[14] The telegraph's rapid deployment in India was coupled with the opening of lines to London by 1865 via land routes through Europe. It took seventeen days for a telegram to reach India from Britain. A new line was opened by Siemens under British con-tract in 1870, reducing this time to six hours.[15] Before the advent of the telegraph, ships carrying letters took anywhere from three to eighteen months to reach Britain via the Cape of Good Hope. "Pax Brittanica" rested on a strong communication base after the telegraph. The demand for expanding the telegraph infrastructure for the rest of the colonial rule came mostly from the British administrative and mercantile inter-ests and the English-language press.[16] By 1948, there were 118,395 kilo-meters of telegraph lines and 3,324 telegraph offices in India.[17] The tele-graph also was readily accepted by rulers in the Indian princely states who, fearing direct British control, had earlier resisted transportation links with British administrative centers.

Since the 1860s, the British claimed to promote the telegraph as a public service. Tariffs were low and subsidized by the government. This may have created a public dependence on the telegraph that made it con-trary to the public interest to cut telegraph lines. Indeed the Department of Posts and Telegraphs was unprofitable until telephones became pop-ular in the major cities in the 1920s.

The rising demand for the telegraph led to the setting up of training centers and production facilities in India. The heat, dust, monsoons, floods, and differences in terrain were among the peculiar geographical factors that required "Indianization" of technology. India led develop-ing countries in indigenizing the technology for tropical climates. Indi-ans also were recruited into the telegraph service by the end of the nine-teenth century. By 1947, Indian engineers and technicians were able to run the infrastructure themselves.

Administratively, the telegraph contributed to a profound change in Indian politics. For the first time, a centralized, hierarchical means of control emerged, first from Calcutta and then from New Delhi after 1912 when it became the seat of the Raj. This system of centralized administrative control outlasted the Raj. Indeed, a highly centralized state acted against the emergence of strong federalism in India, a coun-try often described as "federal in form but unitary in spirit."

The Development of the Telephone in Colonial India

The telegraph was the chief means of administrative and long distance communications in British India. Telephones, introduced by private industry, were limited to meeting intracity commercial and administra-tive demands. In 1948, there were only 82,000 telephones and 17,600 kilometers of trunk lines in India.

Three reasons explain the slow development of telephones.[18] First, the telephone was perceived as a luxury suited to the intracity commu-nication interests of business firms. The existing telegraph network already in place was more cost effective for long distance communica-tion. Telephones were expensive and did not work well over long dis-tances. Second, the British government could censor and control tele-graphic communications. The widespread use of telephones by Indians was thus not politically desirable. As a result, most of the subscribers were British business houses and administrators.[19] Third, the pomp and pageantry of colonial rule made office messengers popular for inter- and intra-office communications. A work culture in which the telephone played a central role was an alien idea in the hierarchically controlled imperial administrations. Officials went so far as to resist telephone installations in their offices. (Even now in many Indian offices, written and oral messages continue to be provided this way even when a simple phone call would suffice.)[20]

Licenses were granted to private British companies in Bombay, Calcutta, Madras (and Rangoon) in 1881 to provide telephone services.[21] For reasons mentioned above, the British government itself had little interest in providing telephone facilities. The decision to allow private companies to provide telephone service was also due to the powerful influence of the British Chambers of Commerce upon the civilian government in the major metropolitan areas. The foremost interest of the British in India was economic, and the influence of the Chambers of Commerce is understandable. Shridharni notes that "the Viceroy's annual address to the Bengal Chamber of Commerce was the supreme occasion for the enunciation of imperial policies."[22] The Chambers of Commerce remained influential till the end of British rule. Speedy nationalization of major industries took place in the 1940s but the nationalization of telephone companies was particularly slow because of the influence of the Chambers of Commerce.

Private ownership of telephones, their spread in major towns, potential of private or state monopoly versus competition, royalties to government, problems of interconnectivity, raised the need for coordination and control that the government assumed. The Electric Telegraph Act of 1854 was superseded by "The Indian Telegraph Act of 1889" which is still the legal framework for telecommunications in India.[23] The act gave the Central Government "the exclusive privilege of establishing, maintaining and working telegraphs" except that the government can grant licenses to private manufacturers when it chooses (Part II: 4.1). In addition, the government can "delegate to the telegraph authority all or any of its powers" (Part II: 4.2).[24] The British government reserved the power to lay trunk routes and build exchanges to suit its needs. Thus by 1914, the little hilltown of Simla (now Shimla), the summer capital of the British from 1864 onwards, had India's first automatic exchange with seven hundred lines, making it the third largest network after Calcutta and Bombay.

Table 5.1 charts the number of telephone subscribers in four Indian cities from 1882–1951, together accounting for 60 percent of the total telephone subscribers in India. Table 5.2 compares the telephone density of India with other countries in 1951. Table 5.3 compares the telephone

TABLE 5.1
Telephone Subscribers in India (1882–1951)
(Four Major Cities)

(Year for which data applies given in parentheses)

City	1882	1890s	1900–1909	1910s	1920s	1951
Bombay	90	n.a	1,600 (1906)	n.a.	6,000 (1921)	44,500
Calcutta	102	437 (1890)	821 (1900)	n.a.	10,000 (1921)	33,829
New Delhi	—	—	—	n.a.	8,000 (1920)	11,844
Madras	24	n.a.	n.a.	250 (1910)	1,224 (1923)	11,102 (1952)

Total number of phones in Jan. 1948: 82,000

January 1951:
Total number of telephones in India: 168,300
Telephones per 100 population: 0.05
Total population in 1951: 361 million (240 million in 1901)
Total number of phones in the four metros: 100,173
Percentage of phones out of the total in the four cities: 60%

Sources:
Shridharni (1953), pp. 102–13 (telephone data).
Department of Telecommunications (1988), p. 1.
Government of India (1990), pp. 8–11 (population data).

density of Bombay, Calcutta, and New Delhi against other major world cities in 1951. The slow diffusion of telephones in India is evident. In 1951, India had only 168,300 out of the 74.8 million telephones in the world (even after a spurt from the 82,000 phones in 1948). The population of India in 1951 was 361 million giving a density of 0.05 phones per 100 population, one of the lowest among developing countries. Nonetheless, telephones were the only section of the Department of Posts and Telegraphs making profits, all of which went toward subsidizing other activities of the department. Even during the depression period, the 1931–32 fiscal year, telephones generated a surplus of Rs 117,916 as against a deficit of Rs 9,385,146 in the department as a whole.

In summary, telecommunications during imperial India provide a good illustration of Harold Innis' famous argument in *Empire and*

TABLE 5.2
Telephones per 100 Population (January 1951)
(Telephone Density)

Country	No. of Telephones	Telephone Density
Argentina	798,391	4.6
Ceylon (Sri Lanka)	16,800	0.2
Cuba	120,668	2.2
Egypt	115,500	0.5
India	168,300	0.05
Ireland	82,031	2.7
Iran	28,620	0.2
Malaya	23,694	0.4
Sweden	1,685,200	23.9
United States	43,000,000	28.1

Source: Shridharni (1953), pp. 112–13.

TABLE 5.3
Population and Telephones in Major World Cities (January 1951)

City	Population (in thousands)	Number of Telephones	Telephone Density
Bombay	3,700	44,550	1.2
Calcutta	5,700	33,829	0.5
New Delhi	1,194	11,844	1.0
Buenos Aires	4,955	502,251	10.1
Cape Town	530	60,068	11.3
London	8,417	1,632,900	19.4
Washington DC	805	487,472	60.6
New York	7,927	3,137,405	39.6

Source: Shridharni (1953), p. 113.

Communications.[25] The telegraph, a written and concrete means of communication, allowed the British to extend administrative control through time. The telephone, a voice medium, could help Indians strengthen their traditions (for example, ideas of Indian heritage and nationalism conveyed over the telephone) and thus the British sought to control its diffusion. Taken together, both media strengthened the tradition of central administrative control at the hands of a technically capable bureaucracy but divorced from many aspects of Indian public life.

THE STATE OF THE STATE (1947–84)

The immediate postcolonial Indian state, riding the current of the Indian nationalist movement, inherited a broad consensus regarding its role in economic development (and the low priority given to telecommunications). By the 1970s, this consensus was challenged by other trends. This political economy of the Indian state is important for understanding the context for the slow development of telecommunications during this period.

The Nehruvian State (1950–67)

The state elite that came to power after 1950 had a broad base of support in India's nationalist coalition—private capital, industrial workers, the educated middle class, and large sections of the peasantry. This base of support and its standing at the forefront of the nationalist movement gave to the government "a sufficiently unified sense of purpose about the desirability of state intervention to promote national economic development."[26] Following categories developed in chapter 2, the Indian state until the mid-1960s may be categorized as being a near-catalytic state. It was sufficiently autonomous to disallow any special interest from dominating its agenda and the vast bureaucratic apparatus allowed it considerable resources to effect its historically defined "responsibility" toward development issues. Most importantly, it was able to shape societal preferences with its control over political-economic resources.

The limited role of the private capital vis-à-vis the state was defined during this period within the broader context of the nationalist coalition. The industrial policy resolutions of 1948 and 1956, while calling for a "mixed economy," in actuality assigned the dominant role for the public sector. The clearest articulation of this program is in the 1955 resolution by the dominant Congress Party to work toward a "socialist pattern of society."[27] Central five-year plans were introduced in 1951. The idea of a mixed economy with the public sector playing the dominant role, as in the case of telecommunications (though it was defined as a "luxury sector" by the 1956 industrial policy resolution), was articulated in the Second Plan (1956–61).[28] Private capital, while occupying a subordinate position to state capital, secured for itself the privilege of catering to India's largely regulated and protected consumer goods markets.[29] By the end of the Third Plan period (1966), the state's share of total investment was 58 percent, the rest taken up by the private sector.[30]

Increasing state involvement in economic affairs increased the power of the Indian civil services, who soon consolidated their position within the state and were guiding, implementing, and managing the state enterprises created by the ISI agenda.[31] In 1956, the Indian Administrative Service (IAS) thwarted an attempt by the national parliament to create an "Industrial Management Service" with a cadre of officials trained in management techniques to run public sector enterprises.[32] However, Nehru's leadership style (analogous to that of M. K. Gandhi) established a wide support for state policies outside the immediate precincts of the decision-making elite—the parliament and the electorate—and also served to contain bureaucratic power.

Private capital, while playing a marginal role in the economy and subservient to state preferences, did strengthen and institutionalize its access to state decision-making instruments, both seeking and benefitting from state protections. In securing such access to the state decision-making processes, the private sector continued the legacy of the British Chambers of Commerce which in postindependent India came to be known as the Federation of Indian Chambers of Commerce and Industry (FICCI) and the Associated Chambers of Commerce and Industry (Assocham). Like their colonial predecessors, these chambers of commerce exercised their influence on state policy by maintaining close contacts with the executive as opposed to the legislative bodies of the state. In the Nehruvian state, the FICCI had access to most of the ministries, including the politicians and the bureaucrats.

There is evidence that rent-seeking was widespread in India by the early 1960s. Krueger[33] calculates that by a conservative estimate, the level of rent-seeking in Indian society was 7.3 percent of the national income in 1964. Moreover, Bauer[34] argued in 1961 that the licensing requirements of Indian industry "bear especially harshly on medium and small scale enterprises. Many of these firms are efficient low-cost producers or distributors; but their owners and managers do not understand the legal position, cannot face prolonged disputes, and are easily overawed by authority, so that their establishment and progress are particularly hamstrung by these measures."[35]

There are other factors that indicate the deterioration of the near-catalytic state in the 1960s. The IAS was criticized for following a colonial-style administration based more on superior attitudes and high-handedness than on following any kind of a social contract with the people. (This argument applies equally to the telecommunications sector.) Jagota noted in 1963 that "the IAS inherits the power, prestige and security of British colonial society."[36] Sovani argued that the bureaucracy comes from a social background (English-speaking middle class), which is favorable to the structure of the Indian political system but not its efficiency.[37]

The impressive 6 percent growth rate in the manufacturing sector during the Nehru years from 1950–63 was largely due to the success of the First Plan (1951–56) as a result of better control over the economic surplus without colonial rule and the recovery of Indian industry after the war. From 1963–76, this growth rate was 3. 35 percent.[38] The droughts in 1965–66 and the war with Pakistan in 1965 strained the economy and by the 1967 parliamentary elections, the state could no longer count on a broad social coalition to support its economic agenda.

The failure of the Third Five-Year Plan (1961–66) to come anywhere near its goals was the biggest factor bringing the ISI strategy under question. The Third Plan emphasized agriculture but the annual average growth rate of agricultural production was –1.4 percent during this period. GNP grew at a rate of 2.5 percent against a target of 5.0 percent.[39] India's share of world exports declined from 2.42 percent to 1.13 percent in 1960 and to a minuscule 0.65 percent in 1970. Import substitution is import intensive but India's ISI did not acknowledge the role of exports until the mid-1970s.[40] Foodgrain shortages, the 1965 drought, inflation, foreign exchange shortages, the war with China (1962), and the war with Pakistan (1965) all led to a bleak economic picture that resulted in the postponement of the Fourth Five-Year Plan for three years. Meanwhile, the foreign exchange crises of 1966–67, 1973–74, and 1980–81 were in part dealt by IMF aid and increasing centralization of power.

Even though Gross Capital Formation as a percentage of the GNP was high during this period (15.6 percent per annum for 1961–66 and 14.1 percent per annum for 1966–69), industrial production grew slowly and erratically (9.0 percent per annum for 1961–66 and 2.0 percent for 1966–69).[41] This was tied to ISI. Lack of technology imports introduced bottlenecks, made efficient specialization impossible, and impeded economies of scale. "The result was the loss of many opportunities and a performance for a long time inferior to that of the average developing countries. Particularly serious was the slow growth of manufactured exports—the most dynamic sector for the developing countries and one in which India was well placed for success in the 1950s."[42] This combination of political and economic failures signals the end of the near-catalytic state in India.

"License-Quota-Permit Raj":[43] 1967–84

The post-1967 period reveals how the state began losing its maneuverability (in terms of both autonomy and capacity) by giving in more and more to special interests (both within and outside its ranks) and its struggles for legitimacy took it further away from a responsible development agenda. The dysfunction between state and private capital on one hand and between state and society on the other became worse during this period. From 1967 onwards, the educated middle class and the agrarian population, two of the prominent groups in the nationalist coalition, became increasingly dissatisfied with slow economic growth. Private capital continued to begrudgingly support the state in return for favorable regulations but also exerted pressure on the state to liberalize and to let it play a bigger role in the successive central plans.

As the nationalist coalition weakened, Indira Gandhi, who became prime minister in 1966, sought to consolidate the survival of the Congress Party within the state by increasing populist appeals to minorities, caste groups, and members of India's diverse religions, by trumpeting the cause of "socialism, secularism and democracy." Rudolph and Rudolph note that such "plebiscitary politics" were a hallmark of Indira Gandhi's leadership ability.[44] Thus, at times the government spewed populist socialist rhetoric (appealing to lower-income groups), at times showed genuine concern for economic reform (to get IMF loans etc.,), and at other times granted favorable concessions to the private sector. Bhagwati and Srinivasan have noted that the state in India was never earnest about its liberalization program. Thus, for example, they write that the 25 percent devaluation of the rupee following an IMF loan in 1966 and the liberal trade policies instituted were short lived. By 1968, most of the restrictive trade policies had been reinstituted.[45]

As the Indian state became increasingly dysfunctional, Indira Gandhi turned to a closely knit group of advisors, chosen politicians, and bureaucrats, for advise and policy-making.[46] Indira Gandhi effectively changed the style of decision-making from one where the elite made policy by seeking (or reflecting) a wide consensus (as during the Nehru era) to one where increasingly personalized politics became the rule. Rudolph and Rudolph note that Indira Gandhi "systematically eliminated actual and potential party rivals. She thus undid the remarkable institutionalization of the party at the state and district levels that had been the distinguishing mark of the Congress since 1920, when Mohandas Gandhi built a political organization unparalleled in Third World countries."[47]

The 1967 election had made the imperative of rethinking Congress Party–dominated state-led ISI strategy apparent. For the first time in national and state elections, the Congress Party's total percentage share of the vote dipped. And while most of the left-wing communist parties (which like the Congress Party supported the state-led ISI agenda), lost their electoral shares in the 1967 elections, the pro-private sector parties on the right—the Swatantra Party and the Jan Sangh (a precursor of the present BJP, the Hindu fundamentalist party)—were able to gain.[48] Financial contributions by private business to the two parties helped them with their electoral gains.

The challenge from the right to the Congress—and thus continuation of the ISI strategy and the associated "socialistic pattern of society"—after the 1967 election led to debate within the Congress Party, with right-wing members calling for a move away from ISI, and left-wing members arguing for a further move toward state-led socialism. Eventually the Congress split largely along the right-left lines (even though many right-wing members opted to stay with what became known as Congress-I for Indira). Congress-I, led by Indira Gandhi, opted to continue the socialist orientation of India's economic strategy, in rhetoric if not in practice. The fact that it was able to do so, however, suggests that the Indian state in the late 1960s and early 1970s did possess at least a modicum of maneuverability, even if from then onwards it would be beholden to the special interests supporting it.

Writing in the early years of the Indira Gandhi administration, Kothari observes: "The first generation of independent nationhood dominated by tall and inspiring men is now coming to an end and a new generation finds itself saddled with, on the one hand, a considerable consolidation of state power and a general consensus on the goals of the transitional polity, but on the other hand lacking the means, the instrumentalities, and the necessary authority to put the power they wield to effective use for the solution of pressing issues."[49] This assessment is only partially correct. While state power might have consolidated, its legitimacy had declined, thus leaving it with fewer ways of imposing its agenda as Indira Gandhi's desperate struggle to stay in power shows. As noted earlier, we see a state with declining maneuverability and with a decreasing sense of responsibility.

The first non-Congress government, led by the Janata Party in 1977, drew upon a loose coalition of agrarian and right-wing interests. However, the Janata Party, while announcing its intent to liberalize the economy, won mostly on a negative vote against the Congress Party and failed to build on the anti-ISI interest groups in the economy, which would have institutionalized the role of not just these groups, but that of the Janata Party itself.[50] The party introduced a few liberalization measures but, before they could take hold, the Janata Party fell due to the infighting among its varied coalitional parties.[51] Indira Gandhi's Congress-I returned to power in 1980 and although the party continued to uphold some of the liberalization measures introduced earlier, the power of the bureaucracy and resistance to a liberalization program remained unchallenged until Rajiv Gandhi's administration came to power in 1984.

In 1947, the Indian state had received a broad mandate for economic change along with impressive institutional structures (a stable political party coupled with state maneuverability) in place. By the

1980s, the state was unable to muster its resources to bring about effective economic change from the top and was continually disrupted by crises of legitimacy. The economic underpinnings of the state's role in society had come undone and the state was being pressured by disparate economic groups with starkly contradictory pressures (such as those between its export groups, private industry and rural constituencies) that the state found hard to resolve. The rest of this chapter examines how the political economy of the Indian state affected telecommunications during the 1947–84 period.

SLOW GROWTH AND ENTRENCHED INTERESTS IN TELECOMMUNICATIONS: 1950–85

Many problems that the ISI strategy faced in general since the 1960s also plagued telecommunications. The telecommunications bureaucracy, relegated to the back burner in India's overall economic strategy, but otherwise secure in its employment, had little incentive to expand the telecommunications infrastructure or meet the demand for telecommunication services. Even though one might expect that at least during the near-catalytic period of the Indian state, telecommunications would grow considerably, this was not the case due to the low priority given to telecommunications in general since the 1950s.

Lack of Investment Funds

From 1950 to 1983, the telecommunications sector, classified as a "luxury sector" by Indian planners, received little investment capital. Table 5.4 provides a summary of the total outlays for telecommunications in India since the first plan (1951–56). These expenditures, while increasing slightly since the late 1960s, were low compared to that of other countries like Brazil, South Korea, or Singapore realizing the importance of telecommunications during this period (see part II). (They are also low compared to the kind of public and private expenditures on telecommunications India was able to incur after the mid-1980s.) The general perceptions about telecommunications among the decision-makers at the time of independence was that it was a luxury India could not afford. Over the years, central planners expressed similar reservations about telecommunications, some of which may be noted as follows:[52]

> The primary need of the people is food, water, and shelter. Telephone development can wait.
> In place of doing any good, development of telecommunication infrastructure has tended to intensify the migration of population from the rural to urban areas.

TABLE 5.4
Total Central Plan Investment Outlays for Telecommunications
(Rs. billions)

Plan/period	Total National Plan Outlay	Telecom Outlay	% of Total Plan Outlay
First Plan (1951–56)	19.60	0.47	2.40
Second Plan (1956–61)	46.72	0.66	1.41
Third Plan (1961–66)	85.77	1.64	1.91
Annual Plans (1966–69)	66.24	1.59	2.40
Fourth Plan (1969–74)	157.79	4.15	2.63
Fifth Plan (1974–78)	286.55	7.81	2.73
Annual Plans (1978–80)	229.50	5.19	2.26
Sixth Plan (1980–85)	1096.46	27.22	2.48
Seventh Plan (1985–90)	1800	90	5
Eighth Plan (1992–97)	4341 (projected)	355 (projected)	8.2

Source:
Department of Telecommunications (1988), p. 17.
Government of India (1996), p. 357.
Government of India (1997), p. 39.

There is a need to curb growth of telecom in the urban areas.

Telecommunication, in any case, has no role to play in rural economy.

Telecommunication is a consumption item particularly of the rich. At best, it deserves the same priority as five star hotels.

These policy statements are understandable, given the colonial history of telephones, the resource constraints faced by the Indian state, and lack of knowledge about the links between telecommunications and development. What is less understandable is the extent of bureaucratic and state resistance to enhancing telecommunications services even when the pressures for these services grew in the 1970s. The state protected itself from these pressures by arguing that telephones were a luxury for India's sprawling rural millions but, as we saw earlier, the state in the 1970s was actually quite ineffective in carrying out even a pro-rural agenda. The rhetoric then was merely designed to give itself breathing room to arbitrate pressures it found increasingly hard to resolve. Overall, there is no reason to believe that the telecommunications sector functioned any more efficiently (or worse) than other protected sectors under an ISI strategy.

Role of the Bureaucracy

The telecommunication bureaucracy had little incentive to meet user demands. The engineers staffing the department of telecommunications are drawn from the All India Engineering Services (the engineering equivalent of the Indian Civil Services) and once selected receive lifetime employment. Chowdary characterized this bureaucracy as "a monopolist, centralized and civil service oriented bureaucracy."[53] He argued that telecommunications restructuring in India was delayed precisely because it was not in the interest of this bureaucracy to institute this reform and risk losing its lifetime employment. A newspaper article in 1989 put it bluntly as such: "The telecom organization in the country belongs to the '40s while it is presently trying to grapple with the technology of the '90s."[54] The ghost of the British Empire was personified in a centralized bureaucracy, much removed from societal demands.

Telecommunications is an industry characterized by high rates of return, but the telecommunications bureaucracy lacked the will and the ability to stop the drain of revenues to the national treasury. The bureaucracy lacked access to the decision-making elite. The Department of Posts and Telegraphs ranked low in the hierarchy of power in New Delhi and its officials had little access to the closely knit group of the state decision-making elite to try to make telecommunications a priority as a result of the rising demand for telecommunication services.[55] The minister of state for communications and the elite members of the Indian civil service—the Indian Administrative Service (IAS)—assigned to the department, considered their appointments as unimportant for their long-term political/career goals, and on their assignment to the department, suffered from a "clear the time syndrome," rather than trying to effect positive changes.[56] One official described the department's position before 1985 as being that of a "pity trader," where high-level politicians and bureaucrats took no responsibility for the state of telecommunications in the country. The state elite itself exerted little pressure on the department to improve its efficiency internally, and its cadre of engineers and other staff came close to reflecting the attitude of its IAS overseers than opposing them.

Most of the profits made by the department were funneled back to the treasury, and plans to expand investments in new or existing services and facilities were consistently ignored by the state's elected officials and the national Planning Commission. This is an extensive form of cross-subsidization that cuts across sectoral lines. In spite of this drain, most of the planned investments in telecommunications came from the department's internal resources. During the First Plan (1951–56), only 20 percent of the investment support came from the department's internal resources but by the Sixth Plan (1980–85), 64 percent of the investment made came from internal resources, going as high as 72 percent during the Fourth Plan (1969–74).[57]

There seems to have been little effort on the part of the technocratic bureaucracy to make an effective case with the decision-making elite to convince the latter about the correlation between telecommunications and development. Since the 1960s, there were a wealth of quantitative studies that provide these economic measurements. It is ironic that from the mid-'70s onwards, when the demand for international services was particularly high from exporters and the service sector, the only studies available locally in India (using Indian data) measured benefits of telecommunications for rural areas.[58] While this may reflect the orientation of the state to address agrarian demands as part of its populist/socialist agenda, the state was also trying to boost exports during this period and should have had an interest in such studies. Exporters still received marginal importance within the ISI strategy and the telecommunications bureaucracy had no interest in furthering their cause. The first study linking exports with telecommunications was commissioned by India's overseas carrier in telecommunications during 1988, five years after telecommunications was made a development priority.[59]

The Department of Posts and Telegraphs did not lack the resources to carry out studies on telecommunications and development to build its case. Historically, India often provided expertise to other developing countries for developing their telecommunications sectors and in 1978 the Telecommunications Consultants of India Limited was set up specifically for this purpose. Thus, while Bruce and coauthors were right in noting, in an influential study, that LDC policymakers "want more precise factual support for their decisions to allocate (scarce) economic resources to telecommunications,"[60] it also needs to be remembered that before 1985, the telecommunications bureaucracy in India had no incentive to try to come up with such evidence. All in all, in the 1970s at least, this bureaucracy reveals the nondevelopmental orientation of the state at the telecommunication sector level and its ability to ignore most user-group pressures (as will be explained later).

Inefficient Utilization of Investments in Public Sector

Emphasis on self-reliance through ISI in telecommunications often led to equipment delays, inefficient manufacturing enterprises, and high capital-output and high labor-output ratios. The creation and workings of Indian Telephone Industries (ITI) in 1948 to manufacture switching equipment and Hindustan Cables Limited (HCL) in 1952 for cable equipment is foremost in this regard. Inefficiencies among these two and other enterprises may now be noted.

First, acquisition of technology and adaptation to Indian conditions created delays and shortages, defeating the goal of self-reliance. In the 1950s, ITI bought Strowger electromechanical equipment technology from Automatic Telephone and Electric (U.K.). The equipment was outdated by the time it was installed. In 1964, ITI acquired new Pentacosta Crossbar equipment technology from Bell Telephone Manufacturing of Belgium. This system was installed without adapting it to Indian conditions and resulted in major problems. Only in 1981, after seventeen years of domestic research, was the Pentacosta system ready for India. By then, it was outdated. Digital equipment had replaced the earlier systems technologically. Similarly, HCL was to meet the demand for network expansion under the successive plans. Transmission cables continued to be imported defeating the need for creating the HCL in the first place.[61]

Second, even where equipment was made available by the public sector firms, it came with many faults. ITI, for example, manufactured customer premises equipment (telephones, telex machines, teleprinters). This equipment had high MTTR (Mean Time to Repair) and low MTBF (Mean Time Between Failures). The prices were much higher than international prices.[62] Telex equipment had no storage or forwarding function, requiring manual presence to be operated at all times, and it also worked at slow speeds.

Third, ISI created productive inefficiencies through high capital-output ratios and this seems to be true of the telecommunications equipment industry, too. Studies of these ratios for telecommunications are not available, but a World Bank discussion paper sent to the Indian government to lay grounds for future assistance noted that, "our discussions with members of the [Telecom] Commission[63] have revealed that techniques in the sector are poor and there is considerable scope for improvement."[64] An indicator of the capital-output ratio in telecommunications is that the per-capita telephone operating expense was about 1.6 times the per-capita national income while for developed countries it is 0.05.[65]

Lastly, one of the goals of ISI was to create employment, but the strategy backfired because most of the resources went into maintaining high levels of employment rather than into new investment or replacement of machinery, which would have provided higher levels of employment in the future. It also introduced production inefficiencies. In India, according to one estimate, there were one hundred people employed for every one thousand telephones, while the figures for the United States and Europe are ten and twenty respectively.[66] As T. H. Chowdary put it:

> The greatest challenge comes in regard to the organization itself. The Indian Telegraph Act is more than 100 years old, and so is the service, the organization and its work methods and ethos. From digging trenches for putting up telephone posts, to the installation of an SPC digital exchange, everything is undertaken by the Department of Telecoms itself. This has led to the employment of a large number of unskilled, low skilled and unupgradable staff, who, over the years, have become more or less permanent and who have aspiration for security, for promotion and other advancement, in line with the social philosophy that rules in the society.[67]

Growth of Telecommunication Services (1950–1985)

The Department of Telecommunications (DoT) claims that in spite of low investment outlays, the increase in telecommunications services was nonetheless impressive for the thirty-five-year period between 1950 and 1985.[68] The growth in three important indicators does corroborate this claim (see table 5.5). First, the number of Direct Exchange Lines (DELs), which exclude multiple telephone sets such as PBXs connected to the same line, multiplied 17.6 times, bringing the telephone density up from 0.05 per 100 population in 1951 to 0.5 in 1985. Second, Telex (mostly used by business subscribers), introduced in the mid-'60s, had 26,253 subscribers in 1985. Moreover 217 STD (Subscriber Trunk Dialing or direct long-distance dialing) routes were opened during this period and international calls (a rough indicator of a country's business links with international markets) increased nearly fourteenfold between 1974 and 1985.

When the performance noted above is compared against the record of other developing countries, the label India earned as possessing the world's worst telecommunications system becomes clear. India's telephone density of 0.4 percent in 1981 was below the 2.8 for developing countries, 2.0 mark for Asia, 5.5 for Latin America, and even the low 0.8 for Africa.[69] (The situation did not improve much by 1988 when India's density of 0.4 compared against 0.9 for Asia, 5.9 for Latin America, 0.7 for Africa, and 1.5 for developing countries as a whole.[70])

TABLE 5.5
Telecommunication Infrastructure in India (1951–85)

Item	1951	1974	1985
No. of DELs (millions)	0.17	1.3	3.0
Telephone Density (tele. per 100 pop.)	0.05	0.29 (1975)	0.50
Direct long-distance dialing routes (STD)	nil	47	217
Outgoing international calls (million calls)	n.a.	0.39	5.35
Telex Exchanges	nil	49	187
Telex Subscribers	nil	8484	26,253

Sources:
Shridharni (1953), pp. 112–13.
Department of Telecommunications (1988), pp. 46–47.
Mody (1989), p. 318.

DEMAND FOR TELECOMMUNICATIONS SERVICES SINCE THE MID-1970s

By the late '70s, in response to appeasing pressures from multilateral institutions and exporters, a very slow move toward a macroeconomic, outward-oriented strategy was evident in India, which put increasing pressure on the government-run telecommunications monopoly.[71] Two other pressures of significance came from the increased demand for telecommunications as a result of growth in the services and manufacturing sectors by large users, and demand for telephones by the growing middle-income groups (concentrated in urban areas). Furthermore, India's increasingly dissatisfied agrarian interests (which were a major force behind a non–Congress-I government coming to power in 1977) were a major force in Indian politics in the 1980s. Although rural areas did not directly pressure the state for telecommunications services, the state (as the next chapter notes), could not justify enhanced expenditures in telecommunications without references or allocations to actual and potential rural users.

Exporters and Telecommunications

The pressures for telecommunications services are suggested by parallel increases in telecommunications and exports in India. Between 1971–72 and 1986–87, the overseas telecommunications traffic in telex and telephones grew faster than India's foreign trade.[72] While foreign trade grew by 9.5 times between 1971 and 1987, telephone traffic grew by 71 times and telex traffic by 23.5 times. Field investigations found that, first, firms developing new markets, promoting new products, firms new to international business, and large firms, use international telecommunications facilities more than others. Second, firms exporting consumer goods use the international telecommunications facilities more than those exporting raw materials, primary commodities, and capital goods because consumer goods markets are more competitive with high price and demand elasticities requiring constant information flows. Also, India's exports of capital goods went to Eastern Europe and Africa, countries with poor telecommunications infrastructures themselves and thus in need of other forms of communication.

International users needed increasingly sophisticated services and showed a high degree of receptivity for superior telecommunications services instead of less cost effective and slower ones.[73] Most impressive of all, telephone traffic multiplied sixty-one times between 1980 and 1997. Telegraph traffic fell as telephone and telex facilities improved. Eventually, telex and telegraph traffic declined after fax became available in 1985. The latter itself began to register a recorded decline after

TABLE 5.6
Growth of International Telecommunications Traffic in India (1980–97)

	Telephone (a)	Telex (a)	Telegraph (b)	Gateway Packet Switching (c)	Fax (d)	International TV (e)
1980–81	22.6	26.3	157	none	none	none
1985–86	109.4	44.9	120	none	3,851	53.6*
1990–91	369.4	46.76	53.10	53.0	214,973	48.31
1995–96	1,147.56	20.4	21.14	560.86	80,356	116.67
1996–97**	1,382	17.39	n.a.	521.00	n.a.	142.53

Key:
(a): Paid minutes in millions
(b): Paid words in millions
(c): Segments in millions
(d): Total number of pages
(e): Paid minutes in thousands

*   1986–87
**   Projected

Sources: Data collected from VSNL during field research in Dec. 1990, July 1993, July 1995, and July 1997.

1989–90, when it became difficult to distinguish between outgoing fax versus voice messages technologically. In the meantime, the poor state of the gateway packet switching (for data services) is indicated by the projected decline in 1996–97 after 1995–96, following the spurt from 1988 to 1989 when it was introduced.

Large Users and Telecommunications

For a long time the government-dominated telecommunication strategy in India ignored the demands of large users of telecommunications services. Many of these large users were government departments and public sector firms that did not think of telecommunications as an important input. A few government users actually resisted or were uninterested in the introduction of better telecommunications services. Thus, for example, introduction of electronic banking in India was heavily contested by workers' and officials' unions as they feared losing their jobs. It resulted in several work stoppages in the largely nationalized banking sector during 1988.

The private sector demanded, and was far more receptive to, sophisticated telecommunications services. This is revealed by the spread of telephones and dedicated networks among private sector large users in the 1980s. Small users in the private sector (textile, microelectronics, garment manufacturing) fared worse. Focusing on other immediate priorities such as obtaining export licenses and favors with the state, it was not in their interest to transform the supply structure in telecommunications even though they badly needed these services. Being too numerous, they also did not form inter-industry alliances.

Chowdary estimated that 7 percent of the users with existing telephone and telex facilities accounted for 70 percent of the total telecommunications traffic, generating 70 to 80 percent of its revenues.[74] For bulk users, he noted, "telecom is not a matter of convenience or comfort or social status but an essential tool for their business occupation or profession itself. Such heavy consumers of telecom are intensely participating in the economic, industrial, financial, entrepreneurial, administrative and managerial processes that are concerned with the exploitation of resources and creation of wealth." However, as subsequent analysis will show, only those large users with access to the state decision-making structure were able to get these facilities.

Through the 1970s and 1980s, demands and pressures for telecommunication services continued to build, especially from private industry groups. As noted earlier, private sector lobbying in India is usually directed at the executive (as in most parliamentary systems) rather than the legislature, and takes various forms. Telecommunications lobbying reveals similar features. First, individual industrialists might have access to powerful ministers winning special favors. This trend, which can be noticed in the 1970s, was particularly true when telecommunications service enhancement and equipment liberalization took place in the 1980s. Second, industry groups usually gain access to the relevant ministries. For example, software exporters in India (who started becoming a force in Indian industrial politics since the late 1970s) consistently complain about the inadequacy and the high cost of the telecommunication infrastructure.[75] Their main access is through the influential Department of Electronics in the Ministry of Industry. Apart from the Ministries of Communications and Industry, other relevant ministries include the Prime Minister's Office and the Ministry of Finance. The latter, through its powers of being the exchequer and foreign exchange controller, exercises control over just about every government project. Third, at the inter-industry level, three national business associations lobby individually and collectively. These are: Confederation of Indian Industry (CII), Federation of Indian Chambers of Commerce and Industry (FICCI), and the Associated Chambers of Commerce and Industry (Assocham). CII is now the most active of the three. Since the 1980s, it has been at the forefront of articulating telecommunication pressures from the industry to the government.

Demand by Urban Users for Telephones

The demand for basic services like the telephone is also a reflection of the growing middle-income groups in India who could afford these services.

TABLE 5.7
Demand for Telephones in India
(1978–96)

Items	1978–79	1980–81	1985–86	1990–91	1995–96
1. Direct Exchange Lines (telephones) (000)	1,867.8	2,149.5	3,165.8	5,074.7	11,978.4
2. Telephone Waiting List (000)	243.0	447.4	985.7	1,961.0	2,277.02
3. Registered demand (1+2) (000)	2,110.8	2,596.9	4,151.5	7,035.7	14,255.6
4. Percentage of 3 met by 1	88.44	82.8	76.3	72.1	84.03

Source: Department of Telecommunications, Annual Reports, various years.

These groups are now estimated to be anywhere between 250 and 400 million people (and were upwards of 100 million in the 1970s). Significantly, even as the demand for existing services was being met, the percentage of registered demand met continued to fall, meaning that the total demand for telephones is greater than the registered waiting list in any given year (see table 5.7). Whereas almost 90 percent of the demand was met in 1979, it fell to almost 75 percent by 1985. Estimates for unregistered demand were even higher because people not expecting to get a telephone connection anytime soon, did not even bother to register for one.

CONCLUSION

Telecommunications was moved from the list of "luxury" to "core "sectors by the Indira Gandhi government in 1983, thus increasing its priority for plan finances. Telecommunications was made a development priority due to the demand pressures as noted above, but the next chapter will show that the state's own prerogatives continued to matter as well. This initial impetus toward restructuring came after more than a century of the development of telecommunications in India in which the telecommunication bureaucracy, used to its underprivileged but nonetheless secure-life-employment status, responded very little to demand pressures or failed to understand the importance of telecommunications to development. This bureaucracy would then obviously resist any change to its status through restructuring. Indeed, the telecommunications bureaucracy was woefully unprepared to meet service enhancement measures in the 1980s.

The historical context given in this chapter also revises the conclusion offered by liberal political analysis that the failure of ISI in India in the 1980s led to economic restructuring, including that in telecommunications. ISI had failed in India by the late 1960s. It took almost two more decades of societal and international pressures and a lot of political uncertainty before India edged away from an ISI strategy. In the meantime, successive governments held onto power by designing populist measures and by catering to a few influential minorities, resulting in a lot of economic mismanagement. In the context of this book's variables, the economic factors clearly only specify the direction of change. The timing and scope of restructuring is specified by the interaction of interest groups (including user groups) and the state.

Finally, the breakdown of the near-catalytic state in India in 1967 is instructive. Like the recent breakdown of catalytic and near-catalytic models in other countries, India too could not sustain this strategy for a long time. Unfortunately, what followed was not a clear consensus toward another clearly articulated economic program, but years of economic mismanagement at the hands of an increasingly dysfunctional state. Economic transitions, unless brought about by effective transitory teams, are difficult. In a state torn apart by the variety and intensity of pressures such as India's, macro- and microeconomic management tasks are hard.

CHAPTER 6

Indian Telecommunications: Service Enhancement, 1984–91

The Indian state faced many difficulties in trying to make the transition from an inward-oriented to a "neoliberal" economy. Specifically, conflicts within the Indian state involved groups and coalitions wanting telecommunication restructuring (or wanting all the benefits of restructuring to be in their favor) versus those wanting to continue the status quo. A few major service enhancement and organizational initiatives were carried out or announced in response to the demands for telecommunication services, Prime Minister Rajiv Gandhi's enthusiasm for high technology, and the state's own internal prerogatives for legitimacy. But interest groups in telecommunications (mostly government employees in telecommunications aided by a few domestic businesses) stalemated major plans for restructuring and the breakup of the government monopoly in telecommunications. In spite of resistance, a few initiatives did take place: internal organizational changes were made within the ministry of communications; investment funding for telecommunications and service provision were enhanced; a para-statal body for telecommunications service was created for Delhi and Bombay (now Mumbai); and a few sections of the equipment market were partially liberalized. However, the many measures protecting telecommunication workers and domestic businesses also reflected the continued holdover of India's inward-oriented development strategy.

THE INDIAN STATE: 1984–91

The state that Rajiv Gandhi inherited in 1984 was overburdened by its economic role[1] and under increasing pressure by the growing middle class and private sector to liberalize and institute measures of economic reform. To some extent, it was also driven by agrarian interests to provide infrastructural facilities,[2] employment, and remunerative agricultural prices for the rural areas. Rajiv Gandhi, however, was neither able to resolve the competing pressures on state resources nor able to break the underlying vested interests of the bureaucracy or protected private capital.

Rajiv Gandhi was even less successful in trying to reinstitutionalize the Congress Party and broaden the arena of the decision-making processes to include the Parliament. Decision-making on national issues remained limited to a handful of elected officials and the prime minister's secretariat, the latter staffed mostly by senior IAS officials. Morris-Jones, summarizing forty years of decision-making through electoral institutions in India, writes: "Whereas Nehru had relished the cut and thrust of debate (in which he was so effective) and had accepted close parliamentary scrutiny of government action, Mrs. Gandhi was contemptuous of the former and resentful of the latter, while her son in Parliament has been ill at ease and ineffective."[3]

In terms of economic reform, the administration did cut taxes, rolled back a few industrial regulations, sought to revitalize domestic financial markets, increased domestic R&D capabilities, and also decreased some of the import regulations (for example, technology requirements) that governed export industries. The Seventh Plan (1985–90) made the first big break with earlier plans by relying more heavily on the private sector, which accounted for almost 60 percent of the total gross capital formation during this period. Most importantly, nearly half the Seventh Plan outlay was to be spent on infrastructural facilities (energy, transport, and telecommunications).[4]

Telecommunications was made a development priority for the Seventh Plan (1985–90) by the Rajiv Gandhi government after being moved off the list of "luxury" sectors and on the list of "core" sectors slotted for development thrust in 1983. However, many of these initial restructurings only benefited, and at other times exacerbated, the multiplying interests of the already protected domestic capitalists.[5] But coming as they were after decades of inward orientation, the economic restructurings received positive endorsements from domestic and international supporters. A fair evaluation is provided by The 1991 World Development Report,[6] which noted that the

> recent experience with partial liberalization—including relaxation of restrictions against entry and expansion, and foreign technology diversification—has been positive. Excessive regulation remains. It includes barriers to adjustment and exit, and labor rules that protect a small number of privileged workers. . . . These objectives will not be achieved easily because the government will have to overcome the opposition of protected enterprises and the regulatory bureaucracy. But past successes indicate that further deregulation could attract reasonable public support.

The Rajiv Gandhi administration lost at the hustings in 1989 due to charges of corruption and kickbacks paid to government officials (allegedly including Gandhi) in a lucrative defense deal with Bofors of Sweden. But the new government, a coalition of parties known as the National Front, failed just as the Janata government did from 1975 to 1977. "Gandhi's major political opponents at the national level don't really represent radical alternatives. They rely on the momentum of political opportunity, the search for allies, the persuasive symbol to win votes and retain constituencies."[7] The National Front soon fell apart and a fresh round of elections in 1991, the bloodiest and most corrupt in Indian parliamentary history, showed the extent to which the rentier state and the politicians who crave its privileges would go to secure power. The Congress-I government of Narasimha Rao, which was installed in June 1991, inherited an economy at the brink of an economic collapse[8] and a state considerably undermined in its legitimacy. Summarizing the legacy of Rajiv Gandhi, assassinated during the 1991 election campaign, *The New York Times*[9] noted that:

> A bright spot in the legacy of Rajiv Gandhi, for many Indians, is that he created an impulse to look outward from a nation that had always found it hard to shake the myths of its romantic and mystical past. Not ashamed to wear jeans and drive a fast car, he appealed to the imagination of a new generation of Indians impatient with the asceticism, puritanism and zealous self-reliance enshrined in the legacy of Mohandas K. Gandhi.

MAJOR POLICY CHANGES AND CHALLENGES

After making telecommunications a development priority, the state remained limited in its efforts to introduce organizational restructuring or to resolve dilemmas it faced with regards to equipment manufacturing and balancing the interests of rural versus urban users. These issues are analyzed below.

Telecommunications: A Development Priority

In 1983, the demand for telecommunications by exporters and large and urban users were foremost among the factors leading the Indira Gandhi government to move telecommunications from the list of "luxury" to "core" sectors. By making telecommunications a development priority, its call on investment financing through the central plans was enhanced. More than 50 percent of the public-sector expenditure during the plan period was on infrastructural improvement including telecommunications. The implementation took place during the seventh plan period [1985–90]. Five percent of the total Seventh Plan outlay was on telecommunications as opposed to 2.48 percent during the Sixth Plan (table 5.4).

Apart from the demands by users, two other factors made it possible for the state to make telecommunications a development priority. Both factors deal with the ability of even the dysfunctional Indian state to impose its agenda (even though, arguably, its maneuverability was declining, leading to ineffective implementation of announced programs). First, telecommunications was part of a broader thinking about India's increasing capabilities in the electronics sector. The electronics industry, launched in the mid-1960s, was seen as "poised for takeoff" in the 1980s.[10] The Sixth Five-Year Plan expected the growth rate in electronics to be 23 percent per annum whereas the computer industry was expected to grow at 40 percent a year.[11] The government body involved in spearheading India's thinking about electronics is the Department of Electronics (DoE), an influential department within the Ministry of Industry. It was realized that the telecommunications network was a necessity for sustaining any growth in the electronics sector. The DoE issued a document entitled *Electronics in India and Comparison with Electronics in South Korea, Taiwan, Singapore, and Hong Kong* in 1982, which placed India favorably with these NICs and served as a basis for the government's *Technology Policy Statement* in January 1983. The latter included the impetus given to telecommunications by making it a "core" sector. The DoE was additionally involved as a key player in the shaping of industrial policy as it affected telecommunications. The Ministry of Industry is a powerful player in the government of India and its help was crucial in making telecommunications a development priority.

Second, the early 1980s also mark the ascendence of Rajiv Gandhi in Indian politics. He became the prime minister in October 1984. An engineer and an airline pilot by profession, Rajiv Gandhi promoted high technology from the time he entered Indian politics in the early 1980s. He also brought in like-minded people into policy-making positions. The case of Satyen (Sam) K. Pitroda is important for telecommunications. Pitroda, a former Rockwell International executive and an engineer of Indian origin, prevailed upon Indira Gandhi and Rajiv Gandhi to let him head India's telecommunications restructuring program. Pitroda presented the blueprints for an R&D center for telecommunications to Indira Gandhi in 1981. The engineering-minded Rajiv Gandhi evinced strong interest in the proposal and he was primarily responsible for bringing Pitroda to India. The R&D center was commissioned in 1984. "More than any other country in the region, India has devoted attention to nurturing the manufacturing capabilities of the telecommunications sector."[12] In 1986, Rajiv Gandhi appointed Pitroda as advisor of his widely publicized "Six Technology Mission" to upgrade the technology and expand productivity in six identified areas, including telecommunications. The telecommunication component came to be known as "Mission: Better Communications." Pitroda also headed the Telecommunications Commission created in 1989 in a move toward separating regulatory functions from operations.

Breaking up the Department of Posts and Telegraphs

Until 1985, telecommunications in India was a classic case of a PTT when the 'P' was divorced from the 'T' in the Department of Posts and Telegraphs. The Department of Telecommunications (DoT) then became an independent department under the Ministry of Communications. After 1985, engineers gained authority over operations and thus supported this move. The IAS officials who had headed the department until 1985 fought to retain their power, keeping influence over day-to-day DoT decision making by having their representatives from the powerful Ministry of Finance (MoF) evaluate every telecommunications project for its financial viability.[13]

Moving Toward Corporatization

The Rajiv Gandhi government also tried to move DoT toward corporatization to try to shake the department out of its decades-long lethargy and inefficiency. The original idea was for the DoT to be broken up into six independent corporations each serving a different part of India. This plan was perceived by DoT officials as a threat to their job security. Once selected by the All-India Engineering Services Exam, those selected serve for life (barring suspensions due to corruption). In government corporations such automatic lifetime employment does not exist and senior officials can be fired with permission from the relevant state or central government (which, however, is seldom granted). Government corporations can also hire outsiders that the technocratic-bureaucracy in DoT perceived as a threat to their own careers.

Due to DoT opposition to corporatization, a more limited experiment was tried. Two corporations, one for domestic services in two of the metro towns and the other for international services, were created in April 1986.[14] Mahanagar Telephone Nigam Limited (MTNL) was created as a semi-public-sector corporation for New Delhi and Bombay (now Mumbai). Ostensibly, this was because Bombay and Delhi are major centers of commercial and political influence and because the two metro towns, officials note, accounted for one third of the total number of DELs in the country.[15] (Moreover, unlike Madras and Calcutta, they were part of the ruling political party Congress-I's strong bases of support.) The services associations (the management and trade unions) in the DoT went on record to oppose this change and people who were moved over to MTNL were not discharged from DoT but went on temporary service (deputation) to MTNL. This feature later created problems of introducing a management culture and powerful pressures from DoT to reincorporate MTNL within its fold. The slight increase in pay given to MTNL employees was a constant source of rancor to the DoT trade unions. Matters came to a head in December 1990 when performance bonuses were given to the seventy thousand MTNL employees. Four hundred thousand employees in the rest of DoT went on strike.

The government appointed Telecommunication Restructuring Committee (known as the Athreya Committee after the person heading it) after the December 1990 worker strikes recommended divorcing policy, regulatory, and service functions of the DoT. It also recommended divestiture and slow privatization for DoT along with private entry by other carriers. These far-reaching recommendations could not obviously be acted upon quickly due to the politics involved, but they attest to the need to shake up the behemoth DoT to get any change. (The Rao government, 1991–96, did implement some of the recommendations beginning with liberalization of equipment manufacturing.)

The creation of the other corporation, the Videsh Sanchar Nigam Limited (VSNL) for international services, was easier because its predecessor, the Overseas Communication Service, existed independently of the Department of Posts and Telegraphs since 1947 under the Ministry of Communications. In 1986, however, VSNL was placed under DoT. (This decision, VSNL officials argue, hurt more than benefited their organization by cutting them off from their direct contact with the ministry.[16])

Creation of the Telecommunication Commission

A semiautonomous policy/regulatory body came into being in 1989 in an attempt to separate telecommunications operations from regulation and policy aspects. The commission was founded by the Rajiv Gandhi administration, not the DoT, which opposed it.[17] The Telecommunications Commission was supposed to take regulatory power away from the DoT for different agencies of telecommunications. The Telecommunications Commission was supposed to be responsible for two major functional areas:

—Formulation of perspective policies on matters relating to telecommunications in India with overall responsibility to modernize India's telecommunications technology, production and services.
—Regulation, control and coordination of all administrative, technical, financial matters relating to telecommunications including—
(i) Development, operation and management of national and international telecom networks and service, (ii) Technology, (iii) Production.[18]

If the Telecommunications Commission had been effective, it would have streamlined Indian telecommunications operations. Figures 6.1 and 6.2 compare the regulatory, policy, and operations organization of telecommunications in 1986 and 1989. The intended streamlining is apparent in the second figure. But the commission con-

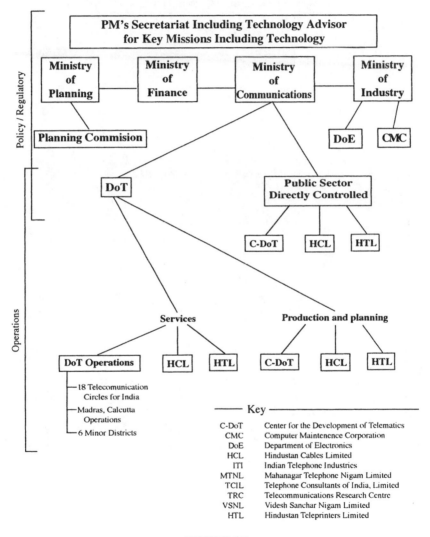

FIGURE 6.1
Policy, Regulatory, Operations Chart
(Telecommunications Sector in India, 1986)

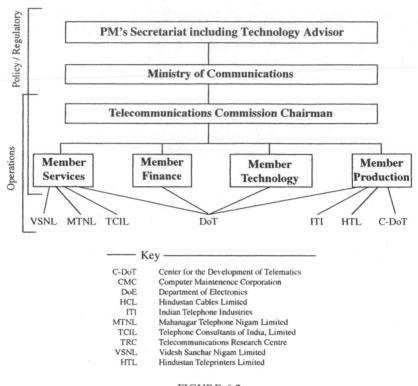

FIGURE 6.2
Policy, Regulatory, Operations Chart
(Telecommunications Sector in India, 1989)

tinued to be beset with problems stemming internally from the DoT as well as outside of it. One of the biggest debates involving Pitroda was the question of manufacturing switches versus importing them (see next section). Pitroda also noted[19] that restructuring effected by the Telecommunications Commission during his tenure was limited by reform in other sectors, particularly the Indian labor laws. The DoT trade unions secured the right of proportionate increases in employment with every new investment project. Negotiating with the labor unions and dealing with the bureaucracy in the DoT were the commission's two most difficult tasks.[20] India's leading business newspaper, wrote: "The work at the Telecommunication Commission set up in May 1989 with high hopes has come to a standstill. The vast power given to it should have enabled it to solve some of the problems. . . . The major stumbling block is the inability to decide on the production of switching equipment."[21]

Pitroda cites eight achievements for the Commission:[22]

1. Negotiations with labor unions leading to workforce reduction concessions
2. Partial liberalization of the telecommunications equipment market to allow for private manufacturing
3. Developing indigenous digital technology
4. Allowing corporations to switch leased lines for data networks
5. Retraining programs for staff
6. Emphasizing management techniques for provision of services
7. Introducing computerization
8. Deregulating value-added services[23] to allow for non-DoT (but state-run) networks and, from July 1991 onwards, to allow private vendors.

Nonetheless, the fate of the Telecommunications Commission after Pitroda left was up for grabs. The DoT persuaded the new V. P. Singh government in late 1989, that Rajiv Gandhi had given far too much power to non-DoT people like Satyen Pitroda, who was the chairman of the Telecommunications Commission. The Singh government perceived Pitroda as a Gandhi loyalist. In 1990, the new administration backed the DoT and the work of the Telecommunications Commission virtually came to a standstill. In 1991, the Rao government appointed the chairman of the commission from DoT's own cadres on grounds of seniority. This new chairman's sympathies were obviously with the DoT and he stymied its workings as much as he could (though he was ultimately unsuccessful given the rush of liberalizations under Rao). By the mid-1990s, the commission's role had become advisory and that of strategic planning within the DoT (as opposed to being its overseer or impartial regulator), and it became coterminous with DoT in terms of regulating other providers in the country (see next chapter).

The workings of the Telecommunications Commission reveal the difficulty of instituting an impartial regulatory authority in messy politics such as India's. The commission, like the state that created it, remained beholden to the various entrenched interests (bureaucracy, labor, public sector enterprises, etc.). Caught in such a battle, providing services to end users often became a secondary concern. The debates on manufacturing switches and providing services to rural users (discussed later) in the end seemed to detract both the Telecommunication Commission and the DoT further away from their agenda.

Developing Indigenous Technology versus Imports

To discourage the drain of scarce foreign-exchange resources and dependence on foreign firms, Rajiv Gandhi and Satyen Pitroda launched a domestic R&D institution, the Centre for the Development of Telematics (C-DoT). It drew on available human resources to develop digital switches and provided technological support to the telecommunications sector.[24] (Chapter 3 noted how South Korea founded similar institutes, a lesson India had not missed.) The technology effort remained controversial throughout the 1980s. Its supporters (academics, a few multilateral institutions, and many domestic businesses that benefited from its technology) admired Pitroda's initiative in applying India's technological and scientific human-resource base toward innovation and practical application. Most of India's R&D efforts go toward reengineering foreign products toward domestic use.[25] The C-DoT effort was thus unique. But C-DoT attracted many critics, a few out of political efficacy and a few due to equipment shortages. The DoT, which risked losing its preferential equipment practices, was foremost in criticizing C-DoT.

It is easy to confuse C-DoT with India's ISI strategy (as did many MNCs) in as much as some of the state-directed initiative's political support came from the same constituency (excepting DoT) that supported ISI. But the effort to create a telecommunications R&D base was different, too. A World Bank official, Asoka Mody, noted: Previous "Indian research efforts have been dispersed and diffuse. . . . [C-DoT] is an exception to the general characterization of the Indian R&D sector. [C-DoT] which is developing small digital exchanges, has had a strong commercial orientation from the start. It has sought to design its products with a common set of components and to work with producers to make component production more efficient."[26]

C-DoT was immensely successful in developing small switches.[27] Shortly after being commissioned, C-DoT had developed a private automated branch exchange (PABX) in 1985 that was licensed to approximately forty private manufacturers for a fee. But C-DoT's most successful innovation (launched in July 1986) was a 128 main line Rural Automatic Exchange (RAX), well suited for the heat, humidity, and dust in India. About thirty manufacturers were licensed for RAX for the Indian market as well as for export (Russia, Vietnam, Yemen, Nigeria, and Nepal). Later, 256 and 512 main line versions of RAX were designed. Eventually C-DoT developed a fifteen hundred-line Main Automatic Exchange (MAX), a MAX-L of up to twenty thousand lines and a MAX-XL of up to forty thousand lines. By 1994, approximately one third of the Indian network was serviced by C-DoT switches, especially RAX. Overall, RAX seems to have been C-DoT's best contribution (at one time even lauded by AT&T officials waiting to get into the Indian telecommunications market).

The controversies regarding C-DoT began with the unavailability of large switches. C-DoT was started in 1985, three years after a (French) CIT-Alcatel and ITI joint venture was launched to manufacture digital electronic switches at Mankapur in Uttar Pradesh.[28] To calm the criticism directed against C-DoT, Pitroda promised that C-DoT would market a large digital exchange switch by late 1987 that would make another Alcatel-ITI venture unnecessary and save the country enormous amounts of foreign exchange. Moreover, these switches would cost Rs 3,000 per line, less than half the cost of Alcatel's, and work in India without air-conditioning, unlike foreign switches. In 1985, Pitroda argued that such switches would be manufactured by ITI, making it independent of foreign imports, and that C-DoT would offer switches for "building a national network on indigenous technology, and not pockets of small networks."[29]

By 1990, however, the 16,000-line Main Automatic Exchange (MAX-L) switch Pitroda had promised was still not ready for large-scale production. But Pitroda had by then successfully blocked an attempt by DoT and Alcatel to set up a second switching factory,[30] and launched renegotiations with IBRD for a $350 million loan, part of which was to go toward acquiring the Alcatel technology, and kept all the other MNCs trying to get into the Indian switching market at bay. For example, in 1985 ATP, then the U.S.-Dutch alliance between AT&T and Philips Communications had offered to supply $1 billion credit, and in 1986 offered to help C-DoT to develop technology. "While C-DoT officials do not comment, sources in telecom circles in Delhi suggest that any effort to gain a foothold in C-DoT by any multinational is not likely to be very welcome."[31] By 1987, when C-DoT introduced its small PBXs and rural exchanges, MNCs focused on the large switching exchanges. ATP offered its 100,000-line exchange that would go far beyond the ones under development by C-DoT or ones being manufactured by ITT-Alcatel.[32]

When the V. P. Singh government came to power, DoT (whose position had been undermined by the Pitroda/Gandhi program of telecommunication efficiency) stepped in quickly. DoT, over the past decades, had developed strong preferences for imports or manufacturing equipment through its enterprises such as Indian Telephone Industries (ITI) and Hindustan Cables Limited (HCL).[33] With C-DoT's preference for licensing its technology to private manufacturers, the DoT monopoly over manufacturing was threatened. The feature is not unique to India. The closely knit relationship between government-run telecommunications monopolies and their equipment suppliers has been called "political telematique."[34]

When C-DoT was unable to supply the large digital exchange technology on schedule, DoT approached the new Singh government to roll back the C-DoT effort. By 1990, the debate on technological requirements flared, eclipsing most other issues. As one newsmagazine put it: "The debate rages everywhere, tempers have risen high, charges are being flung freely and, very soon, it will engage Parliament's attention. And out of the ashes of this battle will emerge the new telecommunication policy for the 1990s—a matter of utmost anxiety for 19 lakh [1.9 million] applicants waiting for connections across the country."[35]

The Singh government's campaign against C-DoT misfired as the scientific and intellectual community supported Pitroda and the R&D effort. Scientists and engineers in India and other countries watching the C-DoT experiment did not think that the delay in the C-DoT technology was anything unusual. It took the MNCs much longer to develop the switches they currently market. Many C-DoT engineers departed in the midst of this controversy, and by late 1990, C-DoT was merged with another DoT organization, the Telecommunications Research Centre, to create a new organization called the Telecommunications Engineering Centre.

The politics of C-DoT are instructive for this book. Unlike South Korea, India was less successful in coming up with an in-house R&D capacity because the state was unable to deal effectively with the opposition to the project. Furthermore, once the state committed itself to the project, it had no choice but to face the opposition by digging itself into a deeper hole than perhaps it intended. For example, it does seem that the Rajiv Gandhi government went too far to keep out foreign suppliers.[36] When shortages developed in equipment supply in 1987, a virtual moratorium was declared on imports of technology. Technology occupied so much attention that matters to do with services, tariffs and finance were neglected.[37]

Large and Urban Users versus Rural Users

The Rajiv Gandhi government, in making telecommunications a development priority emphasized the development of rural networks. This was partly due to the need for maintaining electoral support in rural areas, and partly to deflect from the unfulfilled needs of urban areas and large users and the delay in the development of domestic technology.

Making rural telecommunications a political priority is understandable given the strong political pressures (for infrastructural facilities, among other things) from rural areas since the 1977 election. With almost three quarters of India's population, rural areas have less than one sixth of the total main lines in the country (but is not clear if there were any direct pressures from rural areas for telecommunication services in the 1980s). At an ITU conference in New Delhi in 1989, referring to the target of providing at least one Public Call Office in each of India's 570,000 villages, Rajiv Gandhi declared: "We have geared our objectives to our needs. Our overall target is to put the entire population of 800,000,000 to within five minutes walking distance of the telecom."[38] Rajiv Gandhi seldom referred to the specific needs of large and urban users, choosing instead to highlight the overall objectives of the telecom plan (for example, 20 million phones by the year 2000).

Larger towns that needed switches exceeding twenty thousand lines, and data networks were the casualties of the overemphasis on developing rural networks. It may even be argued that these delays in turn decreased funds for rural expansion that were generated as cross-subsidies from urban and business users. The unavailability of large switches caused project implementation delays, especially in MTNL (discussed later) and in providing specialized services. For example, Pitroda argued that "multinationals will not be interested in transfer of technology"[39] needed for data networks. Building on C-DoT technology was the best bet to develop these networks that would satisfy all of India's telecommunication requirements. In the meantime the DoT was to develop two data networks (named VIKRAM and RABMN) to meet the needs of large users. But by 1989, Pitroda shelved VIKRAM and other such data-oriented networks because they required high levels of imports and needed to await the development of indigenous technology. The delay in putting VIKRAM into operation delayed all other networks awaiting its development, such as the business-users network named Indonet.

In the meantime, DoT opposed any plans to bypass the domestic network for international needs during the 1980s. It disallowed the use of International Business Services (IBS) provided by Intelsat, whereby business users could connect to the Intelsat satellites for international communications without going through the domestic networks and the subsequent international gateway facilities.[40]

Again, India's emphasis on going slow with large and urban users can be seen as the shadow of the ISI strategy. For example, Pitroda characterized cellular phones as elitist in 1988, but changed this position in 1989 supporting cellular for various rural applications.[41] In 1988, T. H. Chowdary, chairman of VSNL, argued that far from being elitist, cellular phones were a necessity for large users who often could not conduct international business because of the poor quality and congestion of local networks in metropolitan towns.[42] Conceding that there were resource constraints, Chowdary felt that such services could be privatized or that "non-resident Indians" (NRIs or Indians living abroad) with foreign exchange might develop them.

The inability of the state to balance the pressures from user (and other interest) groups is apparent here. But the rural versus urban and large user dilemma is illustrative of the gridlock in the state decision-making regarding user-group pressures. This is in contrast to the C-DoT experiment, which for all its delays and failures, did result in the provision of a rural exchange.

SERVICE ENHANCEMENT

We now turn to the record of service enhancement as a result of the major policy initiatives noted above. (For purposes of flow and analytical clarity, the 1990s service-enhancement measures by the DoT and MTNL are also included here briefly.) When telecommunications became a development priority, it received enhanced investment financing. Over the long run, the DoT planned on providing 19 million Direct Exchange Lines (DELs) by 2000, a more than sixfold increase of 17 million over the nearly 3 million DELs available in 1985.[43]

For the Seventh Plan (1985–90), the DoT apparently asked for Rs 135 billion[44] but was first allocated Rs 40 billion, later increased to about Rs 90 billion. MTNL could also raise investment funds on the market through sales of government bonds. At 5 percent of the total plan outlay, the figure is greater than an all time high of 2.48 percent of total outlay given to telecommunications during the Sixth Plan from 1980 to 1985 (see table 5.4). For the Eighth Plan (which was supposed to go from 1990 to 1995 but was launched from 1992 to 1997 due to political changes) the projected expenditure was placed at Rs 355 billion. For the Ninth Plan (1997–2002), it was estimated to be Rs 1,332 billion and for the Tenth Plan (2002–2007), Rs 1,497 billion.[45]

"Mission: Better Communications"

In 1986, Rajiv Gandhi appointed Pitroda the advisor of his widely publicized "Six Technology Mission" to upgrade the technology and expand productivity in the six identified areas, including telecommunications.[46] The telecommunications mission, launched in April 1986, was known as "Mission: Better Communications." Beyond specific number of direct exchange lines, it focused on improving the quality of service (bringing down fault rates, number of attempts made for long-distance dialing, computerized billing services, etc.). It also aimed to cut down the waiting list for telephones in urban areas and extend the network to rural and backward areas. This was consistent with the goals of the Seventh Plan underway, which had targeted the state capitals and 467 district headquarters for direct dialing service, had a goal of fifteen thousand PCOs (Public Call Offices) to be set up in rural areas, and promised provision of two data networks (VIKRAM and RABMN). Mission: Better Communications also reorganized the Seventh Plan objectives focusing on six mini-missions: (1) improving service quality, (2) increasing urban PCOs, (3) improving delivery of telegrams, (4) providing telex on demand, (5) improving rural communication, and (6) building a national digital network.[47]

It is not clear if the trade-offs and resource constraints underlying the six mini-missions noted above had been resolved before announcing the initiative. The inability of the state to come up with appropriate technology or to balance the needs of the rural versus large and urban users was earlier noted. Perhaps the state was trying to please all its constituencies through rhetorical devices like Mission: Better Communications. Athreya, who served as the chairman of the Telecommunication Restructuring Committee mentioned earlier, noted the resources spent on implementing obsolete initiatives like the telegram and telex, when India could have "leapfrogged" technologically.[48]

> There was also a declared bias towards populist ideas, such as the balanced development of telecommunications between all regions and states of the Indian Union, and balanced coverage of metropolitan areas, medium and small towns and rural areas, without recognizing the reality of different rates of development, with entrepreneurial Gujarat and Maharashtra growing faster than Bihar and Bengal in the East, and the aggressive northern states of Punjab, Harayana and Western Uttar Pradesh growing faster than the south, nor of the potential of towns for powering economic growth, including exports of goods and services.

Assessing DoT Achievements

The results achieved by DoT during the Seventh Plan period are impressive at first glance. By December 1989, 1.45 million DELs were provided, more than the revised target 1.1 million. This number was expected to rise to 1.7 million by the end of the Seventh Plan period in March 1990.[49] In addition nearly seventeen thousand PCOs were opened. Of the 467 district headquarters, 302 had national and international direct dialing by April 1989 and all district headquarters were expected to have national long-distance facilities by March 1990.[50] Moreover, marginal improvements took place in the quality of service, especially in the area of telephone faults per month. Whereas nearly one half of the phones did not work in 1980–81, 80 percent of them worked by 1991–92.[51] The success rate of STD calls (straight trunk dialing or directly dialed long-distance) improved from 48 percent in 1987 to 88 percent in 1993.[52]

For the decade 1985–95, nine million DELs existed in the country by March 1995 giving a telephone density of 1 per 100 compared to 0.5 in 1985. By 1997, the government could boast that India had the tenth largest telephone network in the world, when the density was 1.5, and there were 14.4 million DELs in the country.[53] (Between 1992 and 1997, corresponding to the Eighth Plan, 7.5 million DELs were planned, 8.7 million were actually provided, but over 10 million would have needed to be provided if the telephone-on-demand target announced in 1994 were to be met.)

A closer comparison reveals another picture. First, as noted in chapter 5 (table 5.7), the demand for telephones increased more than the growth rate of DELs, meaning that the hidden demand for telephones in India is far greater than the registered demand for it. (Even by August 1997, after years of service enhancement, there was a registered waiting list of 2.9 million telephones in August 1997.[54]) Second, although 70 percent of the subscribers had direct dialing long distance (STD) and international dialing (ISD) facilities by 1990, between 20 and 55 percent of subscribers (depending on the area) got their service blocked because of excessive billing for long distance and international calls that subscribers claimed they never made. Third, subscribers and consumer rights organizations and the media continue to doubt the DoT statistics on the quality of service. *The Economist* noted:[55] "Even in Delhi, the capital, the recent monsoon reduced telephone lines to a cacophony of crackles and gurgles."

Fourth, the emphasis on rural telecommunications placed by successive governments and the DoT was costly, often at the expense of upgrading the urban networks. An MTNL official noted in 1990 that the PCOs in rural areas usually make two or three calls per day; the revenue produced is not commensurate with the Rs 100,000 it takes to provide a phone in rural areas.[56] It is not clear that the Indian planners have debated the pros and cons of the hard choice between demand-led growth in urban areas versus supply-push growth in rural areas, given limited resources.[57]

Out of the total of nearly 12 million DELs available by March 1996, 28 percent of them were located in the four metros, and of the remaining 8.6 million, nearly half were located in the five industrialized states of Andhra Pradesh, Maharashtra, Gujarat, Kerala, and Tamil Nadu (see table 6.1). If demographics are factored in, then almost 7.71 (60 percent) of the total 12.9 million DELs catered to areas with roughly 35 percent of the country's population (in the five states just mentioned and Delhi). If Calcutta's half million DELs and that of Kerala and Punjab are taken out, then only 25 percent of the DELs catered to nearly 58 percent of the population.

TABLE 6.1
Distribution of Population and DELs

Circle/Metros	Percent of Total National Population (1991 census)	Total DELs (March 1996)	DELs as Percent of National Total
Circles			
1. Andeman & Nicobar	0.03	5,077	0.04
2. Andhra Pradesh	7.86	797,326	6.7
3. Assam	2.65	107,051	0.9
4. Bihar	10.21	280.431	2.34
5. Gujarat	4.88	915.563	7.64
6. Haryana	1.94	294,514	2.46
7. Himachal Pradesh	0.61	110,258	0.92
8. Jammu & Kashmir	0.91	52,598	0.44
9. Kerala	3.44	681,234	5.69
10. Karnataka	5.31	783,697	6.54
11. Maharashtra	9.33	984,698	8.22
12. Madhya Pradesh	7.82	622,551	5.20
13. North Eastern (provinces)	about 1.0	75,393	0.63
14. Orissa	3.74	166,415	1.39
15. Punjab	2.4	570,966	4.77
16. Rajasthan	5.2	494,410	4.13
17. Tamil Nadu	6.6	671,412	5.61
18. Uttar Pradesh (East)	16.44	393,284	3.28
19. Uttar Pradesh (West)		416,645	3.48
20. West Bengal	8.04	159,181	1.33
Total for circles		8,582,704	71.66
Metro Districts			
21. Mumbai (Bombay)		1,440,785	12.03
22. Calcutta		445,514	3.72
23. Delhi		1,167,010	9.74
24. Chennai (Madras)		342,382	2.86
Total for Metro Districts		3,395,691	28.34
GRAND TOTAL		11,978,395	100

Source: Department of Telecommunications (1997); Government of India (1996).

Fifth, although government planners began with long-run thinking on how telecommunications would cater to the needs of the economy, implementation was different. Equipment shortages, finance problems, bureaucratic rivalries, and reshuffling priorities all caused problems. Sixth, the telecommunications sector continued to experience difficulties raising financing for projects even though it accounted for high revenues. The use of the sector as a cash cow and the unwillingness of the DoT to let go of services it could not provide accounts for this phenomena during the Seventh Plan period.

Seventh, and perhaps most important, DoT trade unions and officials, like their counterparts in other telecommunication monopolies the world over, acted concertedly to delay any restructuring move that would compromise their position. Political meanderings and court battles delayed the deregulation of basic service provision. The business media noted: "The DoT retains the three functions of regulator, service operator and equipment manufacturer—meaning that it performs none of these roles very well."[58]

Performance of MTNL and VSNL

Since their formation in 1986, both MTNL and VSNL earned high profits and improved their quality and quantity of service. But, like the DoT as a whole, they were also plagued by a shortage of technology and funds for planned expansion of networks. On the other hand, both corporations were pressured to generate revenues for the DoT and at times for the rest of the treasury. DoT and the treasury did so by either new taxes or by raising charges for interconnecting with the DoT network (and, until 1993, through what was termed a "rural levy" for expanding rural networks).

MTNL officials also admit to a problem with introducing a customer-oriented "management culture." MTNL officials and workers are on "deputation" from the DoT and are not permanent officials of the corporation. The training program for employees at DoT is supplemented by training at MTNL, but most staff members initially continued to view themselves as members of DoT rather than MTNL. On the other hand, most MTNL officials over time began to view their identity as distinct from DoT's and saw the latter as their adversary. Organizationally, this is an interesting lesson in that resistance to restructuring diminished once it had actually taken place, with the splinter group forming its own identity.

The high rates of economic returns in providing telecommunication services is clear from the experience of MTNL and VSNL from the date of their incorporation. Both corporations have consistently posted profit margins between 35 and 40 percent over the last decade following 1986.

In fact, the rates of return for MTNL and VSNL are among the highest of all public-sector enterprises in India. The two corporations are consistently among the fewer than twenty-five public-sector corporations that registered improvements in their overall profitability ratios (gross returns on total capital employed, gross returns on net sales, and profits after tax as a percentage of net worth). The high percentages belie the claim that India is strapped for internal resources to meet its telecommunication needs. Both corporations can also raise funds directly from the markets. Privately held equity in 1993 was 20 percent for MTNL and 15 percent for VSNL.

The following points summarize the other achievements and challenges of the two corporations in the last decade. First, media reports reveal that subscribers in Bombay and Delhi complained that despite the high profits of MTNL and VSNL, their subscriber tariffs were among the highest in the world. The cost of installation to subscribers could reach Rs 16,000 (about $1,000 at that time) in metropolitan towns. Consumers joked that MTNL stood for "Mera Telephone Nahin Lagta" (I cannot get my telephone).

Second, MTNL and VSNL contend that their plans were put on hold due to equipment shortages. One MTNL official noted that "DoT is our competitor, controller, everything."[59] Pitroda countered that these corporations have a "vested interest" in getting foreign technology. According to Pitroda, anytime anyone mentioned foreign technology, he thought of vested interest. "I don't care whether it's MNCs, domestic industrialists, politicians, anybody, they all have vested interest."[60] He was firm about utilizing India's human and other resources for technological development. "It's not idealistic, it's a necessity," he said, adding that "there's something to be said for emotionally owning a product." The MTNL official cited above contends that "philosophically Pitroda is right" in insisting on domestic technology, but since it was not forthcoming, it created bottlenecks for network expansion (especially after 1988–89 when MTNL waiting time for telephone connections climbed again).[61] Pitroda lost the battle on indigenous versus foreign technology. As the economic and technological crunch grew, the restrictions on foreign technology began to be removed through successive deregulations after 1991.

Third, the quality of service continued to improve but the fault rates of nearly 11 faults per 100 telephones each month in Bombay and 23 faults for Delhi in 1997 (and 23 since 1994) remained high. MTNL brought down the number of employees per 1,000 telephones in Bombay and Delhi from 56 and 58 respectively to 21 and 26 respectively from 1985 to 1996 (the national average was 59 in 1992).[62] But reducing the employee-telephone ratio was made difficult by rigid labor laws.[63]

The two corporations did register significant improvements in productivity. Between March 1986 and March 1994, MTNL increased DELs from 0.75 million to 1.8 million DELs (a 150 percent increase) out of which Delhi phones increased from 293 to 814 thousand and Bombay from 454 to 1035 thousand. Given the 1991 census figures and the respective figures for MTNL, it gives a telephone density of 6.2 per 100 for Delhi and 5.6 per 100 for Bombay against a national density of 0.6 per 100 in 1991.[64] The most significant improvement is in bringing down the waiting list for telephones in Delhi from twenty years in March 1986 to three years (for most areas) by March 1994 and a "few months" by March 1996.[65] The respective figures for Bombay are fifteen years in 1986 to three years in 1994 and a "few months" by March 1996.[66]

VSNL's record is more impressive than MTNL's because of its greater autonomy, which disallows DoT from continually jeopardizing its plans. First, VSNL has more influence than MTNL over the appointment and workings of its board of directors (a chairman and managing director, three functional directors and three part-time official directors). Unanimity on issues with its board of directors gives VSNL more bargaining leverage with the DoT, the Ministry of Finance, and the Planning Commission. Second, its staff is hired directly rather than through the DoT cadres. Third, its headquarters are in Bombay and the geographical distance restrains everyday interference from the DoT. Fourth, services VSNL provides are important for trade and international groups, lobbies with direct access to the state.

The biggest improvements for VSNL are in the area of basic services. Direct dialing internationally over the telephone increased from eleven destinations in 1986 to 236 by June 1997. The 14,367 international circuits available in May 1997 reflected a 300 percent increase over the 4,789 available in 1993, as India joined the international fiber-optic network (SE-ME-WE-2), and as more gateway facilities opened in the country.[67]

By 1997, VSNL was also providing a variety of specialized services although their countrywide diffusion was limited because of difficulties and costs associated with the domestic network. Nonetheless, the services provided included Internet-based services (data transmission, e-mail, EDI, data search), video services (video conferencing, television, and other forms of broadcasting), and leased or dedicated channel services. The latter took advantage of India's share in Intelsat (for business services) and Inmarsat (for mobile services at sea).

LIBERALIZATION OF MANUFACTURING

The issue of manufacturing versus importing switches was discussed above. The liberalization of customer premises and the transmission market is analyzed below. (Customer premises, transmission, and switching make up the three components of a network.) The equipment market in general reveals the influence and the political machinations of domestic manufacturing in India, which can be taken as another fall out of the "license-quota-permit Raj."

Customer Premises Equipment (CPE)

The CPE market was one of the first to be liberalized in 1985 with the creation of the DoT. It was expected that with the projected 20 million DELs by the year 2000, Indian Telephone Industries (ITI) would not be able to cope with the demand for telephones.[68] But the "liberalized" market soon reflected the ability of the private sector to create protected markets for itself and the government more or less catering to this interest of private capital. The role of foreign manufacturers was limited to technology transfer agreements, something that many analysts note always results in India getting outmoded technologies.

The DoT selected three foreign manufacturers for CPE technology transfer (Ericsson, Siemens, and Face, the latter a subsidiary of Alcatel in Italy) because they agreed to transfer the technology. Both Siemens and Alcatel were already big players in the telecommunications market in India when the CPE deals took place. Private manufacturers in India were asked to sign agreements with these manufacturers and were subsequently licensed by the government for a given amount of production capacity. ITI itself opted for the Face technology even before the market was liberalized[69] and most private manufacturers were licensed to produce either Siemens' or Ericsson's phones. The foreign manufacturers were besieged with proposals by Indian manufacturers for technology tie-ups. Thus from the 12 to 15 proposals that Ericsson received, it chose six. Siemens opted for 10. The government itself licensed 51 manufacturers originally, of which only 14 were around in 1990.

What happened to 37 manufacturers who were originally licensed but were not in the market three years later? While the total market for telephone instruments grew by more than 7.5 percent annually during the Seventh Plan period (crossing the Rs 1 billion mark in 1987), the period also marked a decline in the number of producers who were still in the market a mere three years after production started. By 1990, there was too much licensed and production overcapacity in the telephone market and most of those who were originally licensed could not stay in the market. There are four major buyers of telephone instruments: the DoT, MTNL, the Department of Electronics, and EAPBX manufacturers.[70] The biggest buyers are DoT and MTNL, who still supply the first instrument to the user, and account for nearly 90 percent of the market.

By 1990, ITI was also expected to start producing its telephone instruments and private manufacturers were not hopeful of ever beating ITI's bids made to DoT.[71]

The CPE market in India represents about one fifth of the total equipment market and less than 5 percent of the total telecommunications market. It depends on the total switching capacity and the number of DELs installed (and to a limited extent the number of PBXs). The total licensed capacity in 1989 was more than 9 million phones with private sector accounting for about 4 million, public sector for 2 million and joint sector for the rest.[72] Against this, the demand for telephones before 1990 was always below one million per year. One study shows that seven companies (excluding ITI) accounted for more than Rs 700 million in sales in 1989–90. Of these, two companies accounted for more than 50 percent of the total market share.[73]

Clearly the number of DELs have not kept pace with the capacity of telephone manufacturers. One wonders why the state licensed this excess capacity when by its own Seventh Plan estimates only 1.3 million DELs were expected to be installed. The political economy of protected market stands out as the villain for the excess capacity and the failure of the number of manufacturing units in telephones during this period. The state, with its ambitious telecommunications plans extending to the year 2000, virtually guaranteed a market for private manufacturers, and even obtained the transfer of technology for them from Siemens and Ericsson. The small firms that obtained the licenses for manufacture did little by way of market research on their own and were totally dependent on the government to market their telephones. The licensed overcapacity reflects inflated estimates by the government of this market.

According to Pitroda, outright corruption also played a big role in the telephone market's overcapacity.[74] He noted that state subsidies attracted small producers to the telephone manufacturing market, and that for every rupee that the small manufacturers invested, the government provided five rupees of subsidy. Thus, many manufacturers came into the market without ever intending to produce anything. Because of these subsidies "they have made their money even before they produce one telephone."[75] By 1990, trade media noted that only established business houses (for example, Tatas) had the willingness (given the widespread corruption among many small manufacturers) and the ability (given overcapacity) to survive. An *Indian Express* commentary summed up the market status of the telephone manufacturing market: The "rush of entrepreneurs to enter the newly opened field led to installation of excessive capacity. In fact, horde mentality is a major scourge for the Indian industrial world: whenever any profitable area is discovered, entrepreneurs simultaneously rush to enter that field. . . . Several industries including cement, mini-steel, tyres, polyester staple fibre etc. have gone through this rigmarole."

By 1989, the manufacturers also started asking the government for support (export subsidies, market searches, etc.) in exporting telephones. While two companies managed to get export orders for a few specialized products, India's becoming a telephone exporter is a distant possibility. It would be competing with the MNCs that supplied the technology to India in the first place. The whole idea of exporting telephones is further reminiscent of Bhagwati and Desai's "cynical" summation of India's export policy that "India should produce whatever it can, and export whatever it produces."[76]

A few manufacturers even plagiarized the foreign telephone model and offered it at extremely low prices instead of acquiring the technology from any of the three MNCs. Those holding licenses to the foreign technology were threatened by these low prices and were soon giving in to price-cutting temptations themselves. Even a leading manufacturer like Bharti Telecom acknowledged in 1990 that it was soon going to launch an "indigenous technology" phone that would be cheaper by one hundred rupees.[77]

By 1990, the telephone manufacturers were trying to survive in the market with strategies reminiscent of the heydays of the ISI era. When it came to state procurement, some of them acted in collusion, presenting identical bids at extremely low prices (if the cartel was not inclusive of all firms) and extremely high prices (for an all-inclusive cartel).[78] In 1989, MTNL negotiated a price of Rs 680 per instrument with the cartel even though the identical bid had been Rs 750. In 1990, in trying to break up a cartel, MTNL went so far as to place an order with a company outside of the cartel even though its bid was higher.[79]

The Transmission Market and Private Manufacturing

Partial liberalization took place in the transmission market in 1987. The private sector was allowed to manufacture cables up to a 120-channel capacity. There does not seem to be much of a conflict between DoT and private manufacturers in the transmission components sector. The public sector corporation, Hindustan Cables Limited (HCL) manufacturing transmission equipment, has never been directly controlled by DoT, and the entry of private manufacturers offered no threat to DoT's monopoly over equipment manufacture or procurement. Meanwhile, HCL caters to a number of markets other than telecommunications and did not directly feel threatened by the manufacturers allowed into the telecommunications cables market. ITI did enter the transmission market during the Seventh Plan by beginning to manufacture fiber-optic cables. HCL, however, retained 70 percent of the share of the transmission market. But as with telephones, there was excess capacity in transmission equipment by the end of the Seventh Plan. In 1989, the Telecommunications Commission asked MTNL to review its plans to import cables as it noted that HCL was running at 60 percent of its capacity.[80]

Many cases of cartelization and excess capacity (and corruption thereof) in the transmission equipment market exist. For example, a controversy came about in October 1988 when it was found that the DoT office in Calcutta placed a large order for cables with a "cartel" of twenty manufacturers even though the lowest bid came from three others outside of the cartel. Questions about possible bribery were raised in the Indian Parliament but nothing could be resolved even though the issue continued to be raised in the print media. It seemed to have been forgotten later with the V. P. Singh government when other important controversies and allegations took over.

CONCLUSION

This chapter shows the extent to which state prerogatives and demand pressures for restructuring telecommunications were (or were not) reconciled in a dysfunctional state such as India's during the late 1980s. Top decision-makers in India, like Gandhi and Pitroda, who otherwise came with sincere intentions toward restructuring, were unable to prevail over special-interest groups, many of them located in the policy, production, and service provision wings of the state itself.

Telecommunications was easily made a development priority and DoT separated from the department of posts because it bumped up DoT's status politically. Other moves to restructure the DoT were bitterly contested by its employees. It is arguable whether the Indian state lacked capacity in the 1980s. However, it is clear that it did lack autonomy in enforcing its agenda, thus reducing its maneuverability. It is also clear that apart from a few officials, there was no widespread responsibility toward development goals (beyond populist policies or rhetoric).

The Indian state could not arbitrate effectively among the various user- and interest-groups' demands in the context of telecommunications. India's inward-oriented policies were supported by DoT, and many politicians, to guard their interests and legitimacy, respectively. Exporters, multilateral institutions, and MNCs wanted India to open up, but at least in the 1980s, their efforts were only marginally successful. In between the two constituencies (for or against ISI) were India's domestic manufacturers who wanted market liberalization, but only for themselves, and were dependent on the state for technology procurement, subsidies, and market shares. The shadow of the urban and rural users (or their voting capacities) led the state to undertake many initiatives but many of them either turned out to be rhetoric or they could not be implemented due to battles under way within the state. Service enhancement did extend to these and other user groups but long waiting lists continued to exist. Meanwhile specialized services, demanded by business users, featured the worst shortages following the government's inability to either resolve the various demand pressures, or to direct investments toward high growth areas. It is only in the 1990s that the ISI coalition seems to have collapsed and telecommunication service provision made more responsive to user groups with high demands.

CHAPTER 7

Indian Telecommunications: Privatization and Liberalization, 1991–98

Following a severe fiscal and balance-of-payments crisis in 1991, the demands for liberalization of the economy (including telecommunications) increased while the status-quo constituencies were further weakened. Specialized services (including cellular phones) and equipment markets were liberalized in 1991–92, while land-based basic telephone service (hereafter basic telephone) was liberalized with the announcement of the National Telecommunications Policy (NTP) of 1994. But politics again tempered the exigency of decisions. Both cellular and basic telephone service privatization were soon fraught with charges of nepotism, convoluted legal wranglings, and obstacles constructed by the incumbent department of telecommunications. Private cellular service did not begin until 1995. Private basic telephone service liberalization, derailed further by the hustings in 1996 and 1998, had barely begun by mid-1998. Meanwhile, specialized services like dedicated (data) networks emerged slowly and remained expensive. The uncertainty and bickerings in national politics since mid-1996 further slowed down liberalization. The telecommunication regulatory authority that was announced in 1994 began work eventually in 1997 amid stiff opposition from the DoT, which had by then erected many tariff hurdles for private cellular and basic telephone service operators, and then proceeded to challenge TRAI authority on many grounds.

The many things going on simultaneously in the Indian telecommunications landscape reveal the diverse influences at work on the Indian state. The most powerful liberalization coalition includes international and domestic businesses supported by foreign governments and international organizations. Urban users (and now even rural users) have exerted independent pressures through the media and other agencies, but so far they are not formally part of any coalition. The opposing coalition includes trade unions and many politicians supported by many domestic businesses (the latter continuing to benefit from the past or extant inward-oriented policies or with a stake in keeping MNCs out of the market). The Indian state's juggling between these interest groups (including constituencies within the state itself) is producing one of the most complex liberalization programs ever undertaken. As during the 1980s, while many groups with high demands for services (large businesses, exporters, urban users) continue to be denied services, the state must also hedge between providing services to these groups and rural areas where more than two thirds of Indian voters live.

THE INDIAN STATE: 1991–98

The 1991–98 period may be characterized as featuring further decay of the dysfunctional state in India. Political survival, rather than state responsibility, guided the macro liberalization of the economy since August 1991. The maneuverability of the state was at an all time low. But politicians turned their accessibility to businesses to their personal advantage by accepting large amounts of bribes from businesses seeking to profit from the liberalizing Indian market. Ironically, the current "power" of Indian politicians comes not from exercising state capacities responsibly toward developmental goals, but through the legacy of prior periods of state intervention that have left the politicians in charge of dismantling the behemoth structure of rules and regulations to institute restructuring, a power often misused by them for personal gain.[1] The Congress government lost at the 1996 hustings amid charges (and evidence) of widespread corruption. Twenty-six politicians, including seven cabinet ministers, were indicted for bribery in the four months leading to the April–May elections.[2] No party commanded a simple majority at the elections and within a year, on the eve of India's fifty years of independence from British rule, three prime ministers had ruled in succession. Midterm polls took place in February–March 1998 as the coalition government lost its majority support in December 1997. The Bharatiya Janata Party or BJP, which won just twenty-eight seats short of a majority, came to power with coalitional partners. BJP, whose electoral fortunes have been on the rise since the mid-1980s, presented an electoral platform that deferred from the centrist and secular agendas that previous governments presented. It is right-of-center on economic issues, albeit it favors domestic capitalists over foreign ones, and espouses a "Hindu" ideology in constructing a coalition. Therefore, the BJP is often termed "Hindu-Nationalist." Its electoral agenda included *swadeshi,* meaning self-reliance/domestic production, a phrase harkening back to M. K. Gandhi's struggles against the British.

The Congress government of Narasimha Rao that was installed in

June 1991, inherited an economy at the brink of an economic collapse and a state considerably undermined in its legitimacy. India's foreign debt stood at $70 billion making it the third largest debtor nation in the world and, in May 1991, it had only one week's worth of foreign exchange in the reserves to cover its import bills and debt obligations.[3] (The 1991 GNP growth rate was dismal at one and a quarter percent.) The Rao government moved quickly in terms of economic reform and was able to bring in, to its credit, a few competent people to effect the transition. Of special significance is Manmohan Singh, the finance minister (a former director of the Reserve Bank of India and a liberal economist), who within a month of coming to office, instituted drastic economic reform measures and paved the way for securing a $2 billion dollar standby loan request from the IMF. (He was also heading a Ministry of Finance known to be the hotbed of ISI at one time though by the end of his tenure the ministry was leading India's economic restructuring efforts.) The rupee was devalued by 25 percent. Many licensing requirements for FDI were abolished and foreign capital was allowed to own up to 51 percent of equity in many sectors (up from 40 percent earlier). Finally, the list of companies that are to be exclusively operated by the state was reduced.

Many other restructurings were instituted after 1991. Anti-monopoly (antitrust in the U.S.) legislation, which created the protectionist regulations and licensing procedures benefiting the large industrial houses, was changed to ease the entry requirements for domestic and foreign capital. Industrial tariffs averaged at 65 percent in 1994 from a high of 400 percent before 1991. Apart from foreign exchange and labor restrictions (the latter reflecting the clout of employees in state-owned businesses), other notable barriers include quantitative restrictions on many products, and the consumer-goods market that features many forms of protection. To this one may add corruption of government officials who had to be bribed to effect any results. Economic woes affecting the rest of the economy included the 237 state-run corporations, 150 of which were in the red in 1996. Early reaction to the economic reform measures by foreign investors also critiqued "the country's archaic, cradle-to-grave labor policies and continuing foreign-exchange restrictions."[4]

A thorough reform of the banking sector employing 700,000 workers, which the World Bank in 1990 had specifically pointed out needs privatization, has also not yet emerged. The banking sector's priority lending policies to many inefficient businesses result in marginal or negligible returns on funds.[5] Apart from the vested interest of large industrial houses in securing such credit, the banking sector's policies are also responsible for having spawned a plethora of small industries (including many in telecommunications equipment and components) that are inefficient and thwart economies of scale. The preference for protectionist policies among these industries is high.

However, the surprising element regarding economic restructuring in India is that even the thirteen-party centrist-left coalition (including many socialist, communist, and populist parties), which governed India from May 1996 to March 1998 was unable to stall the process. The coalition took care to appoint another liberal Harvard-educated economist, P. Chidambaran, as the finance minster as an assurance toward continuing the economic reforms underway. Not only the central government, but state governments (many of which have recently featured regional parties as power holders) have also gone out of their way to pledge support to the restructurings under way. Thus, the communist chief minister of West Bengal and the nationalist BJP chief ministers of states like Karnataka and Gujarat have all gone abroad to court foreign investors.[6] (BJP during Rao's time opposed liberalization, but by 1997 was cautiously moving toward endorsing certain types of FDI as, for example, in non–consumer goods industries).

Indian economic restructurings take a new turn with the BJP government although how much the latter, with its window of opportunity through the elections, can really deviate off the path of dependency on dysfunctional Indian politics is not clear. A number of measures have allowed it to consolidate its power but raise many questions about the scope of economic restructurings underway since 1991. The politically popular five nuclear blasts in the desert in May 1998 confirmed the nationalist agenda of the government but brought upon economic sanctions. This was followed by the first fiscal budget presented by the government in June 1998 that, mostly in response to BJP's domestic industrialist supporters, introduced several protectionist measures, including an eight percent import duty and raised the fiscal deficit of the government, which was already deemed high.[7] However, by July 1998 another picture seemed to be emerging. The nationalists in the BJP government seemed to be countered by the "pragmatists" (as the news media called them), who slowed down the nationalist turn. The case of the pragmatists was aided by a flurry of bad economic news: the rupee had taken a nosedive since the blasts and the announcement of bleak economic indicators. The GDP growth rate was expected to be less than 5 percent and the fiscal deficit 5.6 percent for 1998–99, and foreign investment was slowing down considerably. BJP then seemed to backtrack, courting foreign governments and investors, approving several billion dollars worth of foreign direct investment in a month.

Change is slow in a democracy and groups opposing change cannot be easily appeased. The $10 billion of foreign investment that the government expected for 1996 was close to $2 billion for several reasons and was expected to be even lower for 1997 and 1998. MNCs remain wary of the slow implementation of announced restructuring measures. In particular, the maze of regulations, the labor laws and bureaucratic red-tapism, remain hangovers of a prior era.[8] Exports growth slowed down to 2.6 percent in 1997–98 from 21 percent in 1995–96 and 4 percent in 1996–97.[9] Furthermore, the poor state of the infrastructure (power, transportation, ports, and telecommunications) continues to deter businesses. The infrastructure continues to suffer from bureaucratic inertia and incompetence, and the high costs of improvement (in 1996, finance minister Chidambaran noted that the infrastructure needed $200 billion over the next five years). Political uncertainty, frequent physical attacks or threats on MNC facilities (Kentucky Fried Chicken, Cargill seeds, YKK zippers, Pepsi, Coke) aided by populist political parties, and reneging on foreign deals (as in the $2.8 billion Enron project that had to be renegotiated), all represent the difficulties of doing business in a liberalizing democratic polity.[10]

Economic restructuring and other political processes under way in India are producing a few positive economic and political results but their longevity depends on political stability and consistency. Economically, the GNP growth rate, which dwindled between 3.5 and 5 percent from 1992 to 1994, was a healthy average of 7 percent for the three years from 1995 to 1997, but the economy was slowing down just as many had expected it to sustain higher growth rates. As opposed to July 1991 when India had one week's worth of foreign exchange left, in July 1997 India had $24.5 billion worth of reserves that could cover import bills for six months (a substantially healthy mark by any standard). In fact, the rupee appreciated just as the central bank tried to keep it steady or devalued to keep exports competitive. (It began to devalue in November 1997 and in May 1998.) Inflation remained manageable around 5 percent. Foreign investors, while wary of bureaucracy and infrastructure, were finding it easier to get approvals from the investment clearing house, the Foreign Investment Promotion Board, which was also now approving up to 100 percent foreign equity in a few projects. Meanwhile, the government was under intense pressure for infrastructural investment and finding ways to improve spending (including privatization). However, the spending was only expected to be about Rs 20 billion for the 1997–98 fiscal year, of which 60 percent was to come from the state treasury (only a minuscule portion of the $40 billion a year Chidambaran at one time noted was needed). An Infrastructure Investment Promotion Board (IIPB) was created in July 1997 to streamline state projects in roads, power, telecommunications, and industrial enclaves. Overall, economic liberalization continues, even if under the

BJP its preferred beneficiaries are domestic industrialists rather than MNCs.

Politically, the Indian landscape instead of being dominated by a single (rent-seeking) political party, is now a fiercely competitive battle-ground (though still quite corrupt) detracting, in the least, from a cen-tralization of power in few hands. The rise of regional parties also means that India's federalism may now finally be put to practice. Fur-thermore, Indian judiciary is playing a proactive role in prosecuting political offenders. In 1993, via a judicial decision, the judiciary arro-gated to itself the privilege of appointing Supreme Court and High Court justices, giving it more de facto independence from the executive or the legislature than most other judiciaries in democratic systems. Another striking feature of the judicial system is the growing number of public interest litigations (lawsuits), or PILs as they are known in India, against public officials that the courts are entertaining. Many organiza-tions are coming about for the sole purpose of supporting PILs through the courts.

On the whole, many in India look enviously at the supposedly well-functioning Chinese model (comparisons between India and China are frequent in the world's trade media) and often a Chinese-type strategy with its focus on attracting investors and promoting exports is advo-cated for India. Others wonder if India is headed toward Italian-style politics in which politics remain in a state of siege and frequently cor-rupt but the economy continues to grow. The following may be an opti-mistic assessment: "While democratic systems like India's or the U.S.'s frequently seem less decisive and act more slowly than authoritarian ones, when policies are vetted and voted they have a durability that authoritarian arbitrary moves can't match."[11]

GROWING DEMANDS FOR
SERVICES AND RESTRUCTURING

As the "second wave" of Indian economic restructuring began in 1991, the demands for telecommunications services from user groups became quite intense. Two macro coalitions in telecommunications could be dis-cerned but many user groups (urban and rural residential users, and small businesses) while not part of any coalition, could influence politi-cal processes either through direct access to politicians (including the latter's concerns for building legitimacy/voting strength) or through the print media.

The pro-privatization and liberalization coalition includes mostly large domestic and international business users at times supported by international organizations and foreign governments. As noted in the last section, complaints against Indian infrastructural facilities, in which the dearth of and the high cost of sophisticated telecommunications services feature prominently, are a regular feature of Indian politics. Large users, which include domestic and foreign-owned businesses, are interested not just in basic services like telephony (including cellular), but sophisticated services that allow for data transfer and exchange. Networks allowing these users to own, share, and resell space on leased (dedicated) lines continue to be delayed or remain expensive.

Within India, the three industry associations mentioned earlier (CII, FICCI, Assocham) have lobbied the state feverishly for telecommunication restructuring. At a time when the government was in the process of framing a new national policy in telecommunications in 1994, CII (the association with the most political clout and arguably the most effective of the three) complained that only 50 percent of the demand in telecommunications at any given time was met, value-added services were nonexistent, business users were never prioritized individually or collectively, and the quality of service remained low and networks congested. In a major economic policy speech given before the CII, BJP prime minister, Atal Behari Vajpayee, a month after coming to power, promised a major national initiative in information technology policy, which resulted in the appointment of the National Taskforce on Information Technology and Software Development on May 22, 1998 (see below).

Meanwhile individually powerful industries like software manufacturers lobby directly through their organization, NASSCOM, and its direct access to the department of electronics.[12] (Indian software exports grew at above 30 percent per year in the early 1990s, and the government provided many incentives such as the setting up of "technology parks" with sophisticated telecommunications services to lure software firms.[13])

Domestic industry pressures have also intensified after 1991 with the privatization and liberalization programs under way. A number of subsector associations individually or collectively (through national bodies like the CII) now lobby the governments. These include: Cellular Operators Association of India, Indian Paging Service Association (IPSA) and the E-mail and Internet Service Providers Association of India (EISPAI). The newly licensed cellular and telephone service operators were lobbying furiously by 1997–98 to amend the terms of their license agreements that they deemed unfair and burdensome. As most of these private operators have foreign collaborations, they are not necessarily opposed to external liberalization of the economy.

Direct international governmental pressures, which were still quite marginal in the 1980s, became salient in the early 1990s. Of particular significance here is GATT's Uruguay Round of trade negotiations (1986–94) in which services, including telecommunications, featured prominently. Interestingly, contrary to popular wisdom regarding LDC recalcitrance about liberalized services, the commitments India made for specialized services (including cellular) through the General Agreement on Trade in Services (GATS) as part of the Uruguay Round and the WTO (basic services) telecommunications agreement reached in February 1997 followed, rather than drove, Indian liberalization and privatization schedules.[14] On the other hand, India's participation in the WTO now institutionalizes the international commitments toward restructuring, allowing WTO transparency and MFN rules to take effect, which further weaken the Indian bureaucracy's or politicians' capriciousness and favoritism.[15] Meanwhile many foreign governments, and the United States in particular, are applying individual pressures. The U.S. Trade Representative tabled complaints against India's specialized services policies to the GATT in 1990.[16] The FCC chairman, Reed Hundt, visited India in June 1997 specifically to raise issues related to the high charges by the Indian side for international traffic.

It would be easy for the Indian state to meet the demands noted above if there was no other coalition in the country. But the pro-international and restructuring coalition is at times vehemently opposed (either individually or collectively) by the DoT, by many domestic businesses (who gained from prior policies), and by large users within the government. DoT's opposition to restructuring is understandable. Domestic businesses opposed to international liberalization include equipment manufacturers who gained from the first period of manufacturing liberalization and stand to lose from the entry of foreign manufacturers. It also includes a handful of service providers who do not feel the need to collaborate with foreign providers. By the early 1990s, the equipment manufacturers were organized through associations such as the Telecommunications Equipment Manufacturers Association (TEMA), the Telecom Industries Services Association (TESA), and the Electronics Manufacturers Association (EMA). TEMA lobbying (as opposed to that of MNCs and other large industrial houses in India) was quite ineffective and as such was able to win few concessions for the domestic industry through subsequent policy changes.[17] Their fortunes may have improved with the BJP government. Large-government users include ministries within the Indian state that now either run their own networks or depend on the DoT or other government agencies for these networks. Ideologically, these ministries and their employees are sympathetic to the DoT position. The latter itself has become quite adept at playing the government employee card in delaying restructurings.[18] But given that the BJP came to power with the support of large sections of industry, the DoT's future may be more bleak. In fact, both the internationalist and the domestic liberalization coalitions in the country, with the exception of the DoT, favored corporatization of the DoT into a body named India Telecom. The Bharatiya Telecom Employees Federation (BTEF), the trade union in the DoT with BJP sympathies, was at odds with their BJP overseers by July 1998 given the latter's growing interest in corporatization.

User-groups that may be seen neither as part of the pro-liberalization coalition nor as opposing it include the residential users in urban and rural areas. The rising expectations and the frustrations during the 1980s contributed to political mobilization by these users by the 1990s.[19] One could argue that these users may have their sympathies toward a pro-liberalization coalition in as much as it results in getting them services, but there is no systematic or overwhelmingly anecdotal evidence of these sympathies, nor do the large users incorporate residential users in their lobbying or building coalitions. (Scattered news reports do suggest that Indian consumers would welcome enhanced service provision and reduced costs.) In the meantime, user complaints, especially from urban users, are frequently aired through the print media, by political representatives, and through user advisory bodies. Questions regarding telephone installations and waiting lists came up frequently in the national Parliament during the 1990s. And just as Indian judiciary becomes activist, public interest litigations (PIL) and other petitions on the basis of India's Consumer Protection Act are a certainty. For example, a PIL was filed in Bombay challenging DoT and VSNL tariffs and questioning why revenue increases in both organizations had not resulted in tariff decreases for consumers. A handful of consumer-activist organizations and individuals can be seen at the forefront of certain issues. For example, the Forum for Rights to Electronic Expression (FREE) and the "India-GII Listserv," claiming a number of influential members drawn from the media and policy, both advocate freedom of speech and telephony over Internet.

Meanwhile, the pressures from growing waiting lists continue to grow. The waiting list was 2.2 million lines in 1995 (3 million in 1997 and 1998 by DoT's estimates) and expected to grow at a rate of 15 percent per year.[20] This despite the fact that there were 14.5 million telephone lines in March 1998 (giving a teledensity of 1.53), and an annual growth rate of over 20 percent from 1992 to 1998.[21] Official estimates of pent-up demand were between 6 to 9 million lines in addition to the 9 million lines installed.[22] Demand is expected to be 28 million in the year 2000, 60 million in 2005, and 82 million in 2007, increases that are not likely to be accommodated by the current rates of growth. One MTNL official, after noting even the weakness of projecting demands for telephones based on GNP, noted that in India's context, "nobody knows what the real waiting list is."[23] The reason is that as expansion of telecommunications services began to take place, those users who had not even registered for a telephone service earlier (because of long waiting lists) now grew more hopeful and began to register their demand. Furthermore, the last chapter noted many of the complaints users registered against the quality of the network.

Rural users, by the 1990s, were also getting involved in making demands directly. The development of the Rural Automatic Exchange by C-DoT led to intense lobbying by many villages around the country to have these switches installed.[24] Many political parties that came to power in the 1991 and 1996 elections nationally (and many provincial elections) represented rural interests. This rural agenda is reflected in the concrete policy changes (as opposed to rhetoric in the 1980s) in telecommunications favoring rural areas. DoT, too, in the 1990s became a vociferous champion of rural users in stating that only a government authority would be interested in supplying services to rural areas, an argument it used often to guard its interests. O. P. Gupta, the politically powerful spokesperson for the DoT unions, often invoked the DoT responsibility toward providing service to unprofitable areas.[25] One estimate (hard to authenticate) showed that rural areas with only 14 percent of the mainlines account for 86 percent of the waiting list for telephones in the country.[26]

MAJOR POLICY CHANGES

The demands for telecommunication services in the early 1990s were such that neither could they be resolved by the state through marginal measures, nor could the state continue to reassure the many user groups that the DoT in the future would effectively meet their demands. The stage was set for comprehensive restructuring.

1991–92 Telecommunication Restructurings

Specialized and value-added services were liberalized following the macroeconomic liberalization in 1991–92 along with liberalization of equipment manufacturing and imports.[27] Ones attracting immediate and intense commercial attention included paging, cellular, and equipment manufacturing. Bidding and awarding of licenses began in July 1992. By September 1992, the *Far Eastern Economic Review* noted: "Foreign and local competitors for three large contracts—for large digital exchanges, cellular phone networks and paging systems—have been mystified by complicated and sometimes contradictory procedures."[28] The biggest beneficiaries were those with direct access to the instruments of power. This was especially the case with cellular (discussed later), which got mired in a tedious licensing procedure, charges and affirmations of nepotism, and court rulings. Cellular service finally began in 1995. The telecommunications bureaucracy retained its monopoly over provision of basic services until 1994.

The liberalization of equipment manufacturing, which mostly benefited foreign manufacturers of large switches, was less difficult than that of cellular or paging given that it was in both MTNL's and DoT's interest to obtain foreign equipment. During the 1980s, foreign manufacturers were kept at a distance, while C-DoT tried to develop the technology itself. However, given that imports constituted upwards of one quarter of the total Seventh Plan estimates, the Telecommunication Commission did announce in 1989 that it would set up an organization ("Components Bank") to streamline imports. This organization never materialized due to political changes and stiff opposition by the multilateral institutions like World Bank who saw it as another instance of government regulation.[29] In the meantime, foreign manufacturers like AT&T, who had evinced strong interest in the Indian market, and incumbents like Alcatel lobbied to get the Indian market to open up. The same recommendation was made by the Athreya Committee. Following liberalization in 1992, the DoT picked five large switching systems (of 200,000 lines) in July 1993 allowing 51 percent foreign-equity-owned joint ventures by AT&T, Seimens, Alcatel, Fujitsu, and Ericsson.[30] (100 percent foreign ownership was later allowed on a case-by-case basis.) The switches were initially to be installed in the four metropolitan areas: Delhi, Mumbai (then Bombay), Calcutta, and Chennai (then Madras). Domestic manufacturers were to supply the smaller switches needed for the rest of the national market. Domestic manufacturers had opposed foreign entry but, because of their inability to manufacture large switching systems, their arguments did not prevail.

Another liberalized market, the paging market, was soon overcome with bureaucratic delays and nepotism. Eighty-three bids for paging services (including 12 from U.S. firms) for 27 cities were submitted in July 1992 that resulted in 66 licenses being awarded to 14 companies. It was also announced that the rest of the country would be divided into circles for which the rights to provide service would be auctioned off. Motorola initially complained that it had received a verbal permission to set up the paging networks in five cities that it alleged that the Foreign Investment Promotion Board was reneging on. Others note that Motorola's strong-arm tactics in the Indian market proved counterproductive.[31] (Motorola also complained in September 1997 that pager operators were losing $5 million a month because of price caps instituted by the Indian government.) Service began in 1995 and witnessed phenomenal growth within a year, with 200,000 pagers by April 1996 (expected to go up to half a million by the year's end).[32] Apart from its business uses, some of the pagers are being used by nonbusiness customers for social purposes including news updates and keeping in touch with children. One study cites the director of a telecommunication firm as saying, "cellular for the classes and pagers for the masses."[33]

1994 National Telecommunications Policy

The continued pressures for restructuring led to the announcement of the National Telecom Policy (NTP) in May 1994, one part rhetorical and one part substantial. One observer calls it the "middle path" between the coalition of private and domestic capitalists and the state monopoly's advocates.[34] DoT would not be broken up but private competition would be allowed. But this major decision came with a lot of rhetoric. Telephones on demand were to be made available in all urban areas by 1997 and value-added services on demand by 1996. Public phones were to be installed on every major street (which would double the number of public phones to over half a million in the country) and phones were also going to be installed in each of India's over 600,000 villages by 1997. Service provision goals were criticized as being far too ambitious and later on, as expected, did not meet their announced targets. As noted, the waiting list for telephones was 3 million and even the government conceded that only 267, 832 villages had phone service by March 1997 (of which about 200,000 had services in 1994 already).[35] However, given that the government's intent was to also announce a liberalization program that went against the tide of India's earlier economic policies, the announcement of these goals (populist or rhetorical as they may be) was a political necessity to appease many groups in society.

The substance of the 1994 NTP lay in allowing private provision of telephone service and that an independent regulatory authority would be created soon. Foreign equity of up to 49 percent is allowed for basic telephone services and cellular, and 51 percent for value-added services. The guidelines for private participation in basic telephone and cellular (beyond the four metros) were announced in September 1994. For the purposes of basic telephone service, the policy divided the country into twenty regions (known as circles) roughly correspondent to all the major states and federally administered territories (a few small states as in northeast India were clustered together while the large state of Uttar Pradesh was divided into two) with approximately 50 million people in each circle. The twenty circles also corresponded to the extant organizational divisions within the DoT in catering to these regions (see table 6.1). Telephone service providers were asked to bid for each circle separately and would compete with the DoT leading to a duopoly in each market on basic service and intracircle long-distance competition (accounting for nearly two thirds of the long-distance traffic). The initial licenses would be for fifteen years and the restrictions on intercircle long-distance traffic would be reviewed after the initial five. For cellular purposes, the country was divided into eighteen circles and two operators approved for each circle and licenses awarded initially for a period of ten years. The circles for terrestrial telephony and cellular service were also divided into three categories depending on the revenue potential. Thus, category A with six circles included industrialized states such as Maharashtra and Gujarat, category B included intermediate industrial performers like Kerala and Uttar Pradesh with eight circles, and category C included seven circles with poorer states such as Bihar and Orissa. Furthermore, the government prescribed that each bidder must have experience in running at least fifty thousand local lines for five years, which made joint ventures between Indian firms and foreign providers a virtual certainty.[36] (The foreign providers had to own at least 10 percent of the equity in the joint venture.) While most Indian firms welcomed international collaboration, a few would have preferred providing services without it.

Politics explain the emerging market structure and the troubles that followed with basic telephone service provision. They also point to the many important concessions DoT extracted during the 1994 policy announcement. First, attempts to corporatize or break up the DoT into regional carriers in the past had failed.[37] The opposition of the DoT officials and over 450,000 trade union members would be the cause (DoT is the second biggest government employer after the railways). The unions also had the tacit support of more than 18 million employees in other government-owned enterprises. The only option was to have a private carrier compete with DoT in terrestrial telephone service provision. It was a coup for DoT also because DoT was already well positioned organizationally to cater to these twenty circles. Second, that India did not choose a duopoly model similar to the United Kingdom or the long-distance competition model similar to the United States is also explained by trade union pressures and the proclivities of the elite decision-makers in India who left the DoT intact while breaking up its potential competition into twenty circles. DoT argued that allowing national-level competition would result in cream-skimming and monopoly practices. Third, there was also widespread speculation and rumors that the minister of communications had personally benefited from bribes given to him in framing the telecommunications policy. He personally favored 49 percent equity for foreign participation and privatization that would benefit domestic industry. Fourth, delays in announcing revenues sharing rules that seemed to benefit DoT, and lack of transparency in the process, both of which could have been resolved by the creation of an independent regulatory authority, discouraged many foreign bidders (especially the RBOCs) and eventually only fifteen of them came forth.

A distinguishing feature of the Indian market is that, as opposed to most world markets, local competition is allowed, whereas the lucrative intercircle long distance market (accounting for about 40 percent of the long-distance traffic in India) remains a DoT preserve for five years. DoT's interest in this would be obvious. By holding the cards on interconnection (protocols and tariffs), the DoT could bring enormous leverage to bear upon the basic telephone and cellular operators. As explained later, the DoT arrested both types of operators in their tracks by the prohibitively high interconnection rates that it announced in January 1997 (later quashed by the newly formed Telecom Regulatory Authority of India).

The battle over telecommunications policy was reflected well in the tensions between the minister of communications and the chairman of the Telecommunication Commission, who represented different opinions on the scope and pace of privatization. By 1993, Rao government's telecommunication liberalization was being widely criticized as being slow and held up by the Telecommunication Commission chairman who came from the DoT's own cadres. In order to accelerate the reform effort, the Rao government appointed the former secretary of the Department of Electronics, Nagarajan Vittal, to head the Telecommunication Commission in October 1993. He favored quick approvals of foreign and latest technologies to arrest what he called Indian telecommunications' "slow homeopathic method of expansion."[38] Vittal soon clashed with the minister of communications, who, pressured by domestic industry, favored slower privatization. They eventually fell out over foreign equity participation in telephone services with the minister favoring 49 percent and Vittal favoring 51 percent.[39] Vittal resigned in September 1994 after opposition from the DoT staff and differences with the minister.[40] But Vittal's contribution lay in being one of the chief architects of the otherwise sweeping 1994 telecommunications policy.

India's slow and hesitant privatization exercises since 1991 are unique and extend from its pluralistic politics. Of particular importance is its duopoly experiment with trying to make a number of private carriers compete with the incumbent monopoly. These factors led the trade media to term the process "one of the most complex privatization exercises attempted anywhere in the world."[41] The chief opposition party, the BJP, during the summer of 1995, questioned the timing of market opening before the elections were due (explicitly noting that the Congress was collecting funds for the party from the bidders). In late 1996, BJP again strongly objected to the foreign MNCs coming into the country. The whole process of telecommunication licensing was also delayed in late 1996 when India's domestic investigation service, the Central Bureau of Investigation or the CBI, found $1 million in cash and other assets (disproportionate to the income level) in the former Congress communication minister's house, calling all the licensing procedures to question.[42]

In spite of these drawbacks, the restructuring continues, albeit slowly. The stakes are high. The bidding processes themselves generated $7 billion for cellular and nearly $34 billion for telephony. Investment estimates for expanding India's telecommunication infrastructure for a decade have been as high as $150 billion with $60 to $75 billion needed to install the 40 million telephone lines over the current ten million to bring the country on par with the average in other developing countries.[43] Lastly, one sure sign of the strength of restructuring is the temptation among DoT officials to move to private industry.[44]

Telecommunication Regulatory Authority of India (TRAI)

With the deregulation of value-added services in 1991 and basic services in 1994, the pressures for an independent regulatory authority became intense. However, regulatory restructurings like these that usually accompany liberalization present constitutional and bureaucratic obstacles in India. In particular, the 110-year-old Indian Telegraph Act of 1885 defined the legal framework of telecommunications and gave the director general of telegraphs "the exclusive privilege of establishing, maintaining and working telegraphs" (Part II: 4.1). Section 3:6 of the act defining the Telegraph Authority as Director General of Telecommunications needed to be amended to allow for independent regulatory supervision.

Domestic industry as well as multinationals, the World Bank, and even the U.S. commercial attaché in India, lobbied effectively until September 1994 when the government announced plans for an independent regulatory authority. The cabinet granted approval nine months later in May 1995. Initially the authority was created by presidential ordinance (effected January 27, 1996, and fortified with another on January 25, 1997) to be eventually sanctioned through an amendment to the 1885 Telegraph Act. It was called the Telecommunication Regulatory Authority of India (TRAI) and was formally constituted on February 20, 1997.

The government's inability to constitute TRAI through a legislative act until 1997 shows how much DoT influenced the process.[45] The three-member body was initially designed to be nonstatutory, which meant that it would have less clout than other independent government-created bodies, such as the Election Commission.[46] The TRAI act made it statutory. To reassure critics that TRAI would function independently, the government also announced that TRAI's decisions could only be questioned in the state High Courts or the national Supreme Court. It also tried to give credibility by giving its appointments prominence in the political hierarchy. The chairman of TRAI would be a retired or serving judge of the Supreme Court or chief justice of a High Court. The other two members must be at least an Additional Secretary of the government (a high rank below that of the top rank of Secretary in the Indian Civil Services).

The government hedged on the TRAI issue since 1994. If created, TRAI would weaken the power of the DoT as nothing before it. Thus, due to bureaucratic and trade union resistance and the threats of telecommunication service stoppages before the parliamentary elections, the ruling Congress Party–led government delayed the implementation of its own cabinet decision taken in May 1995. In December, two public interest litigations (lawsuits) were filed in the Supreme Court questioning the legality of liberalization efforts given that TRAI had not been created. The Court dismissed these petitions in February 1996 after assurances from the government that the authority would be formed soon after the first presidential ordinance was passed. But Congress was still able to delay the formation due to the upcoming elections and the coalitional government after May 1996 treated the issue like a political hot potato (as it is), effectively delaying legislative enactment and implementation until early 1997.

The TRAI act empowers the regulatory authority to fix tariffs, enforce licensing compliance, resolve disputes among providers including those related to interconnection, provide advice to government, and protect public interest. However, it differs from the mandate given to independent regulatory authorities like the FCC in the United States or Oftel in the United Kingdom on one major count: it can only make a recommendation to the DoT (Telecom Commission) on licensing over which it does not have authority. This was a major concession made to the DoT and pitted TRAI against the DoT. Although TRAI has more power than it was initially given with the presidential ordinances, all depends on how TRAI asserts itself with the DoT and other providers over the coming years.[47]

Two major battles have been fought between the DoT and TRAI within eighteen months of TRAI's operation. The first related to interconnection and access charges and the second related to licensing issues. Given the delay in constituting TRAI, crucial issues about interconnection protocols, access charges, and tariff levels remain undecided for the newly announced basic service providers and other operators (including cellular and paging). DoT benefited from this delay. The most prohibitive tariff hike that the DoT announced (in January 1997) was that of interconnecting from fixed to cellular phones through the DoT. In its first-ever judgment on April 25, 1997, TRAI asked DoT to quash this tariff hike with effect from May 1, 1997. DoT initially did not implement the TRAI order, inviting sharp strictures from TRAI, and another petition at TRAI from the cellular operators. After the second case, in which TRAI ruled on DoT licensing procedures, DoT questioned TRAI's power to regulate this sphere of activity and challenged the petition in the High Court where it was pending in August 1997. DoT argued that TRAI was not supposed to regulate the government providers, only the private ones.

The issues of regulatory supervision became intense as TRAI in early 1998 halted the implementation of DoT's Internet licenses and also called into question the newly awarded cellular licenses to MTNL. TRAI argued in both cases that the TRAI act authorized it to make recommendations to DoT that the latter had not invited. It therefore struck down DoT's Internet policy and invalidated the MTNL cellular licenses. A Delhi High Court ruling in July 1998 on the MTNL issue declared that TRAI could only make nonbinding suggestions, a ruling that was sure to be appealed.

Meanwhile, the very formation of TRAI did make it somewhat easier for telephone and cellular service operators to obtain financing for their projects and TRAI itself sees broadening of its role soon.[48] The task is momentous: its authority will extend over a hundred newly licensed providers in basic and value-added services.[49] It will eventually have six departments dealing with economic affairs, finance, technology, consumer affairs, research and analysis, and administration. But perhaps the biggest agenda item remains its relations with the DoT.

The BJP Government

At the time of writing (July 1998), it was still too early to get a clear picture of the BJP government's telecommunications policies but a couple of things were becoming clear. The sector was to remain prioritized and the privatization/liberalization program was to continue with pressures on DoT to limit its role. Both features, discussed briefly below, came after significant industry pressures for clearly prioritizing information technologies and the growing public awareness in the country about the role of information technologies.

BJP did act quickly to affirm its commitment to prioritizing telecommunications. The first televised address by PM Vajpayee on March 22, 1998, mentioned information technologies as one of the top five priority sectors. An April 28 speech to the CII affirmed commitment toward designing a major policy initiative. Accordingly, the National Taskforce on Information Technology and Software Development was created on May 22 with a mandate toward inviting public opinions and submitting recommendations to the PM within ninety days.[50] Members of the taskforce include representatives from policy, politics, academia, and industry. The taskforce includes many of the most forward looking and bold members of the Indian telecommunications policy scenario including T. H. Chowdary (ex-VSNL director) and N. Seshagiri (director of National Informatics Center—see dedicated networks below). The leapfrogging rationale is obvious in the preamble to the Information Technology Action Plan submitted by the taskforce: "For India, the rise of Information Technology is an opportunity to overcome historical disabilities and once again become the master of one's own national destiny."[51]

However, the preliminary recommendations made by the taskforce are lofty and reminiscent of the 1994 NTP service provision goals that could not be implemented. Apart form a seamless national information infrastructure (the NII vocabulary is taken straight from the United States) and a target of $50 billion worth of software exports by 2008 (they were $1.2 billion in 1995 even after high growth rates), the recommendations speak of "IT for all by 2008."[52] The latter includes universal access to Internet and provision of multimedia services through PCOs. An editorial in a national daily noted that the taskforce's action plan is "disconnected from reality" and went on to note, among other things, that given "basic literacy is still a distant dream for about 40 percent of the population, the taskforce's goal of universal computer literacy 10 years from now must be even more of a dream."[53] It is also questionable if a government like India's, torn asunder by sectarian interests and having little room to maneuver, can implement such bold agendas. In this sense, India comes close to the U.S. model, where, too, the ambitious National Information Infrastructure initiative of Vice President Gore died on the drafting table although it did educate the public about the importance of such technologies. Only governments like Singapore and South Korea in the LDC context (and Japan and France in the developed context) have been able to implement comprehensive information policies.

The government's efforts may be more successful on its second agenda item, namely boosting liberalization and privatization efforts. This is a two-part battle: restraining the DoT and encouraging private industry. The BJP government's communication minister Sushma

Swaraj was able to extract important concessions from the DoT in the first three months of office. Clearly, given the choice between protecting workers or domestic industry, the BJP preferred the latter. Accordingly, the DoT agreed in May 1998 to consult the TRAI before restarting the basic service licensing procedures for the leftover eight circles. DoT itself was undergoing internal reorganization to divorce its policy/regulatory functions more from its operations. The BJP government also seemed to be proceeding with DoT's corporatization initiative and there was speculation that VSNL may be privatized. This left even the pro-BJP trade unions in the DoT without an ally and by the end of July 1998, they were contemplating initiatives to make the government drop the corporatization and privatization initiatives.[54] The government also announced specific initiatives for the information technology industry including tax relief (to soften the protectionist features of the budget), allowing uplinks to satellites for 80 percent Indian-owned firms, rethinking the issue of high license fees that the newly licensed operators were finding hard to pay, and engendering national debates on these issues as noted above.

SERVICES PRIVATIZATION AND PROVISION

The political economy of privatization and service provision is now considered for four important subsectors: telephony, cellular, dedicated networks, and e-mail/Internet services. The analytics of the dedicated networks are traced back to the 1980s when a few of these networks existed but remained either prohibitively expensive or controlled by a privileged few large users (mostly within the government who had political clout to get these networks set up for their respective ministries).

"The Cellular Saga"

The political and legal battles that marked the moves toward private provision of cellular service after the July 1991 deregulation came to be known as "the cellular saga" in India. During this initial phase, cellular service was privatized for the four metros. Service was privatized for the rest of the country in September 1994 following the announcement of the National Telecommunications Policy.

One hundred seventy firms attended the meeting the Telecommunication Commission called in February 1992 after the intent to open the cellular market to private participation for the four metros was first announced. DoT did not lose time in creating barriers. It refused to make the necessary 1:25,000 scale topographical maps available on "security grounds"! The maps can be easily obtained on the international market for Rs 1 million, which bidders complained would add to their costs.[55]

"The cellular saga" began when fourteen firms submitted bids for the four metros to the DoT in August 1992. After DoT evaluated the bids, they were referred to the Telecommunication Commission. Before the latter could reach a decision, the bidding procedure was short-circuited by the minister of communications, who went ahead and awarded licenses to eight companies (two for each metro) in October 1992. The case went to the Delhi High Court and eventually the Supreme Court, in a 500-page ruling in July 1994, upheld the DoT selection process and rejected the minister's preferential decision. While firms like Tatas questioned the efficacy of the DoT evaluation criteria itself, the court decision resulted in a different set of companies to be awarded the licenses eventually.

Service in the four metros began in August 1995. The Indian companies are collaborating with a number of foreign service providers and manufacturers, which reads like a Who's Who of the telecommunications world. They include: Motorola, BellSouth, Nynex, M-Tel, Bell Canada for North America; France Telecom, CGE (U.K.), Alcatel, Ericsson from Europe; NTT, Singapore Telecom, and Telecom Malaysia from Asia (Singapore Telecom pulled out in 1997). India, like other countries, initially underestimated the demand for cellular service in the country (although by 1998 it seemed that the private providers had overestimated it).[56] A MTNL survey calculated the total demand for cellular service in Delhi to be around sixteen hundred in 1991. In hindsight, surveys like these probably kept the DoT's own desire to provide the service itself subdued in the beginning (even though in a later estimate it calculated that the four metros would account for 200,000 customers). The demand estimates in Delhi in 1995, months before cellular service began, were anywhere between 50,000 and 100,000 in the first year of service. The four metros in actuality accounted for 387,000 customers by mid-1997, two years after service began (there were 460,000 customers in the country as a whole).[57] As these estimates poured in, MTNL's desire to provide cellular was rekindled and as noted earlier, DoT granted it a license that was stalled by TRAI and, later, by court wranglings during 1997–98.

Cellular service for the rest of the country was liberalized along with telephone service provision in 1994. Eighteen circles were created for the purpose of cellular service and a duopoly structure was envisioned for each circle. Thirty-two consortia bid nearly $7 billion for licenses in 1995 that were to be given out for an initial period of ten years and renewable for every five years after that. These awards, however, were delayed by political obstacles revolving around selection criteria, nontransparency of the bidding process, DoT-created hurdles, and the communication minister's preferences. The DoT barely had time to respond to the more than 680 clarifications (indicative of nontransparency of the rules) from potential bidders, necessitating the involvement of the prime minister's office and the finance ministry. After the bidding had already taken place in summer 1995, rules were changed in the autumn to allow operators to bid for a maximum of three circles only. This limitation would have benefitted one of the minister's favorite bidders from his home state (had it decided to bid on cellular) by limiting the amount of licence fees the small upstart firm would have to pay. It also harmed US West, which had won five out of the thirty-six licenses (given that two were available for each of the 18 circles). The dust had barely settled when a furor broke out in the Indian Parliament, bringing the entire bidding process for cellular and basic telephone service into question in late 1996.

The final hurdles were the setting up of the regulatory agency (which was delayed due to political factors mentioned earlier) and the issue of license fees (which flared up in 1997–98). The delay in constituting TRAI provided an opportunity to the DoT and it quoted prohibitively high tariff increases for interconnecting cellular calls with the fixed phones it runs. The issue derailed the process for several months as investors and banks were unwilling to commit funds to cellular projects with low revenue potential given high interconnection rates. Finally, TRAI overturned DoT's rate hikes, but DoT initially refused to comply with TRAI's ruling. As for the license fees, many of the operators were unable (or unwilling) to pay the high license fees that they had themselves bid by 1997. A few were in the red by 1998 from the fees they had already paid. They cited delays in their operations due to DoT-created hurdles as their rationale for not paying the fees and faulted the DoT licensing process that extracted such rents from them. The Cellular Operators Association of India lobbied to extend the initial licensing period from ten to fifteen years and for either declaring a moratorium on licensee fee collection or for entering into revenue-sharing agreements with the government (more on this issue later as it affected telephone service providers, too). In August 1998, the Cellular Operators Association of India agreed with DoT to let TRAI rule on whether or not to postpone license fee payments for them.

The TRAI ruling in 1997 did set the ball rolling on financing for the cellular projects and it was expected to be close to $1 billion in the 1997–98 calender year itself based on the strength of the firms involved and revenue projections.[58] Resolving the license fee issue would ease financing further. The operators' case for financing was also helped by the high visibility of Indian and foreign firms involved (e.g., Tatas, Birlas, Modis, Reliance on the Indian side and AT&T, Bell Canada, US West, Swiss PTT on the foreign side to name a few). Furthermore, India now offers one of the biggest cellular equipment markets in the world and the operators' case is helped by the clout of global equipment providers. Equipment orders for the cellular industry were calculated to be $10 billion for the next ten years starting 1995.[59] The subscriber bases for the biggest circles were low in mid-1997 (between 10,000 and 20,000) but most providers expected upwards of one hundred thousand after the next four years, when they expect to break even. The AT&T-Birla alliance for two important circles (Gujarat and Maharashtra) calculates 1.1 million customers after ten years of service, believed to be a conservative estimate. One J. P. Morgan study calculated the latent (unregistered) demand for cellular service to be around six hundred thousand in 1995 and calculated that there would be 2.5 million cellular customers in the country by the year 2000.[60] By 2006, 4.5 million customers were expected.[61]

Telephone Service Privatization

The difficulties that surrounded cellular privatization were magnified severalfold for the telephone service privatization. Troubles began even before the bidding process opened in January 1995. Two days before opening the bidding process, US West was granted approval for a $100 million experimental "pilot project" in the South Indian state of Tamil Nadu. (US West applied for this license to provide multimedia services in September 1993, touching off a scramble among firms that resulted in DoT receiving sixty unsolicited proposals from all over the world with American firms leading the way.) The January 1995 US West license angered other telecommunication firms, who viewed it as an attempt to please Ron Brown, the U.S. secretary of commerce, visiting India at that time. *The Wall Street Journal* termed it as yet another instance of "India's sluggish and sometimes confusing decision-making process."[62] The US West project was eventually shelved in June 1995.

The DoT tried to mar the bidding process through delays and rule changes. At one point it wanted to make the financial bids the sole criteria and make other conditions (regarding universal service and use of indigenous equipment, etc. prespecified and mandatory). Given DoT's record for being unfair, mandatory criteria would have scared away investors. DoT's subsequent proposal was so heavily biased toward itself that the prime minister and the finance minister had to step in. DoT wanted to keep the percentage points to be allowed for each criteria of bidding nontransparent (on the grounds that cartelization would result if bidders knew).

Eventually the criteria announced for telephone service bidding included the requirement that 10 percent of the lines must be in rural areas while 15 percent of the bids' weightage would be for installing lines over this 10 percent requirement. The rest of the bidding points were allocated according to license fees (72 percent), infrastructural plan for the first three years (10 percent), and use of domestic equipment (3 percent). The high weightage given to license fees itself shows the government's eagerness to raise revenues through the licensing process. The low weightage for domestic equipment was due to the inability of Indian manufacturers to deliver the latest technology (in particular, SS-7 technologies, which provide state-of-the-art signaling in exchanges). The low weightage brought to an end the saga of domestic equipment manufacturing that had showcased prominent controversies in the 1980s.

The next hurdle DoT set up was DoT's interconnection rates. The DoT announced that it would charge Rs 0.64 per unit for domestic and Rs 0.80 per unit for international calls. At the average total rate charged customers of Rs 1.25 per unit for domestic calls and Rs 1.40 for international calls, the announced rates would have given DoT operator revenue-sharing ratios of 51:49 for domestic calls and 57:43 for international calls. (In the U.S. the long distance companies typically pay access charges of less than 40 percent of the total revenue and these too continue to decline.) The interconnection rates were brought down Rs 0.50 per unit for domestic and Rs 0. 70 per unit for international, giving DoT-operator ratios of 40:60 and 50:50 for domestic and international calls respectively. Given that access charges are falling the world over, the ratios decided in India also remained in negotiations until July 1997 when differences among DoT and operators seemed to be resolved along the basis of bulk rates used by the department for making ports available.

The announced rules and interconnection rates discouraged many bidders before and after the bidding process started. Reportedly many of the U.S. RBOCs stayed out because they deemed the Indian market nonlucrative and full of barriers. (Bell Atlantic and Nynex were passive shareholders with only 10 percent share of the market and their concern for the India market diminished further as hurdles grew and as plans for their proposed merger in the U.S. took off.) British Telecom, Deutsche Telekom, and New Zealand Telecom opted out for sundry reasons. In the meantime, operators from Southeast Asia (Thailand, Malaysia, and Singapore), hemmed in by their small domestic market, were aggressive in courting the Indian market. (Singapore Telecom dropped out in 1997.) As the bidding began there were only fifteen bidders for the twenty circles leading many to wonder if there would be bids for the nonlucrative circles. Eventually, one circle, Jammu and Kashmir, did not receive a bid, while five circles received only one bid and four circles received only two.

The next hurdle came from the three trade unions in the DoT that went to court to stop the opening of the bids on the grounds that privatization would throw many of them out of jobs and that the operators would only bid in the lucrative circles severely straining universal service in the country. They also argued that as the criteria included only 3 percentage points for indigenous equipment, many others, including those in ITI, would lose their jobs, too. The petitions thus addressed the concerns of telecommunication employees and domestic manufacturers.[63] Interestingly, the petitions were initially filed in the High Courts of Karnataka (a state where ITI is located) and Assam (a state included in the C circle). The Guwahati (Assam) High Court issued a stay against opening the bids. The trade unions also went on strike for four days in June 1995 to protest liberalization. The strike was called off after the minister for communications assuaged union concerns by pledging that most of the revenues generated by the bids and revenue-sharing (among the operators and DoT for calls) would be spent on retraining workers and preparing DoT for competition. He appointed a committee to look into the matter.[64] Eventually the Supreme Court of India intervened overruling the Guwahati stay and authorized the opening of the bids. Significantly, the Supreme Court noted that the grievances filed by the unions needed to have been addressed in the Parliament when this issue came up and not in the courts. The Supreme Court ruled that it was not the judiciary's task to decide if a particular policy is good or bad. The bids were then opened.

Awards for basic services were announced in late 1995 but the terms were reconstituted soon thereafter. Each operator was now allowed to bid for a maximum of three circles only. The latter action favored a small firm, Himachal Futuristic, located in the home state of the minister of communications. The firm, valued at Rs 2.5 billion, had been given lucrative licenses for nine choice circles for Rs 85.9 billion (more than three fourths of the total bid amounts at that time), which were obviously beyond its financial and material capacity. Instead of reawarding the six extra licenses that Himachal Futuristic obtained according to the ranking of the leftover bids, fresh bids (an expensive and time-consuming exercise) were invited in January 1996. This angered many bidders, aroused a heated debate in the popular media and charges of corruption in the national parliament.[65] Meanwhile, the entire privatization exercise had been put on hold due to the 1996 federal and state elections, corruption scandals, and subsequent enquiries. The Indian Parliament was almost paralyzed for two weeks in December 1996 due to questions regarding the botched up bidding process. The operators themselves requested more time to review DoT's interconnection rates before paying their license fees.

By early 1997 the political snafu was simmering down and leftover issues regarding the bids seemed to be resolved. The operators could now begin service but, as with cellular operators, the delay in creating the regulatory authority, DoT's announced interconnection rates, and the high license fees continued to further delay the operators' plans. By mid-1997 interconnection rates had been resolved and the formation of TRAI boosted the standing of operators for raising funds in the markets. *Business India* noted that the delay in telephony licensing might prove to be "a blessing in disguise" in that the global capital markets, already burdened by other Indian telecommunication plans from earlier, might now find it easier to finance the telephone operators.[66]

However, by mid-1998, it was also clear that the liberalization process had been botched and the private operators were not going to begin service anytime soon. The license fee issue became increasingly complex and hard to resolve. During 1997–98, the government only collected Rs 20 billion of the total Rs 36 billion of the license fees for cellular and terrestrial telephony but the DoT was adamant about collecting the rest.[67] DoT efforts to cash in on the bank guarantees signed by the firms backfired as the courts invalidated this move. The operators demanded an extension in license fee periods from fifteen to twenty-five years to ease the debt burden or revenue-sharing arrangements. The Ministry of Finance contemplated a moratorium on license fees but feared that it would send the wrong message.

By 1998, four years after the market was liberalized, license agreements existed in only six out of the twenty-one circles, five were held up in court, two were to be resolved, and the DoT was going to start rebidding for eight. Only one provider, Bharti Telecom in the Madhya Pradesh circle, was ready to start offering telephone service in June 1998 and expected to install 150,000 main lines during the year. The firm claimed that its bid with low license fees helped its operations.[68] The DoT was going to consult with TRAI before restarting the bids for eight circles, which might produce a more streamlined process. But the politics are also likely to get more complicated. Other government departments (railways, energy, VSNL) were planning to compete with DoT and private operators for long-distance (and in some cases) local services. Local and state governments were coming up with additional tax burdens for the newly licensed operators. The court system and TRAI are likely to be burdened with increasing petitions.

Dedicated Leased Line Networks

User pressures weakened the monopoly power of the DoT for the provision of dedicated networks when service was liberalized in 1992. Dedicated leased line networks, as the name implies, cater to exclusive customers either individually (such as a firm) or collectively (such as a group of users with a common identity). They are especially important for data based services. The move toward the market was haphazard and marked by bureaucratic meddling and nepotism. While user demands are being met slowly, the services remain few and expensive. The entry by private firms is expected to ease the situation.

Leased line networks (known as dedicated networks in India) depend on circuits leased to users by the telecommunications provider or on networks set up by the users themselves. The Indian Telegraph Act of 1885 allows the DoT to authorize other organizations to provide such services. But interconnectivity among the networks was not allowed and international access through the gateway switching facility was allowed only for special needs. Thus in the late 1980s, a banking network was allowed access to the Society for Worldwide International Financial Transactions (SWIFT) interbank clearing network and a business network was allowed to link up with international data bases.

India's entry in the data communication market began in the early 1980s. Data networks are critical links to the emerging international economy, which requires instantaneous, cost-effective communications. Indeed, leased communication circuits have defined the international data and information services since the 1960s when national monopolies found it difficult to meet the demands of large users.[69] Although the DoT (and its precursor the Department of Posts and Telegraphs) traditionally provided leased circuits, the provision of leased circuits for data communications began to pick up by the late 1980s. On the services side, the leased circuits and data communications market for 1990–2000 was expected to be Rs 32.78 billion, about 3.8 percent of the total telecommunications services market.

Leased circuits were made available to large users in India, but the proliferation of the dedicated networks was slowed because the DoT failed to deliver on its two public switched data networks, VIKRAM and RABMN, on schedule which were to act as the backbone for other planned networks for large users. Plans for VIKRAM stayed on paper but the DoT did commission RABMN and INET in 1991. RABMN set up a master satellite station and one thousand small earth stations located on customer premises throughout the country. A VSAT (very small aperture terminal) for RABMN use cost Rs 0.7 million (approximately $24,000) plus access charges of Rs 5000 a month ($170) in 1993. As a result, there were only 450 users in 1995.[70] The costs are formidable for any small or medium-sized business to afford and low quality also results from frequent interruptions, delays, noise, and faults in the leased circuits. INET, a terrestrial network, initially provided service to only eight major Indian cities but ninety-five cities were covered by 1998. Access to the networks remains expensive and speeds exceedingly low (initially provided at 1200 bps) . The cost of a dedicated line could be Rs 1 million ($33,000) per year and no resale was allowed (except for selling value-added services like e-mail). INET can now, however, provide speeds up to 64 kbps; 64 kbps speeds were also becoming available as a satellite-based network called Hvnet became operational. ISDN was available to a limited extent in twelve cities by 1998.

The alternative, suggested and implemented by VSNL, allowed Closed User Groups (CUGs) shared use of the Intelsat Business Service (IBS).[71] IBS is especially viable for software exports from India because it allows for reliability and speed currently not available on terrestrial telephony or data networks. In the early 1990s, DoT opposed IBS because it felt that the development of VIKRAM would meet the needs of software exporters without duplicating this effort through installing IBS. VSNL officials objected that "[IBS] can easily be dismantled provided competitive rates are provided."[72] DoT also held that if IBS was provided, DoT should provide it. After a delay of almost five years, it was decided that VSNL should provide IBS.

On the whole, the DoT approach to dedicated circuits emerged on a case by case basis. Existing government and public-sector enterprise networks illustrate the interdepartmental rivalry and relative power position of the various ministries. The first dedicated networks were opportunistic.[73] DoT granted them licenses only because large users, like railways and defense, had clout within the national cabinet.[74] Given their political access and high budgets, the minister of communications and the DoT had to go along. The development of Indian dedicated networks, led by the Indian Railways network (RAILNET) in 1985, parallels the access and decision-making power of the key government ministries. DoT objections only held sway over the plans of weaker ministries. The classic DoT white elephant argument was that additional dedicated networks would waste national resources, that VIKRAM and RABMN alone would provide the needed facilities. Moreover, large private users that asked for Intelsat links, were denied permission.

Development of data communication networks for business in India was also delayed because the Department of Electronics and the DoT argued that India did not possess a data communications culture and that businesses were slow to use existing data communication and information services. This is a weak argument given the variety of pressures from MNCs and academic institutions, and that most large users in India demanding these services were in the public sector. A government agency, Computer Maintenance Corporation, was itself instrumental in designing networks for RBI (the federal bank) and other nationalized banks, electric utilities and government-owned coal mines, steel projects, and public libraries. Another government agency, the National Informatics Center (NIC), after a series of fits and starts, set up one of the largest VSAT-based networks in the world and made databases available to government and corporate agencies in more than five hundred districts in the country. In fact NIC officials note that utilization of NICNET is higher at the district level than in New Delhi where "perceptions of power" inhibit use of the network.[75] Over one million transactions a year are conducted on NICNET. By 1995, NICNET's broadband capabilities, extended to fifteen cities and expected to grow to seventy cities, were being compared to the plans for an information superhighway in the United States. NIC officials proudly noted that their rates were one third that of the DoT.[76] By 1997, most telecommunication intensive government users such as banks, airlines, universities, heavy industry, and other large users had dedicated networks (however inefficient) or were planning to set them up.

Notwithstanding the government claims noted above and the hurdles it created, most service sector private firms with communication needs also had their own networks by 1995. The total networking market was estimated at Rs 4.5 billion in 1995. Twelve hundred organizations with an annual turnover of at least Rs 0.75 billion were using Wide Area Networks or WANs by 1995, a number expected to grow to three thousand by 1997.[77] There was also an installed base of one million computers in the country in 1996, expected to be three million by the year 2000.[78] (However, there were only about 50,000 web users in 1996 and the market is mostly limited to attracting revenues from the estimated 15 million Indian expatriates.[79])

India is emerging as one of the biggest markets for VSATs, the low-cost satellite-based terminals, which have the (leapfrogging) potential of allowing effective and inexpensive provision of data and voice services throughout the country including remote areas where the terrestrial networks are either nonexistent or unreliable. Although NIC was the main VSAT operator initially, the market was expanding and was expected to be close to $170 million by the year 2000 and its growth rate was estimated at 40 percent in 1993.[80] VSAT seems to be an effective alternative for businesses frustrated with the costly and inefficient circuits leased from the DoT. The demand for VSATs was about twenty-five hundred in 1996, almost double the previous year's figure. The high growth of the networking market owes a lot to the deregulation of service provision in 1991. A number of private players entered the market led by HCL-HP (a joint venture with Hewlett Packard). HCL Comnet Systems and Services, with nearly 25 percent of the market share, set up a hub for the Indian Stock Exchange. Other operators include Wipro BT (a joint venture between Wipro and British Telecom), Hughes Escorts Communications Systems, Himachal Futuristic, Telstra-Vcomm (which includes 40 percent share by VSNL) and Comsat Max (50 percent owned by the U.S.-based Comsat).[81] Comsat Max was one of the newest players, though the largest satellite communication service provider in the country by 1996 with clients such as Citibank. As with cellular and terrestrial telephony, the high license fees for VSAT operators made their services unaffordable for but a few.

E-Mail and Internet Provision

The liberalization of the value-added market also led to the proliferation of e-mail providers in India (though VSNL remains the major provider) and, after the mid-1990s, with the growth of the Internet, several potential Internet providers. E-mail providers consistently complained about the high rates of leased line rentals. (By 1997, DoT had received eighteen proposals from e-mail providers and ten had licensed agreements.)[82] A former chairman of the Telecommunication Commission admitted in 1996 that the steep license fee was the only reason constraining the growth of e-mail in the country.[83] Eventually, they formed an association called E-Mail and Internet Service Providers Association of India (EIS-PAI) and jointly petitioned TRAI in July 1997 for rate relief. Members of the EISPAI were expected to start providing competitive e-mail and Internet services by early 1998 but their plans were soon foiled by unfolding politics.

DoT announced its Internet licensing policy on January 15, 1998. It decided to disregard key elements of a government taskforce's recommendations (the so-called Jalan Committee Report) in issuing its requirements. In particular, the Jalan Committee had recommended that the Internet providers be allowed to build their own backbone networks but DoT decided that they would all have to interconnect through its own network. The committee had also recommended breaking the VSNL gateway but this did not happen. DoT also refused to forward the recommendations of the Jalan Committee to TRAI, which eventually challenged the DoT procedures because it had not been consulted. While the DoT-TRAI regulatory dispute continued, potential providers (estimated to be around 200) and India's four hundred thousand Internet users in 1998 waited in the margins.[84] Other potential or partially operational Internet providers included Indian Railways, Department of Electronics through its network Ernet, energy utilities, and NIC.

A second salvo from VSNL came in the form of blocking the Internet web sites of many organizations in 1998 because they were suspected of providing Internet telephony (yet another instance of technologies providing cost-effective alternatives to monopolistic networks).[85] The legality of VSNL's decision was questionable and was likely to be overruled. Interestingly enough, VSNL itself was planning to start offering Internet telephony although it was not likely to be available until the year 2000. (VSNL was also planning on launching a separate subsidiary for provision of value-added services.) Given the regulatory and institutional barriers that needed to be overcome, it was unlikely that universal access to Internet (even as a technological possibility) would be provided in India by 2008, as recommended by Vajpayee's National Taskforce on Information Technology and Software Development.

CONCLUSION

The telecommunications monopoly in India, whose origins may be traced back to 1851 with the introduction of telegraphs by the East India Company, came to an end with the policy changes announced and implemented in the 1990s. Most of the telecommunications restructuring in the late 1980s was limited to service enhancement that failed to meet user demands. Restructuring picked up after 1991 when the state moved toward liberalizing the telecommunications sector to infuse it with private capital and accelerate its growth. While all sections of the telecommunications market were liberalized, the DoT still wielded enormous clout through its sheer numbers and support from other groups within and outside the state.

DoT officials and trade unions were understandably alarmed by ongoing liberalization, which put immense pressures on an organization whose work culture had remained dormant for more than a century. Issues of job security and fears about ability to compete with the private firms made the DoT aggressive in creating barriers toward liberalization. Until the late 1980s, DoT could safely count on the pro-ISI coalition in the country and gained from its tremendous hold over the state. During the 1990s, when the ISI coalition's hold over the state weakened, DoT sought help through disparate constituencies such as other government employees, public sector enterprises, and domestic manufacturers afraid of international competition. DoT used legal challenges, bureaucratic delays, work stoppages, and worker strikes to argue its cause.

In the 1980s, user groups and other interest groups remained more or less heterogeneous and collected few benefits. However, three groups did fare well. First, VSNL picked up pace in the 1980s and provided an array of services to exporters. Second, urban residential consumers in New Delhi and Mumbai (Bombay) gained from the creation of a corporation for service to the two metros. Finally, domestic manufacturers gained from the liberalization of the equipment market to allow for private entry. On the whole, however, despite organizational changes in the DoT, service remained inadequate and expensive. DoT opposition to restructuring eventually prevailed over any countermoves.

After the economic crisis of 1991, entrenched constituencies were further weakened and the Rao government responded to domestic and international pressures to restructure the economy, including telecommunications. After 1991, it is safe to argue that an "international" liberalization coalition continued to strengthen in India comprised of large business users, domestic and international businesses engaged in the Indian market, multilateral institutions like the World Bank and WTO, and foreign governments. Large users, in particular, lobbied the Indian government fiercely through their service organizations.

But while the "international" coalition might be able to receive services and effect restructuring initiatives in its favor, the "masses," urban and rural residential consumers, however, were still fending for themselves when it came to provision of services. While direct lobbying by these groups remained weak and marginal, their best hope still lay in the need for the state to construct its legitimacy among these groups. The state's commitment to these users was still high on the rhetoric and short on service delivery. Furthermore, in 1998 when the BJP came to power, the nationalist coalition (sans DoT) saw its hand strengthened a bit.

As for restructuring initiatives themselves, a few subsectoral liberalizations were easier than others. As expected, those subsectors in which the DoT did not have vested interest or one in which it did not have a sizable presence could be liberalized first. This pertained to many specialized services such as paging, data services, and setting up of PCOs. DoT opposed cellular service liberalization because it would directly compete with DoT's service. MTNL was bitter because it was not allowed to provide cellular. Many of these restructuring initiatives were helped by technological innovations that made it unnecessary for all parts of the network to be controlled by the DoT (though the latter continued to argue its case along precisely these antiquated grounds and continues to do so even now on many issues). The biggest battle in terms of service provision, of course, surrounded that of telephone service. In spite of the coalitional pressures on the Indian government, DoT was still able to extract many useful concessions in the liberalization of this sector. Any plans to break up the DoT into several corporations came to naught earlier.

Finally, in policy terms, the interplay of the two coalitions can be seen in the way TRAI came into being. The government hedged for three years even after announcing in 1994 that it would form a regulatory authority. The internationalist coalition's pressures came directly from sources as diverse as the U.S. commerce secretary and well-placed officials within the Indian government itself. Outside of this coalition, public interest litigations were also filed in Indian courts by consumers. These groups were bitterly opposed by DoT and its political sympathizers. TRAI was eventually sanctioned through legislative act in 1997 but DoT gained significant concessions that curtailed TRAI's jurisdiction.

Overall, while the state still found it hard to effectively arbitrate pressures among the various interest groups, liberalization and privatization as policy options had a firm base in India by 1998, and changes in the state were unlikely to reverse them now. On the other hand, there were still many groups within the state that were not convinced of the direction of liberalization. This is apparent in the statements made by DoT officials and trade unions and many politicians. BJP government's *swadeshi* (self-reliance) policies must be understood in this context. Of particular importance in terms of state decision-making is also the increasingly assertive role played by Indian courts, especially in curtailing the capriciousness of politicians and other government bodies, during the phases of liberalization.

Telecommunications restructuring also owed a lot to the aggressive attempts by many individuals to restructure the Indian telecommunications sector. Taken together, these officials may be included in the "change team," which guided macro aspects of India's telecommunication liberalization. The influence of western liberal ideas and models of telecommunication policy in advanced industrialized countries is quite apparent for most members of this change team.[86] The case of Sam Pitroda and Rajiv Gandhi was mentioned earlier for the 1980s. T. H. Chawdary and M. P. Shukla, who headed VSNL and MTNL respectively when these organizations were created, were responsible for trying to move their organizations from a PTT mindset to that of commercial entities. During the 1990s, the restructuring leadership included finance ministers Manmohan Singh and P. Chidambaran (the architects of many of India's macro liberalization measures), M. B. Athreya (whose telecommunications restructuring report was significant in moving India toward liberalization), Nagarajan Vittal (who as chairman of the Telecommunication Commission pushed through the 1994 policy), and officials like N. Sheshadhari who set up a viable data communications network in the country.

India's telecommunication density of 1.5 in 1998 is impressive when compared with 0.33 in 1980 but it still ranks among the lowest in the developing world. Waiting lists remain long and service quality low. Estimates of future service enhancement are high. If fulfilled, they might enable the country to provide at least telephone service on demand. Service enhancement through the DoT, other government providers (railways and energy utilities in particular), and the private cellular and basic telephone service providers may dictate a take-off stage for the Indian telecommunications market. While DoT calculated that India may have as many as 28 million terrestrial and cellular DELs by the year 2000 to meet the projected demand for that year, a study by J. P. Morgan projected that there would be about 24.35 million lines.[87] New services, such as data communications, while still quite expensive and scarce were now beginning to be provided through user pressures and new value-added service providers.

At the national level, Indian political-economy presented a mixed picture as India turned fifty on August 15, 1997. On the positive side, one can count the 250 million strong middle class, the growth of regional parties and federalism in the country, activist courts and the media, and the bottom-up pressures in a polity long used to operating in an elite top-down fashion. However, there still remained too many question marks. The welfare impact of liberalization remains unclear, politics at times resemble a circus and at times a fragile compact, communalism is on the rise, and leftover baggage of populist parties and a Kafkaesque civil service, taken together portend troubled waters for Indian democracy ahead.

PART IV

Conclusion

CHAPTER 8

The Myth and the
Reality of Leapfrogging

The developing world is now frenzied by the promise of postindustrial technology. The postcolonial governors of the developing world had similarly looked upon industrial technology as the *deus ex machina* toward a future of self-reliance and prosperity. The earlier hopes frittered away with the pressures of history, of politics, and of following independent economic strategies in an increasingly interdependent world. Institutional contexts matter: we learned that they arbitrate the supply and demand of policies and strategies. What now?

Technological "promises" are only now beginning to be explored by political economy scholars. Economists have long considered technology an exogenous force that lifted the lines of production frontiers upwards creating wealth and welfare. Such cataclysmic changes could barely be discerned at the everyday level but, over the "long run," technology carried the banner of time and society forward. One need only look at industrializing Europe for evidence. In their models, economists held technology "constant" in the "short run" enabling them to "exogenize" its influence. This arithmetic relegated technological questions to a few economic historians, best prepared to write about time or the "long run"; who while producing some of the most provocative, rich, and nuanced tales of preindustrial and industrial societies, were simultaneously much admired and marginalized by mainstream scholars.[1] Only recently have the reparations come, through the convergence forged by the historians' statisticalization of their models and the mainstream's need to "endogenize" technology.[2] Another school in economics now raising technological questions contextualizes technology in the overall politics of societies—in the property rights that these societies create, which may or may not lead to development through technology.[3]

Political scientists followed close on the heels of economists, both disciplines in fact tracing their origins to the conditions producing political economy as a discipline: the enlightenment, the industrial revolution, the rise of democratic governance, and the social contract. The instrumental notion of technology, delivering societies out of their dark and horrifying past, is as apparent in the radical scholarship of Karl Marx as it is in the liberal moral philosophy of Adam Smith. The United States of America stands out as the technological republic *par excellence*, at once epitomizing and reinforcing the promise of technology.

Political science is now revaluating its Faustian claims about technology.[4] The mayhem of daily lives (of which technology is a part), the strains on the social contract, proliferation of the weapons of mass destruction, the pillage of the environment, and the failed promise of technology to uplift sections of industrialized society (let alone the developing world) are leading scholars out of notions of simple technological instrumentality.[5] The "progress" of the past that was taken for granted is also now laid bare. Social constructivists explore the contexts that produced the discourses of technological promise; liberal scholars the contexts that produced prosperity (including questions regarding "for whom" and "at whose behest"). Dynamic political-economic contexts now demand a critical evaluation of what technology has wrought. But overall, as Rosenau puts it in the context of technology, "students of global politics have not begun to take account of the transformations at work within societies. . . . [T]he dynamics of post-industrial society tend to be taken for granted."[6]

At the turn of the century, political economy stands united, as it did at the beginning of the nineteenth, in noticing the inextricability of things economic and things political. Dynamic change, as in the case of technology, demands such a synthesis, that of institutional contexts and market preferences. But political economy loses its grandeur, by shoving aside the grand discourses of Adam Smith and Karl Marx, in favor of positing contexts under which technologies may produce development and the contexts under which different sections of society may gain or lose from this development. This contextualization might mar the simplicity and "elegance" of earlier models but it heightens the sense of the variety of options, choices, and constraints governing technology.

The "What now?" question posed at the beginning similarly demands the sobering minutiae of political-economic contexts. That the developing world did not mimic the patterns of European industrialization had less to do with the former "getting it all wrong," than in not realizing that contexts are not readily transferable. Similarly, frequent cries in the media and in scholarship about deploying the East Asian model to realize the potential of information technologies, belong to the same historical museum as that of Europe's industrialized past. Museums serve a useful purpose for self-reflection and caution. The contexts posed in this book, and summarized below, hopefully add to our understanding of the conditions under which developing countries might or might not accelerate, hop, skip, or crawl their way through time with telecommunication technologies.

The most important question for development studies as it prepares itself for the next wave of its scholarship might be the following: How will myriad pressures for economic change be resolved in developing countries with weak political-economic institutions? Simple instrumental notions of technology, showing how groups get empowered through technological diffusion, are insufficient here unless we show how these groups are involved in the political-economic processes and how their involvement is arbitrated by political institutions. The same caveat applies to analyses that show how information technologies are transforming societies without getting into the minutiae of which groups are being transformed and how.

This book argues for contextualizing both instrumental and transformational claims made about technological change. What follows is a summary of the dynamic institutional political-economic contexts brought up in this book that unravel the demand and supply processes underlying telecommunications service enhancement, privatization, and liberalization.

THE MYTHS OF LEAPFROGGING

The word "leapfrogging" gets bandied about a lot in reference to telecommunications. Leapfrogging beliefs in telecommunications include suppositions about accelerating the pace of development, about facilitating the economic transactions by serving as the arteries of an economy (or in ITU's words, the very neural system itself), and about cyberbridges helping the developing world connect with and gain from the fast-evolving global economy. The universal promises of these technologies get considerably sobered when specified in terms of political economy.

The Myth of Technocratic Progress and Efficiency

That 'progress' would come to be synonymous with industrialization in the modern world is understandable (even if controversial for many schools of thought). A corollary, less commonly explored but nonetheless touted often implicitly or explicitly, is that technology can help solve all problems in a society. The connection between the two sentences is direct: technology liberated Europe from its "dark past" by not only delivering vast economic surpluses but by converting the drudgery of menial tasks into the liberation of seeing them done by machines. Notice the difference between hauling boats through the English canals with horses walking on towpaths during early industrialization versus the transformation brought about by railways when industrialization took off.[7]

It then follows that if societal problems can be understood as technological ones, then the manageability of the problem increases. The transformation of the problem of development into "industrialization" speaks to such technocratic beliefs in the postcolonial era. All that was necessary was mustering the resources of the country (preferably by means of the state) and channeling them toward the task of industrialization. Furthermore, the resources would be best expended if used in an "efficient" fashion, the mantra chanted by many neoclassical economists. From the 1940s to the 1960s, a time dubbed by Hirschman as an eminently exciting era in development economics, several strategies were suggested to beget rapid industrialization. Gerschenkron emphasized "great spurt," Rostow "take-off," Liebenstein "critical minimum effort," Rosenstein-Rodan "big push."[8] It is against this backdrop that we must understand the following statement made by Nehru (quoted in chapter 4): "Now India, we are bound to be industrialized, we are trying to be industrialized, we must be industrialized."[9]

The technocratic belief in progress creeps into the formulations about telecommunications. Studies correlating a given amount of telecommunications with a given amount of growth (or vice versa where a given amount of GNP in a country is taken to dictate a certain number of telephones for a country), while contributing to our understanding of the importance of telecommunications, nonetheless, through a slight twist of logic, convert the development problem in to a technical one.[10] Two types of linkages then become common: ones that compare telecommunications indices across countries (investment, number of phones, service quality, etc.) to implicitly argue that more is better, and ones that assume that given a certain amount of telecommunication infrastructure, development benefits to particular groups in society would be automatic.

A related myth is that of technological efficiency, which is often posited as an end in itself. The common practice here is to underscore the high growth rates in countries undertaking restructurings, to note the value of restructuring outcomes. Without careful comparative work—work that compares countries with government providers to those without them, or growth rates in countries before and after privatization or liberalization—these outcome indicators mean very little. But most of all, these indicators tell little about who benefits from these outcomes, and for how long and at whose behest restructurings are taking place. Large quantitative studies here also gloss over the finer nuances available in many cases.

Quantitative studies are particularly ill-suited for evaluating the effects of restructuring. Each country's restructuring experience is varied with respect to scope, pace, and timing. These details are hard to capture in aggregate quantitative indicators. One recent regression, for example, showed privatization and competition to be positively correlated with revenue per main line (the dependent variable) for the 1990–95 period.[11] Of the twelve cases used, the regression included five NICs and LDCs of which countries such as Singapore, South Korea, and China show high revenues but little or no competition and privatization (in terrestrial telephony), the Philippines shows a privatized provider but low revenues per main line, and Mexico shows a decreased growth rate of main lines during the privatization period and had no competition. One wonders how one can generalize, at least for LDCs and NICs, from the regression's coefficients when they clearly do not hold for the five cases in question. Using revenues per main line is also questionable, given high revenues in "cash cow" PTT scenarios. Overall, an indepth look at each of the cases would have yielded better results.

Efficiency indicators on the whole tend to yield inconclusive results because they do not account for the environment in which these restructurings are taking place. This holds true for the cases used in this book (see table 8.1). The clear success story seems to be cellular with its rapid diffusion but here again, China's "success" makes one wonder if market liberalization is the likely cause of this success. Turning now to terrestrial telephony, let us first take the case of the two NICs, South Korea and Singapore, which have eliminated their waiting lists, boast very high teledensities, and falling costs for services. Korea, which has had some form of competition (among government carriers) since the mid-1980s, can be seen to have the most efficient sector, too, as measured by the low ratio of workers per thousand main lines. However, most of the increases in teledensity came about under state auspices. Privatization and liberalization being relatively new in these countries, it is not clear the degree to which the infrastructural growth and efficiency indicators can be attributed to them. Even though liberalization of value-added services and privatization of dominant carriers takes place during 1990–95, this is not reflected in the growth of revenues per main line that were higher during the 1985–90 period.

Other cases raise further puzzles in terms of these indicators. Mexico's growth rate declines during the privatization period (1990–95) while its worker efficiency increases. Malaysian main-line growth rate is faster during the 1990–95 period than the 1980–90 period. Interestingly, Malaysia is dealing with far more pressures than Mexico. As for dysfunctional states, China is the success story but it fares the worst along worker efficiency indicators. As the country with the highest population in the world, such social welfare policies are understandable but the growth rates begotten with such labor-output (main-line) ratios are not understandable. Brazil fares very well on its worker efficiency ratio (a factor that surely helped with the Telebras sale in July 1998) but its

TABLE 8.1
Growth and Efficiency Indicators for Telecommunications

	Years	Singapore	S. Korea	Mexico	Malaysia	China	Brazil	India	Myanmar
Main Lines	1980–90	4.17	15.48	5.79	11.76	5.54	10.58	12.7	5.44
CAGR	1990–95	4.3	6.0	3.87	13.0	41.05	5.54	16.5	15.53
Telecom workers	1986	15	7	10	27	189	89	107	107
per 1000 lines	1990	10	4	9	18	74	12	74	93
	1995	4	3	6	9	12	7	35	45
Telecom revenue	1985	490	288	277	601	269	342	334	—
per main line ($)	1990	1004	382	711	600	313	582	501	869
	1995	1778	469	740	629	334	649	322	1596
Telecom revenue	1985–90	15.4	5.8	20.7	0	3.1	11.2	8.5	—
per main line	1990–95	12.1	4.2	0.8	1.0	1.3	2.2	-8.5	12.9
CAGR									
Cellular subscribers	1990–95	30.16	82.98	60.85	158.3	189	323.7	Started	76.67
CAGR								1995	(1993–95)

Sources:

International Telecommunication Union, *Yearbook of Statistics, Telecommunication Services*, various years, Geneva, October 1997
International Telecommunication Union, *World Telecommunications Indicators on Diskette*

CAGR: Compound Annual Growth Rates (calculation by author)

growth rate during 1990–95 is the lowest except for Mexico's. As for telecom revenues per main line, China fares better than India and Malaysia. The value of privatization (in Malaysia's case) or liberalization (in value-added areas and imminent in other areas) is not reflected in telecom revenues per worker in either India or Malaysia. Predatory Myanmar, were it not for the low teledensity, features high growth rates and has more than halved its workers per thousand main lines.

These indicators also say very little about the effectiveness of restructuring strategies such as privatization and liberalization. While government-led providers do well (Singapore, South Korea), so do ones facing competitive pressures or undergoing privatization (Malaysia, India). The high growth rates in cellular may also be attributed to competition, as in Malaysia, but in China's case, such competitive provision is questionable, unless one counts government-led competition (which applies to Korea, too).

In short, growth rates and efficiency indicators tell very little without plugging in the political-economic environment (the latter calculations needing extreme care, too). First of all, one might be tempted to conclude that authoritarian systems like China's or semi-authoritarian ones like Singapore's are the most desirable for the developing world (and such a case is often made) but in dynamic contexts, the question of how such systems came about in the first place and whether they are sustainable is another important dimension. Second, one can see that in terms of growth rates, systems driven by plural pressures (South Korea, Malaysia, India) do quite well, too. Perhaps, having catalytic governments is the answer but this book posits them not as ideal types but as historical circumstances.

The argument being developed here should caution us against putting the cart before the horse: telecommunications numbers before examining the socioeconomic context of a country. Having argued the case for telecommunications in the seven preceding chapters, the caution here does not amount to throwing out telecommunications as a development goal or discounting all efficiency indicators, but just the bathwater that dictates that "more is good" or that "sectoral efficiency is all that counts."

Placed within the appropriate institutional context, the indicators in table 8.1 can tell a better story. Most of the theories of information and communication are embedded in such contexts and empirical research in telecommunications needs to catch up. For example, the diffusion of innovation literature emphasizes precisely these links between technology and environment. Even ITU's famous Maitland Commission Report emphasized "broad public participation" in the formulation of communication policies to "make men and societies aware of their rights . . . and foster the growth of individuals and communities." Table 8.2 captures the essential insight of the many studies from various paradigms

TABLE 8.2
Theories of Communication and Information: Representative Works

Field	Exemplary Work	Major Concepts	View of Development	View of Telecom.
1. Information Economics				
A. Decision-Making	Simon 1982 Cyert & March 1963	Satisficing, Bounded Rationality	Mkt. equilibrium always suboptimal	Not explicitly stated
B. Organization Econ.	Arrow 1979	Organizational advantages in information gathering (division of labor)	Efficiency or sclerosis of orgns. lies in their ability to receive market signals	Available technologies alter feedback of information in economies
C. Imperfect Markets	Williamson 1985 Akerlof 1970	Markets vs. hierarchies Information creates markets	Better information leads to more efficiency	Not explicitly stated
2. Information Society	Machlup 1962 Porat 1977	Information Sector Growth: productivity & emp.	Share of information activities in GNP increasing	Fundamental to information sector growth
3. Communication Theory				
A. Information Society	Bell 1973 Beniger 1986	Centrality of information in contemporary society	Info. networks produce better coordination among societal ramifications	Fundamental to spread of information society

(continued on next page)

TABLE 8.2 (continued)

Field	Exemplary Work	Major Concepts	View of Development	View of Telecom.
B. Medium Theory	Innis 1950 McLuhan 1989 Deibert 1997	Different media shape society differently	Different technologies produce different space/time biases	Telecommunications destroying space/time constructs: "global village"
C. "Telematique"	Nora & Minc 1980	Convergence between telephone, computers, & mass media	Telematique reduces bureaucratic inefficiency producing decentralization	Important for decentralizing societal relations
4. Diffusion of Tech. Innovations	Rogers 1983	Tech. innovation once begun picks up life of its own: supply push argument	Diffusion fundamental to progress of societies	Fundamental contemporary technological diffusion
5. Information Gap	Pavlic & Hamelink 1985 O'Brien 1983	Info. gap exists: further diffusion benefits info. rich	Structural & world systemic overhaul necessary to correct information gap	Same as above

that inform our understanding of information (telecommunications) and development. Telecommunication "impact" needs to be evaluated with respect to the various societal actors (be they user groups, interest groups, or states). This is true whether we posit telecommunication technologies as increasing efficiency (as in models of information economics) or how societies are transformed through telecommunications (as in communication theory or diffusion of innovations literatures). In this sense, even this book merely makes a beginning in terms of evaluating the possible future impact of restructurings by suggesting the likely beneficiaries from these initiatives.

Our problem is not that we do not know that technological indices by themselves mean little. It is that we have set in place certain political-economic processes that do not dance to the tune of anything else. Rather than links with user-groups and their needs, we still have emphases on numbers and indices of telecommunication that without taking the former into account mean little. This is not a plea for reaching social welfare goals (which also may ultimately be elite driven) but for placing telecommunication policies within the context of user demands, an all-too-often missed point in telecommunication policies. Most studies on telecommunications, while asserting that telecommunications are (or need to be) demand driven, are woefully lacking in either conceptualizing the demand or showing it empirically. The same goes for cross-national or time-series data sets on telecommunications, none of which systematically show demands among various user groups.

Lastly, there is one particular positive context of technological change that does warrant special mention. The empirical chapters have shown how the changes in technology have allowed for entry by new market players leading to service enhancement, for example, in cellular and value-added services. But here again the institutional context of demand and supply is very important. Democratic India and democratizing Brazil both had problems with starting cellular services while China was off to a flying start. On the other hand, Internet poses a particular threat in countries such as China and Singapore that it does not pose in other democratic contexts.

The Myth of Supply Push

The technocratic beliefs underlying the importance of telecommunications for developing countries are often reinforced on three related counts. First, technocratic beliefs are related to the history of supply-push initiatives in telecommunications as a whole. Second, the history of all kinds of infrastructures is often misrepresented as being supply-driven (with corroborating data only telling half the story) and, lastly, the empirical justification for supply-push strategies comes from characterizing the "success stories" East Asian strategies in telecommunications as being exactly that.

As state-run monopolies, the PTTs historically inherited the privilege of making plans that drew their inspiration from engineers running the departments and policymakers who either did not care about these plans or endorsed them without questioning or both. Telecommunications developed as utilities and as highly complex technical systems that revolved around the world of engineers and their calculations.[12] PTT officials and their international *chargé d'affaires* at the International Telecommunications Union (incidentally the oldest international governmental organization in the world), tended to convert all problems of service provision and interconnection as engineering problems. In these plans, if there was prioritization in terms of user-groups, a few large users came first and others more or less did not matter. In fact, the entire setup of these utilities was such that they were notoriously bad at gauging any kind of demand.[13] That former telecommunication monopolies (including the PTTs) missed the boat on cellular, Internet, and multimedia services can all be attributed to the engineering supply-push gestalt of these organizations.

The supply-driven scenario gets reiterated in the developing world. The PTTs were unprepared to meet the demands for telecommunications services from domestic and international users. Faced with these pressures, the restructured telecommunication providers in the developing world, even after commercialization and privatization, are undergoing far-reaching organizational changes to become responsive to these demands. Those that remain government-owned departments, like their PTT predecessors, often dig in their heels and resist change. Singapore Telecom and Korea Telecom are examples of restructured carriers while the Indian DoT is an example of a government-run department.

But the supply push legacy of PTTs was strong even when restructurings began. The legacy dictated that all infrastructural problems be viewed as supply driven. Academics, policymakers, and the PTT officials correctly noted that telecommunications is a vital infrastructure and a development priority (an advance in itself from being marginalized from policy plans until the 1980s), but incorrectly perceived all infrastructural problems as supply push. Thus when telecommunications became a development priority in many countries, infrastructural provision remained unresponsive to demand pressures. In India, telecommunications officials emphasized their "social responsibility" toward rural areas while urban users with high demands languished or these officials decided that India was not ready for data networks even when the demand for these networks grew and actual networks were coming about. The pricing policies followed a "we know better" principle than one reflecting costs or market-based prices.[14] PTTs in general argued that telecommunications was a natural monopoly against all odds. The effect of this thinking was not that service enhancement did not take place (it did), but that the providers did not gauge demands. As noted, sectoral efficiency indicators, of the type presented in table 8.1 are silent on the issue of demand (or it is assumed away).

In believing infrastructural provision to be supply push, telecommunication monopolies were feeding on the popular misunderstanding of the role played by other infrastructural initiatives of the past. The parallels between railways and telecommunications were often drawn. The railways, especially in the United States, were believed to have opened vast frontiers for peoples and commerce and heralded industrialization. Even a cursory attention to evidence now shows that the trains followed rather than created commerce. Fishlow's seminal work in this area shows that railways did not create industrialization but vice versa. He argues that an extensive railroad infrastructure existed in the U.S. South but it failed to produce industrialization because it did not feed into the existing linkages in the antebellum southern economy.[15] In the context of developing countries, Hirschman's advice to policymakers to develop SOC or social overhead capital (infrastructure) where it is demanded rather than trying to anticipate it needs restatement here:

> When the authorities responsible for public utilities and other SOC facilities fail to respond to dangers so clear and present and to needs as obvious as those that are signaled by collapsing bridges, derailed trains, and constant power failures, what hope is there that these same authorities would know how to plan the construction of bridges, railroads, and power stations *ahead of demand*, without the grossest waste of resources?[16]

And

> In situations in which motivations are deficient, it therefore seems safer to rely on development via shortage than on development via excess capacity.[17]

But what to make of this discussion on supply push (if it takes place) in a book that has all along noted demand factors? It is incontrovertible that the least maneuverable of all states in the developing world can still exhibit considerable autonomy either at certain points or all along in certain quarters. Even when they are least maneuverable, states are seldom cohesive and their telecommunications department may often follow policies different from the rest of the state. The holdover of entrenched constituencies in telecommunications (foremost being telecommunications bureaucracies and workers themselves) continues to give a decidedly supply-push orientation to telecommunication restructuring. And, in the case of dysfunctional states, the deviation from the supply-push direction at times only benefits special interest groups.

In the end, the role of technology cannot be understood without understanding how technology is shaped by and shapes human agency. Technology merely proposes change. This change may be reinforced or negated by human actors involved. The natural monopoly argument in telecommunications lived a half century after it had been challenged by technological developments because of the role played by PTTs in keeping the "natural monopoly" alive. The engineers staffing the telecommunication departments in the developing countries around the world are adept at making their arguments salient by clever use of supply-driven logic.

There is thus need to be wary of technology-driven arguments. History is replete with references to technological innovations "whose time had not yet come."[18] Particular technologies and ideas, therefore, may make it easier for a group of individuals to make demands but by themselves they explain nothing. As Nelson and Wright recently stated, "technology is organization specific"[19] or in the words of Cippolla, "it is one thing to lead a horse to water; it is quite another to make it drink."[20]

The Myth of the Benevolent State

There is no need to belabor the point that the state is not a black box and that we cannot by assumption decide that the state would selflessly implement development goals. Most elementary-school-age children in countries such as India now know not to expect too much from their governments or politicians. The idea that states could be entrusted with development goals was debunked by a half century of postcolonial history.

States are not benevolent but they remain necessary or they remain entrenched. In the former case, they must still implement restructuring initiatives. In the latter case, they will implement restructuring initiatives according to their prerogatives or those of groups with the most access to them. Evans drives home the point when he notes: "Dismantling the state is not the answer. It must be reconstructed."[21]

Two myths about the state are particularly pervasive and can be debunked based on the evidence presented in this book. First, state leaders when espousing social welfare ideals may be doing so rhetorically. Evidence of state-led telecommunication restructuring initiatives for the "masses" or underprivileged areas are hard to find. When they are found, it is easier to locate their rationale in societal demands or in the construction of state legitimacy than in any altruism attributed to the state. There is much populism and rhetoric involved in holding on to state legitimacy in developing countries, especially in dysfunctional circumstances. As governance becomes hard, populist rhetoric becomes attractive. Second, in contradistinction to the point just noted, there are states that can implement telecommunication policies quite effectively. This was the case with catalytic and near catalytic states in this book and, to some extent, a dysfunctional state like China that can marginalize many contradictory pressures. Again, the role played by these states must be understood in the sociopolitical context in which it came about. Rather than noting the "generalizability" of the context, we may instead need to examine the specific circumstances that brought about this context in the first place and how these circumstances are becoming increasingly hard to find. A detailed discussion about the role of the state must then wait until the demand factors have been noted. For now, one conclusion is obvious: states are neither inherently benevolent nor inherently predatory. The context in which they operate is important for understanding their role. Given this context, it is hard to say that a minimalist state would do the job just as it became quite obvious after decades of ISI that an interventionist state is not the answer.

THE "REALITY" OF POLITICAL-ECONOMIC CONTEXT

The prime "reality" of the developing world offered here is that while its so-called success stories are not generalizable, its not-so-successful ones say volumes for the present telecommunications (and, hopefully other) policy challenges of the developing world.[22] In other words, well-prepared catalytic states with well-organized cohesive pressures and the not-so-well prepared states with cohesive pressures are becoming a rare breed in the developing world. Where they do exist, these states are finding it either hard to maintain their catalytic position or that they must now deal with pluralistic pressures.

As noted before, the most important question for development studies as it prepares itself for the next wave of its scholarship might be the following: how will myriad pressures for economic change be resolved in developing countries with weak political-economic institutions? The crucial cases worthy of study, as argued in this book, are the contexts surrounding dysfunctional special-interest–driven states and the plural pressures they face. The pressures represent the "reality" of demand and the dysfunctional states that of supply. In terms of telecommunications, gone are the halcyon days where the state, dysfunctional or not, could do what it pleased. Supply-driven PTTs are in the process of being replaced by demand-driven processes, whether or not the PTTs like this change (and whether or not scholars are able to document the demand pressures). Telecommunications carriers in developing countries have to become responsive to the public even as these countries undergo governing crises in trying to arbitrate various pressures or attempting to exercise restraint with respect to those pressures that demand preferential treatment.

The "Reality" of Demand

This book is concerned with demands at the group level (or aggregations from the individual level). Groups cohere in various ways in representing their own members and in interacting with others. Short-run change can be measured by focusing on very specific (micro) sources of demands (to show how this change may or may not respond to these demands), but over the long run such luxury, even if available, may yield incomplete answers. Dynamic political-economic contexts, as is the case with telecommunications restructurings, must then not only be able to show how micro subsectoral demands come about but also connect them with macro sectoral or economy-wide demands. To repeat the quote from Kindleberger in chapter 1, theories of group behavior must present "a system of analysis for inter-relationships among the sub-groups within the larger unit."[23]

Studies of group demands and the context of these demands located in environmental factors (economic, technological, ideational influences) present three sets of findings in this book.First, a focus on user-groups or clubs shows the many heterogeneous pressures at the subsectoral level that may be difficult to resolve completely but may result in piecemeal restructurings like service provision enhancement. Second, coalitions among these clubs and other interest groups may help to minimize the number (but increase the "strength") of pressures that need to be resolved. Third, while this book does not treat this topic at length, even sectoral coalitions must be placed within the overall trajectory of a country's political economy: the broad alliances among societal actors, be they party systems or civil society.

At the subsectoral user-group level, telecommunications can be conceived of as a club-good. Even a descriptive version of club-goods, as employed in this book, helps to discover features of "small exclusive groups" that may not have been possible had this conceptual lens not been employed.[24] In the least, the analysis allows pithy description (in terms of building upon meaningful categories and concepts) instead of reinventing the wheel of terminology and definitions. Here it also shows how elite user groups cohere and capture benefits. And if applied carefully, club-goods analysis shows how telecommunication restructuring efforts deviate from optimal provision to yield second, third, or fourth-best solutions. In other words, it allows us to see how the political economy of telecommunication provision is played out at the user-group level. Finally, while this book itself shies away from a quantitative approach, club-goods analysis allows for determining precise numbers of populations and quantities of service for optimal provision or even second or third best solutions.

Most of the features of club-goods observed in this book arise out of moving away from the simplified version of a club in which members sharing costs of provision and regulating their memberships can provide themselves with optimal quantities of the good in question while avoiding free riding and externalities. But telecommunications sectors in developing countries do not present one club to be examined but several clubs (user-groups), often with heterogeneous populations, and the presence of institutional intervention in the form of the state, which seldom ensures optimal provision.[25]

Membership and provision conditions cannot be derived straight-forwardly from state intervention and heterogeneous clubs. States may supply limited quantities of telecommunication services to limited numbers of users in any particular club (see point B in figure 8.1). Predatory states like Myanmar may approximate this scenario for most of its user-groups. Dysfunctional states may approximate this scenario for non–politically influential user-groups like urban and rural residential users. Or states may not be able to restrict membership but may limit provision (see point A in figure 8.1). Such is the case with politically influential business users in countries like Brazil, China, and India receiving limited amounts of bad quality specialized services like cellular and data networks. A special case of politically influential users might also be where a small number of users in a club can get a large amount of service provision (point C). This might be the case with large businesses or privileged government departments. That states can limit who gets what type of service in what amount does not need club-goods analysis but, if applied carefully, it allows for successive degrees of formalization.

The presence of heterogeneous user-groups also complicates the analysis in other ways. If there was only one club that the state managed it would have limited degrees of freedom in terms of trade-offs and leverage. The presence of many clubs allows the state to cross-subsidize one at the cost of others (business users have historically paid more) or it allows the state to provide more for one club than the other. In such cases the membership and provision conditions of multiple clubs get intertwined.[26] This book suggests that one key to dissecting the who gets

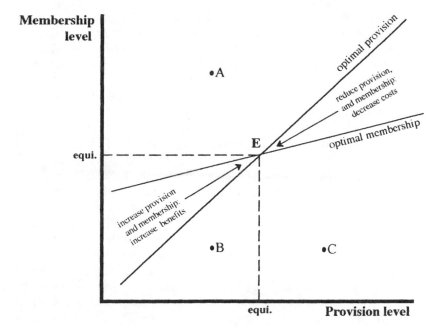

FIGURE 8.1
State Determination of Provision and Membership in Clubs

what here has to do with how the state delivers on its management role, which is seldom contingent upon club-level pressures alone.

At a more general level, the focus on subsectoral demands shows how restructurings may be piecemeal and slow even when they are demand driven (as in state responding to influential clubs) or, of course, when they are not demand driven but dependent on state prerogatives (as in noninfluential clubs). It is because of the vulnerability of heterogeneous clubs at the individual level that many of them take advantage of the many incentives available to them to form coalitions to pressure the state.

Collective action (or alliance formation in this case) is easier for privileged groups in society with small numbers and difficult for larger groups with fewer resources. It is for this reason that most influential restructuring coalitions in developing countries have an elite nature, usually including influential business users, equipment manufacturers, international organizations like the World Bank and WTO, and foreign governments. But while it may be difficult for other groups to form coalitions, other entrenched coalitions (often representative of erstwhile economic strategies), opposed to (or wanting to limit) restructuring, may exist. Not only is restructuring partly a result of the interplay among these coalitional interests, but the problem gets even more complicated when there is not one or two but several coalitions. Only countries like China have the ability to showcase a cohesive coalition in favor of restructuring. In most cases, the kind of plural pressures or coalitions showcased in Brazil and India are more likely to be found.

With multiple coalitions, restructurings may be slow and piecemeal but there is also a positive side to the story. Articulated coalitional demands are forms of restraints on political systems. In arguing for a demand-driven approach to telecommunication restructuring, this book implicitly makes this argument. The inward-oriented strategies in developing countries finally reached the point of unrestrained politics (or rent-seeking) with military rule in Brazil and the so-called "license-quota-permit Raj" (alternatively termed "palace rule") in India. In as much as political systems now begin to respond to wider demand pressures, they are moving away from exclusive considerations, even when the change is slow and piecemeal. Even the service enhancement initiatives launched during the first phase of restructuring in most countries were fraught with difficulties. Therefore, liberalization and corporatization were seen as imperatives by the pro-restructuring coalition(s) to get better service.

To be sure, coalitions in developing countries tend to come about among elite and privileged groups, but the outcome of their political activities need not be so. First, inasmuch as "plural" coalitions exist, they still constrain the state. Second, these coalitions are often part of other nationwide processes and might in the long run turn out to be not so elitist at all. Third, in as much as these coalitions help to privatize telecommunication sectors and make them "market" driven, it may be expected that telecommunications carriers will find it hard to marginalize demands to the extent that states did. (Only in exceptional cases, such as those of a few catalytic states in this book, are states able to provide services without direct coalitional pressures, although indirect regime consolidation pressures may be still relevant.)

Beyond the sectoral level, therefore, even telecommunication based coalitions must be placed in the macro backdrop of the national development trajectories as reflected in nationwide coalitions if they exist or in other broad trends in society. An example of the latter is party systems. This book followed a bottom-up approach toward delineating societal actors, starting and ending with micro- and macro-level telecommunications-based interest groups. As it was not overly concerned with economic restructuring beyond telecommunications, except where the former impacted the latter, going beyond telecommunication restructuring was unnecessary. But, in the least, we do need to know how telecommunications restructuring connects with national restructuring. Figure 1.1 in fact showed how various users and interest groups might be part of larger coalitions and party systems in a country.

Telecommunications restructurings have been at the forefront of national debates in just about all the countries examined in this study. When telecommunications was made a development priority in the developing world, it was not just another sector added to the list of priorities. Telecommunications was going to help these countries "leapfrog." The sector would do what the industrial technologies at one time were supposed to do. Making it a development strategy therefore consumed the same type of national attention that at one time industrialization debates had assumed. No longer would the workings of this sector remain unscrutinized. Telecommunications sectors in developing countries have therefore showcased many of the biggest development projects and the attendant political snafus and scandals in the last few years. In one of the latest developments, for example, the high bids for Telebras in the July 1998 stock offering (the largest privatization ever for Latin America) valued at $18.85 billion (nearly two thirds above the minimum asking price) greatly strengthens President Cardoso's electoral chances for the elections scheduled October 1998.

Party systems offer a good starting point. It would be logical that the debates surrounding telecommunications would be reflected in and shaped by the party systems in developing countries. The lack of a consensus surrounding many issues in the telecommunications sector in fact runs parallel to the breakdown of party systems in developing countries. Most developing countries, just as they are restructuring their economies, are also moving beyond single-party–dominant systems. Thus overall, single-party–dominant systems are now under considerable stress or at the point of breaking down. Singapore, Malaysia, and South Korea offer examples of the former, while Mexico, Brazil, and India provide examples of the latter. Even authoritarian systems like China and Myanmar, inasmuch as they spend considerable resources in minimizing dissent or channeling it through institutional mechanisms (as in the Chinese Communist Party), approximate the scenarios of one-party–dominant systems.

Not only are telecommunications restructurings reflected in the way that parties construct their coalitions but parties may often play a direct or indirect role in helping to shape coalitions in the telecommunications sector. India, the most "representative" case used in this book, offers an instructive example. India's transition from a near-catalytic to a dysfunctional state in the late 1960s is reflected in the consolidation game played by the dominant Congress Party. Congress had inherited the consensus for an inward-oriented development strategy. By the late 1960s, the consensus within Congress came undone with the 1967 hustings and the rising strength of the parties on the right. Given Congress's historical strength, they represented a poor alternative while Congress itself faced the challenge of trying to hold on to power. It did so through populist measures. In spite of a brief period of non-Congress rule from 1977 to 1980 and from 1989 to 1991, Congress was able to maintain power until 1996 when a multiparty coalition took power. But what we see in India is that the breakdown of a single party is not followed by another system able to play a stabilizing role (it is too early to tell if the BJP can play this role). The erstwhile dominant Congress in effect deinstitutionalized other parties in the country. Thus political flux and coalitional governments characteristic of India might be the rule rather than an exception for political systems undergoing transition.

Haggard and Kaufman write that for economic restructuring to succeed it must appeal to a broad constituency. The difficulties associated with constructing such broad constituencies in a country like India are the stuff of daily politics of party systems.[27] When telecommunications was made a development priority in India in 1983, it was a Congress Party prerogative. By the 1996 elections, telecommunications occupied the attention of most political parties. Telecommunications restructuring was one of the most significant restructurings in the country after the liberalization program announced in 1991. The difficulties Congress experienced in placating urban versus rural constituencies, or industrialists versus workers are reflected in the telecommunications sector. Eventually the Congress found it hard to forge the centrist strategy (which had helped it maintain power since independence) resulting in delays with restructuring initiatives. Challenges emerged from the right and left and also from parties that tried to cater to the same constituencies with the same difficulty that the Congress Party was experiencing. It is no surprise that with the coalition governments after July 1996, while on one hand the state tried to carry forth liberalization with the formation of TRAI and easing foreign investment, at the same time it dilly-dallied on the same measures to placate workers and state enterprises.

Any which way the cake is cut, in big pieces or small pieces, the story being told here is that of increasing pressures of demand. But as we have seen, "demands" have often been ignored in the telecommunication sectors of the developing world. Now these demands, in terms of liberalization and privatization, are in effect for a new set of property rights that call for examination of not just how these demands are articulated but also how they are resolved. North sums up the issue well: "When there is radical change in the formal rules that makes them inconsistent with the existing formal constraints, there is unresolved tension between them that will lead to long-run political instability."[28] The other side of our story is therefore that of supply, or in the case of telecommunications, the state that defines the denouement of the story.

The "Reality" of Supply

In development all roads lead to the castle of the state (or away from it). In the postcolonial period, development studies became preoccupied with whether the state is a good giant or a bad giant. Development studies then entered a nonjudgmental period of considerable maturity in acknowledging that a few giants were both good and bad and that while they had existed all along, we had overlooked them in history in our bipolar (good or bad) worldviews. Two trends of thought arose. One side of revisionism, of course, began with charting the "East Asian model" of state-led development and then revisited the history of industrialization where the state's role had always been obvious: the United States, Prussia and, even that most sacrosanct of market systems, Great Britain. One of the dominant strains of this thinking is the historical institutionalist tradition in political economy. Another line of thinking examined the state's role in terms of the property rights or rules and protections governing wealth creation that the state provides. Property rights beneficial to the society at large are better than those that only benefit a handful, this school argued. Britain was a success story in industrializing Europe because of such property rights.

This book synthesizes the two traditions of thought by first critiquing both schools and then preserving a few essential insights. Most reasonable development scholars and policymakers now acknowledge that the answer to development does not lie in taking either the "East Asian model" or the "models of good property rights" provision (or in imposing either of them on other countries). Neither of the models can be imposed from on above. Taken individually, too, the two models are problematic.

The "East Asian model" is a misnomer. It existed in the nineteenth century in the United States and Germany and in the twentieth, for a brief period of time, in countries like India, Brazil, and Mexico. In the current context, it is even breaking down in East Asia. We would then be better off examining the specific conditions under which such a model comes about rather than trying to impose it on other contexts. In the case of developing countries discussed here, it emerged from the postcolonial consensus conferred upon the state to effect development and the enormous capacity that the state inherited in terms of bureaucratic and material resources. Such consensuses (a form of ideological harmony) are hard to maintain in pluralistic circumstances (by extension easier under authoritarian ones, especially ones that can ensure high economic growth to "contain" demands). In countries such as India, this model came undone fairly quickly under pressures of slow economic growth and the pluralistic pressures on its somewhat democratic society. In Brazil, when it broke down, military rule stepped in. In Mexico, PRI was able to hang on to or build a broad societal consensus at least until the end of the 1980s. In East Asia, the state marginalized many societal actors and ensured very high economic returns to the chosen few who were then able to distribute them to vast sections of society (there was a lot to go around). But East Asia now is coming apart with pluralistic pressures and the breakdown of the compact between the state and the chosen few.

The property rights model teaches us that rules that introduce restraints in political systems are better than those that lead to preferential systems. But in showing how bad or good rules comes about, they treat the state as a black box responding passively to societal pressures for these rules. Such passively responding black boxes are rare indeed. Most states are a mixture of the reactive states that the property rights school assumes and the proactive state that the East Asian model posits.

The synthesis effected in this book and building upon others in this tradition, holds the special-interest–driven dysfunctional state operating in a pluralistic environment to be the most prevalent in the developing world today. But like the East Asian model, it also acknowledges that even the dysfunctional state possesses enormous resources and varying degrees of responsibility to development. In fact, in most cases, it represents a good giant gone bad. But that is only one side of the story. We must then place the giant in the jungle of demand to see how it would survive and what kind of rules it would make. Here the rational choice analysis offered by the property rights school comes in handy.

Dysfunctional states only make preferential rules if a narrow static picture is taken. In the narrow scenario, states are beholden to only a few interest groups and in the static scenario, they continue to be beholden. If this picture were true we can expect nothing more than the affluent and the powerful in developing societies to continue to be more so in the future. They have the state's ear and the state is not changing.

In a broad dynamic environment, the results just posited are difficult to obtain. No matter how dysfunctional the state, ultimately in a pluralistic environment the state must forge a broad consensus to survive. But the latter is difficult. Thus, in the past we have seen dysfunctional states in the developing world trying to enhance their legitimacy through populist rhetoric (as in India) or authoritarian rule (as in Brazil) or both (periods of such can be found in both Brazil and India). But even these measures cannot help the state survival for too long. We are in a period where neither is populist rhetoric a guarantee to holding on to power nor is authoritarian rule an option in most circumstances.

What lies in the future? One possibility is that developing countries will continue to head down the path of ungovernability and corruption. Many would argue that they are already doing so. But like the proverbial alcoholic, will these states ever hit bottom and start the road to recovery from the total degeneration of their dysfunction? This offers the other possibility. Inasmuch as a single-party system gives way to multiparty systems in the developing world, we would expect that governments may not be able to hold on to power endlessly to keep responding to special preferences alone. Such states then might move from being dysfunctional to becoming functional.

In terms of telecommunications, such pluralist pressures on states, if the latter can adequately build their maneuverability and sense of responsibility, may not be bad. For example, pluralist-pressured South Korea and Malaysia did just as well, if not better, than cohesively pressured Singapore and Mexico. While one may argue that China's cohesively pressured state is more viable than Brazil's or India's pluralist one, yet the substantiation of the claim may be more complicated.

The case may be examined in terms of India. How does the dysfunctional Indian special-interest–driven state play out its role in the pluralistic environment of telecommunications? The narrow static scenario posited above yields a state in India that seems to be doing one of the two things in responding to the two dominant special-interest–driven coalitions in the country. Its rules either benefit the pro-restructuring coalition that includes businesses, exporters, international organizations, and foreign governments; or the state responds to the inward-oriented coalition headed by the Department of Telecommunications (at least until the BJP came to power), its workers, and those businesses that continue to profit from the hangover of prior economic strategies. Either way, the broader society gets ignored.

In the wider dynamic context, other things enter the picture. Here we see a state responding at least indirectly to pressures other than those of the two coalitions noted above. In this scenario, urban and rural residential users, who comprise mass society, do not get ignored even if they come in second. Finally, in as much as the newly formed private operators cater to the society at large, it might be considered an improvement over the total degeneration of the rent-seeking dysfunctional state in India.

Quite obviously, what this analysis suggests is that instead of trying to see how dysfunctional states become catalytic (as was often done in studies during the 1980s and early 1990s) or how they may marginalize pressures (as is implicitly the case with the East Asian model), we may want to examine how dysfunctional states become functional. Catalytic states exist only in specific circumstances. So would, perhaps, functional ones if they existed in the developing world. But inasmuch as all states in developing countries may be headed toward pluralistic demands and the dilemmas that states face vis-à-vis these demands, it may be worth our while to examine the possibilities of "functional" circumstances rather than catalytic ones.[29]

Functional states, as an ideal type, approximate the conditions of catalytic states in terms of state maneuverability (including capacity) but unlike them, they are unable to marginalize certain types of pressures. Even South Korea and Malaysia, featuring plural pressures, at some point or other marginalized or blatantly repressed pressures in the polity. But it is also remarkable that in these states pluralist pressures did move them toward rapid universal service provision (in South Korea's case) and rural service provision (in Malaysia's case). In contrast, while tiny Singapore matches the experience of South Korea, Mexico fares badly. It is reported that some rural communities in Mexico have only one telephone per thousand people.[30] Similarly, it is arguable if the welfare effects of China's policies are greater than those of India's. If anything, China's policies are much more elite driven than India's. China does exhibit high growth rates, but while its state focuses on marginalizing plural pressures, India's state is being either shaped by them or, of late, seems to be moving toward accommodating them (albeit quite badly). It is hard to say if Brazil and India can become functional polities but it is perhaps even harder for them to emulate Chinese or Singapore experiments. Rebuilding state capacities and applying them toward participatory development agendas will move these states toward becoming functional. Brazil under Cardoso and India with its multiparty system are hopeful developments.

The "Reality" of Leapfrogging

The first part of this chapter charted the myths of leapfrogging. These myths can be summarized as that of supply-push technology effected by a benevolent state to usher in accelerated and efficient development. The "reality" of leapfrogging can be summarized as, first, a caution against the accelerated development scenario and, second, as an end in itself. Instead, we may note how and under what circumstances a state might respond to demand pressures directly or indirectly while constructing its legitimacy. This "reality" presents two conclusions, one limited to telecommunications and the other pertinent to development processes in general.

Table 8.3 summarizes the position of the various user groups in getting their demands met. A letter and a number in each of the cells sum-

TABLE 8.3
Provision of Telecommunication Services
According to User Group Demands and State Supply

User Group	Urban Resident. (1)	Rural Users (2)	Social Delivery Systems* (3)	Small to Medium Business (4)	Large Business Users (5)	Govt. Admn. (6)	Exporters (7)
Singapore	B3	—	B2	C3	C4	C4	C4
S. Korea	C3	B3	B2	C3	C4	C4	C4
Mexico	C3	B2	B2	C2	C3	C3	C3
Malaysia	C3	B3	B2	C2	C3	C3	C3
China	B/D2	B/D2	D1	B2	B3	B2	B3
Brazil	A2	B2	D1	A2	A2	A2	A2/3
India	A2	B2	D1	A2	A2	A3	A2
Myanmar	D1	D1	D1	D1	A2	A2	A2

* Social delivery systems include education, healthcare, and emergency services. The delivery of these services via telecommunications is still in its infancy (even in developed countries) except for emergency services.

Explanation
Micro pressures come from users listed in columns 1, 2, and 3. The weakness of these pressures is reflected in limited services available to these groups relative to other groups.
Macro coalitional pressures come from users listed in columns 4, 5, 6, and 7.

Key
A: State provides services in response predominantly to direct pressures
B: State provides services in response predominantly to indirect pressures (legitimacy consolidation)
C: State provides services in response to both direct and indirect pressures.
D: State does not respond to pressures (even where they do exist)

1: None or very scarce services
2: Limited amount of service availability
3: Service meets demand
4: Abundance of services (beyond demand), often reflecting dirigiste state supply

marize whether these groups will get any services in the first place (the number) and whether they get these services in response to their pressures, state interest in maintaining legitimacy, or both (the letter). While the schema used in the table is somewhat arbitrary and static, they nonetheless help to give the broad etchings of the likely beneficiaries and losers from the telecommunications restructurings under way in developing countries. A rating of C3 or C4, which shows that the state is not only responding to demands but considers meeting these demands to be an important part of constructing legitimacy, is still hard to find in the developing world. On the other hand, inasmuch as a dysfunctional state can move from A1 or A2 to A3, telecommunication restructuring becomes demand driven and what we may expect from a "functional" state. In fact, the rankings obtained in catalytic and near-catalytic states in terms of service provision (C3, C4), however attractive they may be, are not inherently superior in terms of the arguments made in this book. They come about in specific circumstances and, over time, are difficult to maintain politically. The high service provision ratings given to user-groups listed from columns 4–7 also reflect the privileged position of these groups in terms of their access to the state and their ability to form coalitions. Similarly, urban users tend to do better than rural user-groups because of the former's ability to influence the state.

There is also a broader lesson to be learned from this book's explorations. The beneficiaries and losers in the development process depend on the restraints on the state to cater to external (demand) pressures rather than its own agenda alone. The ideal of the story here is "functional pluralistic pressure driven state." In other words, a black box with few internal preferences but a functioning one! When a state is dysfunctional or special-interest driven, rent-seeking or preferential treatment inevitably result.

The argument about constraints being made here fits squarely into the findings of recent works in political economy. Political scientists like Haggard and Kaufman, concerned with democratic and economic consolidation, conclude that either of these consolidations is difficult without strong economic performance and the constraint upon this performance to appeal to a broad constituency. The ability of party systems to exercise these constraints are central to such analyses. Economists like Bhagwati similarly note, in giving importance to the right type of governance, that empirically markets combined with democracy have more broad-based welfare effects than those under authoritarianism.[31] The World Bank, for long a hotbed of casting states as bad giants, now writes of the "effective state" and reinvigorating the state's role in development. An effective state is not just a capable state (one with vast resources) but one that "is a result of using that capability to meet society's demand for those goods. A state may be capable but not very effective if its capability is not used in society's interest."[32] Again, a story of restraint and not very different from the one told in this book in terms of state maneuverability (its capability and autonomy) and responsibility (its effectiveness in meeting societal agenda).

The "value added" of this book lies not just in replicating the research agenda reflected in other studies such as the three just mentioned but in fine-tuning and expanding on this research agenda by the following means. First, this book shows how this research agenda may be applied to particular sectors, in this case telecommunications. Second, so as not to make the story of telecommunications self-involved, it tries to show how to delineate the interlinkages between telecommunications restructurings and other statewide restructurings under way in economies. Third, it refines the categories of state types and pressures upon the state. To say that such types of refinements do not matter would be like noting that the only thing worth learning in development is that states can be effective some of the time. As this and other studies are trying to argue, there is still a lot of work to be done in terms of the varied historical institutionalist contexts in which these "effective" or "functional" states might arise. But we must all start with the "plural" pressures that these states are increasingly facing in their societies.

This is not the first book to speak of constraints in terms of telecommunications. It in fact concurs with the specific conclusions offered in terms of restraint by a recent study of telecommunications. An edited book by Levy and Spiller shows that the extent to which the emerging rules ("regulatory design") in developing countries will bring about enhanced investment and efficiency in telecommunications will depend upon the degree to which governing institutions ("regulatory governance") of a country are constrained in their authority in enforcing these rules so that enforcement does not result in rent-seeking or expropriation on the part of the government.[33] But, whereas the Levy and Spiller book uses institutional economics to provide a picture of the supply of "regulatory design," this book presents a somewhat less technical but broader study of telecommunications restructuring in terms of both demand and supply.

Finally, this book as well as the other studies mentioned above are part of another burgeoning tradition in political economy that, instead of holding the state-defined "public" and socially defined "private" spheres of activity to be mutually exclusive (as in neoliberal traditions) or the same (as in radical Marxian or scholarship), now explores contexts in which the two might work more cooperatively to the benefit of societies.

One of these arenas of research is civil society–state relations. Debates on telecommunications are not only a part of formal political processes like the emergence of interest groups and their coalitions or the construction of such coalitions by party systems in the country, but also that of the interplay of civil society and states. This feature was not directly addressed in this book but nonetheless offers the story of perhaps the broadest and the most abstract of political-economic groupings in any country. Civil society in its traditional definition conveyed the ability of society to participate in governing processes through informal networks, solving of common problems, and building a level of social trust and mutual support.[34] Now foci on civil society are increasingly showcasing the grassroots activism among any country's societal groups and their synergy or conflict with other governing processes such as the state. In as much as these groups involve themselves in the formal or informal governing processes in these countries, they are part of the common problem-solving and social-trust aspects of civil society that the traditional definitions attended to. They in fact modify our views of economic restructuring's being an elite process only.

Current work on civil society and development has focused on contexts under which civil society threatens the state, complements its role, or works independently of it. The relationships between state and civil society in fact "allow us to asses the extent to which state involvement facilitates developmentally effective collective action by common citizens in a diverse collection of settings around the globe (both in the Third World or in what used to be called the Second World)."[35]

The interplay between civil society and the state is directly relevant to the case of telecommunications restructurings in examining the extent to which the latter will involve and benefit the society at large. Unfortunately, telecommunications restructurings in developing countries have been too elite driven so far to document civil society involvement effectively. That does not mean either that counter examples do not exist or that the trend is not changing. The provision of telecommunications services to the society at large in countries like South Korea and Singapore, the demands for telecommunications services in rural areas of India or Malaysia, and, in general, the construction of state legitimacy in the emerging democratic societies of the developing world provide examples of civil society–state conflicts and synergy. In as much as this book shows how these scenarios come about, it may help in furthering refining research on civil society (or vice versa in showing how civil society may help us better explain many of the restructuring initiatives).[36]

I now return to the quote from *Lady Chatterly's Lover* offered at the beginning of this book. A general reading of the quote conveys a sense of the remarkable ingenuity of technological progress. A closer inspection reveals the importance of "the souls in Plato riding up to heaven in a two-horse chariot."[37] Plato tells us in *Phaedrus* that "the ruling power in us men drives a pair of horses, and next that one of these horses is fine and good and of noble stock, and the other the opposite in every way."[38] Plato is here dividing the soul into three elements: the charioteer motivated by love (which is a deeper love here for humans or maybe even family or polis) and the two horses, one motivated by reason and the other by appetite (passion). The white steed "needs no whip" and is driven by "word of command" (reason). But the black steed is "hardly controllable even with whip and goad."[39] An able charioteer (filled with love) must hold the two in balance. We are still trying to find out what makes for an effective charioteer. Unfortunately for the developing world, there are no Fords or Rolls Royces or engines and gas to avoid the difficulty of holding the steeds in balance. Only an effective or functional charioteer can leapfrog to heaven.

NOTES

CHAPTER 1. INTRODUCTION

1. The book focuses primarily on a few important policy/regulatory initiatives including liberalization, privatization, and enhanced service provision initiatives and the attendant organizational changes that accompany these initiatives. While they are crucial issues, they do not exhaust the number of telecommunication restructuring initiatives underway in the developing world.

2. Pierce and Jacquier (1983), p. 19.

3. The focus in this book on demand instruments followed by supply measures to examine restructuring sequencing is consistent with conditions approaching general equilibrium analysis in neoclassical political economy. Capricious restructurings deviate from general equilibrium calculus.

4. Stages of growth argument go back to Rostow (1960), who postulated that economies go through specific stages from the feudal to the industrial age with a short "take-off" stage lasting two to three decades propelling developing societies into industrialization. For its use in the leapfrogging sense, see Karunaratne (1982), p. 212.

5. The idea of accelerating the pace of development through newer technologies and state-led mechanisms goes back to Gerschenkron (1962). For its application in telecommunication literature, see Bruce (1989), p. 45.

6. See Nulty (1989), p. 10; Fredebeul-Krein and Freytag (1997), p. 478.

7. Soete (1985).

8. Deibert (1997); Sapolsky et al. (1992); Pool (1990); Bar (1990); Beniger (1986); Williamson (1985); Pavlic and Hamelink (1985); Rogers (1983); Simon (1982); Nora and Minc (1980); Arrow (1979); Porat (1977); Bell (1973).

9. In economics, Machlup (1962) was the first to write of an "information society" in which, according to him, the rate of growth of the information sector in the U.S. was more than double the rate of growth of GNP.

10. Stone (1991); Saunders et al. (1994).

11. Schmandt et al. (1991); Parker (1989); ITU (1984); ITU (1983); Hudson et al. (1979).

12. DRI/McGraw Hill (1991); Saunders et al. (1983). Forward linkages induce investments by making an input (output) available for later stages of production, while backward linkages come from inducing investments in industries that supply the output (input) to the industry in question.

13. Mueller (1993), p. 156, similarly notes that the "argument that telecommunications 'causes' growth is based on a huge oversimplification of the statistical correlation" and that "in reality the efficiency contributions of

telecommunications investments and usage depend entirely on where and how they are made."

14. Clubs can be run by a variety of institutional arrangements; state-run clubs are one of them. Sandler and Tschirhart (1980), p. 1497.

15. Olson (1982) and Olson (1965).

16. For references on historical institutionalism, see chapter 2.

17. Olson (1990) himself comes close to proposing a synthesis of the two traditions.

18. Olson (1982), pp. 47–48.

19. Sandler (1992), p. 64.

20. The point is acknowledged by Olson in a footnote. Olson (1982), p. 247. "A measure that would reduce economic efficiency if introduced in a Pareto-efficient society could conceivably increase efficiency in a society with prior distortions." Apart from this footnote, Olson's analysis assumes Pareto-efficient societies.

21. The intent to tie in micro-level club demands with macro processes also follows Kindleberger's caveat about this oft-ignored element in theories of group behavior, which, he writes, "must include not only criteria for differentiating the responses of national groups as a unit, but also a system of analysis for interrelationships among the sub groups within the larger unit." Kindleberger (1978), pp. 30–31.

22. The term "incentives" is used here in the general sense of factors prodding groups toward an outcome rather than the specific Olsonian usage of consciously designed mechanisms for collective action. This issue is discussed by Lichbach (1994).

23. For an excellent example of the decline of Keynesianism in the context of a developed country, but relevant for LDCs, see Hall (1989).

24. Biersteker (1995).

25. Aronson and Cowhey (1988), p. 73. Technology also allows for divisibility of goods, which in turn allows for market provision. Sutter (1996), p. 135.

26. Belassa (1989), p. 172.

27. For an important book on the role played by economic crises in the shift toward market economies and democratization, see Haggard and Kaufman (1995).

28. Waterbury (1992), p. 191.

29. Saunders et al. (1994), p.5.

30. Studies from World Bank are seminal in citing the multiple influences for this restructuring. Wellenius and Stern, eds. (1994).

31. There are, however, enough studies that only emphasize particular conditions (economics, technology, or ideas). For references, see chapter 2.

32. A recent study by Levy and Spiller (1996) commissioned by the World Bank in fact concludes that unless the institutional conditions are right, telecommunications privatization efforts will result in failure. Evans (1995) argues that the current "third wave" thinking on the state's role in development follows the earlier periods of postcolonial optimism followed by disenchantment about the state's role.

33. Quite obviously, this borrows from what is known as the method of structured focused comparison and the comparative historical method. For a delineation of this method, see George (1979), Smith (1981), pp. 11–12, and Skocpol (1985), pp. 348–50.

34. George (1979), p. 55.

35. Eckstein (1975), p. 111.

36. The distinction between case and observations is made convincingly by King, Keohane, and Verba (1994), p. 218. They note that, "It may be possible within a single conventionally labeled 'case study' to observe many separate implications of our theory. Indeed, a single case often involves multiple measures of the key variables; hence by definition it contains multiple observations."

37. Indeed, most of the cases chosen in a recent authoritative study of such transitions fit this particular mold. See Haggard and Kaufman (1995). They conclude: "The reconstruction of the state and the formulation of a coherent growth strategy under democratic auspices ultimately hinges on whether political institutions allow for effective management of a market economy while remaining accountable to the interests and aspirations of competing social and economic interests" (p. 310).

38. Eckstein (1975), pp. 111–12.

39. Telephony (Jan. 1992). India has the fourth highest expenditure after Taiwan, Mexico, and South Korea if newly industrializing countries are included.

40. King, Keohane, and Verba (1994), pp. 3–7. The earliest endorsement of the method came from Bruce Russet. George (1979), p. 61, also notes that researchers should "move back and forth between intensive analyses of one or a few case studies to quantitative (and less intensive) analysis of a large number of cases."

41. Kindleberger (1978), p. 57.

42. Chaudhry (1994), p. 4.

43. *The Wall Street Journal* (February 13, 1995), p. A1.

44. Mansell (1996), p. 5, writes that "the ways in which users have become directly and actively involved in complex process of technical and institutional change are largely ignored in the literature on the impact of information and communication technologies." Exceptions to this include Cowhey (1990), Noam (1992), and Mansell (1993).

CHAPTER 2. THE ARGUMENT EXPLAINED

1. It is hard to separate the three influences noted here. Thus, for example, globalization is intricately tied with technology and liberal ideas. The separation effected here for analytical purposes thus must suffer from simplification and repetition at times.

2. The economic underpinnings of ISI strategy were simple: domestic markets with a large import element were identified by the state and protection was afforded to domestic manufacturers. Where the economies of scale were large (as in telecommunications) and private capital was not forthcoming, the state itself

stepped in as a producer. All this necessitated (and was driven by) some degree of central planning.

3. This is the period dubbed by Hirschman as an "eminently exciting era in development economics" in which one economic model after another showed how the "dragon of backwardness" could be slain. Late industrialization and rural underemployment were seen as the two major development obstacles. Hirschman (1981), p. 1.

4. Saunders (1994), p. 5.

5. Schramm (1964). Other well-known early writers to emphasize the links between communication and development include Lerner (1958) and McLuhan (1964).

6. Streeten (1982), O'Brien (1983), ITU (1984), Mowlana (1985), Mowlana (1986/1997).

7. The Declaration of Establishment of NIEO was formally adopted by the UN General Assembly in 1974. It grew from the LDCs' perceived need to alter the terms of trade, which were seen as inimical to their interests (the Prebisch-Singer thesis), which spilled over into other economic and related concerns. These objectives, LDCs argued, could be met only through better control over their own productive assets and the national and international norms that governed trading. For provocative discussions of the debates surrounding NIEO, see Bhagwati (1977), Brandt (1980), and Amin (1976). For a critique of NIEO, see Krasner (1985).

8. Quoted in Pavlic and Hamelink (1985), p. 22.

9. The authors in O'Brien (1983) sum up these arguments.

10. Pavlic and Hamelink (1983).

11. On a more general level in communications, this is reflected in the writings of Streeten (1982), Galtung (1982), and Mowlana (1990). Pitroda (1976) argued that a creation of a Technology Development Center in developing countries could go a long way toward making these countries self-reliant while making sure that technology remains labor intensive and sensitive to the shortage of capital. Some of these types of concerns are also addressed by Okundi (1975) and Mody (1989).

12. Mowlana (1990), p. 60.

13. This case is also supported by Braman (1993), p. 136. She writes: "Calls for a New World Information Order—based on the insight that redistribution of global economic resources would not come into being without a redistribution of global information flows—demonstrated that a generalized consciousness of the centrality of information to society was already felt beyond the Western industrialized world. By the late 1980s, the example of newly industrializing countries (NICs) such as Singapore demonstrated the one route to economic success for developing nations was through participation in the information economy."

14. See Saunders et al. (1994). The first edition of this book came out in 1983 summing up studies in telecommunications and development until then.

15. ITU (1984).

16. Estimates of economic rates of return vary between 17 and 50 percent and averaging about 17 percent. The World Bank also estimated internal financial

rates of return on 13 projects in telecommunications it funded as ranging between 13 and 25 percent and averaging 20 percent. The projects were able to draw internally upon 60 percent of the funds needed. Saunders et al. (1994), p. 15.

17. An ITU report cited in Saunders et al. (1994), p. 21.

18. Vernon (1990). Import substitution by itself called for either imports of technology or development of such technology indigenously. The former led to foreign exchange shortages, unwillingness by technology owners to transfer it, and finally, foreign debt. Trying to develop technology indigenously led to its underdevelopment, scarcities, high costs, and, often, inflation.

19. Chowdary noted that "it is increasingly recognized that there are disadvantages in having telecommunications services provided by government. The disadvantages relate to the financing, pricing, development and regulation of these services." He wrote that while it is difficult for governments to invest in telecommunications from their limited financial resources "if, however, these providers were non-government corporations, they would have much more freedom, for example, to market shares and bonds." Chowdary (1989), p. 107.

20. Belassa (1989).

21. Belassa (1989), p. 176.

22. The World Bank (1997), pp. 236–37.

23. Aronson and Cowhey (1988), p. 5.

24. Keohane and Nye (1977), p. 18.

25. The positing of efficiency here is more than just an academic exercise. Information flows (as argued in chapter 1) are crucial for any economic transaction to take place and in this sense a well-functioning telecommunications infrastructure reduces transaction costs by eliminating the barriers to information flows.

26. See Belassa (1989); Bhagwati (1977); Bhagwati and Srinivasan (1975); Bhagwati and Desai (1970). Multilateral organizations such as IBRD and IMF have also long championed this strategy. For an emphatic endorsement, see World Bank (1991).

27. As such, it begs the question asked by Haggard: "If neoclassical policies are superior, why are they so infrequently adopted?" See Haggard (1990), p. 9.

28. Many of these changes have themselves come about as a result of the revolutions in technologies that will be discussed later as part of the "ideas and technology" explanation.

29. The international division of labor is noted by any standard text in international political economy. For its application in terms of post-Fordism, especially in the context of telecommunications, see various articles in *Journal of Communication* (1995).

30. Stallings (1995), p. 8.

31. Tyson and Castells (1988), p. 57.

32. Tyson (1992); Tyson and Zysman (1983). Mody (1989) writes specifically of niche markets.

33. Ohmae (1985). The launching of Microsoft Windows 95 is a well-known example.

34. Gereffi (1995), p. 113.

35. Aaron (1995).

36. This is not the same as the debate among the international relations theorists versus neoclassical economists, which is along descriptive versus prescriptive grounds. Here, both dimensions are descriptive albeit with reference to different variables.

37. See Comor (1994) for neo-Marxist arguments, McDowell (1997) for social constructivist arguments, Krasner (1991) and Waltz (1978) for neorealist arguments, and Sandholtz (1992) and Cowhey (1990) for neoliberal arguments.

38. Krasner (1991).

39. Keohane and Nye (1977). For application of this argument to North-South bargaining, see Singh (forthcoming a and b).

40. Cowhey (1990), p. 198. Cowhey's analysis includes the role played by domestic actors, ideas, and technology in the creation and maintenance of international regimes. As such, it traverses more than one category of analysis in this section. It is placed under the globalization of markets here only for pedagogical purposes.

41. Large users "typically, less than 5 percent of all users constitute over half of the long distance traffic and about one-fifth of local traffic." Cowhey (1990), p. 187.

42. Woodrow (1991) has even argued that although the ITU was initially opposed to regime range, it eventually came round to it (especially after Pekka Tarjanne took over as secretary-general in late 1989) and was thus not so opposed to it as Cowhey (1990) makes it out to be.

43. It is because of the focus on domestic restructurings that the jargon of "regime theory" as expounded by international relations scholars is avoided here. Instead, the globalization analysis just presented abstracts from regime theory approach that, in a now famous definition, posits regimes as "principles, norms, rules and decision-making procedures around which actor expectations converge." Krasner (1985), p. 4. The relationship between domestic and international factors remains important in international relations as a whole and regime theory in particular. This book's analysis, centered around state supply of restructuring initiatives, focuses on domestic changes (while taking international influences into account). As such, the analysis here is not overly concerned with the domestic sources of international change (see Putnam [1988], Keohane and Milner [1996], and Milner [1997] for this) but does pay attention to the international sources of domestic change. See Gourevitch (1985).

44. The approach I have taken here is consistent with Strange's assertion that we can capture the dynamic character of "who-gets-what" of an international economy "by looking not at the surface but underneath, at the bargains on which it is based." See Strange (1982), p. 496.

45. For an excellent example of the decline of Keynesianism in the context of a developed country, see Hall (1992).

46. Zacher with Sutton (1996), p. 11.

47. Saunders et al. (1983).

48. Wellenius et al. (1993). Other documents from The World Bank that are consistent with these goals include Saunders et al. (1983/1994); Ambrose et al. (1990); and Ivanek et al. (1991).

49. This author remembers discussing telecommunication policy options with a senior telecom official in New Delhi in 1990 and showing him a chart of various telecommunication sector options out of Aronson & Cowhey (1989). The official noted how his agency had been involved in collecting precisely the type of information that I was showing him and proceeded to get photocopies made of the chart.

50. Kahler (1990), p. 59.

51. Biersteker (1995), pp. 183–84.

52. Cowhey (1990), p. 199.

53. Rogers (1983), p. 10.

54. Biersteker (1995), p. 185.

55. Elihu Katz quoted in Rogers (1983), p. 25.

56. Altschuler (1992).

57. In India, for example, ideas of neoclassical economists such as Bhagwati, Belassa, Desai, and Srinivasan have for three decades asked for a move away from an ISI strategy but were an anathema among the planners until recently.

58. Olson (1982), p. 62. Socioeconomic contexts work similarly. It is thus no coincidence that in the 1930s, it was Keynes and not Schumpeter who found a ready audience. Even though Schumpeter's theory was more encompassing, it was Keynes who directly addressed himself to saving capitalism from the ravages of the Great Depression.

59. Aronson and Cowhey (1988), p. 73.

60. Noam (1989).

61. Nora and Minc (1980).

62. Cowhey (1990), pp. 183–84. Nonexistence of natural monopoly does not mean that economies of scale do not exist either. The issue of economies of scale extends beyond the natural monopoly issue. It implies that a strict general equilibrium situation in which supply and demand equal each other is difficult to obtain in telecommunications. Falling average or marginal costs make it difficult to derive optimal demand and supply results as well as making marginal cost pricing difficult. With advances in digital switching and fiber optics etc. enabling over 100,000 lines to be provided from a single switch, one might even expect situations where installed capacity will outpace demand. Thus, the difficulty of economies of scale and marginal pricing thereof calls for institutional intervention in telecommunications pricing.

63. Landes (1980), p. 115. As Landes states, this is not a theory of invention but of production even if it sounds similar. "Necessity may be the mother of invention, especially if backed by money, but there is no substitute for the kind of environment that generates novelty" (p. 114). For a fuller treatment of this subject, see Landes (1969).

64. There are very few available sources that treat telecommunications as a club-good. The best known is Noam (1992)

65. Buchanan (1965). Other examples of club-goods include political coalitions, international alliances and cartels, common markets, supranational organizations, all of which can exclude nonmembers from benefits.

66. See Sutter (1996), p. 135.

67. A classic statement of telecommunications as a public-good is provided by Leff (1984).

68. At a broader level, Hirschman's critiques why the government should not try to internalize externalities (as would be the case by characterizing telecommunications as a public good) in infrastructural provision. See Hirschman (1958), pp. 55–61.

69. Nonetheless, advocacy of telecommunications as a public-good continues in order to obtain public subsidies. Saunders et al. (1994), p. 170.

70. The World Bank (1994), p. 25; Saunders et al. (1994).

71. Zacher notes that in the past "any self-respecting nation owned and controlled its air transport, telecommunications, and postal industries." Zacher with Sutton (1996), p. 220.

72. Aronson and Cowhey (1989).

73. Sandler (1992); Sandler and Tschirhart (1982); Sutter (1996). Increasing returns flow from the high fixed cost needed for installation of network with relatively low cost for adding members to the network up to a certain point.

74. The impact of heterogeneous user needs on telecommunication service provision is also acknowledged by Mansell (1993).

75. Telecommunication service tariffs, because of problems associated with calculating costs due to increasing returns, have evolved historically in most places often making it difficult to "unbundle" its components. Many countries, however, allowed for rate or return regulation allowing for prefixed returns over cost. This practice encouraged cost inefficiencies (a practice known as "gold plating"). British Telecom moved toward a more inefficient pricing scheme in 1982 with what came to be known as price cap regulation, which allowed for prices to rise every year in accordance with a price index after accounting for technological inefficiencies with a factor fixed by the regulator (Price increase = price index – technological efficiency factor X). Marginal cost pricing, considered the most efficient by neoclassical economics, is difficult in telecommunications because of the difficulty attached with unbundling, economies of scale, and political pressures.

76. Noam (1992) and Mansell (1993) reach similar conclusions.

77. Duch (1991), p. 28.

78. "Alliance valence" of groups stands for their "propensity to form alliances with other groups to support particular policies." Gourevitch (1986), p. 159.

79. Statements like the following are now increasingly noticeable. *The New York Times* quotes a successful entrepreneur as saying: "Every country needs two things to develop economically: transportation and communications. . . . [C]ommunication is not a luxury in emerging markets; it is a necessity." See *The New York Times* (January 5, 1997), p. 3:1. Or consider the following: "'You can't develop a market economy and attract foreign investors,' said a prominent reformer in Czechoslovakia, 'if you can't get a telephone call through or receive a fax.'" Quoted in Crawford (1991), p. 1.

80. Migdal (1994).

81. Haggard (1990), p. 34.

82. North (1994), p. 361. We could, however, expect efficient outcomes in

more democratic contexts. See Wittman (1995). Most LDCs do not approximate Wittman's scenario.

83. These analyses also continually resort to behavioral and historical variables in explaining outcomes. For a good example of old institutionalist analysis in telecommunications see Cowhey (1994).

84. For a telecommunications study involving the U.K's pluralist institutions and France's statism and Germany's corporatism, see Duch (1991).

85. Haggard (1990), for example, shows that inward-oriented development strategies in Latin America did not necessarily result from authoritarian rule.

86. Relevant representative works include, Haggard and Kaufman (1995); Evans (1995); Steinmo et al. (1995); Haggard and Kaufman, eds. (1992); Haggard (1990); Evans et al. (1985).

87. The behavioral underpinnings of group preferences and institutional development, are now, in fact, getting increasingly emphasized. See North (1990), ch. 3; Ostrom (1998).

88. Kohli (1994) traces the origins of the South Korean "developmentalist" state to the Japanese occupation of the country (1905–45) and the consolidation of administrative control under the Yi dynasty prior to Japanese occupation. Haggard (1990), p. 4, notes the following: "The State is not only an actor but a set of institutions that exhibit continuity over time."

89. Bratton (1994) notes that state autonomy and capacity must be analyzed distinctly and that the temptation by many writers is to compact both. The use of state capacity for maintaining maneuverability versus fulfilling development objectives helps to preserve this distinction in this book.

90. Feigenbaum and Henig write of state responsibility in a narrow sense as "de facto assignment of responsibility as determined by public values and expectations as well as formal legal definition." See Feigenbaum and Henig (1994), p. 208. Haggard and Kaufman (1995), pp. 269–71, are writing of something similar to my concept of state responsibility when they refer to the development orientation of the state.

91. White, ed. (1988).

92. The concept of "embedded autonomy" is developed by Evans (1995).

93. Migdal, Kohli, and Shue, eds. (1994) provide an excellent introduction to state-society relations in LDCs.

94. The terminology is consistent with Olson (1993). North also writes of a predatory state as one not based on social contract, but it is not clear in his conception why such a state would undertake development-oriented tasks. See North (1981), chapter 3. The answer is provided by Olson (1993), who shows that even autocrats might have an encompassing interest in providing public goods if only to maximize their revenues and taxes. Thus, in the conception given here, a special interest–dominated state, as opposed to a predatory state, can act responsibly depending on historical and revenue maximization factors.

95. The concepts of "windows of opportunity" and "change teams" were first developed by Waterbury (1992) in his discussion of the Mexican economic crises in the 1980s that allowed the Salinas administration to bring in a change team of technocrats to reorient the economy. Haggard and Kaufman (1995) use

these concepts to explain policy changes initiated by governments undergoing dual transitions toward political and economic liberalizations.

96. Kohli notes in a similar vein: "The irony of India's political-economic situation is tragic: The state is highly centralized and omnipresent, but the leverage of its leaders to initiate meaningful change has diminished." Kohli (1990), p. 16.

97. For a case study on how governments use telecommunications restructuring to consolidate power, see Mody (1995).

98. This does not mean that states enjoy a high degree of legitimacy (ranging from none in Myanmar to relatively high in Malaysia) or that they are not responsive to a diversity of pressures beyond telecommunications. Cohesive pressures, once unbundled, might actually reveal a variety of pressures.

99. Haggard and Kaufman (1995), p. 311.

100. The "encompassing interest" of an autocratic state in improving economic productivity is acknowledged by Olson (1993), although he also notes that these regimes have uncertain rules and structure governing transition of rulers, and thus the rulers' interest in productive measures seldom lasts beyond a generation. This last point, while casting a shadow upon the states termed catalytic and near-catalytic in this book, is nonetheless consistent with their overwhelming interest in development. It remains to be seen if South Korea, Singapore, Malaysia, and Mexico, beridden with political succession problems, will continue their economic policies beyond a generation.

CHAPTER 3. TELECOMMUNICATIONS RESTRUCTURING IN CATALYTIC AND NEAR-CATALYTIC STATES

1. Haggard (1990), pp. 102–103. The political economy of the Singapore state given here mostly follows Haggard's analysis.

2. Haggard (1990), p. 110.

3. The World Bank (1997), p. 96.

4. Haggard (1990), p. 115.

5. Singapore is different from the other cases described in this chapter where only two phases may be observed. This is a result of Singapore's making telecommunications a priority back in the early 1970s, allowing the country's telecommunications infrastructure more than twenty-five years of restructuring.

6. Telephone service started in 1879, and until 1955 it was run by the Oriental Telephone and Electric Company (OTEC), which catered mostly to the British trading interests. From 1955 until 1974, the domestic service was provided by the Singapore Telephone Board and international service by Telecommunication Authority of Singapore when the two were merged into TAS, which after 1989 came to be known as Singapore Telecom.

7. Interview, Singapore Telecom official, July 1995.

8. Kuo (1994), pp. 278–79.

9. Sisodia (1992).

10. Singapore Telecom (May 25, 1995).

11. Bruce and Cunard (1994), p. 207.

12. Euromoney (April 1993).

13. Interviews.

14. *Asiaweek* (May 16, 1997); *Communications International* (June 1997).

15. *The Wall Street Journal* (May 12, 1995).

16. Bruce and Cunard (1994), p. 207.

17. *The Wall Street Journal* (June 30, 1998), p. A15.

18. *Communications International* (July 1998), p. 18.

19. Sisodia (1992), p. 48.

20. *The Guardian* (December 12, 1994).

21. Kohli (1994); Evans (1995).

22. Haggard (1990).

23. The World Bank (1993), pp. 221, 245. During the next decade (1980–90), South Korean growth rates for industry and merchandise exports were 12.2 and 12.8 percent respectively (ibid.).

24. Hahn and Plein (1995).

25. Mody (1989).

26. Haggard and Kaufman (1995), pp. 83–84.

27. Larson (1995), p. 11.

28. UNDP (1996), p. 176.

29. Kim, Kim, and Yoon (1992), p. 1,830.

30. Sung (1994), p. 309. This may be a conservative estimate. Larson (1995), p. 40, quotes a study noting that it took only the top ten *chaebol* to account for 50 percent of the GNP in 1977 and it took the top five to do the same in 1984. *The Wall Street Journal* (November 24, 1997) noted that one third of the country's wealth lay with the top 30 *chaebol*.

31. Choo and Kang (1994), p. 300–301.

32. Larson (1995), p. 8.

33. Hahn and Plein (1995), pp. 57–58.

34. Quoted in Choo and Kang (1994), p. 299.

35. Choo and Kang (1994), p. 289.

36. Sung (1994), p. 304.

37. *The Wall Street Journal* (September 30, 1997), p. A16.

38. Quoted in Choo and Kang (1994), p. 295.

39. Larson (1995), p. 36.

40. Choo and Kang (1994), pp. 292–95

41. Quoted in *The Economist* (June 10, 1995), p. 35.

42. Haggard and Kaufman (1995), p. 239.

43. Kim and Ro (1993), p. 483.

44. Cho and Huh (1994), p. 250.

45. Ibid., p. 247.

46. Larson (1995), pp. 199–200.

47. Individual share holdings after 2001 will be limited to 3 percent in KT, 10 percent in other wireline services, and 33 percent in wireless after 2001.

48. *Business Korea* (March 1997), pp. 26–27.

49. *The Wall Street Journal* (February 25, 1998), p. A 14.

50. *The Wall Street Journal* (July 31, 1998), p. A9.

51. This section draws upon the following sources for the overall Mexican

political situation: Haggard (1990); and Haggard and Kaufman (1995).

52. Haggard and Kaufman concede a similar point in noting why the state did not act predatorily. See Haggard and Kaufman (1995), p. 269.

53. Waterbury (1992).

54. The World Bank (1997), p. 63.

55. This historical sketch draws from Petrazzini (1995), chapter 5.

56. Szekely (1989).

57. Wellenius (1994), p. 120; Mendoza (1989), p. 94.

58. Cowhey (1994), p. 556.

59. *The Wall Street Journal* (May 14, 1998), p. A17.

60. Glover and Lotvedt (1997), p. 25.

61. Wellenius and Staple (1996), p. 16.

62. *The Wall Street Journal* (June 17, 1996), p. A11.

63. Wellenius and Staple (1996), p. 5.

64. Figure quoted from *The Wall Street Journal* (January 7, 1997), p. A8.

65. *The Wall Street Journal* (May 14, 1998), p. A17. The government-owned satellite provider, SatMex, was sold for $554 million in 1997 and the radio spectrum was auctioned for $1 billion in 1998.

66. Monterrey, Guadalajara, and Mexico City, along with a few *maquiladoras*, boast of the best telecommunication services in the country. Venable (June 1996), p. 573.

67. *The New York Times*, (January 1997) and *The Journal of Commerce* (October 13, 1993).

68. Bell Atlantic took over management control of the firm in February 1997, which was widely interpreted as a new era for U.S.-based firms that would no longer require domestic partnerships with Mexican firms in order to do business. *The Wall Street Journal* (November 17, 1997), p. A23.

69. Landa (1997) documents well the various incumbent tactics used by Telmex (and regulators thereof) to forestall liberalization.

70. Rowney (January 28, 1998); Rowney (February 17, 1998); Moats (February 6, 1998); Moats (February 17, 1998).

71. *The Wall Street Journal* (July 16, 1998), p. A12.

72. This point only relates to the weakened ability of the state to play a dirigiste role and not to advocate a role for comprehensive planning. The ability of the markets to work effectively with or without the state will be debated in the concluding chapter.

73. *The Wall Street Journal* (November 3, 1998), p. A14.

74. *The Wall Street Journal* (November 14, 1997), p. A19. President Ernesto Zedillo is quoted in the article as saying: "We are now on the learning curve of democracy. As in any democracy, there will be moments of danger and controversy, but I think one should be fundamentally optimistic about the final result."

75. Nantha (1995), p. 66. In the decade following the Second World War, the British rebuilt the telecommunications infrastructure destroyed by Japanese occupation resulting in Malaysia's possessing a technologically up to date infrastructure when it got independence (ibid.).

76. Sundaram (1993), pp. 555–57.

77. Malaysia's population is over 20 million, of which about 55 percent is Malay, 34 percent ethnic Chinese, and the rest ethnic Indian.

78. Haggard and Kaufman (1995), p. 358.

79. Jesudason (1995), p. 327.

80. The World Bank (1997), p. 113.

81. Jesudason (1995), p. 348.

82. National security was another concern behind investing in SEACOM. The cable links improved communications between peninsular Malaysia and Malaysian territories in Northern Borneo (Sabah and Sarawak). Of direct threat was Indonesia, which opposed the formation of the federation of Malaysia. Onn (1994), pp. 138–39.

83. Lim (1995), p. 256.

84. The World Bank (1997), p. 231.

85. Telekom Malaysia Berhad (1995), pp. 34–36 (operational review)

86. Onn (1994), p. 143.

87. The policy emulation is noted by most observers of Malaysian telecommunications. See, for example, Lowe (1994), p. 119–20 and Petrazzini (1995), p. 144. The London-based consulting firm hired by the government for advice had been involved with privatization of British Telecom under Thatcher. Other policy emulations frequently noted in Malaysian context include justifying the role of the state along the lines of Japanese government involvement and the later tilt toward copying the U.S. policies in many matters. U.S. firms are significant investors in Malaysia and the number of U.S. consultants advising top officials is on the rise. Most top positions in the government are occupied by officials trained in U.S. universities. Based on interviews and disparate sources.

88. Interviews and Mohamad (1994) and Isahak (1989).

89. Interview.

90. Interview.

91. Interview.

92. This does not mean that privatization went smoothly. The country's ethnic Indian minister for energy, telecommunications, and posts who headed Telekom Malaysia's privatization effort came under investigation in 1992 for offering 9 million shares to three companies owned by other ethnic Indians. *Far Eastern Economic Review* (July 16, 1992), p. 56.

93. *Far Eastern Economic Review* (June 15, 1995), p. 64.

94. *Far Eastern Economic Review* (June 15, 1995), p. 65.

95. Interview.

96. *The Wall Street Journal* (June 10, 1997), p. A1.

97. Interview.

98. Malaysian officials downplay Singapore's experience with infrastructural development by noting that it is limited to a small city-state. Interviews.

99. Another study comparing telecommunications in these two countries holds them to be essentially similar by focusing on similar state types, though overlooking the differences in societal pressures. See Petrazzini (1995), p. 145.

100. *The Wall Street Journal* (April 23, 1998, and July 14, 1998).

101. However, as the financial crisis grew, Mahathir Mohamad also noted the "subsidy mentality" of businesses that he noted threatened to unravel social

policies. Quoted in *The Wall Street Journal* (April 23, 1998), p. A15.

102. The populist rhetoric pertained to blaming its economic crisis on international (Western) influences. Interestingly, the Malaysian state while quite open to MNCs, regularly uses "inimical Western influences" trumpcard (or its counterpart "the Asian model") to shore up its political position at home or in providing a rationale for containing political dissent.

CHAPTER 4. TELECOMMUNICATIONS RESTRUCTURING IN DYSFUNCTIONAL AND PREDATORY STATES

1. Olson (1993) makes a similar point about such states aiding development efforts within the bounds of the construction of their legitimacy.

2. Braudel (1993), p. 215. In fact the British administrative system was based on the Chinese mandarin system. Wittfogel, now considerably debunked for his once popular thesis about the need for large bureaucracies to build large infrastructural projects like dams and the Great Wall, was one of the first scholars to underscore the presence of large and efficient bureaucracies in ancient China.

3. Many studies are now beginning to show how the Chinese state consolidated itself vis-à-vis society. Perry (1994) shows how Chinese labor, the linchpin of the communist state, was not as cohesive as assumed. She shows how Shanghai labor and its influence over the state can be divided along whether it came from the industrial (skilled) or the guild-based (semi-skilled) cadres. The latter being more communal-based accepted the Communist Party easily.

4. *The Wall Street Journal* (September 15, 1997), p. C1.

5. Joseph (1993), p. 133. In an unusual move at its 1997 meeting, the Chinese Communist Party (CCP) argued that China needs to undergo fully developed capitalism before it can embark on success with communism!

6. Skocpol notes that this feature of the CCP distinguishes the Chinese revolution from its counterpart in the Soviet Union which never quite became as mass based. Skocpol (1979), pp. 263–81.

7. Ibid., p. 276.

8. Xiong-Jian and You Nong (1994), p. 73.

9. Ibid., p. 74.

10. Lu Hui (March 1997), p. 30.

11. ITU (1997).

12. Zita (1994), p. 87.

13. Tan (1994), p. 180

14. Ibid., p. 174.

15. Bruce and Cunard (1994), pp. 224–26.

16. Zita (1994), p. 90.

17. Lee (1991).

18. Ibid., p. 537.

19. Ibid., p. 539.

20. Bruce and Cunard (1994), p. 224.

21. Jiangzhou (November 1997), p. 72.

22. Lee (1991), p. 536.

23. Zita (1994), p. 88.

24. *Far Eastern Economic Review* (October 5, 1995), pp. 56–57.

25. *The Wall Street Journal* (October 6, 1998), p. A18.

26. Lu Hui (March 1997), p. 29.

27. Mueller (1994), p. 171. The Mueller essay serves as the introduction to *Telecommunication Policy*'s special issue on China.

28. The *latifundiara* bourgeoisie that dominated Brazil until 1930 was an immigrant elite that continued to identify with the elite culture in Europe. Most Brazilian exports, dominated by coffee, went to Europe during this period.

29. Frank (1979).

30. The seminal work is Cardoso and Faletto (1979).

31. Evans (1979), p. 4.

32. See Smith (1981) for a critique for a nonradical/Marxian critique and Warren (1981) for a classical Marxian critique of dependency theory.

33. Net Domestic Product growth rate that was 6.7 percent from 1957–62 fell to 2.6 percent from 1962–66 and inflation that had maintained an annual rate of 20 percent grew rapidly after 1961. Pereira (1984), pp. 89, 101.

34. Evans (1979), p. 93.

35. In 1972, the lowest quintile of Brazil's population earned two percent of the total household income in the country, while the top quintile earned 66.6 percent. Bardhan (1984), p. 89.

36. Haggard and Kaufman (1995), p. 73.

37. Henrique Cardoso, one of the founders of dependency theory, is a well-respected academic-turned-politician. He has moved away from dependency theory now as he introduces market-driven policies in the Brazilian economy.

38. Inflation had dropped below 7 percent in 1997 (the lowest in 40 years) from a high of 2,560 percent in 1993. *Financial Times* (July 3, 1997), p. 13.

39. *The Wall Street Journal* (October 10, 1997), p. C1.

40. *The Wall Street Journal* (April 23, 1997), p. A15.

41. *The Wall Street Journal* (April 30, 1997), p. A10 and *The Wall Street Journal* (September 19, 1997), p. A15.

42. Mazucco (1996), p. 16.

43. Roy (1992), p. 2.

44. Calculated from International Telecommunication Union, 1997.

45. Population figure from the World Bank (1997), p. 215. Teledensity statistics from ITU (1997).

46. Quoted in Saunders et al. (1994), p. 99.

47. Ibid., p. 279.

48. Roy (1992), p. 3.

49. Lerner (1988), p. 62.

50. The net flow of funds from telecommunications (comprising 3–40 percent of the operating revenues) to the treasury was $600 million in 1984. Saunders et al. (1994), p. 34.

51. Wellenius (1994), p. 135.

52. Dibble (1992), p. 32.

53. Ibid., p. 32.

54. *The Wall Street Journal* (March 31, 1998), p. A16.

55. Dibble, pp. 30–31.

56. Roy (1992), p. 11.

57. *The Wall Street Journal* (September 19, 1997), p. A15.

58. Dibble (1992), p. 30.

59. *The Wall Street Journal* (September 19, 1997), p. A15.

60. At that time, Telebras was seen as one of the best available telecommunication stock options by several brokerage firms worldwide.

61. Motta died in April 1998 and was replaced by Luiz Carlos Mendonca de Barros.

62. See Mazucco (1996) for details on the new law.

63. *The Wall Street Journal* (January 23, 1998), p. A18. Although these figures seem ominous, by Brazilian standards of the past they are not so.

64. On the other hand, Telebras stock was expected to do well. It was the most hotly traded foreign stock on the New York Stock Exchange in 1997 and trailed only IBM and Compaq in being the most traded overall. *The Wall Street Journal* (April 6, 1998), p. A11.

65. *The Wall Street Journal*, July 30, 1998, p. A13.

66. *The Wall Street Journal*, July 29, 1998, p. A10.

67. National account statistics on Myanmar are unavailable. The World Bank merely lists it as a low-income country with GNP per capita below $750. The World Bank (1997), p. 248.

68. Shridharni (1943), p. 89.

69. Steinberg (1990).

70. Pepsi, Apple Computer, and Liz Clairborne of the U.S. either got out of or cut back in their Myanmar operations. Carlberg of Denmark canceled a joint venture in July 1996 after the death of the Danish honorary consul in a Burmese prison. The issue of the effectiveness of economic sanctions, of course, extends beyond Myanmar. It is not clear if pressures via foreign businesses already operating there or via an economic boycott of the regime would make it change its practices to any great extent.

71. Saunders et al. (1994), pp. 25–26. These studies were also quoted in the earlier edition of the book, which came out in 1984.

72. Saunders et al. (1994), pp. 177–78.

73. Khin Muang Win (1994), p. 116.

74. Goforth (WWW, accessed January 12, 1997).

75. ITU (1997), p. 145.

76. Khin Muang Win (1984), p. 118.

77. Wellenius and Stern (1994), p. 638.

CHAPTER 5. INDIAN TELECOMMUNICATIONS: SHADOW OF THE EMPIRE (1851–1984)

1. Nehru was prime minister of India until 1964 but there was no major change to the policies his government instituted until after the 1967 parliamentary elections.

2. This section draws heavily upon a fascinating account of Indian telecommunications during the British days by Shridharni (1953). For a classic on the interplay between empires and communication media, see Innis (1950).

3. The same year as Western Union was founded in the United States. Indian telegraphs are the oldest public utility in the world. In Britain, at that time, telegraph was run privately. Shridharni (1953).

4. Dr. William O'Shaughnessey, a doctor of medicine from Ireland teaching in Calcutta, began experimenting with the telegraph in 1839. Later appointed the Director General of Telegraphs, he is credited with introducing telegraphs in India and convincing the East India Company's directors in London of its usefulness in the 1850s to ensure its expansion.

5. Shridharni (1953), p. 21.

6. Total length of railway lines in India in 1853 when introduced was 34 kilometers growing to 53,596 kilometers in 1950. Government of India (1990), pp. 606–8.

7. Quoted in Shridharni (1953), p. 20.

8. Shridharni (1953), p. 167

9. India was governed under the doctrine of "dual control" exercised by the British government and the East India Company since 1784.

10. It explains why mercantilist policies were applied to India and free trade used with Latin America where the British lacked direct political control. Gallagher and Robinson note that "the main work of imperialism in the so-called expansionist era was in the more intensive development of areas already linked with the world economy, rather than in the extensive annexations of the remaining marginal regions of Africa." See Gallagher and Robinson (1953), p. 127.

11. The demand for Western education came from Hindu reformers, beginning in the 1830s, who viewed Western liberal education as a way out of the stagnation of the Hindu religion.

12. Unknown source quoted in Moore (1966), p. 372.

13. "In a country where any kind of government employment carried appropriate prestige, membership of the highest civil service of all [the ICS] lifted a man into a social stratosphere." Morris-Jones (1987), p. 25.

14. An interesting by-product of this was a call by many Britishers to make telegraphs a public monopoly in Britain. An editorial dated Jan. 17, 1855, in the influential *Bombay Times and Journal of Commerce* noted: "Wherever it [the telegraph] is set up it becomes the most perfect means of communication, it modifies the arrangements of trade, and influences every feature of society. That such an engine should remain in private hands is repugnant to the instinctive commonsense of mankind." Quoted in Shridharni (1953), p. 6.

15. This is the same time that the transatlantic submarine cable was completed. At the inauguration of both these cables, the Viceroy of India sent President Grant a cable in Washington, D.C., from Simla, India's first telegraphic contact with the United States. President Grant replied: "I congratulate you upon the successful connection of your country with the rest of the world." Quoted from Shridharni (1953), p.33.

16. Telegrams in Hindi could not be sent until 1949. Thus, the telegraph

was a powerful means of censoring and containing political dissent. The vernacular press, on which the Indian nationalist movement relied for information, had little access to the telegraph.

17. Shridharni, (1953), pp. 2, 8.

18. Some of these reasons are given in Shridharni (1953) and others are based on interviews conducted with officials in the Department of Telecommunications in India during Nov.–Dec. 1990.

19. An interesting exception (and the importance of telephones) is provided by the otherwise Spartan M. K. Gandhi who, beginning with the 1920s, allowed himself only two modern luxuries, a watch and a telephone. Prominent Indians had telephones beginning with the 1920s.

20. The lack of dependence on the telephone also reflected the way European states in general perceived the telephone. For example, Hudson noted that North Americans "use the telephone as a virtually indispensable part of personal and organizational activities" but that this might not be the case with Europeans and people in developing countries "that have taken their cue from the Europeans." Quoted from Hudson (1982), p. 176. In this article she also noted that, "a telecommunication system that allows for consultation among and between various levels in a government agency may be viewed as counterproductive or even a threat to the established centralized bureaucracy," an observation that holds true for many developing countries (p. 167).

21. Telephone service was introduced to New Delhi, the area adjoining Delhi, in 1912 when the capital of the Raj was moved there from Calcutta.

22. Shridharani (1953), p. 88.

23. As defined by this act, the 'telegraph' stands for any form of telecommunications transmission and any kind of equipment used for doing so. See the Indian Telegraph Act, Part I: 1.3.1. The act was amended thrice before independence and seven times thereafter mainly to include newer technologies in its wording and, in 1972, to include supposed security interests giving government the power to intercept messages.

24. This is an important measure because in 1985, the Ministry of Communications by means of a simple directive, was able to allow the Department of Telecommunications the power to issue licenses to private manufacturers of equipment. Similarly, divorcing the Bombay and Delhi operations from the department in 1988 posed no legal problems. In many other countries, deregulation/corporatization/privatization (as the case may be) entailed difficult legislative debates. (See, for example, the articles on Sri Lanka and Malaysia in Wellenius et al. [1989], which mention the difficult legislative processes along the road to deregulation and privatization. In Britain, privatization was effected through the Telecommunications Act of 1984.)

25. Innis (1950). He charts the dialectic between oral and written traditions emphasized by different communication technologies. Oral traditions, with their origins in traditions and folklore, help maintain empires through space. Written traditions tend to be authoritative and legal and help to extend empires (edicts posted by empire builders are examples) through time. A preponderance of one tradition leads to the downfall of empires. This is a crude rendering of Innis' analysis. His work merely illustrates the tensions produced in civilizations by differ-

ent media rather than being deterministic of their trajectory.

26. Bardhan (1984), p. 38. Similarly, Rudolph and Rudolph characterize the period from 1952 to 1964 as that of "command polity" where "the state is sovereign—differentiated, autonomous and authoritative. Command politics can orient policy toward future societal benefits and public capital goods or toward the appropriation by state political elites, and employees of state-generated wealth, power and status." Rudolph and Rudolph (1987) p. 14. A second period of command politics noted by the authors (and one that typifies to them the aggrandizement of wealth, power, and status by state officials) is that of "emergency [authoritarian] rule" under Indira Gandhi from 1975 to 1977.

27. Quoted in Morris-Jones (1987), p. 201. In 1949, Nehru had noted the urgency of government-led industrialization and the need to catch up with the West in the following words: "Now India, we are bound to be industrialized, we are trying to be industrialized, we must be industrialized." Quoted in Byres (1982), p. 135.

28. "The public sector has to expand rapidly. It has not only to initiate developments which the private sector is either unwilling or unable to undertake; it has to play the dominant role in shaping the entire pattern of investments in the economy, whether it makes the investments directly or whether these are made by the private sector." Second Plan document quoted in Bannerjee and Ghosh (1988), p. 105.

29. The industrial sector (public and private) accounted for only 11 percent of the total employment in the 1960s. State-run industries account for two thirds of this employment. Balasubramaniam (1984), p. 112.

30. Ibid., p. 116.

31. Rudolph and Rudolph note: "As Nehru's coauthors and implementors civil servants were the vanguard of the lobby for an industrial strategy, collaborating in the creation of basic and heavy industry under the second and third five year plan." See Rudolph and Rudolph (1987), p. 77.

32. The IAS (the postcolonial descendent of the ICS) is of particular importance for analyzing the role played by the bureaucracy in the Indian economy. It remains the most prestigious body among the Indian bureaucratic services and serves as a role model for the others, including the Indian Telecommunications Service. Each year 40,000 to 50,000 candidates compete for the 200–300 positions in the IAS. Despite the IAS presence in almost every sphere of administrative and economic activity, the total number of IAS "officers" in 1985 was only 4,284 (see Goyal [1989], pp. 425–26). In 1948, there were 800 officers and 2,600 in 1969. Morris-Jones (1987), p. 129.

33. Krueger (1974), p. 294. Seventy percent of this rent came from the auction of import licenses while 20 percent of it came from control over commodities like steel, cement, coal, passenger cars, scooters, food, etc. She notes that her estimates are crude and do not include rent-seeking from investment licensing (which is probably as important as import licenses) for lack of data. Bannerjee and Ghosh (1988) note that the practice by powerful industrial houses of blocking entry in competitive markets by obtaining all available licenses for a product began during this period.

34. Bauer (1961), p. 89. See chapter 4 of Bauer's book titled "The Private

Sector under the Plan" for the effect of the Second Plan and the Industrial Policy Resolution of 1956 upon private industry.

35. See also Bauer's critique of Gunnar Myrdal along similar lines. In his famous work, *Asian Drama*, Myrdal had argued that private capital can do little to lift South Asian economies out of economic backwardness and viewed wealth maximization as being correlated to political power and exploitation. Bauer (1976), pp. 197–98, 217–19.

36. Quoted from Jagota (1963), p. 57. He continues to note that, "hence it [IAS] continues to attract young men of non-bureaucratic inclinations who if other avenues were open might be Sanskrit poets, artists, scientists, or successful men of commerce."

37. Sovani (1963), p. 269.

38. Brahmananda (1979), pp. 4–5.

39. Morawetz (1977).

40. Bhagwati and Srinivasan (1975).

41. Morawetz (1977).

42. Wolf (1982), p. 12.

43. A popular label used to describe the result of economic policies followed by the successive Indira Gandhi governments between 1967 and 1984.

44. Rudolph and Rudolph (1987), p. 78.

45. Bhagwati and Srinivasan (1975).

46. Rudolph and Rudolph (1967) summarize this trend, which reached a crescendo after 1980 with Indira Gandhi's increasing reliance "on palace advisors, many of whom were senior civil servants. In Nehru's time, confidential advise and deliberation on policy and politics had been the province of cabinet colleagues, state chief ministers, the Planning Commission members, and senior party leaders."

47. Rudolph and Rudolph (1987), p. 7. In Morris-Jones words "it resulted in de-institutionalization, not only of Congress but of the party system as a whole" as rival parties sought to capture state power by resorting to populist politics as Indira Gandhi had done. Morris-Jones (1987), p. 264.

48. The Swatantra Party represented private business and small land-holding capitalist farmer interests but remained a politically marginal force before 1967. See Erdman (1967) for the influence of the Swatantra Party and the way it sought to represent business and capitalist farmer interests. See Kochanek (1974) for the way private capital and state interacted in the Nehruvian state and the decade following Nehru's death.

49. Kothari (1970), p. 4.

50. "Its [India's] 500 million voters are as sophisticated as the members of any democracy anywhere—not good on details, but quite able to get the sense and drift of major events when things go badly wrong. This is why Rajiv's mother, Indira, got the boot in 1977. . . . India's tragedy is, like many other democracies before it, that it has not always got the direction and policies from the top its democratic impulses deserve. When the politicians don't give an honest and inspiring lead, the voters are able to say *no*, but saying *yes* is more difficult, since they have no idea what they are supposed to be saying *yes* to." Quoted from Power (May 23, 1991).

51. A few import licensing requirements were removed and other incentives granted to export-oriented industries.

52. Quoted in Department of Telecommunications (1988), p. 44.

53. Chowdary (1989), p. 109.

54. Quoted from *Financial Express* (May 12, 1989), p. 4.

55. Based on interviews.

56. Quoted from an interview.

57. Department of Telecommunications (1988), pp. 53–57.

58. See Kaul (1979) and Economic Study Cell (1981). These studies point out the importance of telecommunications for business purposes by rural users and the savings in transport costs.

59. Indian Institute of Foreign Trade (1988).

60. Bruce et al. (1988), p. 425.

61. For example, between 1962 and 1984, the IBRD extended $4,802 million worth of loans on eight occasions for telecommunication projects. A part of the loan for each project was utilized for importing co-axial cables.

62. *Indian Post* (February 2, 1989).

63. Telecom Commission was created in 1988 as the apex decision-making body for the telecommunications sector.

64. Quoted from Robinson (1990). While conceivably economies of scale might produce incremental units of output at declining fixed costs, time series studies on annual average and incremental capital-output ratios do not confirm this trend in India. See Balasubramaniam (1984), pp. 72–73. He quotes two studies: one shows that the ratio of net investment to changes in GNP (incremental capital-output ratio measured at 1960–61 prices) increased from 2.39 in the 1950s to 4.63 in the 1970s while the average capital-output ratio increased from 2.7 in the 1950s to 2.9 in the 1960s and 3.33 for the 1970s.

65. Chowdary (1989), p.107. The argument that the per capita operating expense in India is higher because it has not yet experienced economies of scale found in the developed countries did not hold because the network utilization capacities in India are high and there are long waiting lists for telephones.

66. Statistics quoted from *The Indian Post* (February 2, 1989).

67. Chowdary (1988), p. 9.

68. DoT was divorced from the Department of Posts and Telegraphs in 1985. I have relied upon a Department of Telecommunications (1988) publication summing up the contributions made by the department since 1947. It declares: "We, in telecommunications, are proud of our heritage and contribution, to the telecommunications, in the face of very heady obstacles" (Department of Telecommunications [1988], p. viii).

69. Saunders et al. (1983), pp. 4–5.

70. Saunders et al. (1994), pp. 6–7. The fall in Asian figures is probably due to data availability for more Asian countries by 1988, which brought the figures down. India still ranks low by either of the two Asian figures. India's overall density remained the same as the growth in telecommunication lines was negligible compared to its population growth. Interestingly, government of India statistics show the density to be 0.5 in 1985.

71. It is analytically hard to note the demands only until 1985. Therefore,

demands beyond 1985 are explained in a few cases. Pressures during the 1990s will be referred to again in chapter 7.

72. Indian Institute of Foreign Trade (1988).

73. Data in this paragraph collected from VSNL on research trips to India.

74. Chowdary (January 18, 1988). Aronson and Cowhey write that in industrial countries 5 to 10 percent of the users account for more than half the long distance traffic. Aronson and Cowhey (1988), p. 27.

75. The software industry is organized through the National Association for Software and Service Companies (NASSCOM).

CHAPTER 6. INDIAN TELECOMMUNICATIONS: SERVICE ENHANCEMENT, 1984–91

1. *The New York Times Magazine* (April 20, 1986) noted that the "license-permit-quota Raj" (by the time of Rajiv Gandhi government) was increasingly backed by "the giant cadre of 16 million permanent officials, clerks, bureaucrats and other workers who either run the nation's publicly owned businesses or administer the rules of its clanking government." Similarly, Srinivasan has noted that in an economy such as India's, burdened with decades of state regulation and production, "a chaotic incentive structure and the unleashing of rapacious rent-seeking were the inevitable outcomes." Quoted in World Bank (1991), p. 38.

2. These include roads, electric power, drinking water, etc. I have found no documented evidence noting high demand for telecommunications facilities in rural areas during the 1980s.

3. Morris-Jones (1987), p. 270.

4. Echeverri-Gent notes that since "the late 1960s, infrastructural bottlenecks have acted as major constraints on development." Echeverri-Gent (1990), p. 108. For the politics of the reform process during Rajiv Gandhi's tenure, see Kohli (1989). For an analysis of the pressures by large and small scale manufacturers for liberalization, see Kochanek (1986).

5. "While Rajiv Gandhi appears to favor a more open economy, and the mid-eighties witnessed an increase in foreign import agreements such as cars and for communications equipment and other high-technology products, the vested interests in protection of both public and private sectors are powerful." Rudolph and Rudolph (1987), p. 13. None of the 29 public sector enterprises targeted for sales by the Rajiv Gandhi administration had been actually sold by 1987. See Belassa (1989), p. 181.

6. The World Bank (1991), p. 154.

7. Lelyveld (May 26, 1991).

8. A. M. Khusro, an eminent economics columnist, noted in December 1990 that "[t]he economy is riddled with open and hidden subsidies, low and lower interest rates, tax exemptions and investment allowances, rebates and concessions, and cash compensations and duty drawbacks. Each such concession brings the State and Central Governments, the banks and financial institutions, closer and closer to bankruptcy. Some public sector banks are close to disaster." Khusro (December 16, 1990).

9. *New York Times* (May 26, 1991).

10. Morehouse and Chopra (1983), p. 5.

11. Morehouse and Chopra (1983), p. 5. Grieco argues that India had a national policy governing computers by the late 1970s. See Grieco (1982), pp. 626–27.

12. Bruce and Cunard (1994), p. 220.

13. The Ministry of Finance works closely with the Planning Commission for the central plans' outlays. Moreover, it plays an important role in import licensing, undoubtedly crucial for a sector like telecommunications with the need for high technological requirements from abroad. Dominated by the IAS, the MoF was the linchpin of vested bureaucratic interests and resistance to reform in the 1980s.

14. Bombay (now Mumbai), Calcutta, Delhi (including Old and New Delhi), and Madras (now Chennai), the four largest cites, are known as the four metro towns in India.

15. Cowhey et al. note that modernization efforts in telecommunications in developing countries continue to pour into "the urban centers of political influence." They specifically mention New Delhi and Bombay. Cowhey et al. (1989), p. 8. Bombay and Delhi accounted for 749 thousand (or less than 25 percent) of the 3,166 thousand phones in India in 1986. Neither the DoT nor MTNL has published the DELs figure for 1986, but it can be easily derived by cross-checking the various annual reports and making a few calculations. It then becomes clear that MTNL was created for Delhi because of its political importance and Bombay for its financial and commercial influence.

16. Interviews. VSNL (like its predecessor, the Overseas Communication Service or OCS) retains the power to hire and fire its officials independently of DoT.

17. Over the 1980s, the DoT became increasingly resentful of change. By 1989, the DoT had been slowly losing its monopoly over equipment manufacturing, and it was under pressure to improve its efficiency. For example, the relative efficiency of MTNL and VSNL as compared to the DoT put enormous pressure on the DoT to improve its services.

18. Quoted from Press Information Bureau, Government of India (March 13, 1989), p. 1.

19. Based on interview.

20. Pitroda noted that 50 percent of DoT's 350,000 workers needed retraining. Quoted in *Independent* (May 23, 1989). In July 1989, the Telecommunications Commission declared "that decentralization and disbursal of powers to the regional heads would improve the functioning of the telecom network" (quoted from *Economic Times*, 8.2). This objective did not sit well with the DoT.

21. Quoted from *Economic Times* (June 6, 1990).

22. Interview.

23. Telecommunications services, in countries following U.S. convention, are distinguished as basic (telephone, telex, fax, and others that do not alter the content of the message during transmission) and value-added or enhanced, which do.

24. India has the third largest engineering force in the world and a sizable (even if highly inefficient) industrial base. Bruce et al. term the "reservoir of highly skilled technical, operational, and management personnel" as India's "primary resource." Bruce et al. (1988), p. 413. See Pitroda (1976) for an early statement on the need for developing countries such as India to tap into their resources and develop self-reliant R&D centers.

25. For a comprehensive article on the strengths and weaknesses of Indian science and technology, see Zorpette (1994).

26. Mody (1989), p. 317.

27. This paragraph draws upon Pradhan (1994).

28. The way CIT-Alcatel technology was procured is itself a classic story of the workings of the state and the bureaucracy in India. The decision to install only digital switches in the future was made in 1976 but no foreign manufacturer was willing to transfer the technology on the conditions demanded by the Indian government (total transfer of technology for indigenous production including subsequent improvements in the technology). The CIT-Alcatel deal was signed in 1982 but production did not start until 1986 (a decade after the decision to install only digital technology!). Moreover, by the time these switches, the E-10–B switch as it is known, came to India, they were already outdated internationally. *The Economic Times* (August 1, 1990) summed up the issue in an editorial when the Singh administration seemed to be emphasizing foreign technology after five years of C-DoT: "It should not be expected that significant [foreign] equity participation would result by simply insisting on it. Further, the experience of the Indian Telephone Industries from the collaboration with Alcatel has also proved that the expectations of the foreign collaborator meeting the obligations of R and D, indigenization and export, is a case of wishful thinking."

29. Quoted in *Business India* (July 13–26, 1986), p. 110.

30. In 1990, Alcatel is reported to have hired a Paris based public relations firm for $5 million to make its case with the Indian government.

31. *Business India* (December 15–28, 1986), p. 114

32. ITT (U.S.) and Alcatel (France) formed a transnational alliance in 1985.

33. Some of DoT's preference patterns and its strong support for them by the Singh government have to do with the large amount of bribes public officials demand from MNCs when signing joint ventures. The trade press did not fail to underscore this issue as the C-DoT versus foreign technology issue developed.

34. Noam (1989).

35. *The Week* (April 22, 1990), p. 29.

36. It might be argued that it was necessary for the Gandhi government to put up such a strong front in order to break the vested interest of the bureaucracy. But it delayed implementation of many telecommunication goals because of equipment shortages and turned away multilateral institutions and MNCs who had promised India credit for its telecommunications program.

37. The *Times of India* (February 2, 1990) put it succinctly in the early stages of the C-DoT versus Singh government controversy: "At stake is a slowdown in the programme expansion of two million lines a year on an average in

the Eighth Plan period, culminating in 20 million lines by the year 2,000. . . . The uncomfortable fact that the new policy makers are struggling to accept is that the development of the required main exchanges handling 20,000 to 40,000 lines each will take a few years."

38. Quoted in Chatterjee (May 20, 1989), p. 28.

39. Quoted in *Sunday* (September 17–23, 1989), p. 61.

40. Texas Instruments was the only user to have been allowed this facility in the South Indian city of Bengalore in 1987.

41. In October 1989, Pitroda unveiled a plan whereby DoT would work with a group of Stanford University researchers to develop cellular mobile radio phones and low-cost digital radio multiplexers for rural applications. Based on a news report in *Financial Express* (October 2, 1989).

42. See Chowdary (January 18, 1988). He wrote: "Those who frequently travel by air and spend much of their time shuttling between the airport and their office on the ground or those whose telephones work only now and then and hardly ever in the monsoon season know how much they need a mobile telephone."

43. In all media reports and press conferences, the total of 20 million DELs was given for the year 2000. I was unable to derive this figure from the published projected growth rates in the 1980s.

44. Quoted from interviews.

45. Government of India (1997), p. 24.

46. Other areas were health, immunization, drinking water, oilseeds, and literacy. The launching of these missions earned Rajiv Gandhi the title of "Technology Prime Minister." Pitroda successfully introduced new technologies and management techniques in these areas. The mission on oilseeds is said to have been the most successful, saving the country billions of rupees in import costs.

47. Quoted from Department of Telecommunications (1988), p. 71.

48. Athreya (1996), pp. 12–13.

49. *Financial Express* (April 20, 1990).

50. Press Information Bureau (April 5, 1989).

51. Department of Telecommunications (1990) and (1993).

52. Department of Telecommunications (1994).

53. Figures quoted from Government of India (1997).

54. Figure cited from data collected at the DoT during July and August 1997.

55. *The Economist* (November 11, 1995), p. 64.

56. Interview. The cost of providing a telephone in urban areas is about Rs 30,000.

57. A more practical solution is proposed as a result of the 1994 telecommunications policy. Private carriers are to install 10 percent of their lines in rural areas. Fifteen percentage points of the bids for private telephone service in 1995 was also given to firms who could install lines above the 10 percent requirement. See chapter 6 for details.

58. *Far Eastern Economic Review* (April 7, 1994), p. 45.

59. Interview.

60. Interview.

61. Bruce and Cunard (1994, p. 220) reach the same conclusions.

62. MTNL (1995) and (1996). Compare this with six of the cases described in chapters 3 and 4: Singapore (9), South Korea (4), Mexico (7), Malaysia (16), China (63), and Brazil (7).

63. MTNL, various annual reports.

64. Calculated from DoT, MTNL, and 1991 Census figures.

65. MTNL (1996), p. 10.

66. Ibid.

67. Source: VSNL data and interviews. India also has a 1.8 percent share in the Intelsat system and a 0.44 percent share in Inmarsat, the global maritime communications satellite system.

68. ITI, in collaboration with ATE Liverpool, manufactured telephone instruments since 1948.

69. Alcatel, of course, was ITI's collaborator for producing the large switches.

70. PBXs, or private branch exchanges, are small (usually intra-office) exchanges. In 1986, thirty-six manufacturers opted for C-DoT's 128-line EAPBX technology. There were about one thousand EAPBXs operational in India by 1990.

71. The bidding is done by the manufacturers after the government publicly asks for these by means of tenders. The government chooses the lowest cost bid. In practice, there is considerable corruption. The position of the private manufacturers reflected the fear that DoT and ITI would act collusively to keep private manufacturers out.

72. *Independent* (February 2, 1990).

73. *Economic Times* (July 30, 1990). The two companies were: Tata Telecom and Bharti Telecom, both getting the technology from Siemens. The two were largely responsible for the increase in profit margins from 5.4 percent in 1988–89 to 9.9 in 1989–90 among the seven companies. The two companies had a diversified portfolio in telecommunications manufacturing, including supply of components for dedicated networks. Relevant to the discussion here is that both were also EAPBX manufacturers and were able to use their own telephone instruments for these.

74. Interview.

75. Pitroda. Quoted from interview.

76. Bhagwati and Desai (1970), p. 466.

77. Pressures by domestic manufacturers who can disassemble foreign technology and offer it at low prices accounts for the militant stance adopted by policymakers from countries like India in negotiating intellectual property rights. The other classic case of not respecting international patents in a modern industry is that of a few manufacturers in the software industry who have copied and sold international software products at extremely low prices. One of the three things the U.S. Trade Negotiator's Office placed India on a watch for while invoking Super 301 in 1989 was India's lack of protection for intellectual property rights. (The others were restrictions on foreign direct investment and the government monopoly in the insurance industry.) See Sell (1998) for a discussion of North-South intellectual property issues.

78. This would mean that if the bids are accepted, the cartel would divide the share among themselves edging others out of the market. The strategy is questionable. At such low prices, the firms may or may not recover their average costs and the marginal costs might be higher than marginal revenue. The only advantage would be survival in the market, in the hope of capturing larger market shares at higher prices later. Firms are tenacious about staying in the market because if they leave they not only lose their fixed costs but also lose out on limited investment opportunities in other areas. By 1990, the price of phones had already fallen to about Rs 600 per instrument from a high of Rs 1,200 in 1987.

79. A cartel of companies made identical bids of Rs 495 for an order of fifty thousand telephones. MTNL decided to order it from a company with a bid of Rs 595 but one that was outside of the cartel. The company awarded the contract had actually broken away from the cartel, otherwise the award would have had to go the cartel.

80. There was another reason. It was part of the Telecommunications Commission's efforts to renegotiate the $350 million World Bank loan (noted earlier), a part of which would have gone toward importing cables.

CHAPTER 7. INDIAN TELECOMMUNICATIONS: PRIVATIZATION AND LIBERALIZATION, 1991–98

1. Kohli notes in a similar vein: "The irony of India's political-economic situation is tragic: the state is highly centralized and omnipresent, but the leverage of its leaders to initiate meaningful change has diminished." Kohli, (1990), p. 16.

2. *The Wall Street Journal* (May 6, 1996), p. A1.

3. Statistics quoted from *Los Angeles Times* (July 29, 1991) and (July 30, 1991).

4. *Los Angeles Times* (July 30, 1991).

5. A World Bank confidential note leaked to the print media in India called for a privatization of Indian banking that, among other things, noted that Indian "banks are undercapitalized, have high statutory requirements for reserve ratios and low profitability on existing assets." Quoted from *The Business & Political Observer* (December 1, 1990).

6. *The Wall Street Journal* (December 29, 1995), p. A1.

7. *The Economic Times* (June 1, 1998), India's leading business newspaper, opened its front-page story on the budget with the following statement: "It's a Swadeshi Budget, protectionist and inflationary."

8. "Even as politicians clear barriers, the bureaucracy erects new ones by changing the rules." *The Wall Street Journal* (February 19, 1997), p. A14.

9. *The Hindu* (July 11, 1998), p. 12.

10. In July 1997, Jeffrey Sachs, asked by the government of India for advice on foreign direct investment, noted that trouble with highly publicized FDI projects hurt Indian credibility (he was specifically referring to a deal between Tatas and Singapore Airlines that was called off due to bureaucratic and ministerial

change of mind; however, the Enron renegotiations in 1995 are the most famous case in India). Sachs also noted that tariffs and corporate taxes remain high in India compared to East Asian economies.

11. House (February 24, 1995).

12. See McDowell (1995) for pressures from the Indian software industry for telecommunications.

13. *India Today* (February 15, 1996), pp. 78–84.

14. For a history of Indian position on telecommunications during the early years of the Uruguay Round, see McDowell (1997). For recent history, see Singh (forthcoming, a).

15. Transparency means that all rules and legislation must be openly available while MFN (Most Favored Nation) disallows any special treatment to any one nation. Taken together the two features allow for GATS' goals of market access and national treatment (the latter allowing the same treatment for foreign business as for the domestic ones).

16. McDowell (1994), p. 117.

17. Interviews.

18. Telecommunication officials often refer to the 450,000 employees of DoT and the millions of others in other government departments frequently. (Based on news reports and on interviews.)

19. At a general level, Kohli (1990) makes the point that Indian democracy, which was always elite driven, is now trickling down and many groups are now making demands on the political system.

20. *Economist* (November 15, 1995), p. 64.

21. Source: DoT press release quoted on India-gii listserv, india-gii@cpsr.org, June 22, 1998.

22. *Far Eastern Economic Review* (April 7, 1994), p. 45. Unofficial estimates run as high as twice the supply (1995), which would make pent-up demand upwards of 18 million lines (Interviews).

23. Interview.

24. Pradhan (1994), p. 46.

25. Quoted from *Telematics India* (June 1995), p. 5.

26. Cited in Pradhan (1994), p. 43.

27. Basic services such as telephone service do not alter the content of the message sent. Value-added services (such as data delivery) change the content as required for transmission and distribution purposes. Specialized services can be a combination of both basic and value-added and are required by few users or provided by a specialized carriers (for example, radio paging).

28. *Far Eastern Economic Review* (September 10, 1992), p. 62.

29. A World Bank position paper questioned why the Components Bank "should be the sole prerogative of the public sector to establish." Quoted from Robinson (1990), p. 4.

30. Nonetheless, for reasons unknown and unannounced, the lowest bidder, Britain's GPT was not included in the initial selection.

31. Based on news reports and interviews with trade media journalists.

32. *India Today* (April 15, 1996), pp. 61–63.

33. Bath (1997), p. 154.

34. Mody (1995), p. 115.

35. Ministry of Finance (1998).

36. The local line requirement raised doubts about the long-distance carrier AT&T's participation but eventually the fact that AT&T does run ISDN lines was deemed sufficient.

37. Plans in 1995 to convert DoT into a body named "India Telecom," to give the organization more managerial autonomy without corporatizing it, failed as the intent of the exercise was never clear. Earlier recommendations by a committee (A. N. Varma committee), which drawing upon the Athreya Committee report, recommended dividing DoT in to four corporations also met stiff opposition and were shelved.

38. Quoted in *Far Eastern Economic Review* (April 7, 1994).

39. The irony is that by 1998, although NTP called for 49 percent foreign equity, international firms in India got around this requirement by setting up holding companies and diluting domestic ownership requirements. (I thank Richard French of Tata Communications for bringing this point to my attention.)

40. See Chowdary (1998), pp. 15–16 for details on the Vittal appointment issue.

41. *Business India* (June 5–18, 1995), p. 54.

42. Additional corruption charges continued to pile up against the former communications minister until 1998. Interestingly, after being ousted from the Congress Party, this former minister started supporting the BJP!

43. *Economist* (November 11, 1995), p. 64.

44. Interviews. Many retired DoT officials now serve as consultants to private firms. Concerns about conflict of interest began to be raised about this Indian revolving back door. The latest was an announcement by the private operator, Reliance Telecom, in end-July 1998 that it was hiring B. K. Syngal, the recently retired chairman and managing director of VSNL (against whom there were pending charges of corruption).

45. This paragraph draws on the discussion of TRAI in Sinha (1996), p. 36.

46. A public-interest litigation filed in the Delhi High Court at once questioned the efficacy of creating a nonstatutory regulatory authority.

47. Jain (1997).

48. This paragraph is based on an interview with the chairman of TRAI published in *The Indian Express* (July 14, 1997).

49. Bath (1997), p. 155.

50. Many important documents now attest to such bold efforts by other countries: see NTIA (1992) for the U.S. and Nora and Minc (1980) for France.

51. National Informatics Center (1998).

52. Ibid.

53. *The Hindu* (July 11, 1998), p. 12.

54. *The Hindu* (July 23, 1998).

55. *Telematics India* (April 1992), p. 25.

56. Bell Lab's now infamously low estimate of 900,000 cellular subscribers in the U.S. by the year 2000 is well known. There were more than 30 million

subscribers in 1996 and the growth rate was well over 25 percent a year. *The Wall Street Journal* (January 11, 1996). Worldwide demand was 77 million in 1995, up from 10 million five years earlier and was expected to be 330 million by 2000. *The Wall Street Journal* (October 13, 1995).

57. Data source: DoT internal data collected July–August 1997. The breakdown for the four metros was Mumbai 130,000; Chennai 35,000; New Delhi 170,000; Calcutta 45,000.

58. This paragraph borrows from *Business India* (July 14–27, 1997), pp. 80–84.

59. *The Economist* (November 11, 1995).

60. *Business India* (June 5–18, 1995), p. 58. Estimates vary. Bath (1997), p. 153, mentions five million customers for 2000.

61. An *India Abroad* news story quoted on India-gii listserv: india-gii@cpsr.org, October 12, 1997.

62. *The Wall Street Journal* (January 24, 1995), p. B4.

63. DoT officials often note that as incumbent players, they face lots of hurdles whereas the private firms are coming in with a "clean slate." Among the hurdles, DoT cites the high level of workforce and their accountability to the public as a government department. Interviews.

64. Others wondered if DoT workers could ever be retrained. An article by a former Telecom Commission member in the influential *Economic Times* outlined an entire laundry list of DoT travails and noted; "DoT requires a complete overhaul from decision making to the working level." It noted that the department's work culture has remained unchanged for the last fifty years. See Nanda (July 24, 1995) .

65. Following the Parliamentary elections in June 1996 where the incumbent Congress Party lost, the minister of communications from the erstwhile Rao government was arrested on corruption charges and later released on bail.

66. *Business India* (July 14–27), p. 83.

67. *India Today* (May 18, 1998).

68. *The Hindu* (May 30, 1998).

69. Aronson and Cowhey (1988), p. 78.

70. Interview.

71. IBS consists of small rooftop antennae providing 64 kbps data links through Intelsat satellites.

72. Interview.

73. This parallels the story of dedicated networks in other developing countries such as China noted in chapter 3.

74. The Ministry of Railways supervises the second largest railways network in the world after Russia and plays a key role in national politics. The railway budget precedes and is presented separately from the national budget and often indicates the shape of the national budget.

75. Interviews.

76. Interviews

77. Malhotra and Ranjan (April 1995).

78. *India Today* (July 15, 1996), p. 55.

79. *India Today* (July 6, 1996), pp. 86–90.

80. *Telematics India* (July 1993), p. 24.

81. Heywood (1996).

82. Bath (1997), p. 154.

83. R. K. Takkar quoted in *India Today* (February 29, 1996), p. 101.

84. Statistics from http://www.intenetnews.com/site cited on India-gii list-serv: india-gii@cpsr.org, June 5, 1998.

85. Most of these calls were international. VSNL charges high rates for international calls. It is twice as expensive to call the United States from India than vice versa.

86. Based on news reports, published writings (of officials like Athreya, Chowdary and Seshadhari) and interviews. An exception might be Sam Pitroda who remains skeptical of fulfilling social development goals through liberalization alone.

87. DoT figures quoted from the Government of India (1997), p. 19 and p. 26. J. P. Morgan study quoted in *Business India* (June 5–18, 1995), p. 59.

CHAPTER 8. THE MYTH AND THE REALITY OF LEAPFROGGING

1. For endlessly admired works, see Gerschenkron (1962), Fishlow (1965), Landes (1969), Cippolla (1980), Rosenberg and Birdzell (1986).

2. See symposium titled "New Growth Theory" in *The Journal of Political Economy* (1994). Archibugi and Michie (1997) offer a well-rounded introduction.

3. The seminal work remains, North and Thomas (1973).

4. A good starting point for recent studies are studies by Meltzer et al. (1993), Sclove (1995), and Sarewitz (1996).

5. Of course, these enquiries are hardly new. Similar questions in the past were asked, in one form or another, by Winner (1977), Mumford (1970), and Ellul (1964).

6. Rosenau (1990), p. 17.

7. See Deane (1968) for the contribution of canals and railways to industrializing Britain.

8. Gerschenkron (1962), Rostow (1960), Leibenstein (1978), Rosenstein-Rodan (1943).

9. Quoted in Byres (1982), p. 135.

10. Early macro correlational studies were of this variety. ITU cross-sectional analyses, for example, showed not only that GDP per capita and teledensity are correlated but that the slope is 1.4. This meant that for every 10 percent increase in GDP, teledensity grows 14 percent. See Saunders et al. (1994), pp. 86–88.

11. Cho and Lee (1998).

12. Genschel and Werle (1993).

13. Singh and Sheth (1997).

14. Cost-based pricing in telecommunications is hard for a number of reasons but there has been a steady movement toward it since the 1980s. See chapter 2 for details.

15. Fishlow (1965), pp. 306–11.

16. Hirschman (1958), p. 97.

17. Ibid., p. 93

18. Water mill revolutionized agriculture and manufacture in medieval times. However, Cippolla writes: "The Romans were aware of the water mill, but they built relatively few of them and continued to make far wider use of mills employing animal and human powers." Cippolla (1980), p. 167.

19. Nelson and Wright (December 1992), p. 1961.

20. Cippolla (1980), p. 190.

21. Evans in Haggard and Kaufman (1995), p. 141.

22. The word 'reality' is used carefully here to show that our understanding of this 'reality' itself, rather than being the assertion of a universal 'truth', must be the positing of a contextual circumstance.

23. Kindleberger (1978), pp. 30–31.

24. This author is aware of the many criticisms leveled against rational choice theory's constructs, among which is the notion that its concepts merely add useless fluff and jargon to otherwise simple or simplistic analyses. See symposium titled "Controversy in the Discipline: Area Studies and Comparative Politics" in *PS: Political Science & Politics* (June 1997). In as much as this book tries to avoid the "complexity of rational choice" it is hoped that it falls somewhere between simple street wisdom of area studies and other types of political-economic theories/conceptualizations available.

25. Clubs' heterogeneity and institutional provision are, of course, conditions that can be formalized to derive more precise results.

26. Sandler (1992), p. 75.

27. Haggard and Kaufman (1995), part 3.

28. North (1990), p. 140.

29. The liberal democratic model of Locke and Rousseau is that of a functional state.

30. Glover and Lotvedt (1997), p. 1.

31. Bhagwati (1998).

32. The World Bank (1997), p. 3.

33. Levy and Spiller (1996).

34. Such traditional definitions form the backbone of writings by Tocqueville (1835/1945), Almond and Verba (1963), and Putnam (1993 and 1995).

35. Evans (1996), p. 1034. This article provides a nice summary of the debates leading up to this issue.

36. Studies on civil society involvement in telecommunications are lacking. For an exception, see Horwitz (1998) and Janisch and Kotlowitz (1998).

37. Lawrence (1959), p. 167.

38. Plato (translated 1973), p. 51.

39. Plato (translated 1973), p. 62.

REFERENCES

Aaron, David L. February 2, 1995. "After GATT, U.S. Pushes Direct Investment." *The Wall Street Journal*, p. A14.

Akerlof, George. August 1970. "The Market for Lemons: Qualitative Uncertainty and the Market Mechanism." *Quarterly Journal of Economics* 84.

Almond, Gabriel A., and Sidney Verba. 1963. *The Civic Culture*. Princeton, N.J.: Princeton University Press.

Altschuler, Alan. 1992. "The Politics of Deregulation." In Harvey M. Sapolsky et al., eds., *The Telecommunications Revolution: Past, Present and Future*. London: Routledge.

Ambrose, William W., et al. 1990. *Privatizing Telecommunications Systems: Business Opportunities in Developing Countries*. The World Bank: International Finance Corporation. Discussion Paper No. 10.

Amin, Samir. 1979. "NIEO: How to Put Third World Surpluses to Effective Use." *Third World Quarterly* 1.

Archibugi, Daniele, and Jonathan Michie, eds. 1997. *Technology, Globalization and Economic Performance*. Cambridge: Cambridge University Press.

Aronson, Jonathan D. 1992. "Telecommunications Infrastructure and U.S. International Competitiveness." In *A National Information Network: Changing Our Lives in the 21st Century. Institute for Information Studies*. Fallschurch, Va.: Institute for Information Studies and The Aspen Institute.

———. 1988. "The Service Industries: Growth, Trade and Development Prospects." In J. Sewell et al., eds., *Growth, Exports, and Jobs in a Changing World Economy*. Overseas Development Council: U.S.-Third World Policy Perspectives, No. 9.

Aronson, Jonathan D., and Peter F. Cowhey. 1988. *When Countries Talk: International Trade in Telecommunications Services*. Washington, D.C.: The American Enterprise Institute.

Arrow, Kenneth J. 1979. "The Economics of Information." In Michael L. Dertouzos and Joel Moses, eds., *The Computer Age: A Twenty Year View*. Cambridge: MIT Press.

———. 1969. "The Organization of Economic Activity: Issues Pertinent to the Choice of Markets Versus Nonmarket Allocation." *The Analysis and Evaluation of Public Expenditures: The PPB System*. Joint Economic Committee, U.S. Congress. Reprinted in Breit et al., eds., *Readings in Microeconomics*. St. Louis: Times Mirror, 1986.

Asiaweek. May 16, 1997. "A Monopoly Fights Back: But Does Singtel Have What It Takes to Win?"

Athreya, M. B. January/February 1996. "India's Telecommunications Policy: A Paradigm Shift." *Telecommunications Policy* 20.

Bagchi, Amiya Kumar, ed. 1988. *Economy, Society and Polity: Essays in the Political Economy of Indian Planning.* Calcutta: Oxford University Press.

Balasubramaniam, V. N. 1984. *The Economy of India.* Boulder, Colo.: Westview Press.

Bar, Francois. 1990. *Configuring the Telecommunications Infrastructure for the Computer Age: The Economics of Network Control.* Ph.D diss. University of California at Berkeley.

Bardhan, Pranab. 1989. "Alternative Approaches to Development Economics: An Evaluation." In Hollis B. Chenery, and T. N. Srinivasan, eds., *Handbook of Development Economics.*

———. 1984. *The Political Economy of India.* Oxford: Basil Blackwell.

Bath, Dimple Sahi. August 1997. "Telecommunications in India: Policy and Regulatory Issues for Investors." *Computer and Telecommunications Law Review* 2, no. 1.

Bauer, P.T. 1976. *Dissent on Development.* Revised edition. Cambridge, Mass.: Harvard University Press.

———. 1961. *Indian Economic Policy and Development.* New York: Frederick A. Praeger.

Belassa, Bela. 1989. *New Directions in the World Economy.* New York: New York University Press.

Bell, Daniel. 1973. *The Coming of Post-Industrial Society: A Venture in Social Forecasting.* New York: Basic Books.

Beniger, James R. 1988. "Information Society and Global Science." *The Annals of the American Academy of Political and Social Science.* January 1988.

———. 1986. *The Control Revolution: Technological and Economic Origins of Information Society.* Cambridge, Mass.: Harvard University Press.

Bhagwati, Jagdish. 1998. *A Stream of Windows: Unsettling Reflections on Trade, Immigration and Democracy.* Cambridge, Mass.: The MIT Press.

———, ed. 1977. *The New International Economic Order: The North-South Debate.* Cambridge, Mass.: MIT Press.

Bhagwati, Jagdish, and Padma Desai. 1970. *India: Planning for Industrialization.* London: Oxford University Press.

Bhagwati, Jagdish, and T. N. Srinivasan. 1975. *Foreign Trade Regimes and Economic Development.* New York: Columbia University Press.

Biersteker, Thomas. 1995. "The 'Triumph' of Liberal Economic Ideas in the Developing World." In Barbara Stallings, ed., *Global Change, Regional Response: The New International Context of Development.* Cambridge, Mass.: Cambridge University Press.

Brahmananda, P. R. 1979. *Planning for a Futureless Economy.* Bombay: Himalaya Publishing House.

Braibanti, Ralph, and John Spengler, eds. 1963. *Administrative and Economic Development in India.* Durham, N.C.: Duke University Press.

Braman, Sandra. Summer 1993. "Harmonization of Systems: The Third Stage of the Information Society." *Journal of Communications* 43.

Brandt Commission. 1980. *A Program for Survival.* New York: United Nations.

Bratton, Michael. 1994. "Peasant-State Relations in Postcolonial Africa: Patterns of Engagement and Disengagement." In Joel S. Migdal, Atul Kohli, and Vivienne Shue, eds., *State Power and Social Forces: Domination and Transformation in the Third World*. Cambridge: Cambridge University Press.

Braudel, Fernand. 1993/1987. *A History of Civilizations*. Translated by Richard Mayne. New York: Penguin Books.

Bruce, Robert. 1989. "Options and Development in the Telecommunications Sector." In Bjorn Wellenius, Peter A. Stern, Timothy E. Nulty, and Richard D. Stern, eds. *Restructuring and Managing the Telecommunications Sector: A World Bank Symposium*. Washington, D.C.: The World Bank.

Bruce, Robert R., and Jeffrey P. Cunard. 1994. "Restructuring the Telecommunications Sector in Asia: An Overview of Approaches and Options." In Bjorn Wellenius and Peter A. Stern, eds., *Implementing Reforms in the Telecommunications Sector: Lessons from Experience*. Washington, D.C.: The World Bank.

Bruce, Robert R., Jeffrey P. Cunard, and Mark D. Director. 1988. *The Telecom Mosaic: Assembling the New International Structure*. Fromme, Somerset: Butterworth Scientific for International Institute of Communications.

Buchanan, James M. 1972. "A Public Choice Approach to Public Utility Pricing." In James M. Buchanan and Robert D. Tollison, eds., *Theory of Public Choice: Political Applications of Economics*. Ann Arbor: The University of Michigan Press.

———. February 1965. "An Economic Theory of Clubs." *Economica*.

Business & Political Observer. December 6, 1990. "Telecom Corporate Set-Up Unlikely: DoT Sees Additional Burden for Govt. in Delinking Services."

———. December 1, 1990. "Priority before Privatisation." Editorial.

———. December 15–28, 1986. "AT&T and Philips: Knocking on India's Door."

Business India. June 5–18, 1995. "Open Sesame!"

———. July 13–26, 1986. "C-DoT's Trials."

Business Korea. March 1997. "A Landmark Deal."

Business Standard. May 15, 1989. "Imports in Telecom Sector Inevitable."

Byres, T. J. 1982. "India: Capitalist Industrialization or Structural Stasis." In Bienefeld and Godfrey, eds., *The Struggle for Development*. New York: John Wiley & Sons.

Cardoso, Fernando, and Enrique Felatto. 1971/1979. *Dependency and Development in Latin America*. Berkeley: University of California Press.

Castells, Manuel, and Laura D'Andrea Tyson. 1988. "High Technology Choices Ahead: Restructuring Interdependence." In John W. Sewell, Stuart K. Tucker, and Contributors, *U.S. Policy and the Developing Countries: Growth, Exports, & Jobs in a Changing World Economy: Agenda 1988*. Washington, D.C.: Overseas Development Council, U.S.-Third World Policy Perspectives, No.9.

Chatterjee, Gautam. May 20, 1989. "Role of ITU for Global Telecom Development." *Mainstream*.

Chaudhry, Kiren Aziz. October 1994. "Economic Liberalization and the Lineages of the Rentier State." *Comparative Politics* 27.

Cho, Shin, and Myeongho Lee. 1998. "Competition and Deregulation: An APEC Perspective." In Gary Clyde Hufbauer and Erika Wada, eds., *Unfinished Business: Telecommunications after the Uruguay Round*. Washington, D.C.: Institute for International Economics.

Cho, Wha-Joon, and Suk-Zoon Huh. 1994. "Modernization of Rural Telecommunications in Korea." In *Report of the Seminar on Rural Telecommunications*. Asia-Pacific Telecommunity. Christchurch, New Zealand, 8–12 December 1994.

Choo, Kwang-Yung, and Myung-Koo Kang. 1994. "South Korea: Structure and Changes." In Eli Noam, Seisuke Komatsuzaki, and Douglas A. Conn., eds., *Telecommunications in the Pacific Basin: An Evolutionary Approach*. New York: Oxford University Press.

Chowdary, T. H. 1998. "Politics and Economics of Telecom Liberalization in India." *Telecommunication Policy* 22, no. 1.

———. 1989. "An Indian Perspective on Sector Reform." In Bjorn Wellenius, Peter A. Stern, Timothy E. Nulty, and Richard D. Stern, eds., *Restructuring and Managing the Telecommunications Sector: A World Bank Symposium*. Washington, D.C.: The World Bank.

———. Jan. 1988. "International Telecommunications: Strategic Considerations for Development." Videsh Sanchar Nigam Limited. Unpublished paper.

———. Jan. 18, 1988. "Improving Telecom Services." *Financial Express*.

Cippolla, Carlo M. 1980. *Before the Industrial Revolution: European Society and Economy, 1000–1700*. Second edition. New York: W.W. Norton and Company.

Comor, Edward, ed. 1994. *The Global Political Economy of Communication*. Houndmills, U.K.: Macmillan.

Communication International. July 1997. "The Road from Singapore."

Cowhey, Peter F. 1994. "The Political Economy of Telecommunications Reform in Developing Countries." Bjorn Wellenius and Peter A. Stern, eds., *Implementing Reforms in the Telecommunications Sector: Lessons from Experience*. Washington, D.C.: The World Bank.

———. 1990. "The International Telecommunications Regime: The Political Roots of Regimes for High Technology." *International Organization* 44, no. 2.

Cowhey, Peter F., and Jonathan Aronson. 1993. *Managing the World Economy: The Consequences of Corporate Alliances*. New York: Council of Foreign Relations.

Cowhey, Peter F., Jonathan Aronson, and Gabriel Gzekely, eds. 1989. *Changing Networks: Mexico's Telecommunications Options*. San Diego: Center for U.S.-Mexican Studies, University of California. Monograph Series, 32.

Crandall, Robert W., and Kenneth Flamm, eds. 1989. *Changing the Rules: Technological Change, International Competition and Regulation in Communications*. Washington, D.C.: The Brookings Institution.

Crawford, Morris H. 1991. *Communication Networks for Finance and Trade in the USSR and Eastern Europe*. Program on Information Resources Policy, Harvard University.

Cyert, R. M. and J. G. March. 1963. *A Behavioural Theory of the Firm*. Englewood Cliffs, N.J.: Prentice Hall.

Deane, Phyllis. 1965. *The First Industrial Revolution.* Cambridge: Cambridge University Press.

Deibert, Ronald. 1997. *Parchment, Printing, and Hypermedia: Communication and World Order Transformation.* New York: Columbia University Press.

Department of Telecommunications. Ministry of Communications, Government of India. 1994. *Annual Report 1993–94.*

———. 1993. *Annual Report 1992–93.*

———. 1990. *Annual Report 1988–89. Activities 1989–90.*

———. 1989. *Annual Report 1987–88. Activities 1988–89.*

———. 1988. *Forty Years of Telecommunications in Independent India.* New Delhi: Department of Telecommunications, Government of India.

Dibble, Anne C. April 6, 1992. "Telecommunications Deregulation in Brazil Rings Up Sales for U.S. Firms." *Telephony.*

DRI/McGraw-Hill. 1991. *The Contribution of Telecommunications Infrastructure to Aggregate and Sectoral Efficiency.* DRI/McGraw-Hill.

Duch, Raymond M. 1991. *Privatizing the Economy: Telecommunications Policy in Comparative Perspective.* Ann Arbor: University of Michigan Press.

Dutta-Roy, Amit. Feb. 1992. *The State of Brazilian Telecommunications Services.* Harvard University, Program on Information Policy Research.

Echevveri-Gent, John. 1990. "Economic Reforms in India: A Long and Winding Road." In Richard E. Feinberg, John Echeverri-Gent, Friedmann Muller, and contributors. *U.S. Foreign Policy and the USSR, China, and India: Economic Reform in Three Giants.* Washington, D.C.: Overseas Development Council, U.S.-Third World Policy Perspectives, no. 14.

Eckstein, Harry. 1975. "Case Study and Theory in Political Science." In F.I. Greenstein and N.W. Polsby, eds., *Handbook of Political Science, vol. 7.* Reading, Mass.: Addison-Wesley.

Economic Study Cell, Posts and Telegraphs Board. 1981. "India's Rural Telephone Network."

Economic Times. June 1, 1998. "Sinha's Budget Today May Entice Foreign Funds, NRIs."

———. Nov. 9, 1990. "AT&T Keen on Indian Market."

———. August 1, 1990. "Telecom Policy."

———. July 30, 1990. "Telecom Equipment Manufacturing Companies: Mixed Performance."

———. June 25, 1990. "Telecom Commission."

———. Feb. 9, 1990. "Wrong Numbers: Ruthless Competition Strangles Those Who Heard the Call to Make Telephones."

———. Sept. 11, 1989. "RAX Tendering Policy Liberalized."

———. July 21, 1989. "Telecom Plan Cost Moves Up."

———. June 7, 1989. "Telecom Tariff Structure: BICP to Suggest Changes."

———. May 22, 1989. "Performance of Six PSUs in 1987–88."

———. Feb. 5, 1989. "Packaged Rural Exchanges."

———. Oct. 21, 1988. "Rapid Growth in Telecom Traffic."

The Economist. November 11, 1995. "Indian Telecoms: Clearing the Line."

———. June 10, 1995. "South Korea: Not So Militant."

Ellul, Jacques. 1964. *The Technological Society*. Translated by John Wilkinson. New York: Alfred K. Knopf.

Erdman, Howard. 1967. *The Swatantra Party and Indian Conservatism*. Cambridge: Cambridge University Press.

Evans, Peter. 1995. *Embedded Autonomy: State and Industrial Transformation*. Princeton, N.J.: Princeton University Press.

———. 1979. *Dependent Development: The Alliance of Multinational, State and Local Capital in Brazil*. Princeton, N.J.: Princeton University Press.

Evans, Peter B., Dietrich Rueschemeyer, and Theda Skocpol., eds. 1985. *Bringing the State Back In*. Cambridge: Cambridge University Press.

Far Eastern Economic Review. October 5, 1995. "China: Numbers Please."

———. June 15, 1995. "Privatization: Hold the Phones."

———. April 7, 1994. "India: Seeking a Quick Fix."

———. September 10, 1992. "Telephone Tag: Indian Contract Procedures Frustrate Bidders."

Feigenbaum, Harvey B., and Jeffrey R. Henig. January 1994. "The Political Underpinnings of Privatization: A Typlogy." *World Politics* 46.

Feinberg, Richard E., John Echeverri-Gent, Friedmann Muller, and Contributors. 1990. *U.S. Foreign Policy and the USSR, China, and India: Economic Reform in Three Giants*. Washington, D.C.: Overseas Development Council, U.S.-Third World Policy Perspectives, no. 14.

Financial Express. April 20, 1990. "7th Plan Progress."

———. Oct. 2, 1989. "Telecom Commission Plan Finalized: Output to be Quadrupled."

———. July 15, 1989. "Role for Private Sector in Telecom."

———. July 13, 1989. "Rs 48,000 cr. Telecom Plan."

———. June 29, 1989. "Ministry of Communications: Performance of Departmental Enterprises."

———. May 12, 1989. "Significant Developments Change the Face of Industry."

Financial Times. July 3, 1997. "Tarnished Triumph."

Fishlow, Albert. 1965. *American Railroads and the Transformation of the Ante-Bellum Economy*. Cambridge, Mass.: Harvard University Press.

Fredebeul-Krein, Markus, and Andreas Freytag. 1997. "Telecommunications and WTO Discipline: An assessment of the WTO Agreement on Telecommunication Services." *Telecommunications Policy* 20.

Gallagher, John, and Ronald Robinson. 1953. "The Imperialism of Free Trade." *Economic History Review* 6.

Galtung, Johan. 1982. "The New International Order: Economics and Communications." In Meheroo Jussawalla and D. M. Lamberton, eds., *Communication, Economics and Development*. Honolulu: East-West Center.

Genschel, Philipp, and Raymond Werle. 1993. "From National Hierarchies to International Standardization: Modal Changes in the Governance of Telecommunications." *Journal of Public Policy* 13.

George, Alexander L. 1979. "Case Studies and Theory Development: The Method of Structured, Focused Comparison." In Paul Gordon Lauren, ed., *Diplomacy: New Approaches in History, Theory and Policy*. New York: The Free Press.

Gerschenkron, Alexander. 1962. *Economic Backwardness in Historical Perspective.* Cambridge, Mass.: Harvard University Press.

Glover, Stephen I., and JoEllen Lotvedt. Winter 1997. "The Mexican Telecommunications Market: The Interplay of Internal Reform and NAFTA." *NAFTA: Law and Business Review of the Americas* 3, no. 1.

Goforth, Ray. January 12, 1997. "Burma/Myanmar Bans Modems and Fax Machines." World Wide Web. http://members.tripod.com/~goforth/one. Accessed on January 12, 1997.

Gourevitch, Peter. 1986. *Politics in Hard Times: Comparative Responses to International Economic Crises.* Ithaca, N.Y.: Cornell University Press.

Government of India. 1997. *Perspective Plan for Telecommunication Services (1997–2007).* Ministry of Communications, Department of Telecommunications, New Delhi.

———. 1996. *India 1995.* New Delhi: Research and Reference Division, Ministry of Information and Broadcasting.

———. 1990. *India 1990.* New Delhi: Research and Reference Division, Ministry of Information and Broadcasting.

Grieco, Joseph M. Summer 1982. "Between Dependency and Autonomy: India's Experience with the International Computer Industry." *International Organization* 36.

The Guardian. December 12, 1994. "Speeding toward the Infobahn."

Haggard, Stephen. 1990. *Pathways from the Periphery: The Politics of Growth in the Newly Industrializing Countries.* Ithaca, N.Y.: Cornell University Press.

Haggard, Stephan, and Robert F. Kaufman. 1995. *The Political Economy of Democratic Transitions.* Princeton, N.J.: Princeton University Press.

———, eds. 1992. *The Politics of Economic Adjustment: International Constraints, Distributive Conflicts, and the State.* Princeton, N.J.: Princeton University Press.

Hahm, Sung Deuk, and L. Christopher Plein. October 1995. "Institutions and Technological Development in Korea: The Role of the Presidency." *Comparative Politics* 28.

Hall, Peter. 1989. *The Political Power of Economic Ideas.* Princeton, N.J.: Princeton University Press.

———. 1986. *Governing the Economy: The Politics of State Intervention in Britain and France.* New York: Oxford University Press.

Hanna, Nagy K. 1991. *The Information Technology Revolution and Economic Development.* World Bank Discussion Papers, no. 120.

Hardin, Russell. 1982. *Collective Action.* Baltimore: Johns Hopkins University Press.

Heywood, Peter. April 1996. "India Inc." *Data Communications.*

The Hindu. July 23, 1998. "Telecom Union Opposes Move to Convert DoT into Corporation."

———. July 11, 1998. "A Mirage on IT." Editorial.

———. May 30, 1998. "First Private Basic Service from June."

Hirschman, Albert. 1981. "The Rise and Decline of Development Economics." In Albert Hirschman, *Essays in Trespassing: Economics to Politics and Beyond.* Cambridge: Cambridge University Press.

——. 1958. *The Strategy of Economic Development*. New Haven, Conn.: Yale University Press.

Horwitz, Robert B. 1997. "Telecommunications Policy in the New South Africa: Participatory Politics and Sectoral Reform." *Media, Culture and Society*.

House, Karen Elliott. February 24, 1995. "Two Asian Giants, Growing Apart." *The Wall Street Journal*.

Hudson, Heather E. 1982. "Toward a Model for Predicting Development Benefits from Telecommunication Investment." In Mehroo Jussawalla and D. M. Lamberton, *Communication Economics and Development*. Honolulu: East-West Center.

Hudson, Heather E. et al. 1979. *The Role of Telecommunications in Socioeconomic Development*. Report prepared for the ITU. Boston: Information Gatekeepers Inc.

Indian Express. 1989. "Despite Red Tapism: Vast Scope for Pvt. Sector in Telecom."

Indian Institute of Foreign Trade (IIFT). December 1988. *India's Overseas Telecommunication Services: Relationship With Foreign Trade*. Prepared for Videsh Sanchar Nigam Limited, IIFT, New Delhi.

Indian Post. Feb. 2, 1989. "An Indian Post Supplement on the Industry of the Future: Telecommunications."

——. March 17, 1989. "Are VSNL and MTNL Being Forced to Cook Their Books?"

——. May 23, 1989. "Telecom Commission Sets Tasks for Improving Communications."

——. Feb. 2, 1990. "Telephone Instruments: Coping with Excess Capacity."

——. May 17, 1990. "Telecom Department Makes Staggering Profits While Quality Improves Marginally."

Innis, Harold. 1950. *Empire and Communications*. Oxford: Clarendon Press.

International Telecommunication Union. 1998. *World Telecommunication Indicators on Diskette*.

——. 1997. *Yearbook of Public Telecommunication Statistics*. 24th edition. Geneva: International Telecommunication Union.

——. 1992. *Yearbook of Public Telecommunication Statistics*. 19th edition. Geneva: International Telecommunication Union.

——. 1984. *The Missing Link: Report of the Independent Commission for World Wide Telecommunications Development*. Geneva: International Telecommunications Union.

Isahak, Daud bin. 1989. "Meeting the Challenges of Privatization in Malaysia." In Bjorn Wellenius, Peter A. Stern, Timothy E. Nulty, and Richard D. Stern, eds., *Restructuring and Managing the Telecommunications Sector: A World Bank Symposium*. Washington, D.C.: The World Bank.

Ivanek, Ferdo et al. 1991. *Manufacturing Telecommunications Equipment in Newly Industrializing Countries: The Effect of Technological Progress*. World Bank Technical Paper no. 145. Washington, D.C.: The World Bank.

Jagota, S. P. 1963. "Training of Civil Servants in India." In Ralph Braibanti and John Spengler, eds., *Administrative and Economic Development in India*. Durham, N.C.: Duke University Press.

Jain, Rekha. September 1997. "Operationalizing a Regulatory Framework in India." Paper presented at the 25th Telecommunications Policy Research Conference, Alexandria, Virginia.

Janisch, Hudson N., and Danny Kotlowitz. June 1998. "African Renaissance, Market Romance: Post-Apartheid Privatization and Liberalization in South African Broadcasting and Telecommunications." Paper presented at the conference on "Has Privatization Worked? The International Experience." Columbia Institute of Tele-Information, Columbia University, New York.

Jesudason, James V. November 1995. "Statist Democracy and the Limits to Civil Society in Malaysia." *Journal of Commonwealth & Comparative Politics* 33, no. 3.

Joseph, William A. 1993. "China." In Joel Kreiger, ed., *The Oxford Companion to Politics of the World*. New York: Oxford University Press.

Journal of Commerce. October 13, 1993. "U.S. Telecom Companies Prepare for '96 Opening of Mexico."

Journal of Communication. Autumn 1995. "Symposium: Horizons of the State: Information Policy and Power." Special Issue. *Journal of Communication* 45.

Journal of Economic Perspectives. 1994. Symposium: "New Growth Theory." *Journal of Economic Perspectives* 8.

Jussawalla, Mehroo, and H. Ebenfeld. 1984. *Communication and Information Economics: New Perspectives*. Amsterdam, N.Y.: North-Holland.

Jussawalla, Mehroo, and D. M. Lamberton, eds. 1982. *Communications, Economics and Development*. East-West Center. Honolulu: Pergamon Policy Series on International Development.

Kahler, Miles. 1990. "Orthodoxy and Its Alternatives: Explaining Approaches to Stabilization and Adjustment." In Joan M. Nelson, ed., *Economic Crisis and Policy Choice: The Politics of Adjustment in the Third World*. Princeton, N.J.: Princeton University Press.

Karunaratne, Neil Dias. 1982. "Telecommunication and Information in Development Planning Strategy." In Mehroo Jussawalla and D. M. Lamberton, eds., *Communications, Economics and Development*. Honolulu: East-West Center. Pergamon Policy Series on International Development.

Kaul, S. N. April 1979. "Planning of Telecommunications Services for Development." *NCAER Margin* 2.3.

Keohane, Robert O., and Helen Milner, eds. 1996. *Internationalization and Domestic Politics*. Cambridge: Cambridge University Press.

Keohane, Robert, and Joseph Nye. 1977. *Power and Interdependence*. Boston: Little, Brown.

Khusro, A. M. Dec. 17, 1990. "Writing on the Wall." *Indian Express.*

———. Dec. 16, 1990. "No Soft Options." *Indian Express.*

Kim, Jae Cheol, and Tae-Soek Ro. September/October 1993. "Current Policy Issues in the Korean Telecommunications Industry." *Telecommunications Policy.*

Kim, Cae-One, Yong Kon Kim, and Chung-Bun Yoon. 1992. "Korean Telecommunications Development." *World Development* 20.

Kindleberger, Charles. 1978. *Economic Response: Comparative Studies in Trade, Finance and Growth*. Cambridge, Mass.: Harvard University Press.

King, Gary, Robert O. Keohane, and Sidney Verba. 1994. *Designing Social Enquiry: Scientific Inference in Qualitative Research*. Princeton, N.J.: Princeton University Press.

Kochanek, Stanley A. Dec. 1986. "Regulation and Liberalization Theology in India." *Asian Survey* 26.

————. 1974. *Business and Politics in India*. Berkeley: University of California Press.

Kohli, Atul. 1990. *Democracy and Discontent: India's Growing Crisis of Ungovernability*. Cambridge: Cambridge University Press.

————. March 1989. "Politics of Economic Liberalization in India." *World Development* 17.

Kothari, Rajni. 1970. *Politics in India*. New Delhi: Orient Longman.

Krasner, Stephen. April 1991. "Global Communications and National Power: Life on the Pareto Frontier." *World Politics* 43.

Krasner, Stephen D. 1985. *Structural Conflict: The Third World against Global Liberalism*. Berkeley: University of California Press.

Krueger, Anne O. 1974. "The Political Economy of the Rent-seeking Society." *American Economic Review* 64.

Kuo, Eddie C. Y. 1994. "Singapore." In Eli Noam, Seisuke Komatsuzaki, and Douglas A. Conn, eds., *Telecommunications in the Pacific Basin: An Evolutionary Approach*. New York: Oxford University Press.

Landa, Ramiro Tovar. October 1997. "Policy Reforms in Networks Infrastructure: The Case of Mexico." *Telecommunications Policy* 21, no. 8.

Landes, David. 1980. "The Creation of Knowledge and Technique: Today's Task and Yesterday's Experience." *Daedalus* 109, 1.

————. 1969. *The Unbound Prometheus: Technological Change and Industrial Development in Western Europe from 1750 to the Present*. Cambridge, Mass.: Harvard University Press.

Larson, James F. 1995. *The Telecommunications Revolution in Korea*. Hong Kong: Oxford University Press.

Lawrence, D. H. 1959. *Lady Chatterley's Lover*. New York: A Signet Classic.

Lee, Paul S. N. December 1991. "Dualism of Communications in China." *Telecommunications Policy*.

Leff, Nathaniel H. January 1984. "Externalities, Information Costs, and Social Benefit-Cost Analysis for Economic Development: An Example from Telecommunications." *Economic Development and Cultural Change* 32.

Leibenstein, Harvey. 1978. *General X-Efficiency Theory & Economic Development*. New York: Oxford University Press.

Lelyveld, David. May 26, 1991. "India's Fate." *Los Angeles Times*.

Lerner, Daniel. 1958. *The Passing of Traditional Society*. Glenco, Ill.: Free Press.

Lerner, Norman C. October 24, 1988. "Formidable Aspirations Lead Brazil Forward." *Telephony*.

Levy, Brian, and Pablo T. Spiller, eds. 1996. *Regulations, Institutions and Commitment: Comparative Studies of Telecommunications*. Cambridge: Cambridge University Press.

Lichbach, Mark I. April 1994. "What Makes Rational Peasants Revolutionary? Dilemma, Paradox, and Irony in Peasant Collective Action." *World Politics* 46.

Lim, Linda Y. C. 1995. "Southeast Asia: Success through International Openness." In Barbara Stallings, ed., *Global Change, Regional Response: The New International Context of Development*. Cambridge: Cambridge University Press.

Los Angeles Times. July 30, 1991. "India's New Economics May Be First Shot in a Revolution."

———. Nov. 11, 1985. "Sign of Pitiful Public Sector: In Zaire, Walkie-Talkies Proliferate as Phones Fail."

Lowe, Vincent. 1988. "Malaysia and Indonesia: Telecommunications Restructuring." In Eli Noam, Seisuke Komatsuzaki, and Douglas A. Conn, eds., *Telecommunications in the Pacific Basin: An Evolutionary Approach*. New York: Oxford University Press.

Lu, Hui. March 3, 1997. "China's Telecommunications Market." *China Today*.

Machlup, Fritz. 1962. *The Production and Distribution of Knowledge in the United States*. Princeton, N.J.: Princeton University Press.

Mahanagar Telephone Nigam Limited, Ministry of Communications, Government of India. 1996. *Annual Report 1995–96*.

———. 1995. *Annual Report 1994–95*.

———. 1993. *MTNL Completes Seven Years*. Monograph.

———. *Annual Report 1991–92*.

———. *Annual Report 1988–89*.

———. *Annual Report 1987–88*.

———. *Annual Report 1986–87*.

Mansell, Robin. 1993. *The New Telecommunications: A Political Economy of Network Evolution*. London: Sage Publications.

Mansell, Robin, and Roger Silverstone, eds. 1996. *Communication by Design: The Politics of Information and Communication Technologies*. Oxford: Oxford University Press.

Mazucco, Antonio C. C. February 1996. "Telecoms Regulation in Brazil: Trends and Prospects." *Computer and Telecommunications Law Review* 3, no. 4.

McDowell, Stephen. 1997. *Globalization, Liberalization and Policy Change: A Political Economy of India's Communications Sector*. Houndmills, U.K.: Macmillan.

———. Autumn 1995. "The Decline of the License Raj: Indian Software Export Policies." *Journal of Communication* 45.

———. 1994. "International Services Liberalization and Indian Telecommunications Policy." In Edward Comor, ed., *The Global Political Economy of Communication*. Houndmills, U.K.: Macmillan.

McLuhan, Marshall. 1964/1997. *Understanding Media: The Extensions of Man*. Cambridge, Mass.: The MIT Press.

Mcluhan, Marshall, and Bruce R. Powers. 1989. *The Global Village*. New York: Oxford University Press.

Meltzer, Arthur M., Jerry Weinberger, and M. Richard Zinman. 1993. *Technology in the Western Political Tradition*. Ithaca, N.Y.: Cornell University Press.

Mendoza, Alfredo Perez de. 1989. "Teléfonos de Mexico: Development and Perspectives." In Peter F. Cowhey, Jonathan Aronson, and Gabriel Gzekely, eds.,

Changing Networks: Mexico's Telecommunications Options. San Diego: Center for U.S.-Mexican Studies, University of California. Monograph Series, 32.

Migdal, Joel S. 1994. "The State in Society: An Approach to Struggles for Domination." In Joel S. Migdal, Atul Kohli, and Vivienne Shue, eds., *State Power and Social Forces: Domination and Transformation in the Third World*. Cambridge: Cambridge University Press.

Migdal, Joel S., Atul Kohli, and Vivienne Shue, eds. 1994. *State Power and Social Forces: Domination and Transformation in the Third World*. Cambridge: Cambridge University Press.

Milner, Helen V. 1997. *Interests, Institutions and Information: Domestic Politics and International Relations*. Princeton, N.J.: Princeton University Press.

Ministry of Finance. 1998. "Economic Survey: 1997–98." Accessed through http://www.nic.in/indiabudget.

Moats, Bruce R. February 17, 1998. Letter written to USTR by the Director of Federal Government Affairs, AT&T. Obtained from USTR files, Washington, D.C.

———. February 6, 1998. Letter written to USTR by the Director of Federal Government Affairs, AT&T. Obtained from USTR files, Washington, D.C.

Mody, Asoka. 1989. "Information Industries in the NICs." In Robert W. Crandall and Kenneth Flamm, eds., *Changing the Rules: Technological Change, International Competition and Regulations in Telecommunications*. Washington, D.C.: The Brookings Institution.

Mody, Bella. Autumn 1995. "State Consolidation through Liberlaization of Telecommunications Services." *Journal of Communications* 45.

Mohamed, Syed Hussein. 1994. "Corporatization and Partial Privatization of Telecommunications in Malaysia." In Bjorn Wellenius and Peter A. Stern, eds. 1994. *Implementing Reforms in the Telecommunications Sector: Lessons from Experience*. Washington, D.C.: The World Bank.

Moore, Barrington. 1966. *Social Origins of Dictatorship and Democracy: Lord and Peasant in the Making of the Modern World*. Boston: Beacon Press.

Morehouse, W., and R. Chopra. 1983. *Chicken and Egg: Electronics and Social Change in India*. Lund, Sweden: Research Policy Studies, Technology and Culture.

Morris-Jones, W. H. 1987. *The Government and Politics of India*. New Delhi: Universal Book Stall.

Mowlana, Hamid. 1997. *Global Information and World Communication: New Frontiers in International Relations*, Second edition. London: Sage.

———. 1985. *International Flow of Information: A Global Report and Analysis*. Paris: Unesco.

Mowlana, Hamid, and Laurie J. Wilson. 1990. *The Passing of Modernity: Communication and the Transformation of Society*. New York: Longman.

Mueller, Milton. 1994. "China: Still the Enigmatic Giant." *Telecommunications Policy* 18.

———. Spring 1993. "Telecommunications as Infrastructure: A Skeptical View." *Journal of Communication* 43.

Mumford, Lewis. 1970. *The Myth of the Machine: The Pentagon of Power*. New York: Harcourt Brace Jovanovich.

Myrdal, Gunnar. 1968. *Asian Drama*. New York: Pantheon Books.

Nelson, Richard R., and Gavin Wright. Dec. 1992. "The Rise and Fall of American Technological Leadership." *Journal of Economic Literature* 30.

The New York Times. January 5, 1997. "Thinking Wireless, John Kluge Builds His Next Empire out of Thin Air."

———. January 1997. "Mexican Rivals Campaign for Callers."

———. May 26, 1991. "Heir to Tragedy: India Confronts Gandhi's Death and Flawed Legacy."

Noam, Eli. Winter 1992. "Private Networks and Public Objectives." *Aspen Quarterly*.

———. 1989. "International Telecommunications in Transition." In Robert W. Crandall, and Kenneth Flamm, eds. *Changing the Rules: Technological Change, International Competition and Regulation in Communications*. Washington, D.C.: The Brookings Institution.

Noam, Eli, Seisuke Komatsuzaki, and Douglas A. Conn, eds. 1994. *Telecommunications in the Pacific Basin: An Evolutionary Approach*. New York: Oxford University Press.

Nanda, D. N. July 24, 1995. "DoT & the Challenges of Competition." *Economic Times*.

Nantha, Francis C. July 15, 1995. "Telecommunications over the Years." *New Straights Times*.

National Informatics Centre. 1998. "Information Technology Action Plan." Accessed through http://it-taskforce.nic.in/it-taslforce/prem.htm.

Nora, Simon, and Alain Minc. 1980. *The Computerization of Society: A Report to the President of France*. Cambridge, Mass.: MIT Press.

North, Douglass C. June 1994. "Economic Performance through Time." *The American Economic Review* 84.

———. 1990. *Institutions, Institutional Change and Economic Performance*. Cambridge: Cambridge University Press.

———. 1981. *Structure and Change in Economic History*. New York: W.W. Norton.

North, Douglass C., and Robert T. Thomas. 1973. *The Rise of the Western World: A New Economic History*. Cambridge: Cambridge University Press.

NTIA. 1991. *The NTIA Infrastructure Report: Telecommunications in the Age of Information*. U.S. Department of Commerce. National Telecommunications and Information Administration.

Nulty, Timothy. 1989. "Emerging Issues in World Telecommunications." In Bjorn Wellenius, Peter A. Stern, Timothy E. Nulty, and Richard D. Stern, eds., *Restructuring and Managing the Telecommunications Sector: A World Bank Symposium*. Washington, D.C.: The World Bank.

O'Brien, Rita Cruise, ed. 1983. *Information, Economics and Power: The North-South Dimension*. Boulder, Colo.: Westview Press.

Ohmae, Keniichi. 1990. *The Borderless World: Power and Strategy in the Interlinked Economy*. New York: Harper Business.

Okundi, Philip O. October 1975. "Pan-African Telecommunications Network: A Case for Telecommunications in the Development of Africa." *World Telecommunication Forum*. Geneva: International Telecommunication Union.

Olson, Mancur. September 1993. "Dictatorship, Democracy, and Development." *American Political Science Review* 87.

———. 1982. *The Rise and Decline of Nations: Economic Growth, Stagflation, and Social Rigidities*. New Haven, Conn.: Yale University Press.

———. 1965. *The Logic of Collective Action: Public Goods and the Theory of Groups*. Cambridge, Mass.: Harvard University Press.

Onn, Fong Chan. 1994. "Malaysia." In Eli Noam, Seisuke Komatsuzaki, and Douglas A. Conn, eds., *Telecommunications in the Pacific Basin: An Evolutionary Approach*. New York: Oxford University Press.

Ostrom, Elinor. March 1998. "A Behavioral Approach to the Rational Choice Theory of Collective Action." *American Political Science Review* 92, no. 1.

Parker, Edwin B., Heather Hudson, et al. 1989. *Rural America in the Information Age: Telecommunications Policy for Rural Development*. Lanham, MO: University Press of America and The Aspen Institute.

Pavlic, Breda, and Cees J. Hamelink. 1985. *The New International Economic Order: Links between Economics and Communications*. Paris: Unesco.

Pereira, L. 1984. *Development and Crisis in Brazil: 1930–1983*. Boulder, Colo.: Westview Press.

Perry, Elizabeth J. 1994. "Labor Divided: Sources of State Formation in Modern China." In Joel S. Migdal, Atul Kohli, and Vivienne Shue, eds., *State Power and Social Forces: Domination and Transformation in the Third World*. Cambridge: Cambridge University Press.

Petrazinni, Ben. 1995. *The Political Economy of Telecommunications Reform in Developing Countries: Privatization and Liberalization in Comparative Perspective*. Westport, Conn.: Praeger.

Pierce, William, and Nicholas Jacquier. 1983. *Telecommunications for Development*. Geneva: International Telecommunications Union.

Pitroda, Satyen G. July 1976. "Telecommunications Development—The Third Way." *IEEE Transactions on Communications* (COM-24:7).

Plato. 1973. *Phaedrus and The Seventh and The Eighth Letters*. Translated by Walter Hamilton. London: Penguin Classics.

Pool, Ithiel de Sola. 1990. *Technologies without Boundaries: On Telecommunications in a Global Age*. Cambridge, Mass.: Harvard University Press.

Porat, Marc Uri. 1977. *The Information Economy: Definition and Measurement*. Washington, D.C.: Office of Telecommunications, U.S. Department of Commerce.

Power, Jonathan. May 23, 1991. "A National Tragedy, Beyond Gandhi." *Los Angeles Times*.

Pradhan, Bishnu D. March 1994. "Telecommunications: At Least a Phone in Every Village."

Press Information Bureau, Government of India. April 5, 1989. "DoT Exceeds Seventh Plan Targets." Press release.

———. March 13, 1989. "Setting up of Telecommunications Commission." Press release.

PS: Political Science and Politics. June 1997. "Symposium: Controversy in the Discipline: Area Studies and Comparative Politcs" 30.

Putnam, Robert. January 1995. "Bowling Alone: America's Declining Social Capital." *Journal of Democracy* 4.

———. 1993. *Making Democracy Work: Civic Traditions in Modern Italy.* Princeton, N.J.: Princeton University Press.

———. Summer 1988. "Diplomacy and Domestic Politics: The Logic of Two-Level Games." *International Organization* 42.

Ravi, N. May 12, 1989. "Significant Developments Change the Face of Industry." *Financial Express.*

Robinson, S. J. 1990. "Possible World Bank Assistance for Telecommunications Development in India." World Bank position paper sent to the Government of India.

Rogers, Everett. 1983. *Diffusion of Innovations.* Third edition. New York: The Free Press.

Rosenau, James N. 1990. *Turbulence in World Politics: A Theory of Change and Continuity.* Princeton, N.J.: Princeton University Press.

Rosenberg, Nathan, and L. E. Birdzell Jr. 1986. *How the West Grew Rich: The Economic Transformation of the Industrial World.* New York: Basic Books.

Rosenstein-Rodan, P. N. June–Sept. 1943. "Problems of Industrialization of Eastern and South-Eastern Europe." *The Economic Journal* 53.

Rostow, Walt W. 1960. *The Stages of Economic Growth: An Anti-Communist Manifesto.* Cambridge: Cambridge University Press.

Rowney, Michael J. February 17, 1998. Letter written by Executive Vice President of MCI to USTR. Obtained from USTR office, Washington, D.C.

———. January 28, 1998. "Making Competition Work in Mexico and on the US-Mexico Route." Presentation obtained from USTR files, Washington, D.C.

Rudolph, Lloyd I., and Susanne Hoeber Rudolph. 1987. *In Pursuit of Lakshmi: The Political Economy of the Indian State.* Chicago: University of Chicago Press.

Sandholtz, Wayne. 1992. *High-Tech Europe: The Politics of International Cooperation.* Berkeley: University of California Press.

Sandler, Todd. 1992. *Collective Action: Theory and Applications.* Ann Arbor: University of Michigan Press.

Sandler, Todd, and John T. Tschirhart. December 1980. "The Economic Theory of Clubs: An Evaluative Survey." *Journal of Economic Literature* 18.

Sapolsky, Harvey M. et al., eds. 1992. *The Telecommunications Revolution: Past, Present and Future.* London: Routledge.

Sarewitz, Daniel. 1996. *Frontiers of Illusion: Science, Technology, and the Politics of Progress.* Philadelphia: Temple University Press.

Saunders, Robert J., Jeremy J. Warford, and Bjorn Wellenius. 1994 (second edition)/1983. *Telecommunications and Economic Development.* Washington, D.C.: The World Bank.

Schmandt, Jurgen et al. 1991. *Telecommunications and Rural Development: A Study of Private and Public Sector Innovation.* New York: Praeger.

Schramm, Wilbur. 1964. *Mass Media and National Development.* Stanford, Calif.: Stanford University Press.

Sclove, Richard. 1995. *Democracy and Technology.* New York: Guilford Press.

Sell, Susan. 1998. *Power and Ideas: North-South Politics of Intellectual Property and Antitrust.* Albany, N.Y.: State University of New York Press.

Shridharni, Krishanlal. 1953. *Story of the Indian Telegraphs: A Century of Progress.* New Delhi: Posts and Telegraphs Department, Government of India.

Simon, Herbert A. 1982. *Models of Bounded Rationality.* 2 vols. Cambridge: MIT Press.

Singapore Telecom. May 25, 1995. "Highlights of the Singapore Telecom Group's Unaudited Results for the Year Ended 31 March 1995." News Release.

Singh, J. P. Forthcoming, a. "Negotiating Regime Change: The Weak, the Strong and the WTO Telecom Accord." In James N. Rosenau and J. P. Singh, eds., *Information Technologies and Global Politics: The Changing Scope of Power and Governance.* Albany, N.Y.: State University of New York Press.

———. Forthcoming, b. "Weak Powers and Globalism: Impact of Plurality on Weak-Strong Negotiations in the International Economy." *International Negotiation.*

———. June 1998. "Evaluating Telecommunication Privatization and Liberalization in India and Far East." Paper presented at the conference on "Has Privatization Worked? The International Experience." Columbia Institute of Tele-Information, Columbia University, New York.

Singh, J. P. and Jagdish Sheth. 1997. "Exclusion and Territoriality in Global Telecommunications: Influence of Industrial Age State-Business Relations in the Information Age." Paper presented at the International Studies Association, Toronto, March 18–22, 1997.

Sinha, Nikhil. 1996. January/February 1996. "The Political Economy of India's Telecommunications Reforms." *Telecommunications Policy* 20, 1.

Sisodia, Rajendra S. May–June 1992. "Singapore Invests in the Nation-Corporation." *Harvard Business Review.*

Skocpol, Theda. 1979. *States & Social Revolutions: A Comparative Analysis of France, Russia & China.* Cambridge: Cambridge University Press.

Smith, Tony. 1981. *The Pattern of Imperialism: The United Sates, Great Britain, and the Late-Industrializing World since 1815.* Cambridge: Cambridge University Press.

Soete, Luc. March 1985. "International Diffusion of Technology; Industrial Development, and Technological Leapfrogging." *World Development* 13.

Sovani. 1963. "Non-Economic Aspects of India's Economic Development." In Ralph Braibanti and John Spengler, eds., *Administrative and Economic Development in India.* Durham, N.C.: Duke University Press.

Steinmo, Sven, Kathleen Thelen, and Frank Longstreth, eds. *Structuring Politics: Historical Institutionalism in Comparative Analysis.* Cambridge: Cambridge University Press.

Stigler, George. 1971. "The Theory of Economic Regulation." *Bell Journal of Economics and Management Science* 2.

Stone, Philip B. 1991. *The Relative Importance of Telecommunications Investments on Selected Measures of Socio-Economic Development.* Research Report no. 13. Center for Telecommunications Management, School for Business Administration, University of Southern California.

Strange, Susan. 1982. "Cave! Hic Dragones: A Critique of Regime Analysis." *International Organization* 2.

Streeten, Paul. 1982. "The Conflict between Communication Gaps and Suitability Gaps." In Mehroo Jussawalla and D. M. Lamberton, eds., *Communications, Economics, and Development*. Honolulu: East-West Center. Pergamon Series on International Development.

Sundaram, Jomo Kwame. 1993. "Malaysia." In Joel Krieger, ed., *The Oxford Companion to Politics of the World*. New York: Oxford University Press.

Sunday. May 13–19, 1990. "Telecommunications: The Minister and the Messiah."

Sunday Observer. April 9, 1989. "What's Pitroda's Claim to Fame?"

Sunday Times of India. Dec. 9, 1990. "City Phone Service below Mark, Says Study."

Sung, Keuk Je. 1994. "South Korea: Telecommunications Policies into the 1990s." In Eli Noam, Seisuke Komatsuzaki, and Douglas A. Conn, eds., *Telecommunications in the Pacific Basin: An Evolutionary Approach*. New York: Oxford University Press.

Sutter, Daniel. July 1996. "Public Goods, Indivisible Goods, and Market Failure." *Economics and Politics* 8.

Szekely, Gabriel. 1989. "Mexico's Challenge: Developing a New International Economic Strategy." In Peter F. Cowhey, Jonathan Aronson, and Gabriel Gzekely, eds., *Changing Networks: Mexico's Telecommunications Options*. San Diego: Center for U.S.-Mexican Studies, University of California. Monograph Series, 32.

Tan, Zixiang. April 1994. "Challenges to the MPT's Monopoly." *Telecommunications Policy* 18.

Telekom Malaysia Berhad. 1995. *1994 Annual Report*.

Telephony. Nov. 2, 1992. "Business is Booming for Chile's Telecom Industry."

———. July 6, 1992. "The Curtain Rises on Telecommunications in Eastern Europe."

———. Jan. 6, 1992. "Global Economy, Changing Political Scene Play Havoc with Spending."

Times of India. Aug. 28, 1989. "Videsh Sanchar to Offer Database Services."

Tocqueville, Alexis de. 1835/1945. *Democracy in America*. Translated by Henry Reeve. New York: Alfred A. Knopf.

Tyson, Laura D'Andrea. 1992. *Who's Bashing Whom? Trade Conflict in High-Technology Industries*. Washington, D.C.: Institute for International Economics.

Tyson, Laura D'Andrea, and John Zysman, eds. 1983. *American Industry in International Competition: Government Policies and Corporate Strategies*. Ithaca, N.Y.: Cornell University Press.

United Nations Development Program. 1996. *Human Development Report*. New York: Oxford University Press.

Venable, Tim. June 1996. "North American Telecom Pushes the Right Business Buttons . . . But Not Necessarily Everywhere." *Site Selection*.

Vernon, Robert. ed. 1990. *The Promise of Privatization: A Challenge for American Foreign Policy*. New York: Council on Foreign Relations.

The Wall Street Journal. July 31, 1998. "South Korea Gets Gloomy Prognosis from OECD."

———. July 30, 1998. "Brazil's Telebras Stake Goes for $18.85 Billion."

———. July 29, 1998. "Brazil Girds for Crucial Test in Big Telebras Sale."

———. July 16, 1998. "Mexican Long-Distance Fight Nearing an End."

———. July 14, 1998. "Malaysia Affirms That a Recession is Approaching."

———. June 30, 1998. "Singapore to spend $1.2 Billion to Stimulate Flagging Economy."

———. May 14, 1998. "Battle Over Mexican Phone Market Heats Up."

———. April 23, 1998. "Malaysian Social Experiment Faces Threatening Ripples of Asian Crisis."

———. April 6, 1998. "Big Board Is Seen Listing Telebras 'Babies.'"

———. March 31, 1998. "Cellular Sale to Resume in Brazil."

———. February 25, 1998. "South Korea's Kim Must Lure Foreign Funds."

———. January 23, 1998. "Brazil's President Thrives Amid Turmoil."

———. November 24, 1997. "Korea's Past Policies Are Unable to Remedy Today's Economic Ills."

———. November 14, 1997. "Political Pluralism Arrives in Mexico." Article written by Robert l. Bartley, editor.

———. November 3, 1997. "Mexico Expects to Withstand Turmoil."

———. October 10, 1997. "Latin Stocks to Shine through '98."

———. October 6, 1997. "China's Telecom's IPO Lures Investors, But Some See Risks in $3 Billion Sale."

———. September 30, 1997. "Korea Inc.'s Gamble on Cellular-Phone Technology May Pay Off."

———. September 19, 1997. "Brazil Should Open Telecom to Full Competition."

———. September 17, 1997. "Brazil Sets Tight Schedule to Sell Phone Company."

———. September 15, 1997. "Newest Reforms in China May Be the Hardest Yet."

———. June 10, 1997. "Silicon Valley East: Malaysia is Gambling on a Costly Plunge into a Cyber Future."

———. April 30, 1997. "Legal Challenges Force Brazil to Delay Privatization of Mining Giant CVRD."

———. February 19, 1997. "India's Gowda Belatedly Advances Economic Reform."

———. January 7, 1997. "Mexico's Long Distance Providers Claim Early Victories as Phone Wars Begin."

———. June 17, 1996. "Mexican Ruling Party Cools on Support of Government's Free-Market Policies."

———. December 29, 1995. "Beyond Gandhi: Economic Reforms Seem Secure in India, Election Rhetoric Aside."

———. May 12, 1995. "Singapore's New Telecom Licenses Hold Promise, But Not for Investors Seeking Quick Gratification."

———. February 13, 1995. "The Outlook: Mexico's Woes Show Risks of Partial Reform."

Waltz, Kenneth. 1979. *Theory of World Politics*. Reading, Mass.: Addison-Wesley.

Warren, Bill. 1980. *Imperialism: Pioneer of Capitalism*. London: Verso.

Week. April 22, 1990. "Taking a Hot Line: CBI to Follow Up on Unnikrishnan's 'Charge-Sheet' against Sam Pitroda?

Wellenius, Bjorn. 1994. "Telecommunications Restructuring in Latin America: An Overview." In Bjorn Wellenius and Peter A. Stern, eds., *Implementing Reforms in the Telecommunications Sector: Lessons From Experience*. Washington, D.C.: The World Bank.

Wellenius, Bjorn, and Gregory Staple. 1996. *Beyond Privatization: The Second Wave of Telecommunications Reforms in Mexico*. World Bank Discussion Paper no. 341.

Wellenius, Bjorn, and Peter A. Stern, eds. 1994. *Implementing Reforms in the Telecommunications Sector: Lessons From Experience*. Washington, D.C.: The World Bank.

Wellenius, Bjorn and others. 1993. *Telecommunications: World Bank Experience and Strategy*. World Bank Discussion Papers, 192.

Wellenius, Bjorn, Peter A. Stern, Timothy E. Nulty, Richard D. Stern, eds. 1989. *Restructuring and Managing the Telecommunications Sector: A World Bank Symposium*. Washington, D.C.: The World Bank.

White, Gordon. ed. 1988. *Development States in East Asia*. London: Macmillan.

Williamson, Oliver E. 1985. *The Economic Institutions of Capitalism*. New York: Free Press.

Win, Khin Maung. 1994. "Rural Communications in Myanmar." In *Report of the Seminar on Rural Telecommunications*. Asia-Pacific Telecommunity. Christchurch, New Zealand, 8–12.

Winner, Langdon. 1977. *Autonomous Technology: Technics-out-of-Control as a Theme in Political Thought*. Cambridge: The MIT Press.

Wittman, Donald. 1995. *The Myth of Democratic Failure: Why Political Institutions Are Efficient*. Chicago: University of Chicago Press.

Wolf, Martin. 1982. *India's Exports*. Washington, D.C.: The World Bank.

Woodrow, Brian R. August 1991. "Tilting Towards a Trade Regime: The ITU and the Uruguay Round Services Negotiations." *Telecommunications Policy*.

The World Bank. 1998/99. *World Development Report: Knowledge for Development*. Washington, D.C.: The World Bank.

———. 1997. *World Development Report 1997: The State in a Changing World*. Washington, D.C.: The World Bank.

———. 1994. *World Development Report 1994: Infrastructure for Development*. Washington, D.C.: The World Bank.

———. 1993. *World Development Report 1993: Investing in Health*. Washington, D.C.: The World Bank.

———. 1992. *World Development Report 1990*. Washington, D.C.: The World Bank.

———. 1991. *World Development Report 1991: The Challenge of Development*. Washington, D.C.: The World Bank.

Xiong-Jian, Lian, and Zhu You-Nong. 1994. "China." In Eli Noam, Seisuke Komatsuzaki, and Douglas A. Conn, eds., *Telecommunications in the Pacific Basin: An Evolutionary Approach*. New York: Oxford University Press.

Zacher, Mark, with Brent A. Sutton. 1996. *Governing Global Networks: International Regimes for Transportation and Communications*. Cambridge: Cambridge University Press.

Zita, Ken. 1994. "China: Steps toward Political and Financial Reform." In Eli Noam, Seisuke Komatsuzaki, and Douglas A. Conn, eds., *Telecommunications in the Pacific Basin: An Evolutionary Approach*. New York: Oxford University Press.

Zorpette, Glen. March 1994. "Technology in India." *IEEE Spectrum* 31, 3.

INDEX

administrative users. *See* government administrations as users

AirTouch Communication, 104

Akerlof, George, 208

Alcatel,
in China, 94
in India, 149, 159, 175, 184, 254n. 28 (149)

Almond, Gabriel, 262n. 34 (228)

Ameritech,
in Brazil, 103

Amin, Samir, 234n. 7 (22)

Archibugi, Daniele, 261n. 2 (201)

Aronson, Jonathan D.,
breakdown of natural monopoly, 232n. 25 (12)
ideational influences, 237n. 49 (30)
large users and data networks, 260n. 69 (190)
on large users, 252n. 74 (135)
services sector, 235n. 23 (25)
technological influences, 32–33
telecommunications as cash cows, 238n. 72 (35)
urban centers of political influence, 253n. 15 (143)

Arrow, Kenneth, 208, 231n. 8 (5)

ASEAN (Association of South East Asian Nations), 107

AT&T,
and Singapore, 60
break-up of, 29
in Brazil, 102–103
in China, 93–94
in India, 175, 186, 259n. 36 (177)
in Mexico, 76–78
technological influences upon, 32

Athreya Committee (India), 144, 175

Athreya, M.B., 153, 196

banks. *See also* services sector
control of Mexican telecommunications, 73
data networks in India, 192
electronic banking in India, 135
reform awaited in India, 167
SWIFT and India, 190

Bar, Francois, 231n. 8 (5)

Bardhan, Pranab,
on state intervention in India, 122

Bauer, P.T., 123

Belassa, Bela,
economic conditions, 12,
export orientation, 235n. 26 (26)
ideational influence, 237n. 57 (31)
privatization in India, 252n. 5 (140)
resource constraints for import substitution, 24, 234n. 20–21 (24)

Bell Atlantic
in Brazil, 103
in India, 187
in Mexico, 77, 242n. 68

Bell Canada,
in India, 184, 186
in Mexico, 76

Bell Labs, 259n. 56 (184)

Bell, Daniel, 208, 231n. 8 (5)

BellSouth,
in Brazil, 103–104
in India, 184

Beniger, James, 208, 231n. 8 (5)

Bhagwati, Jagdish,
export orientation, 235n. 26 (26)

Bhagwati, Jagdish *(continued)*
  ideational influences, 237n. 49
    (31)
  Indian export policy, 161
  ISI and exports, 250n. 40 (124)
  on NIEO, 234n. 7 (22)
  welfare effects of markets, 226
Bharti Telecom, 161, 189
Biersteker, Thomas, 30–31
Birlas, 185–186
BJP government in India, 166–170
Braman, Sandra,
  NIEO and information economy
    consciousness, 234n. 13 (23)
Brandt, William, 234n. 7 (22)
Braudel, Fernand, 244n. 2 (90)
Brazil, 97–106
  indicators for specialized services,
    59–60
  political economy, 97–101
  summary of restructuring, 53, 98
  telecommunication efficiency
    indicators, 205–207
British Telecom,
  in India, 187, 193
  in Singapore, 58
  policy emulation in Malaysia,
    243n. 87 (83)
  privatization, 29
broadband. *See also* ISDN
  Singapore, 61
Bruce, Robert F.,
  factual support for policy-makers,
    251n. 60 (130)
  large users in Singapore, 241n. 16
    (61)
  on equipment shortages in India,
    256n. 61 (157)
  R&D in India, 142
  services in China, 244n. 15 (93),
    244n. 20 (94)
  telecom strategy in Singapore,
    240n. 11 (58)
Buchanan, James M., 33
Bureaucracy in India. *See* Indian
  Administrative Service, India:
  telecommunications bureaucracy

Burma. *See* Myanmar
Bush administration,
  pressures on Brazil, 102–103
Business lobbying in India,
  1970s and 1980s, 135–136
  by equipment manufacturers, 172
  by service providers, 171
  cellular operators lobbying, 185
  CII clout, 171
  from 1967 onwards, 125
  in colonial and postcolonial times,
    123
  NASSCOM, 171
  software industry, 171
  three current industry associations,
    171
business users. *See also* large users,
    small business users
  colonial India, 118
  demands documented well, 50
  influential, 216
  lobby separately, 37
  Malaysia, 82
  Mexico, 75

C-DoT (Centre for Development of
    Telematics, India), 148–150
  keeps away foreign manufacturers,
    175
Cable & Wireless,
  in China, 94
cable television,
  Mexico, 77
capital-output ratios, 131–132
Cardoso, Fernando,
  electoral prospects, 219
  presidency in Brazil, 100, 106
  seminal work on dependency
    theory, 245n. 30 (99)
cartels in India,
  equipment manufacturing,
    161–162
  telephone service bids, 186
Castells, Manuel, 235n. 31 (26)
catalytic states. *See also* Singapore,
    South Korea
  defined, 10, 20

maneuverability and responsibility, 42
streamlined initiatives, 20, 45
telecommunication restructuring in, 51–70
cellular,
Bell Lbs estimate, 259n. 56 (184)
Brazil, 59, 100, 102–103
China, 59–60, 94–96
growth rates for cases examined, 205–207
India, 59–60, 174, 181, 183–186
Malalysia, 59–60, 84–85
Mexico, 59, 76–77
Myanmar, 59, 108
Singapore, 58–60
South Korea, 59–60, 68
subscribers in cases examined, 59
central planning in India. *See* India: central planning
CGE in India, 184
change teams. *See* window of opportunity
Chidambaran, P., 168–169, 196
China, People's Republic of, 89–97
indicators for specialized services, 59–60
political economy, 89–92
summary of restructuring, 53, 91
telecommunication efficiency indicators, 205–207
Chowdary, T.H.,
government provision of telecommunications, 235n. 19 (24)
large users in India, 135
leadership role, 196
on BJP IT Taskforce, 182
on funding from expatriates, 151
telecommunication organization in India, 132
Cippolla, Carlo M., 213, 261n. 1 (201)
circles for telecommunications in India,
for cellular, 177–179, 184–185
for telephone services, 176–179

civil society, 227–228
club goods. *See also* user groups
Buchanan, James M., 33
concept of, 8–10
crowding and congestion effects, 34
demands met, 39
institutional context, importance and outcomes, 215–221
Mansell, Robin, 238n. 74 (35)
membership and provision conditions in institutional contexts, 216–217
membership and provision conditions, 35–36
nature of, 33–35
Noam, Eli, 237n. 64(33)
Olson, Mancur, 11
politics of, 12, 34–37
privileged groups, 39–40, 89
Sandler, Todd, 10
Sutter, Daniel, 237n. 66 (34)
types of, 10
collective action,
reform coalition in China, 93
and clubs, 34–37
and ideas and technology, 38
and privileged groups, 217
and societal groups, 40
and states, 37–40
coalitions in India, 165–166, 170–171
difficult with plural coalitions, 46
during second phase of restructuring in developing countries, 110
politics of, 12
problems of, 10
South Korea, 67
colonial communications. *See also* telephone service introduction, telegraph service introduction
India, 115–121
Malaysia, 79
Myanmar, 106–107
South Korea, 62
telegraph in India, 116–118
telephone in India, 118–121

Comor, Edward, 236n. 37 (27)
competition policies,
    Brazil, 102–104
    India, 174–186
    Malaysia, 84–85
    Mexico, 77
    Singapore, 58, 61
    South Korea, 68
comprehensive policies for
        telecommunications. *See also*
        policy-making and planning
        agencies
    China, 90
    in catalytic and near-catalytic
        states, 86–87
    India, 182
    lacking in Brazil, 106
    Malaysia, 85–86
    Mexico, 79
    presence or lack of in cases
        examined, 52–53
    Singapore, 56–61
    South Korea, 69
Comsat Max,
    in India, 193
Congo, 37, 106
Consultative Committee on
    Telephones and Telegraph
    (CCITT), 24
corporatization.
    India Telecom proposal, 259n. 37
        (177)
    Malaysia, 82
    moves toward in India, 143–144.
        See also Athreya Committee,
        MTNL, VSNL
    obstacles in India, 177
    Singapore, 56–57
    South Korea, 66
costs of installation. *See also* pricing
    Brazil, 101
    India, 157
    Mexico, 76
Cowhey, Peter F.,
    breakdown of natural monopoly,
        232n. 25 (12)
    ideational influences, 237n. 49 (30)

    importance of user groups, 233n.
        44 (17)
    institutionalist analysis of
        telecommunications, 239n. 83
        (41)
    large users and data networks,
        260n. 69 (190)
    Mexican growth rates, 242n. 58
        (74–75)
    neo-liberal argument in telecom-
        munications, 236n. 37 (27)
    on ideational influences, 30–31
    on large users, 252n. 74 (135)
    on technological influences, 32–33
    regime change in
        telecommunications, 28
    services sector, 235n. 23 (25)
    telecommunications as cash cows,
        238n. 72 (35)
    urban centers of political
        influence, 253n. 15 (143)
cross-subsidization. *See* pricing
Cunard, Jeffrey P.,
    large users in Singapore, 241n. 16
        (61)
    on equipment shortages in India,
        256n. 61 (157)
    R&D in India, 142
    services in China, 244n. 15 (93),
        244n. 20 (94)
    telecom strategy in Singapore,
        240n. 11 (58)
customer premises equipment in
    India, 159–161
Cyert, R.M., 208

DACOM, 37, 66, 68
data networks,
    Brazil, 102–103
    China, 93
    India, 151, 158, 189–193
    Mexico, 74, 76
    Myanmar, 108
    RABMN in India, 153
    Singapore, 58
    South Korea, 67, 69
    VIKRAM in India, 153

Deane, Phyllis, 261n. 7 (203)
debt crisis,
    Mexico, 73–74
dedicated networks. *See* data
    networks
Deibert, Ronald, 209, 231n. 8 (5)
demand conditions. *See also* user
        groups, clubs
    Brazil, 101–103
    China, 92–93, 95
    detailed, 33–40
    empirical evidence sparse, 50
    importance of, 210
    in India, 133–137, 150–152,
        170–174
    indicators used, 50
    Malaysia, 81–84
    Myanmar, 107–108
    Mexico, 74–77
    "reality" of, 215–221
    Singapore, 55–56, 58
    South Korea, 65–68
    summarized, 4, 20, 52–53
    summary for user groups
        examined, 224–226
dependency writers, 97, 99
Desai, Padma,
    export orientation, 235n. 26 (26)
    ideational influence, 237n. 57 (31)
    Indian export policy, 161
Deutsche Telecom in India,187
development priority for
        telecommunications,
    consensus on, 211
    factors responsible for, 23
    India, 137, 141–143, 211
    reasons for lack of importance, 21
    reasons for importance, 22
    Singapore, 56
    South Korea, 64
    strategic prioritization, xxi, 3
development, economic and
        telecommunications. *See also*
        development priority for
        telecommunications
    empirical investigations, 5–8
    implications, xxii

levels of analysis, 6–8
    myths and realities of, 201–229
    supply side, xxi
diffusion of innovations, 30–31
Duch, Raymond M., 238n. 77 (36)
duopoly,
    adopted in cellular for India, 178
    Mexico, 76
    Singapore, 58, 60
    South Korea, 66
    rejected in basic telephony for
        India, 177
dysfunctional states. *See also* China,
        Brazil, India
    defined, 11, 20
    maneuverability and responsibility,
        42–43
    most representative of developing
        world, 14–15, 89, 110–111
    problematic restructurings, 20, 45
    restructurings in, 89–106

E-Mail provision in India, 193–194
East Asian model,
    limited generalizability of,
        221–223
    success of, 202, 211
East India Company, 116–117
Eckstein, Harry, 14–15
economic conditions,
    basis for demand and supply,
        49–50
    domestic, 19–25
    global, 25–29
    summary for cases examined, 109
economic linkages. *See also*
        globalization
    backward and forward, 5
    global, 25–29
economies of scale,
    and natural monopoly, 31, 237n. 62
    inhibited in India, 168
electronics sector in India,
    data networks, 191
    policy-making, 142
    prioritization, 142
    software exports, 182

enlightenment , 210
Ericsson,
    in Brazil, 103
    in India, 159, 175, 184
Evans, Peter B.,
    civil society, 262n. 35 (228)
    embedded autonomy, 239n. 92
        (42)
    on Brazil, 99
    reconstructing the state, 213
    state decision-making, 239n. 86
        (41)
    state's role in development, 232n.
        32 (12)
export-oriented strategy. See also
        exporters
    China, 93–94
    Malaysia, 83
    Mexico, 74
    Singapore, 55–56, 58–62
    South Korea, 64
exporters,
    Brazil, 40
    China, 40
    get better services, 40
    Hong Kong, 40
    India, 40, 130, 133–134
    Indonesia, 40
    Singapore, 40
    summary of provision for cases
        examined, 224–226
externalities, 34

Faustian claims about technology,
    202
fax (facsimile),
    Brazil, 102
    India, 134–135
    Myanmar, 108
FCC (Federal Communications
        Commission),
    and MCI, 32
    and Mexico, 78
    pressures on India, 172
fiber optics,
    India, 158
    Singapore, 61

Financial crisis,
    in Asia, 61, 86
    in Brazil, 105
    in Mexico, 76
Fishlow, Albert, 212, 261n. 1 (201)
foreign direct investment. See foreign
        investors
foreign investors,
    demand for telecommunications,
        40, 238n. 79
    in Singapore, 56
France Telecom,
    in India, 184
    in Mexico, 75
Frank, Andre Gunder, 97
Fujitsu,
    in China, 94
    in India, 175
functional states, 224, 226–229

Gandhi, Indira,
    dynamics of Congress after 1966,
        125
    increasing dysfunction of state,
        125–127
Gandhi, M.K.,
    leadership style, 123
    swadeshi and BJP, 166
    use of telephone, 248n. 19
Gandhi, Rajiv,
    the state under, 139–141
General Agreement on Tariffs and
        Trade (GATT). See World Trade
        Organization
general equilibrium,
    conditions approaching, 221n. 3 (4)
    in club goods, 35
    supply and demand, 6
George, Alexander L., 14–15
Gereffi, Gary, 235n. 34 (27)
Gerschenkron, Alexander, 204, 231n.
        5 (5), 261n. 1 (201)
global alliances,
    in Brazil, 103–104
    in China, 94–95
    in India, 148–150, 159, 184–186,
        193–194

in Malaysia, 82, 85
in Mexico, 78
Singapore Telecom seeks, 60
globalization. *See also* economic
   linkages
and exporters, 40
connecting globally, 3, 12, 203
economic conditions, 25–29
technologies of, 21
Gourevitch, Peter, 38, 236n. 43 (28)
government administrations as users,
   China, 92, 96
colonial India, 118
India, 191
Malaysia, 82
summary of provision for cases
   examined, 224–226
GTE,
   in Brazil, 103
   in Mexico, 78

Haggard, Stephan,
   creeping authoritarianism, 243n.
     78 (81)
   business-government relations in
     South Korea, 241n. 42 (69)
   consolidating reforms, 226
   critique of neo-classical economics,
     235n. 27 (26)
   demonstrating societal influences,
     40
   dual transitions, 233n. 37 (14)
   impetus for reform, 46
   legitimacy of reform, 220
   on Brazilian politics, 99–100
   on Mexico, 241–242n. 51 (71)
   on Singapore, 55
   regime type and development
     strategy, 239n. 85 (41)
   role of economic crises, 232n. 27
     (12)
   state decision-making, 239n. 86
     (41)
   state responsibility, 239n. 90 (42)
   window of opportunity,
     239–240n. 95 (44)
Hamelink, Cees, 209, 231n. 8 (5)

HCL (Hindustan Cables Limited),
   self-reliance ideal, 131
   transmission market, 161–162
Hewlett Packard
   in India, 192
Himachal Futuristic, 188, 193
Hirschman, Albert,
   emphasis on demand, 212
   evaluating development
     economics, 234n. 3 (21)
   on governments internalizing
     internalities, 238n. 68 (34)
historical institutionalism,
   and societal preferences, 11, 16
   context for examining state, 214,
     221
   representative works, 239n. 86
   state decision-making, 41–45
Hitachi,
   in China, 94
House, Karen Elliott, 258n. 11 (170)
Hudson, Heather E.,
   benefits of telecommunications, 7
   culture of telephone usage, 248n.
     20 (119)
human rights issues,
   abuses in Myanmar, 107–108
   Kwangju student uprising, 64
   Tiannenman, 90
Hyundai, 66

IBS (International Business Services),
   151, 191
ideational influences,
   explained, 29–31
   Malaysia, 83
   Mexico, 74
   summarized for India, 196
   summary for cases examined,
     109–110
   types of 11–12
IMF (International Monetary Fund),
   aid to India, 124, 167
   package for Mexico in 1994, 76
import substitution industrialization
   (ISI),
   and NWICO, 23

import substitution industrialization
    (ISI) *(continued)*
  Brazil, 99
  defined, 233n. 1 (21)
  in general, 21
  in telecommunications, 21–25
  India, in general, 122–127
  India, in telecommunications,
    127–138
  lack of finances for, 235n. 18 (24)
  Mexico, 73–74, 76
  rent-seeking, 218
  South Korea, 64
India Telecom proposal, 259n. 37 (177)
India,
  indicators for specialized services,
    59–60
  political economy, 122–127,
    139–141,166–170
  telecommunication efficiency
    indicators, 205–207
India, central planning in,
  Eighth, Ninth, Tenth Plans, 162
  plan outlays in
    telecommunications, 127–128
  Seventh Plan (1985–90), 140,
    152–162
  under Nehru, 122–127
India: telecommunications
  bureaucracy, 129–131, 137,
  143–147, 156, 177–178, 181
Indian Administrative Service (IAS),
  accrues power in postcolonial
    India, 123
  and telecommunications, 129
  competitive, 249n. 32
  in PM's secretariat, 140
  leave DoT, 143
  precursor in colonial India, 117
Inmarsat, 158
Innis, Harold,
  applied to Indian colonial
    communication, 120
  medium theory, 209
Intelsat,
  India, 151, 158
  the old regime, 28

interconnection issues,
  Brazil, 105
  colonial India, 119
  India, 178, 180, 187
  Mexico, 77–78
international division of labor, 26
international services,
  India, 132, 134, 154, 156. *See also*
    VSNL
  Singapore, 58
Internet,
  advocacy group in India, 173
  Brazil, 59,
  China, 59–60, 96
  in cases examined, 59
  India, 59–60, 158, 181, 193–194
  Malaysia, 59–60
  Mexico, 59, 76
  Singapore, 59–60
  South Korea, 59–60
ISDN
  India, 191
  Singapore, 56–58
ITI (Indian Telephone Industries),
    159
  and trade unions, 188
  self-reliance ideal, 131
  transmission market, 161–162
ITU (International
    Telecommunications Union),
  as interest group, 28
  conference in New Delhi, 151
  finding on underinvestment, 24
  importance of
    telecommunications, 3
  reporting of figures, 82
  studies on telecommunications and
    development, 23
  technocratic reasoning, 211, 261n.
    10 (204)
  the old regime, 28

Jalan Committee Report (India), 193
joint ventures. *See* global alliances
Judiciary in India,
  and cellular bids, 184
  and telephone service bids, 188

and TRAI, 180
playing a proactive role, 170, 173, 196

Kahler, Miles, 30, 237n. 50 (30)
Kaufman, Robert F.,
  business-government relations in South Korea, 241n. 42 (69)
  consolidating reforms, 226
  creeping authoritarianism, 243n. 78 (81)
  dual transitions, 233n. 37 (14)
  impetus for reform, 46
  legitimacy of reforms, 220
  on Brazilian politics, 99–100
  role of economic crises, 232n. 27 (12)
  state decision-making, 239n. 86 (41)
  state responsibility, 239n. 90 (42)
  window of opportunity, 239–240n. 95 (44)
KDD
  and Singapore, 60
Keohane, Robert O.,
  domestic sources of change, 236n. 43 (28)
  issue-structures, 28
  on research design, 15
Keynesian ideas, 29, 31
Khusro, A.M., 252n. 8 (141)
Kindleberger, Charles,
  group behavior, 215, 232n. 21 (11)
  role of politics, 16
King, Gary, 15
Kohli, Atul,
  developmentalist state in South Korea, 239n. 88 (41)
  future of democracy in India, 258n. 19 (173)
  historical strength of states, 240n. 96 (44)
  state-society relations, 239n. 93 (42)
Kothari, Rajni, 126
Krasner, Stephen,
  critique of NIEO, 234n. 7 (22)

definition of regimes, 236n. 43 (28)
  on global influences, 27
Krueger, Anne O., 123

labor issues,
  Brazil, 100, 103
  China, 244n. 3 (90)
  high employment in India, 132
  labor laws in India, 169
  Malaysia, 83
  Mexico, 73
  Singapore, 55
  South Korea, 64, 68–69
  strength in India, 258n. 18 (172)
  trade union in Indian telecommunications, 173–174
  trade unions in India, 143, 146, 156, 177, 188, 194
  under BJP in India, 183
Landes, David,
  importance of demand, 33
  on technology and economic history, 261n. 1 (201)
  theory of production, 237n. 58 (33)
large users,
  Brazil, 102–103
  China, 92
  India, 135–136, 150–152, 190
  Singapore, 61
  South Korea, 65–67
  summary of provision for cases examined, 224–226
Largest city main lines,
  historical, 121
  in cases examined, 57
Larson, James F., 65, 241n. 46 (69)
Lawrence, D.H., v, 228–229
leapfrogging,
  accelerating development, 3
  and user groups, 17
  defined, 4–5
  economic, 5
  in India, 153, 182
  "myths" of, 203–214
  not done in Myanmar, 107

leapfrogging *(continued)*
    possibility of, 4
    "reality" of, 214–229
    stages of growth, 5
    technological, 5
leased line networks. *See* data
    networks
legislative issues in
        telecommunications,
    Brazil, 104–105
    colonial India, 117, 119
    India, 179–180
    Malaysia, 83
    Mexico, 78
    Myanmar, 108
Leibenstein, Harvey, 204
Lerner, Daniel, 234n. 5 (22)
Levy, Brian, 227, 232n. 32 (12)
liberal internationalists, 27–28
license fees for service providers in
    India, 187, 189
lobbying in India. *See* business
    lobbying in India
local telephony,
    Mexico, 75–77
    Singapore, 58
Locke, John, 262n. 29 (224)
long-distance telephony,
    DoT preserve in India, 178
    India, 132, 154
    Telmex loses monopoly, 75, 77
Lucky Goldstar, 64, 66

M-Tel in India, 184
MacBride Commission Report, 22.
    See also NWICO
Machlup, Fritz, 208, 231n. 9 (5)
MAFF talks, 32, 67, 77
Maitland Commission Report, 23, 207
Malaysia, 74–86
    crisis of legitimacy, 44
    indicators for specialized services,
        59–60
    political economy, 79–81
    summary of restructuring, 52, 80
    telecommunication efficiency
        indicators, 205–207

Mansell, Robin, 233n. 33 (17), 238n.
    76 (36)
March, J.G., 208
market efficiency,
    competitiveness of firms, 27
    disciplining monopolies, 50
    importance of
        telecommunications, 3, 26
    in democratic markets, 238–239n.
        82
    inefficient political markets, 41
    role of information, 5
Marx, Karl, 202
Marxists, 27, 227
McDowell, Stephen,
    India and GATT, 258n. 14 (172)
    pressures from Indian software
        industry, 258n. 12 (171)
    USTR pressures on India, 258n. 16
        (172)
MCI,
    and AT&T, 32
    in Brazil, 106
    in Mexico, 76, 78
McLuhan, Marshall, 209, 234n. 5
    (22)
Meltzer, Arthur M., 261n. 4 (202)
Mexico, 71–79
    economic conditions, 38
    indicators for specialized services,
        59
    political economy, 71–74
    summary of restructuring, 52, 72
    telecommunication efficiency
        indicators, 205–207
Michie, Jonathan, 261n. 2 (201)
Migdal, Joel S., 238n. 80 (40), 239n.
    93 (42)
Minc, Alain, 32, 209, 231n. 8 (5)
Ministry of Finance in India,
    cellular licensing, 185
    power over DoT, 143
Mitsubishi,
    in China, 94
Modis, 185–186
Mody, Asoka, 133, 148, 241n. 25
    (65)

Mody, Bella,
  1994 telecommunications policy in
    India, 259n. 34 (176)
  political consolidation through
    restructuring, 240n. 97 (45)
Moore, Barrington, 247n. 12 (117)
Morris-Jones, W.H.,
  deinstitutionalization of Congress,
    250n. 47 (125)
  on successive Indian governments,
    140
Motorola,
  in Brazil, 103
  in China, 94
  in India, 175, 184
  in Mexico, 76
Mowlana, Hamid, 23, 234n. 6 (22),
    234n. 11 (23), 234n. 12 (23)
MTNL (Mahanagar Telephone
    Nigam Limited),
  buyer of equipment, 159, 161
  corporatization, 143
  desire to provide cellular, 184
  equipment shortages, 151
  performance, 156
Mueller, Milton,
  on China's economic policies, 97
  politics of telecommunications and
    development, 231n. 13 (8)
multi-national corporations. *See*
  foreign investors
Mumford, Lewis, 261n. 5 (202)
Myanmar, 106–108
  indicators for specialized services,
    59–60
  political economy, 106
  summary of restructuring, 53
  telecommunication efficiency
    indicators, 205–207

NAFTA, 77–78
National Front government in India,
    166–168
National Telecommunication Policy,
    1994 (India), 176–179
natural monopoly argument. *See*
  technological influences

near-catalytic states. *See* Mexico,
  Malaysia
India, 1950–67, 122–124
  telecommunication restructuring
    in, 71–86
NEC,
  in Brazil, 103
  in China, 94
Nehru, Jawaharlal,
  on industrialization in India, 204
  state under, 115, 122–124
Nelson, Richard R., 213
neo-classical economics,
  as ideational influence, 30–31
  globalization perspective, 26
  Haggard's critique of, 235n. 27
    (26)
  technological efficiency, 204
  zeitgeist of, 29
nepotism,
  Brazil, 101
  India, 166, 190. *See also* rent-
    seeking in India
  Malaysia, 82–83
  South Korea, 68
  under communication minister in
    India, 178–179
New World Information and
  Communication Order (NWICO),
    22–23
New Zealand Telecom in India, 187
NICNET, 192
Noam, Eli,
  club goods theory, 233n. 44 (17),
    237n. 64 (33), 238n. 76 (36)
  political telematique, 32
Nokia,
  in China, 94
Nora, Simon, 32, 209, 231n. 8 (5)
North, Douglass C.,
  behavioral underpinnings of the
    state, 239n. 86 (41)
  importance of property rights,
    261n. 3 (201)
  political markets, 41
  property rights and political
    instability, 220–221

Northern Telecom,
  in Brazil, 103
  in China, 94
NTT,
  in India, 184
  in Singapore, 58
  privatization, 29
Nye, Joseph, 28
Nynex in India, 184, 187

O'Brien, Rita Cruise, 209, 234n. 6
  (22), 234n. 9 (23)
Olson, Mancur,
  concepts related to club goods
    analysis, 11
  ideational influences, 237n. 58 (31)
  Pareto optimality, 232n. 20 (11)
  predatory state, 239n. 94 (43)
  responsible autocrats, 240n. 100
    (46)
Ostrom, Elinor, 239n. 87 (41)

paging,
  Brazil, 59,
  China, 59, 93, 96
  India, 59, 174,
  Malaysia, 59, 84
  Malaysia, 59, 84
  Mexico, 59
  Singapore, 59
  South Korea, 59
  subscribers in cases examined, 59
Pareto optimality,
  club goods and, 10–11, 35
  market distortion, 8
Parker, Edwin B.,
  benefits of telecommunications, 7,
    9
party systems. See political parties
Pavlic, Breda, 209, 231n. 8 (5)
payphones. See PCOs
PCOs (public call offices),
  in cases examined, 57
  in India, 151, 153
  in rural India, 152–154
  multimedia service provision in
    India, 182

PCs (personal computers)
  Brazil, 59
  China, 59–60
  India, 59–60, 192
  Malaysia, 59–60
  Mexico, 59
  Singapore, 59–60
  South Korea, 59–60
Petrazzini, Ben,
  history of Mexican
    telecommunications, 342n. 55
    (73)
  ideational influences in Malaysia,
    243n. 87 (83)
Philips,
  in China, 94
Pitroda, Satyen (Sam) K.,
  boosting R&D in India, 142,
    148–150
  C-DoT, 148–150
  calls cellular elitist, 151
  corruption in manufacturing, 161
  leadership role, 196
  "Mission: Better
    Communications", 152–153
  on vested interests in India, 157
  "Six Technology Mission",
    142–143
  support for in India, 150
  Telecommunications Commission,
    143, 146
Plato, v, 228–229
policy-making and planning. See also
    comprehensive policies for
    telecommunications, India,
    Central Planning in
  Blue House (South Korea), 64
  Brazil, 100, 106
  EDB (Singapore), 55–56
  EPB (South Korea), 64
  flow charts for India, 145–146
  in colonial India, 117–119
  KISDI (South Korea), 67
  major policy changes in India,
    141–152, 174–183
  Malaysia, 83
  ministries in China, 93

ministries in Singapore, 56
ministries in India, 136
MOST (South Korea), 64
NCB (Singapore), 56
postcolonial India, 127–131
State Council (China), 93
technicos (Mexico), 73–74
political parties,
 BJP, 166–70, 178–179
 CCP in China, 90–92, 95
 Congress in India, 122–127, 140,
  166, 219–220
 DAP in Malaysia, 81
 in Brazil, 99–100
 in developing countries, 219–221
 Janata Party in India, 126
 National Front in India, 141,
  166–168
 PAN in Mexico, 73, 76–77
 PAP in Singapore, 51, 55
 PRD in Mexico, 77
 Precursor to BJP in India, 125–125
 PRI in Mexico, 71–79
 UMNO in Malaysia, 81, 83
Pool, Ithiel de Sola, 231n. 8 (5)
Porat, Marc Uri, 208, 231n. 8 (5)
Portugal Telecom, 106
Pradhan, Bishnu D., 254n. 27 (148),
 258n. 24 (174)
predatory states. *See also* Myanmar,
 Congo
 defined, 21, 43
 restructuring in, 106–108
pricing,
 Brazil, 101–103, 105
 cross-subsidization among clubs,
  216
 cross-subsidization in India, 130
 data networks in India, 191
 difficulties with marginal costs, 35,
  212, 237n. 62, 238n. 75
 equipment in India, 131
 flat rates, 35
 Mexico, 75, 77–78
 TRAI preserve in India, 180
 VSNL, 261n. 85 (194)
private goods, 33–34

privatization,
 Brazil, 100, 103–106
 cellular in India, 183–186
 China, 95
 Malaysia, 82
 Mexico, 74–75
 Singapore, 58,61
 South Korea, 66, 68, 70
 telephone service in India, 186–189
product cycle and
 telecommunications, 26
property rights in
  telecommunications,
 concerning liberalization and
  privatization, 38
 inefficient political markets, 41
 regulatory design and governance,
  227
 role of the state, 221
 under political uncertainty, 220–221
PTTs (post, telegraph and telephone)
  monopolies,
 ideational influences on, 30
 traditional suppliers of
  telecommunication, 10
public goods, 33–34
Putnam, Robert, 236n. 43 (28), 262n.
 34 (228)

quality of service in India,
 marginal improvement, 153
 MTNL, 157
quantitative studies in
  telecommunications,
 strengths, 5–8
 supply-side emphasized, xxi
 weaknesses, 204–207

R&D
 China, 94
 colonial India, 118
 comparing India and South Korea,
  150
 South Korea, 64, 66
 telecommunication in India, 142,
  148–150
 under Rajiv Gandhi in India, 140

RABMN (India), 153, 190–191
railways,
    as service provider in China, 95
    as service provider in India, 189
    data networks in India, 191, 193
    in colonial India, 117
    Malaysia, 79
    networks in China, 93
    parallels with telecommunications
        infrastructure, 212
Rao government in India,
    economic crisis, 141, 167
    on telecommunications, 144
    state under, 166–167
rates of return in telecommunications,
    rationale for state intervention, 35
    World Bank estimates, 234–235n.
        16 (23)
rational choice,
    critiques of, 262n. 24 (2150
    institutionalism, 11
RBOCs in India, 178, 187. See also
    Ameritech, Bell Atlantic,
    BellSouth, SBC Communications,
    Nynex, US West
Realists, 27
regime theory, 26, 236n. 43 (28)
regulatory agency,
    Brazilian Telecommunication
        Agency, 105
    COFTEL in Mexico, 78–79
    DoT in India, 157
    JTM in Malaysia, 83
    pressures for in India, 176,
        178–179
    SCT in Mexico, 77, 79
    Telecommunication Commission
        (India), 144–147
    TRAI in India, 179–181
Reliance (India), 185–186
rent-seeking in India, 123, 160. See
    also nepotism
    communication minister under
        Rao government, 179
    corruption of officials, 167
    related to political party, 170
research and development. See R&D

research design,
    choice of cases, 14
    most-likely case, 14–15, 89,
        110–111, 214
    structured focused comparison, 14
restructuring of telecommunications,
    defined, 3, 231n. 1 (3)
    demand driven, 4, 10, 19–20, 27,
        33–40
    factors determining, 13
    first moves toward, 25
    issues involved, 3
    micro and macro, 8–11, 13, 33–40
    summarized, 20–21, 52–53
    supply driven, 16–17, 20, 41–45
revenues from telecommunications,
    cash cow in India, 156
    colonial India, 119–120
    funds for treasury in India, 130
    indicators for cases examined,
        205–207
    Telebras as cash cow, 102
    Telmex as cash cow, 74
    Telmex overpriced and inefficient,
        76
    through sales of enterprises, 50
Rogers, Everett, 209, 231n. 8 (5)
Rosenau, James N., 202
Rosenberg, Nathan, 261n. 1 (201)
Rosenstein-Rodan, P.N., 204
Rostow, W.W., 204, 231n. 5 (5)
Rousseau, Jean Jacques, 39, 262n. 29
    (224)
Rudolph, Lloyd I.,
    on Indira Gandhi, 125
    on Rajiv Gandhi, 252n. 5 (140)
Rudolph, Susanne Hoeber,
    on Indira Gandhi, 125
    on Rajiv Gandhi, 252n. 5 (140)
rural users
    Brazil, 102
    China, 93–94
    India, 130, 133, 150–152,
        173–174, 176, 187, 194–195
    Malaysia, 82, 84
    Mexico, 224
    Myanmar, 107

South Korea, 69
summary of provision for cases
    examined, 224–226

Samsung, 64, 66
    in China, 94
Sandholtz, Wayne, 236n. 37 (27)
Sandler, Todd,
    membership and provision in
        multiple clubs, 262n. 26 (216)
    state supply of club goods, 10
Sapolsky, Harvey M., 231n. 8 (5)
Sarewitz, Daniel, 261n. 4 (202)
satellite,
    data networks in India, 190
    IBS in India, 151
    Intelsat in India, 151
    Mexico, 77
    uplinks allowed in India, 183
    VSATs in India, 190–192
Saunders, Robert J.
    benefits of telecommunications, 7,
        9
    teledensities in developing
        countries, 251n. 70 (133)
SBC Communications,
    in Mexico, 75
Schramm, Wilbur, 22
Sclove, Richard, 261n. 4 (202)
Seimen's,
    in China, 94
    in colonial India, 117
    in India, 159, 175
Sell, Susan, 256n. 77 (161)
services sector,
    Brazil, 101
    importance for developing
        countries, 24–25
Seshagiri, N., 182, 196
Sheth, Jagdish, 261n. 13 (211)
Shridharni, Krishanlal,
    history of colonial
        telecommunication in India,
        116–121
    telecommunications in colonial
        Burma, 246n. 68 (106)
    teledensity in India, 1951, 133

Shukla, M.P., 196
Simla, 119
Simon, Herbert, 208, 231n. 8 (5)
Singapore Telecom in India, 184, 187.
    See also Singapore
Singapore, 51–62
    indicators for specialized services,
        59–60
    political economy, 51–55
    summary of restructuring, 52, 54
    telecommunication efficiency
        indicators, 205–207
Singh, J.P.
    historical neglect of demand, 261n.
        13 (211)
    India and WTO, 258n. 14 (172)
    North-South bargaining, 236n. 39
        (28)
Singh, Manmohan, 167, 196
Singh, V.P., government,
    C-DoT, 149–150
    Telecommunication Commission,
        147
Skocpol, Theda,
    on CCP, 244n. 6 (92)
    on research design, 233n. 33 (14)
small business users,
    India, 135
    summary of provision for cases
        examined, 224–226
Smith, Adam, 202
Smith, Tony, 245n. 32 (99)
social constructuvists, 202
social contract and technology,
    201–202
social delivery systems as users,
    South Korea, 69
    summary of provision for cases
        examined, 224–226
societal unrest,
    Singapore, 61–62
    South Korea, 69–70
South Korea, 62–70
    crisis of legitimacy, 44
    indicators for specialized services,
        59–60
    MAFF talks, 32, 67, 77

South Korea *(continued)*
  political economy, 62–65
  summary of restructuring, 52, 62,
    64
  telecommunication efficiency
    indicators, 205–207
specialized services. *See also* cable
    television, cellular, data
    networks, E-Mail, fax, Internet,
    paging, PCOs, PCs, satellite,
    telegraph, telex
  China, 93
  Mexico, 74, 76
  Singapore, 59
  South Korea, 67–69
Spiller, Pablo T., 227, 232n. 32 (12)
Sprint,
  in Brazil, 103
Srinivasan, T.N., 235n. 26 (26),
  237n. 57 (31) 250n. 40 (124)
state,
  as a black box, 222
  autonomy, 41–42
  behavioral factors, 41, 239n. 87
  capacity, 41–42
  decision-making, 41–45
  development orientation, 41–42
  functional, 224, 226–229
  historical context, 214
  legitimacy, 42–44
  maneuverability, 42–44
  myth of benevolence, 213–214
  responsibility, 42–44
  summary of restructurings, 52–53
  window of opportunity, 44
Steinmo, Sven, 239n. 86 (41)
Stern, Peter A., 246n. 77 (108)
stock offerings from privatization,
  Brazil, 105, 219
  Mexico, 75
  Singapore, 58
Strange, Susan, 236n. 44 (28)
Streeten, Paul, 234n. 6 (22)
subsidies,
  Singapore, 61
supply conditions,
  "myth" of supply-push, 210–213

"reality" of, 221–224
  summarized, 20
Sutter, Daniel, 237n. 66 (34)
SWIFT, 190
Swiss PTT, 186

tariffs. *See* pricing
Tatas,
  and cellular, 184–186
  in Indian telecommunications
    market, 160
TCIL (Telecommunication
    Consultants of India Limited), 130
technological efficiency,
  mantra chanted, 204
technological influences,
  and globalization, 26
  Brazil, 103
  explained, 31–33
  fall in costs, 31–32
  Mexico, 74
  natural monopoly argument, 12,
    24, 28, 31, 33, 213
  summary for cases examined, 109
  summary for India, 195
technological instrumentality,
  myth of, 210–213
  supply side, xxi
Telecom Italia, 106
Telecom Malaysia, 184. *See also*
    Malaysia
Telecommunications Commission
    (India). *See also* Pitroda
  and cellular bids, 184
  and MTNL, 162
  creation, 144–147
  idea for Components Bank, 175
  trade union obstacles, 146
teledensity,
  Asia, 132
  Brazil, 57
  China, 57
  historical comparisons, 121
  in Indian provinces, 156
  India, 57, 132–133
  Latin America, 132
  Malaysia, 57

Mexico, 57
Myanmar, 57
Singapore, 57
South Korea, 57
Telefonica, 106
telegraph in India, 116–118,
    prioritization in the 1980s, 153
telegraph service introduction
    China, 92
    India, 115
    Malaysia, 79
    Myanmar, 106
    South Korea, 62
telephone service introduction
    China, 92
    Malaysia, 79
    Mexico, 73
    Myanmar, 106
    Singapore, 240n. 6
    South Korea, 62
telex in India, 134,
    prioritization in the 1980s, 153
Telia, 104
Texas Instruments, 255n. 40 (151)
Thomas, Robert T., 261n. 3 (201)
Tocqueville, Alexis de, 262n. 34 (228)
trade unions. *See* labor issues
TRAI (Telecommunication
    Regulatory Authority of India),
    179–181
    cellular operators, 181, 185
    comparison with FCC, 180
    Internet, 181
    telephone service bids, 189
Tyson, Laura D'Andrea, 235n. 31
    (26), 235n. 32 (27)

universal service,
    Singapore, 56
    South Korea, 69
urban residential users,
    Brazil, 102
    China, 92, 224–226
    India, 136–137, 150–152,
        173–174, 176, 194–195
    Malaysia, 82
    Mexico, 75

Singapore, 56
South Korea, 65
summary of provision for cases
    examined, 224–226
US West, 185–186
user groups. *See also* clubs, large
    users, small business users,
    exporters, urban users, rural
    users, government
    administrations, social delivery
    systems
    and collective action, 10)
    benefits from telecommunications
        for, 5–9
    coalition building, 38–39
    demands met in cases examined,
        224–226
    ideational influences on, 30
    importance of, 5–6
    politics of, 8
    technological influences upon, 33
    types of, 10
USTR (United States Trade
    Representative),
    and Mexico, 78
    and South Korea, 32, 67
    pressures on India, 172
    Super 301 for India, 256n. 77
        (161)

Vajpayee, A.B. *See also* BJP
    government in India
    prioritizes telecommunications,
        171, 182
value-added services. *See also* data
    networks, E-Mail, fax, Internet,
    paging, PCs, satellite
    India, 147, 176
    Singapore, 56
    South Korea, 66–69
Varma Committee, 259n. 37 (177)
Verba, Sidney,
    on civil society, 262n. 34 (228)
    on research design, 15
Vernon, Robert, 235n. 18 (24)
video services in India, 158
VIKRAM, 153, 190–191

Vittal, N., 178, 196
VSAT (very small aperture terminals),
    China, 93
    India, 190–192
VSNL (Videsh Sanchar Nigam
        Limited),
    and data networks, 191
    and Internet, 193–194
    competing with DoT, 189
    corporatization, 143
    growth of traffic, 134–135
    performance, 156–158

waiting lists,
    as indicators of demand, 50
    Brazil, 57, 101
    China, 57
    in developing countries, 57
    in Singapore, 56–57
    India, 57, 173–174, 176
    Malaysia, 57, 82–84
    Mexico, 57, 74–76
    MTNL in India, 158
    Myanmar, 57, 108
    South Korea, 57, 66, 70
Waltz, Kenneth, 236n. 37 (27)
Warford, Jeremy,
    benefits of telecommunications, 7,
        9
Warren, Bill, 245n. 32 (99)
Waterbury, John, 239n. 95 (44)
Wellenius, Bjorn,
    benefits of telecommunications, 7,
        9
    ideational influences, 236n. 48
        (30)
    influences on restructuring, 232n.
        30 (12)
    Mexican telecommunications,
        242n. 57 (74)
    on Brazilian tariffs, 102
    on Myanmar, 246n. 77 (108)

Williamson, Oliver, 208, 231n. 8 (5)
window of opportunity, 44
    India, 138, 142, 167–168
    Mexico, 73, 75
    South Korea, 70
Winner, Langdon, 261n. 5 (202)
wireless,
    Mexico, 74
Wittman, Donald, 238–239n. 82 (41)
workers. See labor issues
World Bank,
    as interest group, 28, 179, 195
    capital-output ratios in India, 131
    changes in thinking regarding
        telecommunications, 23
    critiques government interference
        in India, 175
    effective states, 226
    ideational influences, 30, 31,
        236n. 48 (30)
    Indian R&D, 148
    pressures on Brazil, 103
    role of information technologies,
        xxi–xxii
    study on Myanmar, 108
    telecommunication equipment
        negotiations for India, 148
    urges bank reform in India, 167
World Wide Web. See also internet
    English language dominance, 61
Wright, Gavin, 213
WTO (World Trade Organization),
    and India, 172, 195
    and Malaysia, 85
    and Mexico, 78
    and Singapore, 60–61
    as interest group, 54
    GATS agreement, 172
    telecommunications accord, 27, 70

Zacher, Mark, 29, 238n. 71 (34)
Zaire. See Congo